T0149615

GLORIA PITZER'S

Cookbook –

THE BEST OF THE RECIPE DETECTIVE

Famous Foods From Famous Places

GLORIA PITZER

BALBOA
PRESS
A DIVISION OF HAY HOUSE

Balboa Press books may be ordered through booksellers or by contacting:

Balboa Press
A Division of Hay House
1663 Liberty Drive
Bloomington, IN 47403
www.balboapress.com
1 (877) 407-4847

Because of the dynamic nature of the Internet, any web addresses or links contained in this book may have changed since publication and may no longer be valid. The views expressed in this work are solely those of the author and do not necessarily reflect the views of the publisher, and the publisher hereby disclaims any responsibility for them.

The author of this book does not dispense medical advice or prescribe the use of any technique as a form of treatment for physical, emotional, or medical problems without the advice of a physician, either directly or indirectly. The intent of the author is only to offer information of a general nature to help you in your quest for emotional and spiritual well-being. In the event you use any of the information in this book for yourself, which is your constitutional right, the author and the publisher assume no responsibility for your actions.

Any people depicted in stock imagery provided by Thinkstock are models, and such images are being used for illustrative purposes only.
Certain stock imagery © Thinkstock.

ISBN: 978-1-5043-9121-4 (sc)
ISBN: 978-1-5043-9122-1 (e)

Print information available on the last page.

Library of Congress Control Number: 2017917591

Balboa Press rev. date: 01/15/2018

GLORIA PITZER
The Recipe Detective

Secret Recipes
For
Famous Foods
From
Semi-↑ Famous Places

Secret Recipes

From *Gloria Pitzer's Better Cookery Cookbook* (St. Clair, MI: Secret Recipes Ltd., May 1983 – 3rd printing). Edited by Laura Emerich for new edition.

Gloria Pitzer's Cookbook

The Best of the Recipe Detective

Famous Foods from Famous Places

A special edition based on the original text and illustrations from Gloria Pitzer's
Better Cookery Cookbook (St. Clair, MI: Secret Recipes Ltd., May 1983 – 3rd
printing) – as copyrighted by Gloria Pitzer – 1982, as PUBLISHED BY Secret Recipes Limited.
Re-written and edited (with Gloria's permission) by her daughter, Laura Emerich. All
rights reserved. No portion of this book may be copied, reprinted, or reproduced in
any way, for any purpose, without the author's express, written permission.

A New Special Edition

REDEDICATION

This book is [still] dedicated to my 5 children,
Without whose absence
It could never have [originally] been written!
And to my [late] husband, Paul,
Who admitted he may have his faults -
But, being wrong was not one of them!

GLORIA PITZER

The Secret Recipe Detective

GENERAL THRILLS FOODS

1983

❀ ❀ ❀ ❀ ❀

From *Gloria Pitzer's Better Cookery Cookbook* (St. Clair, MI: Secret Recipes Ltd., May 1983 – 3rd printing). Edited by Laura Emerich for new edition.

THANK YOU, [again...]

...Bob Allison & his "Ask Your Neighbor" radio program on WWJ-Radio, Detroit, MI – which has been broadcasting since 1962, for moral support and interest in my research and development of recipes that imitate restaurant and commercial food products. You've been a great friend over the years.

...Art Lewis & his "Listen to the Mrs." program on WSGW-Radio, Saginaw, MI – which has been on the air since 1952, and **...Warren Pierce** of WJR-Radio, Detroit, MI, which has been on the air since 1976 – for putting me in touch with some of the most responsive and enthusiastic listening audiences.

...Jim White, Ann Keefe & Art Fleming of KMOX-Radio, St. Louis, MO – for all the great years we visited on the air, sharing secrets of some giants in the food industry with your nationwide audience.

...Bob Cudmore of WGY, Schenectady, NY – whose listeners have become good friends over the many years of our radio visits with your wonderful audience.

...Ralph Story of KNX-Radio, Los Angeles, CA – for introducing me to your west coast audience, which offered me many new restaurants to investigate

...Bob Barry of WEMP-Radio, Milwaukee, WI – whose newsletter to the radio personalities included notes of my progress and opened many doors for me.

...Paul Harvey, broadcaster for the ABC Radio Networks, for his kind words about my work.

...The Michigan Federation of Press Women – for MANY years of meaningful membership.

...Marian Burros, author of *"Pure and Simple"* - for your encouragement and enthusiastic endorsement as Food Editor of *the Washington [DC] Post*, making my research of the food industry's secrets an exciting and interesting labor of love.

...Ed Busch of WFAA, Dallas, TX and KSL-Radio, Salt Lake City, UT; **Toby Gold** of WSAY-Radio, Rochester, NY; **Toni Harblin** of WTNY, Watertown, NY; **Fred Krell** of WSGW-Radio, Saginaw, MI; **Bunny Morse** of WCMY-Radio, Ottawa, IL; **Pat Rogers** of WOAI-Radio, San Antonio, TX; **Eddie Schwartz** of WGN-Radio, Chicago, IL; and **Bob Sweeney** of WHIO-Radio, Dayton, OH.

*...BUT MOST OF ALL TO **PM Magazine** and their television crew in Detroit, MI for having created new interests in my recipes ...and to **The Phil Donahue Show** and its amazing television audience for an overwhelming response to my "Eating Out at Home" ideas.*

CONTENTS

 *IT ALL STARTED WITH THE STROKE OF A PEN*

DEAR FRIENDS,

I DO, WITH RECIPES, WHAT RICH LITTLE DOES WITH VOICES! Imitating the "Secret Recipes" of the food industry has been an exciting experience for me. The critics felt that "fast foods" and restaurant dishes were not worth the effort to duplicate at home, when you can just as easily buy the products already prepared!

The critics who contend that "fast foods" are "junk foods" and not good for us, have probably never prepared these foods themselves. Certainly, they have no access to the closely guarded recipes from the food companies that created these dishes, as there are only a few people in each operation that are permitted the privilege of such information! So, 99% of the critics' speculations are based on their own opinions. To know what these dishes contained, they'd have to be better chemists than I, as I have tested over 20,000 recipes with only the finished product as my guide to determine what each contained. "Fast foods" are not "junk foods" unless they're not properly prepared. Any food that is poorly prepared (and just as badly presented) is junk! Unfortunately, "fast food" has carried a reputation, by default, of containing ingredients that are "harmful" to us. Yet, they contain the same ingredients as those foods served in the "finer" restaurants with wine stewards, linen table cloths, candlelight, coat-check attendants, and parking valets; which separate the plastic palaces of "fast food" from the expensive dining establishments. One "eats" at McDonald's, but "dines" at The Four Seasons. Steak and potato or hamburger and French fries – the ingredients are practically the same. How they are prepared makes the difference!

In the early 70s, I was trying to juggle marriage, motherhood, homemaking and a newspaper column syndicated through Columbia Features, when it seemed obvious to me that there wasn't a single cookbook on the market that could help me take the monotony out of mealtime. There was not a single recipe in the newspaper's food section that did not smack of down-home dullness! "Okay," they said at the newspaper I worked for, "YOU write the column on foods and recipes that YOU think would really excite the readers and make them happy!" I did, but that didn't make the Editors happy, because it made their [food industry] advertisers miserable. When I was told that I'd have to go back to monotonous meatloaf and uninteresting side-dishes that made mealtime a ritual rather than a celebration or "pick up my check", I told them to "MAIL it to me!" I went home to start my own paper!

It was probably a dumb thing to do, amid an economic depression with the highest rate of unemployment I had ever experienced, but it was worth the risk. I was a dedicated writer that new someone had to give homemakers something more than what they were being given in the colored glossy magazines, where a bowl of library paste could even be photographed to look appetizing! There had to be more to mealtime than Lima beans and macaroni and cheese with Spam and parsley garnishes. There also had to be more to desserts than chocolate cake recipes that came right off the cocoa can. The food industry gave us more appealing products than did the cookbooks we trusted.

THEY LAUGHED! THEY DOUBTED! They even tried to take me to court when some famous food companies insisted that I stop giving away their secrets. They couldn't believe me when I said that I did NOT know, nor did I want to know, what they put in their so-called secret recipes. I did know that there are very few recipes that can't be duplicated or imitated at home. And we could do them for much less than purchasing the original product. I proved…it can be and should be done!

FAMOUS FOODS FROM FAMOUS PLACES have intrigued good cooks for a long time – even before fast foods of the 1950's were a curiosity. When cookbooks offer us a sampling of good foods, they seldom devote themselves to the dishes of famous restaurants. There is speculation among the critics as to the virtues of re-creating, at home, the foods that you can buy "eating out", such as the fast food fares of the popular franchise restaurants. To each, his own! Who would want to imitate "fast food" at home? I found that over a million people who saw me demonstrate replicating some famous fast food products on The Phil Donahue Show (July 7, 1981) DID – and their letters poured in at a rate of over 15,000 a day for months on end! And while I have investigated the recipes, dishes, and cooking techniques of "fine" dining rooms around the world, I received more requests from people who wanted to know how to make things like McDonald's Special Sauce or General Foods Shake-N-Bake coating mix or White Castle's hamburgers than I received for those things like Club 21's Coq Au Vin.

A COOKBOOK SHOULD BE AS EXCITING AS A GOOD MYSTERY! Most are drably written by well-meaning cooks who might know how to put together a good dish, but know nothing about making the reader feel as if they're right there, in the kitchen with them, peeling, cutting, chopping, stirring, sifting and all the other interesting things one does when preparing food. It is my intention in this book of the food industry's "Secret Recipes", to make you feel at home in my kitchen, just as if we're preparing the dishes together…to later enjoy with those who share our tables with us.

THIS COOKBOOK IS NOT A BARGAIN BASEMENT COLLECTION! It is not a miss-mosh of recipes from here and there. It's not at all like any other cookbook you will probably find, unless the publisher has used mine as a pattern – and a few have. But, it is nice to know that in having sold several hundred thousand copies of my monthly publication and my other 5 books, as well as the 10 or 15 books I did prior to "Secret Recipes" - that my readers have also been my friends.

I make a living with my writing – but, it's my writing that makes living worthwhile!

Best wishes for great cooking adventures!

Gloria

WHAT THIS BOOK INCLUDES

Although I've been writing longer than I've been cooking, the notion to investigate the secrets of the food industry didn't become a full-time labor-of-love until I was working for a small-town newspaper [about 1971.] As the only "married lady" on the staff, I was always assigned the food page and recipe column, and I was willing to try the dishes at home and present a column or article about their results to the paper. When you work for a small-town paper, you wear many hats. You set type, sell advertising, proof read, design headlines, create art work, campaign for subscribers; and, before you know it, you acquire skills you didn't even know you possessed. The food department became such a welcomed relief from the local politics that I poured my heart and soul into it, learning some of the essentials of good cooking purely by default!

Everything went well until I initiated an idea to create advertising interest among local restaurants. It started when I answered a reader's request in my column for a recipe like McDonald's "Special Sauce". I knew it was a kissin' cousin of a good Thousand Island dressing, so the development of the recipe wasn't difficult. The response from our readers was so appreciative that I contacted local restaurants for their advertising in exchange for my printing one of their recipes and menu in my column and a complimentary review of their place. No one was willing to part with any of their "secrets!" So, I decide to see if I could "guess" how they prepared their specialties of the house.

I came across a hotel in town that advertised "home-baked" cheesecake, and I felt they should be telling their customers "homemade." The difference to the public is very slight, but they wanted the public to "think" it was homemade, from scratch, when it was, in fact, simply taken from a carton and popped into the oven like brown-and-serve rolls. That was before our "truth in menu" laws, but no one at the paper wanted to make an issue out of it. The restaurant insisted it was an old family recipe. I said the cheesecake smacked of commercial automation, stainless steel computerized kitchens and the family they referred to was probably that of Sara Lee! At any rate, that was when I parted company with the paper and set out on my own to create the "Secret Recipe Report," which I dearly miss now.

FOOD FOR THOUGHT

When you're cooking, the recipe is not as important as the attitude of the cook. Good cooks are not born, but "shaped" through pure experience and a good memory. It's one thing to be able to read and follow a recipe while you're cooking – it's quite another to follow a recipe and know instinctively if it will be good; or, at least, as good as you would like it to be! The only way you can achieve this kind of success in the kitchen is to taste your dish as you prepare it. You should always taste the food you're preparing WHILE you're preparing it, after you've added the last required ingredient and after each addition you make of your own and again just before you serve it. Even if you're working with a truly dependable recipe, you may want to adjust it to fit your taste or that of whom you're serving it to.

COOKBOOKS ARE APPARENTLY NOT ENOUGH to create a better standard for food preparation, any more than "The Bible" can create a moral atmosphere in the world. It's more than reading the words and following the instructions, when we're up to it. We need to put something of ourselves, our enthusiasm, into cooking as much as we do in our other activities. To be a good cook, you need to have a good attitude about what you're preparing, how you want it to taste and what you want it to look like when you present it to those with whom you share your table. It takes more than a good recipe to make a good cook!

RECIPES ARE NOT INFALLABLE

No matter how the recipe may taste to the one who records it for publication, the chances of pleasing everyone with it are slim. Never be shy about making additions or flavor changes in a recipe. The only changes you shouldn't make are those in proportions of ingredients in bake goods. When you work with baked goods, leavening and yeast, the ratio of leavening to shortening and starches (flour, etc.) are rather exact if the recipes have been tested prior to publishing. The cookbooks that admit the recipes were not tested, but, rather, collected from dubious sources may require some cautious experimenting on your part before you trust them to prepare for company.

The amount of shortening in such a recipe should also get your respect. To alter the amount of shortening, alone, in a recipe means that you also must alter the amounts of flour, eggs, etc.; so, do be cautious in this regard! However, the flavorings can be inter-changed with other flavorings. For example, if you want DIFFERENT flavors, you can use alternate extracts if the "amount" called for in the recipe is the same. The substitutions will have to be in accordance with the recipe requirements. If you want LESS flavor, use less extract and add water to equal the required "liquid amount." If the balance of the liquid amount has not been compromised, then the result should be satisfying.

HI, NEIGHBOR!
BOB ALLISON'S "ASK YOUR NEIGHBOR"

One of the nicest things about being a writer is that you can work at home. Back in the late 60's and early 70's, as soon as my kids were out the door to the school bus, I set up my $39.95 Smith Corona portable typewriter at the kitchen table, where I was one step away from the stove, refrigerator and recipes I was curious to test and write about. The view from the kitchen table included the front yard and the North Channel of the St. Clair River (part of the St. Lawrence Seaway to everyone else) – the river-side was the front yard and the road-side was the back yard. The old house had its faults, I'll grant you, but nobody could refuse a view like we had, living on the banks of that river! There was always something going on outside, sufficient to inspire a feeling of well-being, which every writer must have to do their job well. In keeping with "write about what you know best", I could put every economical recipe I used to feed my family of seven to good use, sharing the Secrets with others.

One of my addictions in those days was a daily recipe radio show called *Ask Your Neighbor*, hosted by Bob Allison over the WWJ-Detroit radio airwaves. He always opened his two-hour show by saying, "if you have a household problem you cannot solve, then call… (and he'd give a phone number) …and ask your neighbor!" I called him frequently with answers to his other listeners' recipe questions, until I became "a regular" on the show. With Bob's generous help in mentioning my monthly newsletter, my subscriptions began to climb to 300, and 400. I was finally showing a profit! That gave my husband, Paul, some relief from his skepticism that I would eventually outgrow my obsession with writing.

From Bob Allison's listeners alone, Paul and I had received over 1000 letters in one day! When, 106 months later, we closed our subscriptions to the monthly newsletter, we were already serving over 15,000 subscribers and had probably returned subscription requests to over 10,000 people, because that's when, like Dick and Mack McDonald, we decided that we did not want to "get big!" It is as much a thrill for me today, to hear somebody on Bob's *Ask Your Neighbor* show request that "Gloria, The Secret Recipe Detective" try to duplicate a recipe, as it was for me decades ago when it all began.

HAMBURGERS AND FRIES

MOST POPULAR

From the sidewalk diners of the 30's and the 40's, where "fountain service" was offered at "luncheonettes", to today's ultra modern, beautifully designed family restaurants, we have seen in our lifetime, the successful growth of an industry.

Ray Kroc
Founder of McDonald's

WE ALL NEED GOOD EXAMPLES TO FOLLOW whether it's the influence in the fashions we wear, the homes we decorate, the tables we set. Why not imitate the giants of the industry as a gesture of flattery? The critics who cry the loudest about the doubtful fast food industry have yet to find a success story equal to it. The restaurant and commercial food industry will always have its competition!

Reproduced with permission from Gloria Pitzer, *Gloria Pitzer's Better Cookery Cookbook* (St. Clair, MI: Secret Recipes Ltd., May 1983 – 3rd printing), p. 14.

WE CAN'T TALK ABOUT HAMBURGERS without talking about the most successful of the fast food chains – McDonald's! It's the only company in the fast food industry that has succeeded in cornering the market on family food and fast service restaurants – the world over! McDonald's was the trend-setter; the hometown hospitality example in the industry. They took meat and potatoes and turned it into a billion-dollar enterprise.

Hamburgers, French fries and milkshakes were making their menu debut at "drive-in" restaurants, where car hops took your orders and returned with trays of food that hooked on to the window of your car. Kids cruised these places in their parents' Edsel, Hudson and Kaiser-Fraser sedans back then. Hamburger "joints" were less than desirable to most people who appreciated good food and a pleasant dining-out experience. But, these drive-ins had one interesting thing in common that appealed to the public – they were AFFORDABLE!

It was 1954 and Ray Kroc, founder of McDonald's, was 52 years old. Hardly the time in one's life when they'd start to think about launching a new enterprise, but rather a time when most began to think about retiring! On one of his sales trips, Ray Kroc, a Dixie Cup salesman, met the owners of a thriving hamburger restaurant in California. Eventually, Kroc purchased the business from Maurice (Mac) McDonald and his brother, Richard. Mac & Dick had a fetish for cleanliness. Their place in San Bernardino was spotless! And much like Ray Kroc in his own experience years later, they weren't too keen about teenagers. They avoided catering to the teenage market exclusively because kids loitered, were noisy and threw food around. The McDonald's concept was for "the family!" McDonald's wasn't the first company to create a fast food concept; but, by far, it was the most recognized and the most profitable in the industry. While fast food has taken it on the chin for every conceivable infraction of culinary achievement that the critics could possibly contrive, McDonald's still came out on top!

THE BIG MATCH ATTACH – This is the double-decked, at-home-hamburger recipe that promises you will shock the socks off everyone who tries your improvisation of the famous "Golden Arch's" very own "Big Mac".

All you need for one 'Big Match' is: 2 all beef patties, "Special Sauce", lettuce, cheese, onions, pickles & 2 sesame seed buns. Sear both sides of the 2 patties in a bit of oil on a hot griddle, cooking to medium-well. Place each patty on the 2 bottom halves of the buns. To each of these, add a tablespoon of Special Sauce (see below), lettuce, cheese, onions and pickles to taste. Assemble one atop the other and add one of the bun tops to the top of that. Serve at once to anyone having a Big Match Attach!

THE BIG MATCH SPECIAL SAUCE

1 cup Miracle Whip Salad Dressing
1/3 cup creamy French dressing
¼ cup sweet pickle relish
1 tablespoon sugar
¼ teaspoon pepper
1 teaspoon dry, minced onions

In a small mixing bowl, stir all ingredients together with a spoon, as listed. Makes 2-cups sauce. Keeps up to a week or so if refrigerated & well-covered. Do not freeze this.

White Castle information, reproduced with permission from Gloria Pitzer, *Gloria Pitzer's Better Cookery Cookbook* (St. Clair, MI: Secret Recipes Ltd., May 1983 – 3rd printing), p. 22.

KRYSTAL HAMBURGERS is based in Chattanooga, Tenn. It originated in 1932 when Rody Davenport, Jr and Glenn Sherrill opened a 10-stool diner called "Krystal Kleen" in downtown Chattenooga. They specialized in soft drinks, coffee, home-baked pies, eggs, toast, bacon and waffles, plus a few menu ideas inspired by a competing chain, "White Castle", which originated 11 years earlier in Columbus, Oh. Davenport was looking for a "depression-proof" business at the time and visited the White Castle operation, which greatly impressed him. White Castle's clean concept was the incentive which led to the development of his own chain.

WHITE CASTLE ORIGINATED THE FAST FOOD CONCEPT and today it employs more people than any other industry in America, generates more business than any other industry over the longest period of time. The "dime store" lunch counters of the Forties, with the multiple sections of stools and counters, expanded the idea of "fast food"–affordable food for folks who couldn't "eat out" otherwise. The small rectangular hamburger patties on the square buns and the 4-oz presentation on the sesame seed bun, complete with trimmings, depicts the essence of an industry that has outlived every other franchised food fare. The "all natural ingredients" label is probably the only weapon the critics now have who attempt to undermine the virtues of the fast food industry, but that promotional phrase is the biggest paradox to come down the pike since the "one size fits all" slogan. Fast food franchiesing will survive the critics!

WHITE CASTLE – In 1916, Walter Anderson started his career in the restaurant field by opening a rented, re-modeled streetcar and giving the food industry its very first "fast food" place. In 1921, he ran into some difficulties when he tried to lease another place to expand his operation. So, he turned to a Realtor by the name of Billy Ingram, who secured the needed lease for Anderson, and soon became partners with him in the hamburger restaurant. Eventually, the operation became entirely Billy Ingram's, and today White Castle is a respected name that represents "quality" in the food industry.

Originating in Wichita, Kansas during "The Depression", Ingram so-named his operation "White Castle" because it stood for purity, cleanliness, strength and dignity. He was a business man with high ethics. He was responsible for many changes in the business that initiated health inspections, to ensure that all restaurants complied with what Ingram personally felt was a responsibility to the customer. He invented utensils never used, such as the spatula and the grills that are still considered the most practical equipment.

White Castle has no special, secret recipe – but, the technique used to prepare their small hamburger is unique and unequaled by competitors. You must like onions to appreciate White Castle patties. The quality of the beef they specifically use that we couldn't possibly equal it with what we buy in the supermarkets; so, I set to work to try to enhance the ordinary "ground chuck" available to us with a few ingredients that create a recipe reminiscent of Ingram's "White Castles."

A letter of appreciation from Gail Turley, Director of Advertising and Public Relations with White Castle Systems in their Columbus, Ohio headquarters reflected the feelings not often expressed by the major food companies, whose products I attempt to imitate with "make at home" recipes. "On behalf of White Castle System," the letter said, "We are honored that you deemed the White Castle Hamburger worthy of an attempt at replication of the early days of White Castle and Billy Ingram..." And she enclosed a check to cover the cost of purchasing 15 copies of my first Secret Recipes Book to distribute to their Regional Managers. A far cry from the reaction I received from Orange Julius and Stouffer's, who threatened legal action against me.

WHITE TASSLE BURGERS

Supposedly, the original beef mixture used in the famous White Castle patties during the early 30's was of such high quality that there was no way to equal it [50 years later.] Today we send beef to the market much younger, before it has aged. Young beef has less fat, which Americans want. The marbleizing fat in older beef is what gives it flavor. To compensate for this, it seemed to me, ground beef's flavor could be enhanced by adding another pure beef product – strained baby food. It worked!

3-ounce jar baby food, strained veal
1 ½ pounds ground round steak
1 tablespoon onion powder
½ teaspoon pepper

Combine all ingredients thoroughly. Shape into 12 rectangular, thin patties. Fry briskly on a hot, lightly oiled flat grill, making 5-6 small holes in each patty with the end of a spatula handle. After turning patties once, place bottom half of bun over cooked side of patty and place the top half of the bun over the bottom half. Fry quickly to desired *"done-ness"* and remove. Add pickle slices and a few tablespoons of chopped, grilled onions to each serving. Makes 1 dozen burgers.

COUNTRY CLUB BURGERS

I don't know why, but so many country clubs can easily fracture a simple hamburger! They serve them too thick to ensure that they are properly done, turning them out either too rare or too well-done and, therefore, dry. Or they have no flavor. Well, when I complained to one manager about the texture and flavor of the burgers they served, and offered him a suggestion for improving them, he took me up on it. I developed a recipe for marinating the patties and shaping them differently. The first day that he added these to the menu, he said he had more compliments than he could keep track. Here's that recipe (makes 15 patties.)

5 pounds ground round
3 ½ ounce jar baby food, strained veal
3 ½ ounce jar baby food, strained beef
10 ½ ounce can Campbell's Beef Broth
1 teaspoon onion salt
½ teaspoon pepper

In a roomy mixing bowl, combine everything as listed, working ingredients together well with your hands. Separate mixture into 15 6-oz patties, 1-inch thick and as big around as the bun you'll be using. I use a 1-cup measuring cup and pack it firmly, 2/3 full. Place each patty into a sandwich-sized plastic food bag. Sprinkle both sides liberally with season salt AFTER you have placed it in the bag.

THEY FREEZE WELL up to 6 months. Store them in coffee cans with tight-fitting plastic lids or in store-bought plastic freezer containers. Thaw patty at room temperature before searing on a hot, lightly oiled grill to desired doneness. To sear properly, use 1-tsp oil and 1-tsp margarine for each patty; melting it and getting the grill hot, but not hot enough to burn the margarine. Don't use butter with oil because that changes color too quickly with heat. Make a small slit in the patty as it sears on the second side, to check the color of the meat. You can also broil the patties on a rack in a shallow pan, placing them about 3" from the broiler heat, allowing about 5-minutes on each side (or as you desire doneness.)

ANOTHER LITTLE TIP: if you like the patties pink in the center and "done" everyplace else, place a chip of ice in the center of the patties before cooking them. Keep the chip about the size of an M&M candy. It melts as the patty cooks, keeping the center from over-cooking.

PATTY MELT – COUNTRY CLUB STYLE

An old-fashioned restaurant favorite is to serve seared hamburger patties on open-faced, grilled rye or pumpernickel bread with a slice of American, cheddar or Swiss cheese, broiler-melted over the top. Add some sautéed onions and a spoonful of hamburger sauce or bleu cheese dressing just as you go to serve it. You can also garnish the plate with a dill pickle spear and a few olives on top of a small ruffle of lettuce. Use an ice cream scoop to dip out a nicely rounded mound of macaroni or potato salad along-side the sandwich, as well, and sprinkle with a little paprika. Now you have a sandwich equal to what is being served in the best country clubs around!

MARKUS–STYLE FRANK–BURGERS

Detroit, Michigan (circa 1940's and 1950's) – The proprietor of a popular lunch spot had his bakery supplier rush over an order of rolls for his burgers, only to find that they had delivered the wrong kind – they had delivered hot dog buns! There wasn't time to have the order corrected, with the place already filling up for the lunch hour rush. So, "instead of raising the bridge, he lowered the river." Once again, a mistake that could have been a set-back to someone else, became a step forward for this fellow. He shaped his burgers to fit the buns and his "Frank Burgers" became not only an instant success, but also his trademark.

I still re-create these at home, using the same mixture I use for "White Tassel Burgers" (see Index), but I add to it one beaten egg. Then, I shape the meat mixture to resemble hot dogs and brown them like sausage links in a little bit of oil in a shallow skillet. To this, add just enough water to the skillet until it's about 1/2-inch deep in the pan and cover it with a tight-fitting lid. Turn burner heat to low to keep it simmering gently for about 5 minutes. Using tongs, remove them from the pan onto toasted hot dog buns. One recipe of "White Tassel" plus the egg makes about 8 "Frank Burgers".

THE BEST RECIPE for making a proper hamburger is to use the right kind of ground beef. I use what is called "hamburger" for everything BUT hamburgers! In sauces and meatloaf, this grade of ground beef is fine; but, as a patty, it has too much fat and gristle, and less flavor than ground round. Ground beef or hamburger is less expensive than ground round, but there is no bargain in the waste in it.

If you want to know exactly how good the quality of the ground beef is that you're buying, try this test: Pack about 1 cup of ground beef into a 2-cup Pyrex measuring pitcher. Seal it in foil and place it on a cookie sheet on the center rack of your pre-heated, 350-F oven – bake it for 20 minutes. Remove from oven and uncover the pitcher. You should see that some liquid has come to the top of the beef. If you allow it to cool about 30 minutes the liquid will separate so that the liquid fats rise to the top and the liquid mixture of the water and juices form a second layer underneath. If you have more than 1" deep of liquid on top of the meat (or the equivalent of a 1/4-cup combined liquid,) complain to your butcher! In the old days, when ethics were not practiced seriously in the meat business, it was not unusual for ground beef to be packaged with the addition of water, which gave added weight and only surfaced when it was cooked. You must conduct this test before you freeze the beef, however; because once the beef has been frozen, the ice crystals will convert to more water in the thawing process.

To make hamburgers the way they do at your favorite places, you must have a flat grill. Skillets do not produce a decent burger. After much experimenting, I finally bought the next best thing to a grill – a 10x10, flat griddle with a 1/4-inch rim, a handle and a no-scratch surface (that requires very little oiling) that you can place on a burner on the stove. (Teflon and Stone-Ware make good ones.) I use it for nothing but hamburgers. It's dishwasher safe and stores nicely in the cupboard without using as much space as the skillet. The reason skillets don't produce good hamburgers is that the collar (or rim) around the skillet traps the steam from the meat and "fries" the patties rather than "sears" them. You want to keep the grill hot, but not too hot, and barely oiled. Apply a few tablespoons of corn oil to the hot surface of the grill (or griddle pan) and wipe up the excess with a paper towel. When a few drops of water "dance" on the surface, the heat is just right for adding the patties – don't crowd the patties either, keeping at least 2-inches between them and turning them only once, salting only the seared sides. Kosher salt and Sea Salt are best to use because the iodine in table salt makes the meat tough and evaporates the liquids and natural juices too quickly.

FRENCH FRIES

"NOBODY DOES IT LIKE McDONALD's CAN" - [was] the popular television jingle that advertised some of the best French-fried shoestring potatoes to come down the pike in a long while. The French did not invent French fries – American fur trappers did. Potatoes were not well-thought of in the early days of this country. But, fur trappers would melt down bear grease in large open kettles over their campfires and, when the grease began to bubble, they'd spear chunks of their dressed game meat, roots and potatoes on the end of a sharply pointed stick, setting them in the hot grease to cook to the individual's liking and then eat off the stick – much like modern-day shish kabobs or fondue.

TO MAKE FRENCH FRIES at home – long, white Russets work best! Peel and cut in half lengthwise. Place cut sides on a cutting board and remove a thin slice from each end, as well as from the rounded long-sides. You now have sort of rectangle blocks to work with. Slice these into 1/4-inch thick strips and place in a deep refrigerator container. Mix 1-quart water with ½ cup vinegar and pour over potatoes, repeating this process until you have enough to cover the potatoes. Cover and chill for several hours to draw out the starch that makes a fried potato hold the grease and become limp.

After chilling, drain them well on paper towels. Drop a few at a time, using a French-frying basket, into 425°F oil that's at least 4" deep. A good combination is 1-pint corn oil to 1 cup Crisco, using as much as is needed for the amount you are preparing, keeping it 4 inches deep; and, if the oil is not hot enough, the fries will turn out greasy. Let the potatoes "Blanche" in the oil rather than fry completely, removing them after just one minute. Drop them on a cookie sheet and put in your freezer for 10 minutes. Return them to the oil to fry until golden brown and drain them well on paper towels. Salt them as you wish, which also helps to evaporate any excess grease on the finished potatoes. Most of the salt will fall off when the fries are transferred to serving plates.

SALT-SPICE MIX

¼ cup sea salt
1 tablespoon Accent
1 teaspoon each: dill weed, black pepper and onion powder
finely-grated rind of 1 lemon
¼ teaspoon each: chili powder, paprika, oregano leaves, dried marjoram leaves, & rubbed sage

Combine all the ingredients and store in a grinder or put through the blender on high-speed until finely powdered. Makes about 1/2-cup mix. Keeps indefinitely at room temperature.

CELERY SALT MIX

Combine 1/2-cup table salt with 1/2-cup dehydrated celery leaves and 1/4-cup celery seed in a blender on high-speed until powdered. Makes 1 ¼ cups. Keeps for ages at room temperature.

HAMBURGERS can be seasoned as differently as there are restaurants to serve them. Some of my own favorites include a mixture like my Steak Tartare and Country Club Burgers in this chapter. But these are easier to put together - and much juicier! They are reminiscent, in fact, of a famous fast food restaurant!

WEDNESDAY'S HOT & JUICY HAMBURGERS

5 pounds of lean ground beef
3 ½ ounce jar baby food, strained veal
3 ½ ounce jar baby food, strained beef
10 ½ ounce can Campbell's Beef Broth
1 teaspoon each: onion salt and season salt
½ teaspoon each: lemon pepper and finely crushed, dry, minced onions
2 tablespoons of my Cup of Thoup Powder – Tomato Flavor (see Index)

Mix all the ingredients together thoroughly, covering your hands with plastic food bags to knead it well. Or dig right in like Grandma did; remember that fingers were made before forks! Shape into patties by measuring out 2/3-cup of mixture for each and keeping them about 1/2-inch thick and square in shape (about the size of a graham cracker.) The mixture makes about 15 patties, which can be individually wrapped and frozen to use within 6 months, thawing for about 30 minutes at room temperature. Do not refrigerate for more than 2 days.

LUMP'S GOLLY BURGERS - *Best when, first, kept in this liquid marinade overnight:*

3 tablespoons lemon juice
1 teaspoon pepper
1 ½ teaspoons season salt
1 tablespoon each: Worcestershire sauce, soy sauce, A-1 Steak Sauce and corn oil
½ cup canned beef broth (or 1 teaspoon beef bouillon powder, dissolved in ½ cup boiling water)
1 teaspoon Heinz 57 Sauce
¼ teaspoon garlic salt
1 teaspoon vinegar

Shape 1 ½ to 2 pounds ground round - into 6-8 round patties, 3/4-inch thick & 3 ½ inches across. Mix the above ingredients together in a refrigerator container that will also accommodate the patties and seal tightly with a lid. Refrigerate at least 12 hours, turning the patties frequently in the marinade. Just before preparing, remove from the marinade and sear as suggested in my Country Club Burger recipe in this chapter.

IMPROVISING ON SOME INGREDIENTS

Before we go much further, I want to give you a few recipes that can be used in place of commercial food products that may not be available to you in your area. When Paul & I were publishing my monthly Secret Recipes Report, our subscribers in Europe and Australia and some remote places in Alaska, were grateful they could make their own substitutions for ingredients they couldn't buy. Lipton's Tomato Cup-A-Soup was one product that seemed to be difficult to come by [and has, since, been discontinued by Lipton.] Although I couldn't pulverize my mixture into a silky, fine powder like the commercial product; I could do a good job with a blender and a mixture that, once baked and broken into pieces like crisp cookies, did yield a very good likeness to the original soup powder.

CUP-OF-THOUP POWDER – Tomato Flavor

6-ounce can tomato paste
½ cup each: cornstarch and Creamora creamer powder
2 tablespoons season salt
1 cup finely powdered Saltine crackers
1 teaspoon bottled, finely grated lemon peel

Mix all the ingredients together well, using a fork, until it's the consistency of hamburger. It will look just like ground beef when you've finished combining it properly. Line a cookie sheet in brown wrapping paper; or, cut up a paper grocery bag to fit, having the inside facing up. Spread out mixture on paper so that no single piece is larger than a blueberry, and place cookie sheet on oven rack 4" from the bottom of the oven, baking slowly at 200°F for about 1 ½ - 2 hours, or until completely dry. Do not let the mixture brown. [*If the least little bit of browning develops before the mixture is completely dry, reduce heat to 150°F, or turn it off altogether for a while and back on again in 10 or 15 minutes.*] When completely dried, put the mixture through your blender until finely powdered, using an on/off speed on high. The powdered mixture should be stored in a covered container at room temperature; where it will keep for several months, if away from direct heat or humidity and out of direct sunlight.

TO USE THE SOUP POWDER: Allow 1/4-cup of homemade soup powder for 1 envelope of the commercial kind. To prepare a cup of soup with the homemade powder, mix 1/4-cup of soup powder with 7 or 8 ounces of boiling water, stirring well until it's dissolved. You can add more powder if you like the soup thicker, or add more water if you want it thinner.

LEMON PEPPER

Using the smallest holes of your grater, remove the yellow peel of one whole lemon; being careful not to take off too much of the white pulp, beneath, as it's very bitter. Measure the grated peel and mix with an equal amount of coarse ground black pepper. Measure that mixture and add half as much salt. Mix thoroughly. Store in a shaker-style container out of direct sunlight, away from heat and humidity. Keeps for ages! (If it gets sticky add a few grains of rice to the shaker to keep it free-flowing.)

LOUDLY'S SEASON SALT

2 tablespoons pepper
1 tablespoon each: chicken bouillon powder, garlic salt, dry-minced parsley and chili powder
1 teaspoon each: onion salt, onion powder, cumin powder, dry marjoram leaves and paprika
½ teaspoon curry powder
1/3 cup table salt

Mix ingredients together thoroughly. Put into a 1-qt jar with tight-fitting lid and shake the mixture until blended thoroughly. Keep at room temperature, to use within 3 months. Makes about 1-cup salt.

BIG PLOY'S SEASON SALT

2 tablespoons sugar
2 teaspoons each: dry mustard, dry sweet pepper flakes, onion salt, garlic salt and black pepper
1 ¼ cups table salt
1 tablespoon each: celery salt and paprika
1 teaspoon each: finely grated lemon peel and dry-minced parsley flakes

Mix well and store at room temperature in a covered container. Keeps for ages! Makes 1¾ cup of salt.

LIP BONE ONION SOUP MIX

2 jars (3 ½ ounces each) beef bouillon powder
¼ cup instant tea powder
½ teaspoon pepper
1 cup dry, minced onion
¼ cup each: onion powder and parsley flakes
1/8 cup onion salt (or 7 teaspoons)

Combine as listed, mixing well. Keep at room temperature in a covered jar. Makes 2-cups. *TO USE THE MIX FOR SOUP: Allow 1/4-cup mix for 4-cups boiling water, stirring well until soup mix is dissolved Serves 4. (1/4 cup mix = 1 envelope commercial soup mix product.)*

GOOD TEASIN'S ITALIAN DRESSING MIX

2 teaspoons onion powder
1 tablespoon sugar [or 1 packet (.035-oz) Sweet & Low artificial sweetener]
1/8 teaspoon each: black pepper, powdered allspice, paprika and marjoram leaves (crushed)
1 teaspoon each: dry minced onions and dehydrated celery flakes
¼ teaspoon each: garlic salt and dry oregano leaves (crushed)
1 clove garlic, peeled and sliced fine (or 2 teaspoons bottled minced garlic)
2 [1 ½ inch-square, each] soda crackers

Put everything in your blender, using an on/off agitation on high speed, blend until mixture is the consistency of the original [or force through a fine mesh strainer until powdered.] Keep mixture in covered container at room temperature, away from direct sunlight, up to 3 months. Recipe yields equivalent of one envelope of the commercial product.

TO USE THE DRESSING MIX: Combine with 1/4-cup vinegar, 2/3-cup water, and 1/3-cup corn oil. Keeps in covered container in refrigerator up to a month. Shake well before using the dressing. Makes about 1 ½ cups of prepared dressing.

WITCH BONE ITALIAN DRESSING – *This is one of the most versatile seasoning ingredients, as well as a good salad dressing.*

Put into your blender:

1/3 cup light vinegar
2 [1 ½ inch-square] Saltine crackers
2 tablespoons light corn syrup
1 teaspoon instant tea powder

Blend for 20 seconds and pour into a small mixing bowl, adding:

1 teaspoon each: lemon juice, garlic salt and onion salt
1 tablespoon dry, minced onions
½ teaspoon dry oregano leaves
½ cup, plus 1 tablespoon, corn oil

Funnel mix into a bottle (that accommodates 8 ounces with shaking-room). Shake mixture well to combine and, again, before each use. Refrigerate up to 3 months. Makes 1-cup (8-oz) dressing.

CANNING HAS NEVER BEEN one of my favorite culinary projects – mostly because it requires so much time and because the equipment and ingredients seem to overwhelm me to the point that I dream I'm making a liar out of Geritol! It wouldn't help me!

*THIS RECIPE FOR KOSHER PICKLES (and the next one for Bread & Butter Pickles) requires no canning, no hot water baths, and no calling in the Marines to help with the work! In the Kosher Dill recipe, you will notice that it requires no vinegar... just **a salt water brine** strong enough that, when the salt has been dissolved in the simmering water, it will "float an egg." This means that if you drop a fresh egg (in-shell) into the water solution when it's at lukewarm (or room) temperature, it should float to the top and "bob" around if the brine is strong enough. If the egg sinks to the bottom, retrieve it and bring the water back to a boil, adding 2- or 3-TB more of Kosher-style salt. Continue the process until you can "float an egg" in it. By the way, always use Kosher salt because it's not iodized. Iodized salt will give you rubbery pickles and probably scum on top of the brine too!*

ELASTIC BRAND DELI KOSHER DILLS

3 quarts of water
½ cup Kosher salt
1 dozen dill sprigs
1 large bulb garlic
10 to 12 cucumbers (do not peel these)

Put water and salt into a stainless-steel kettle or large saucepan. Never use aluminum cookware for this brine. There is something about the acidity that offends aluminum! Bring the water to a boil and let it simmer about 15 minutes without a lid. Be sure the salt is completely dissolved. Let it cool to Luke-warm or room temperature. Perform the egg test described above until brine is strong enough to "float" the egg.

Meanwhile, put half of the dill sprigs into a 1-gallon, wide-mouth, plastic (or glass) container with a nice fitting lid. Do not use a metal container with the salt brine. Separate the bulb of garlic into individual cloves and put half of them into the container as well. Cut each of the cucumbers in half, horizontally, and then each half into about 6-8 spears. Arrange spears in the container, packing them in tightly with the narrow tips up. On top of the spears, place the remaining sprigs of dill and cloves of garlic and then pour in brine to completely cover the cukes. Cap it loosely and let it stand at room temperature for 3 days and 3 nights. You may have to put a plate under the container in case the fermentation of the brine bubbles up and spills out the top. This sometimes happens, but don't worry about it. It merely means the stuff is working the way it should.

On the third day, check the brine to see if it's bubbly. It should be a bit like soda pop when you pour it into a glass. Take a bite of one of the spears to see if it is crisp enough for you. If not, leave them another day or two, or until they are. Then to halt the fermentation, you just cap it tightly and refrigerate it. Once it is in the refrigerator, the fermentation stops and the pickles stay as you have them. They will keep up to 3 months in the refrigerator – maybe longer.

NOTE: To be certain the cucumbers are not bitter, cut them up one at a time and take one slice off the center, tasting it to be certain it's not bitter. I have had an entire batch of pickles spoiled because I didn't taste each cuke that I sliced, and it only takes one bitter cuke to ruin the entire batch!

BREAD & BUTTER PICKLES

1 small onion – the size of an egg – sliced thin
6 cucumbers – unpeeled and sliced into 1/4-inch thick slices
Enough water to cover the slices in a plastic container
¼ cup Kosher salt

Combine in an accommodating plastic container and allow to stand, uncovered, for at least 12 hours.

The Brine:

6 cups light vinegar
5 cups sugar
4 tablespoons mustard seed
2 teaspoons turmeric
4 teaspoons each: celery seed and celery salt

Combine the Brine ingredients in a large sauce pan and bring them to a gentle boil. Stir and simmer for 5 minutes. When sugar is completely dissolved, remove from heat and allow to cool to Luke-warm or room temperature.

Drain the cukes and onions, but don't rinse them. Pack them into a 1-gallon plastic or glass container and pour the brine mixture over them. They must be completely submerged in the Brine. If the cukes are especially large, you may have to increase the Brine recipe to accommodate this. Cover tightly and refrigerate immediately. Do not serve for at least 72 hours. They'll keep refrigerated up to 3 months.

HIGH-END'S MUSTARD SAUCE

This is a unique product that can be used alone or in addition to mayonnaise or other dressings, as a salad dressing or sandwich spread.

½ cup cold water
4 tablespoons cornstarch
½ cup, plus 2 tablespoons of dark vinegar
2 tablespoons salt (sounds like a lot, but it isn't)
½ cup sugar (or equivalent of artificial sweetener)
1 egg
4 tablespoons each: French's prepared mustard and margarine (in tiny bits)

Place all ingredients, as listed, in blender on high speed (2 minutes) until smooth. Transfer to top of double boiler and cook over gently boiling water, stirring often, for 12-15 minutes, or until thickened. Refrigerate in covered container 24-hrs before using. Makes 2 cups. Keeps refrigerated up to 3 months.

HIGH-END'S KETCHUP – *WITHOUT CANNING*

This is the kind of ketchup you prepare, using a blender, when you only need a quart or two – enough to last about a month for a family of four. It can be used as an ingredient in other recipes calling for "ketchup" and it doesn't require canning or hot water baths or multiple jars, equipment and energy.

14 ½ ounce can (approx.) stewed-tomatoes
¾ cup light vinegar
4 teaspoons season salt
½ teaspoon cinnamon
2 tablespoons cornstarch
6-ounce can tomato paste
¾ cup packed brown sugar
2 teaspoons onion powder
¼ teaspoon powdered cloves
2 tablespoons butter (or margarine)

Put everything into your blender one ingredient at a time, blending well with each addition. Turn off from time to time and scrape down sides and around blades to ensure proper blending. When smooth, transfer to a 2 ½-quart heavy sauce pan. Cook on medium-low heat, stirring constantly. Bring to a boil, continuing to stir... *If the Avon Lady rings the bell and you're interrupted, remove this from the heat before you let her in! If it's your mother-in-law, you can always ask her to wait until you're finished with the ketchup...* Only allow the ketchup to boil for about half of a minute, then remove it from the heat. Let it cool in the pan about 30 minutes without a lid. Pour it into a quart-sized container and refrigerate up to a month (maybe even longer.) It freezes beautifully for up to a year. Makes 1-qt.

FRESH'S MILD MUSTARD

Simple mustard that is every bit as good as what you can buy at the supermarket. Takes only a little time and effort, and requires NO canning!

Put these ingredients, as listed, through blender on high speed until smooth: ½ cup light vinegar, ½ teaspoon salt, ¼ cup flour, 1 ½ teaspoons turmeric, ¼ cup softened butter (or margarine), 1 egg, ½ cup water, 1 teaspoon dry mustard and ¼ cup sugar. Transfer to 2-quart saucepan. Cook on medium heat until smooth and thick, stirring constantly. It should have the consistency of pudding. Remove from heat. Pour into a non-metal container with a tight-fitting lid. Keep refrigerated up to 2 months. Makes about 1 cup of mustard.

BIG PLOY'S HAMBURGER SAUCE

1 cup mayonnaise
¼ cup each: chili sauce and ketchup
3 tablespoons sugar
½ cup sweet relish
1/8 teaspoon garlic salt
½ teaspoon onion powder
1 teaspoon dry, minced onion

Use an electric mixer on low to medium speed to carefully combine all the ingredients as listed. Blend for 1 minute on medium with the last addition. Store in a covered container in the refrigerator up to a month. Makes 2 cups of sauce. DO NOT freeze.

HAMBURGER ASSISTANT

In a box on the Grocer's shelves, it would be a convenience food by another name. This is my answer to dinner-in-a-rush!

2 pounds ground chuck
4 cups water
4 envelopes Tomato Cup-a-Soup powder (or 1 cup of my Cup-of-Thoup mix, see Index)
1 tablespoon each: dry minced onions and cornstarch
1 teaspoon each: onion powder, chili powder and season salt
¼ teaspoon pepper
½ teaspoon each: garlic salt and oregano powder
8-ounce package thin spaghetti, uncooked

Brown the chuck in a large skillet without any additional oil added to the pan. Crumble the beef with the back of a fork and, when the pink color disappears, stir in the water, soup powder, onion, cornstarch, and remaining seasonings. Stir it thoroughly to blend it all well. Cover and simmer for 3 minutes. Break the uncooked spaghetti into 2- or 3-inch pieces and stir it in to the simmering sauce. Cover and continue simmering for 10 more minutes, or until spaghetti is tender. Serve piping hot! Feeds 4 or 5, depending on their appetites!

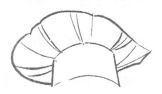

STEAK TARTARE

Originally the hamburger was of German origin, being served hundreds of years ago, by only the aristocrats as a dish of raw beef, scraped with a dull knife into highly seasoned hot oil and swallowed with a piece of bread and a chunk of cheese, then, washed down with a mug of ale. Today, we call the "scraped beef" dish, steak tartare and it's still considered a gourmet's choice. The only remarkable difference between this and the all-American hamburger, is that the hamburger is hardly seasoned and it is also cooked to varying degrees. But, it still goes good with bread, and sometimes cheese, and the seasonings are added to it in the form of relish, mustard, ketchup, onions and such. When Europeans began to immigrate to this country, they brought with them their own food customs and traditions, of which included steak tartare. Served in the colonies, as it was in their homeland near the port of Hamburg, Germany – some found the taste of spoilage was camouflaged if the meat was heated and then seasoned. Thus, the birth of the American hamburger! My own favorite recipes for making steak tartare at home, developed from one dish I had sampled at a country club gathering.

I was a little skeptical about trying this very gourmet appetizer the 1ˢᵗ time I was introduced to it years ago; but after studying the chemistry of food science, I realized that the ingredients with the raw ground beef were preserving the meat, even though it was served uncooked. This is the great-grandfather of the all-American hamburger, brought to this country by people who found the ingredients they were used to in Europe, unavailable in the new land. They did what they could with what they had. The steak tartare was a staple on the colonial table. Today it is a gourmet treat!

You'll want to make this up at least 4-5 hours before you plan to serve it. It's even better if you make it up the day before serving, so the wine can thoroughly marinate the meat. *Note: Don't substitute on the cut of beef; the leaner, the better. If you can get your butcher to grind the meat twice, all the better!*

1 ½ pounds of ground round steak
1 envelope onion soup mix
1 envelope Lipton's [or Knorr's] Tomato Cup-a-Soup powder
(for my homemade equivalent, see Index)
½ cups Burgundy or Sweet Vermouth
1 tablespoon Italian Dressing Mix powder
1 teaspoon Worcestershire Sauce
***lettuce and pimiento-stuffed green olives for garnishments

Mix it all thoroughly, as listed. Work it well with your hands. Pack the mixture into a lightly oiled 4-cup ring mold (or a pretty bowl, lightly oiled.) Cover well and refrigerate 4 to 5 hours – or overnight.

Loosen edge of meat mixture with the tip of a sharp knife. Cover the bowl with a pretty plate and invert it, shaking them tightly together to loosen the meat from the mold. Arrange little ruffles of leafy lettuce around the edge of the mold, tucking the ragged edges under the meat so they don't show. Accent here and there around the lettuce ruffle and on top of the meat with pimiento-stuffed green olives. Serve it icy cold as a spread for Melba toast or crackers. Serves 6-8 adequately.

SALADS AND SALAD DRESSINGS

WHEN RESTAURANTS ADDED THE SELF-SERVE SALAD BAR to their operations and menus, it became one of the most popular features, if not profitable, for the food industry, even for "fast food" and middle-priced "family" restaurants. If you didn't feel up to any of the main selections on a menu, you could always build your own meal from the assorted offerings at the salad bar; and it was a blessing for people on special diets. Some restaurants have gone beyond the usual offerings of greens, toppings and salad dressings to also include potato and pasta salads, dessert-type dishes, fruits, and appetizer selections.

THE HOUSE DRESSING has remained one of the popular choices and selling features of most of the good restaurants. While the most unusual dressings still belong to the Backus Red Fox restaurants in the Lansing and Birmingham areas of Michigan, there is a close runner-up with Marie Callender's unusual French Dressing in their California Restaurants. Bob Evans also updated their celery seed dressing to a coveted position and sold them in jars at their register counters. And, when you ordered popovers at Bullock's Department Stores' dining rooms in Southern California's Lakewood or Torrance areas, you were also served a side-dish of their own special poppy seed dressing in which to dip the popovers.

When McDonald's took the humble Thousand Island dressing and added their own clever touches to it, it became a burger sauce. At the famous Canadian chain, Crock & Block, they used a spicy Oriental topping for their salads and assortment of sandwiches. Unique products such as Marzetti's Slaw Dressing remain a supermarket product, but each of the popular recipes can and do take the monotony out of mealtime when you imitate them at home.

GRASP'S MAYONNAISE

2 raw egg yolks
juice of 1 lemon
¼ cup non-dairy powdered creamer
¼ cup sugar (or equivalent in artificial sweetener)
1 teaspoon salt
2 teaspoons 1 cup corn oil

ONE AT A TIME add each ingredient, as listed, into a blender on medium speed – do not stop the motor except to periodically clear mixture away from the blades and scrape down the inside walls of the pitcher. THE OIL MUST BE ADDED VERY SLOWLY, using a very thin, but slow and steady stream. When thickened, scrape mixture into a 1-pt jar and cap it tightly. Refrigerate for 24 hours before using it. This will keep well in the refrigerator for a month – DO NOT freeze!

RUSSIAN DRESSING

Mix together, 1/3 cup each: apple butter, ketchup and Catalina dressing. Stir in 1 cup of mayonnaise and 1 tablespoon dry, minced onion. The authentic Russian dressing also has 2 tablespoons of caviar in it, which is the distinguishing ingredient; but, who can afford it these days! Try it without the caviar and chances are you'll be *rushin'* around tellin' everyone how great it is! Makes about 2 cups.

HELP-ANN'S MAYONNAISE

4 egg yolks
2 whole eggs
¼ cup lemon juice
1/3 cup light vinegar
¾ cup sugar
4 teaspoons salt (Yes! 4!)
¼ teaspoon pepper
¾ cup of canned, skimmed Pet Evaporated Milk
3 cups corn oil
½-pound stick margarine (cut into bits)

Place first 8 ingredients in a blender, using on/off speed for 3 to 4 minutes or until perfectly smooth. Turn off the motor every minute to clear mixture from the blades and scrape down the inside walls of the pitcher. Keeping motor at a medium speed, begin to add the oil, using a very thin, but slow and steady stream. Then, while continuing to blend, add the bits of margarine until smooth. Stop the motor again every minute or so to scrape and continue blending until smooth. Refrigerate it 24-hrs before using to let it stabilize and allow the flavors to get well-acquainted. Makes 3-pts. DO NOT freeze!

MACARONI (OR POTATO) SALAD – *LIKE THE COLONEL'S - There was a time when the best deli-style macaroni salad was from The Colonel's KFC, but over the years that recipe changed. This is my own favorite version from the one they used in the 60's.*

Dressing mixture:

½ cup sour cream
½ cup Miracle Whip
1 cup Hellman's mayonnaise
2 tablespoons prepared mustard
3 tablespoons sugar
1 teaspoon onion salt
½ teaspoon pepper

Combine dressing mixture in an accommodating bowl, as listed (above), and set aside. In a larger bowl, combine the following:

2 tablespoons dry, chopped onion
2/3 cup celery, chopped
2/3 cup sweet midget pickles, chopped
    (don't substitute with relish – it's too juicy)
2 tablespoons pimiento, chopped
    (or half of a small tomato, seeded & chopped)

Add the dressing mixture to this, mixing well, and use to coat 8 cups (cooked, drained and chilled) elbow noodles (3 cups, uncooked) – or cubed potatoes. Cover tightly and refrigerate for an hour before serving. Serves 8 adequately (or 14 weight-watchers!)

CROCK & BLOCK – CANADIAN RESTAURANTS - These are the most unique of the family food restaurants – based in Toronto [around 30 units in 1983.] The decor was turn-of-the-century English, with a soft motif and restful atmosphere. The wonderful sauce they served with their sandwiches on their luncheon menu was spicy and semi-sweet, but unusual...a challenge to be sure!

CHOP AND DROP SECRET SAUCE

1/3 cup each: Miracle Whip and orange marmalade
2/3 cup Catalina dressing
1 tablespoon each: dry, minced onions and Worcestershire sauce
1 teaspoon onion salt
1/16 teaspoon pepper

Combine all ingredients, whipping it vigorously with a sturdy spoon. Makes about 1½ cups of sauce. Keep tightly covered in the refrigerator up to 2 weeks. Use as a sandwich sauce or salad dressing.

CREAMY FRENCH DRESSING

When my American readers, overseas, can't buy American-brand products, they've assured me that recipes for good substitutions make it a lot easier for them to cook. This is one of those products!

2/3 cup light vinegar
1 cup of vegetable oil
6-ounce can tomato paste
1 cup sugar
½ teaspoon paprika
2 teaspoons salt
½ teaspoon pepper
2 teaspoons onion juice
½ teaspoon garlic powder
½ cup whole milk

Put each ingredient into a blender, as listed, blending well with each addition. After last addition, blend on high for 1 minute. Pour into a quart-sized jar with a tight-fitting cap. Keep refrigerated up to 60 days or so. Makes almost a quart.

HONEY MUSTARD DRESSING

Beat together with electric mixer on low speed: 1 cup mayonnaise, ½ cup honey and ¼ cup prepared mustard until blended thoroughly. Cover and refrigerate up to 3 weeks. Makes about 1 ¾ cups sauce.

CATALINA DRESSING – *Like Ponderosa Steak House – this hearty, spicy dressing is also a good pinch-hitter for the Kraft brand bottled dressing.*

10-ounce can tomato soup
1 ½ cups corn oil
½ cup vinegar
1/3 cup sugar
2 tablespoons Worcestershire sauce
1 tablespoon dry mustard
1 ½ teaspoons salt
3 tablespoons dry, minced onion
½ teaspoon each: celery salt and paprika
1 tablespoon soy sauce
¼ teaspoon pepper
3 tablespoons light corn syrup
½ cup ketchup

Put each ingredient as listed, in a blender on medium speed, blending well with each addition. Pour into a quart-sized jar with a tight-fitting cap. Keep refrigerated up to 60 days. Makes almost a quart.

MACKUS RED FOX HOUSE DRESSING

This is one of those unique combinations of ingredients that has been copied by other restaurants under various names. Some places used celery seed and others used poppy seed, but the basic idea was for a cornstarch thickening in a cooked pudding-like mixture that's cooled and seasoned.

1 cup water
1/3 cup vinegar
2 tablespoons cornstarch
5 tablespoons sugar
1 envelope Good Seasons Italian Dressing mix

Put it all in a blender, blending thoroughly until smooth. Transfer mixture to a sauce pan on medium heat, stirring until it comes to a boil and begins to thicken, resembling a pudding. Remove from heat as soon as you see the first bubble of a boil surface. Cool and refrigerate several hours before using to allow it to stabilize. Makes about 1 3/4-cups.

CELERY SEED DRESSING – *LIKE WOMEN'S CITY CLUB, DETROIT*

To the Mackus dressing (above), upon removing it from the heat, stir in 1 teaspoon celery salt and 1 tablespoon celery seed. Refrigerate as directed above.

MAURICE DRESSING – *LIKE HUDSON'S*

I know there are many people who claim to have the authentic recipe, right from the kitchens of the J. L. Hudson Company, where this secret formula had its beginnings; but, their recipe did not produce the same dressing as served in the company's dining rooms. This is what I devised.

Mix together: 2 cups mayonnaise, 2 teaspoons dry minced parsley, ½ cup minced dill pickles, 4 teaspoons Dijon mustard, 2 teaspoons onion powder, a 3.3-ounce jar (baby food) strained egg yolks, 1 teaspoon garlic salt, 1 teaspoon sugar, and a pinch of pepper. Serve over torn greens, covered in matchstick-size pieces of ham, turkey and Swiss cheese – as it was once served in Detroit's greatest store ever!

GREEN GODDESS DRESSING

Some call this "green mayonnaise" – but, it's known under several brands as "Green Goddess."

Put into a blender on high-speed: ¼ cup Wish Bone Italian salad dressing, 2 tablespoons dry minced-parsley, ¼ teaspoon dry mustard, ¼ teaspoon turmeric, and 1 tablespoon sugar. Blend for about 1 minute or until smooth. Transfer to a small bowl and stir in 2/3 cup mayonnaise until well-combined. Makes about 1 cup of dressing. Keeps refrigerated about 2 weeks in a tightly covered container.

THOUSAND ISLAND – *Like Waldorf Astoria's dressing & Big Chief's hamburger sauce!*

This salad dressing was the creation of Chef Oscar – of the famous New York City hotel of the 20's and 30's era, The Waldorf Astoria. The original Waldorf building was located where the Empire State Building now stands; but, when plans were drawn up to establish a "new" Waldorf, amid one of the most fashionable residential neighborhoods, the citizens of that area put up quite a fuss! They treated the Astor family, for whom The Waldorf Astoria was named, as if they were bringing in a McDonald's. But, with the market crash in the late 20's, the project was sold to the citizens as a patriotic means by which they could become employed – from the construction of the building to the staff that would operate the ultra-posh hotel. During this period, the Astor family took their troubles with them to their hide-away in the Thousand Islands and, of course, their personal chef, Oscar, and his kitchen staff accompanied them. When preparing a salad with the usual ingredients, Chef Oscar discovered he was out of some of his favorite food items; so, on the spot, he created a mayonnaise-based dressing that became known as "Thousand Island Dressing." Basically, it's mayonnaise, or a form of it, with a tomato-like addition such as ketchup, chili sauce or a similar condiment. The final distinguishing mark of his dressing was the addition of pickle relish – either sweet or dill, with or without the touch of onions. From there, other enterprising chefs and cooks have added their own personal signatures to this basic dressing by adding ingredients such as grated hard-cooked eggs, or just the yolks, jams, jellies, marmalade, apple butter, hot pepper sauce, and a hundred others that set theirs apart from all the others... As a salad dressing or on a hamburger, try my version, which is as close to The Big Chief's sauce as I can remember.

1 ½ cups mayonnaise
1/3 cup each: ketchup, applesauce and sweet pickle relish (drained)
1/8 teaspoon pepper
½ teaspoon seasoned salt
1 tablespoon sugar (or an equivalent artificial sweetener)

Mix all ingredients well, just as listed, using a spoon or fork rather than an electric mixer. Store in a covered container in the refrigerator up to 2 weeks. Do NOT freeze. Makes 2 ½ cups of dressing.

BIG PLOY'S TOMATO-GARLIC DRESSING

½ cup light vinegar
2 envelopes Lipton Cup-A-Soup, tomato-flavored
    (or use equivalent amount of my "Cup-of-Thoup, Tomato", see Index)
1 ½ teaspoons chili powder
1 teaspoon each: seasoned salt and garlic salt
¼ teaspoon pepper
½ teaspoon paprika
1 teaspoon dry, minced onion – crushed (pound them fine with a hammer)
corn oil or vegetable oil

In a small sauce pan, bring the vinegar to a boil for 30 seconds. Remove from heat and, at once, stir in the soup powder, chili powder, seasoned and garlic salts, pepper and paprika. Whip it well, with a sturdy spoon, until it's a smooth paste; then, beat in the crushed onion. Refrigerate this paste in a covered container until about 15 minutes before using it. At that time, mix 1-part paste to 2-parts oil in a jar with a tight-fitting lid. Shake it vigorously to blend well – it tends to separate when it stands for a bit, so revitalize with another shake before using. Add oil to the paste only when you're ready to use the dressing. Makes about 1 pint of dressing. Prepared dressing can be kept in the refrigerator, tightly-covered, for up to 3 days; but, shake well before each use.

MERRY CALL WHIPPED SALAD DRESSING

4 raw egg yolks
¼ cup lemon juice
¾ cup, plus 1 tablespoon light vinegar
1 tablespoon salt (Yes! 1 tablespoon!)
¾ cup sugar
¼ cup Creamora powdered creamer
4 teaspoons Grey Poupon Dijon prepared mustard
¾ cup stick margin, chopped into tiny bits
small can (3.55-ounce) PET evaporated milk
½ teaspoon paprika
2 ¼ cups corn oil

As listed, put all ingredients (except the oil) into a blender on high speed, blending well for 20 seconds with each addition, stopping only to scrape down the sides and blades as needed. Add the oil about a teaspoonful at a time, continuing the blending without interruption. It will be on the thin side, but don't be discouraged – it will be fine! Bottle it and cap tightly, refrigerating it 6-8 hours to allow it to thicken and stabilize. Makes about 6 cups. Keeps for 2 months, refrigerated. Don't freeze it!

EGO BRAND SWEETENED CONDENSED MILK

This recipe took me over 8 years to perfect, and during my various experiments with compatible ingredients for this unique product imitation, I found that you can use 2 completely different sets of ingredients and produce almost identical results. The "first" recipe was one I accepted as a challenging request from my friend, Bob Allison, and his "Ask Your Neighbor" radio audience in the Detroit area. When one of his callers complained to him on the air one day that my original imitation tasted like it should, but was still "too gritty", I pulled out my blender and set to work improving it. Before Bob went off the air that day, I gave his listeners this revised recipe, adding the butter to smooth it out. That was the secret ingredient!

THE IMPROVED "FIRST" RECIPE FOR EGO BRAND MILK

¼ cup hot tap water
¾ cup granulated sugar
1 ¼ cups non-fat, dry milk powder
4 tablespoons butter

Place the hot tap water and granulated sugar in a blender on an on/off, medium-high speed for one minute, or until sugar has partially dissolved. Add the milk powder, blending the same way until smooth. Add the butter 1 tablespoon at a time, blending the same way (scraping mixture away from blades as needed) until smooth. Refrigerate in a covered container for at least 24 hours before using, as this thickens quite a bit while it's being chilled. This makes about 1 ½ cups – or a little bit more than the equivalent of a 14-ounce can. Keeps refrigerated up to a month, but it will also freeze well for up to a year if it's tightly sealed.

THE "ALTERNATE" EGO BRAND MILK RECIPE

1 cup hot tap water
1 ½ cups granulated sugar
¼ cup light corn syrup
¼ teaspoon vanilla
¼ teaspoon salt

Put everything into a blender as listed, cap tightly and blend on high-speed for about a minute. Use the on/off agitation until smooth.

Add to the mixture, a little at a time, an 8-ounce tub of soft, corn-oil margarine (or one that is butter-flavored), which has been melted first and is still barely warm – do not let the margarine foam or change color during the melting process or it will ruin the milk! Blend until smooth. Next, a little at a time, add 2 cups of dry milk powder (or 2 pouches, 3.2-oz each), blending well with each addition. Scrape mixture away from blades frequently. Blend until satiny smooth and refrigerate in a covered container for 24 hours before using. Makes 3 cups. Freezes up to a year if tightly sealed.

MARZESTY SLAW DRESSING

It wasn't until I lived in California, for a few months in 1982, that I couldn't find Marzetti Brand dressing! I was frantic! So, out came the blender and my trusty home-made formula for re-creating it. I can't run my kitchen without this, as either a slaw dressing or an ingredient in other recipes.

4 eggs
14-ounce can Eagle Brand Sweetened Condensed Milk
    (or my equivalent version – see index)
2 teaspoons salt
1 teaspoon dry mustard
1 cup light vinegar

8-ounce tub of soft, corn-oil margarine (or one that is butter-flavored),
    which has been melted first and is still barely warm

Start by breaking 4 raw eggs into a blender and adding the Sweetened Condensed Milk. Cap the blender tightly and blend on high-speed for 30 seconds. Add the salt, dry mustard and vinegar, blending on high-speed for another 30 seconds. Uncover and blend on lowest possible speed while you add the melted margarine in a slow, constant, steady stream. With the last drop added, re-cover and blend on high-speed with an on/off motion for 1 minute. Scrape down sides and away from blades periodically, resuming blending until mixture is smooth. Refrigerate in a covered container for at least 24 hours before using. Makes almost a quart. Keeps refrigerated up to a month or so; but, do NOT freeze this!

MARZESTY II

2/3 cup mayonnaise
1 cup Kraft Miracle Whip (do not substitute on the brand)
4 tablespoons sugar
3 tablespoons light corn syrup
3 tablespoons light vinegar
2 teaspoons salt
1 teaspoon prepared mustard

As listed, mix all ingredients thoroughly with a sturdy spoon (don't use a mixer on this.) Makes 1 pint. Keeps refrigerated for about 6 weeks. Do NOT freeze this!

HAMBURGER SAUCE or salad dressing combinations can do much to enhance your own at-home versions of famous restaurant creations. Combine 1/2-cup Marzesty Dressing (above) with 1/2-cup ketchup and 1/4-cup crumbled bleu cheese to make a good open-faced burger sauce like the St. Clair Inn once served. It's also like the Bleu-French dressing that you could once find on the salad bar at the Chuck Muer River Crab restaurant. As a unique baked potato topping, you can mix together equal parts of Marzesty Dressing to sour cream and stir in scissor-snipped green onion stems to taste. Works great as a hamburger sauce also!

FAVORITES!

HOUSE DRESSING, MARIE CALIBER'S

The very interesting additions to the salad bar of this California-based restaurant chain sets it apart from all the others that give us just the "standard" offerings. One of the most unusual and tastiest salad dressings, is mimicked in this home-made version – inspired by the Marie Callender's product.

16-ounce can stewed-tomatoes
8-ounce bottle each: Italian and creamy French salad dressings
1 tablespoon sugar (or equivalent in artificial sweetener)

Drain the juice from the tomatoes and pour it into a 1 ½ quart mixing bowl. Cut up the tomatoes into small bits and add them back to the juice along with the remaining ingredients. Stir well. Keeps refrigerated up to a month in a covered container. Do NOT freeze this!

BEEF FEEDER CREAMY GARLIC DRESSING

They once called The Beef Carver Restaurants "The Sign of the Beef-Eater", and their creamy garlic salad dressing was the most, to say the least!

1 ½ cup mayonnaise (not salad dressing)
½ cup milk
1 teaspoon each: garlic salt, prepared mustard and dry Oregano leaves
¼ teaspoon each: pepper, light Dijon-style mustard and Tabasco sauce

Use a sturdy spoon to beat all ingredients together until smooth. Keeps refrigerated up to a month in a covered container. Makes about 2-cups dressing. Substitute ½ cup of thick sour cream for the milk to equal what they serve at the Marie Callender's restaurants. Substitute ½ cup of buttermilk for the milk in this recipe to equal what they serve at what I lovingly refer to as the "Big Ploy's" restaurants!

POUND OF ROSES SWEET & SPICY FRENCH DRESSING

1 ½ cups corn oil
2/3 cup ketchup
½ cup sugar
¼ cup vinegar
3 tablespoons granulated beef bouillon powder
½ teaspoon each: garlic salt and onion salt
1 tablespoon each: soy sauce and Worcestershire

As listed, place each ingredient into a blender one at a time, blending for 10 seconds with each addition. After the last ingredient is added, blend for 2 minutes on high-speed, using an on/off agitation. Pour it into a quart-sized jar and cap tightly. Refrigerate for several hours before using – allowing the flavors to get nicely acquainted with each other. Makes 1 quart. Do NOT freeze this!

* * * * * *EGGS FOR SALAD BARS* * * * *

One of my Chef-friends warned me once, "do not grate your hard-cooked eggs! They look so rigid. You want them to have grace and courage on the salad bar table – so force them through the wires of a French-frying basket and note how much nicer they look." You can also force them through the holes of a colander, and they have a softer, more gentle appearance. Try it!

EGG SALAD

Mix 1 cup of "grated" eggs, using the process above, with a few tablespoons of Maurice Salad Dressing (for my version, see Index) and stir in about 2 tablespoons sweet pickle relish, as well as 1 teaspoon of dry, minced onion. Should be sufficient to fill 3 to 4 sandwiches.

SEVEN LAYER SALAD – *This is a great salad to make for a party or for taking to a pot-luck since it can be – must be – prepared 24 hours ahead of serving-time.*

Begin with a lightly-oiled Pyrex dish, 9 x 12 x 2". Arrange half a head of finely shredded lettuce over the bottom of the dish. Sprinkle it well with chopped, partially-seeded tomatoes, sufficient to cover the lettuce in a single layer. Next, sprinkle on an even layer of diced, seeded and peeled cucumbers to cover the tomato layer. Cover the cucumber layer with a package of frozen peas, thawed but not cooked – the marinating process will soften them nicely. Over the peas, arrange a layer of shredded cheddar cheese and, over that, a layer of more shredded lettuce (almost the rest of the other half a head will do.) Finally, apply a 1/2-inch thick layer of mayonnaise to sufficiently cover the lettuce like a finely-whipped frosting. DO NOT STIR THIS. Cover and refrigerate the salad for 24 hours. About an hour before serving, sprinkle the top mayonnaise layer with 1 pound of bacon that has been fried crispy, thoroughly drained of grease, and crumbled into bits. Don't spoil it all with phony bacon bits! To serve, have guests individually spoon out a portion with a large serving spoon – but, never try to stir it up! Serves 8 to 10 nicely.

POPPY-SEED DRESSING & POPOVERS – *Like Bullock's*

When you ordered the Canton Chicken Salad at the Bullock's Department Store dining room in either their Lakewood or Torrance, CA locations, you had the opportunity to sample their equally famous giant popovers with a side-dish of poppy-seed dressing for dunking!

The dressing:

1 cup corn oil
¾ cup sugar
1 teaspoon each: dry mustard and salt
1/3 cup vinegar
4 teaspoons bottled onion juice

With an electric mixer on low-speed, beat together until smooth and add 4 teaspoons of poppy seeds. Refrigerate in a covered container for at least 24 hours before using, to allow the flavors to mingle. Makes about a pint of dressing.

The Popovers:

Put 4 eggs into a blender with 1 cup milk, 1 cup flour and 1 teaspoon salt. While you're doing this, have the oven pre-heated to 450°F and set a greased muffin tin in the oven so that it is good and hot when you divide up the batter between the 12 individual wells, filling each well 2/3 full. Bake for 10 minutes without opening the oven door at all, then drop the heat to 350°F and continue baking for 20 to 25 minutes or until golden brown and crispy looking on the surface. Slide the muffin tin out just far enough that you can insert the tip of a sharp knife into the center of each popover to let steam escape; then, return it to bake for another 5 minutes. Serve them at once. Makes 1 dozen. You can freeze these to use within 6 weeks.

CHICKEN-ALMOND SALAD – *This was the specialty in JL Hudson's Detroit store's dining room.*

6 chicken breasts, boneless & skinless – simmered until tender, well-chilled & cubed
1 cup sliced almonds – sautéed in 2 tablespoons butter for 5 minutes,
    then oven-roasted on a sheet pan at 400°F for 5 minutes
1 cup diced watermelon pickles
4 green onions – stems only – finely scissor-snipped
1-pound can pineapple chunks, well-drained
1 head very crisp lettuce, broken into bite-sized pieces

Toss everything together very lightly and place in an attractive bowl. Drench with a dressing made of equal parts Marzetti's Slaw Dressing (or use my "Marzesty" version, see Index) and real mayonnaise (not salad dressing.) Serves 6-8 nicely.

COLESLAW SECRETS

When you make coleslaw the way the restaurants do, keep in mind a few simple steps that will promise you a stunning success every time! For instance, if you like the small, confetti-sized pieces of cabbage, hand-chopping is the best way to prepare it; even though, it takes a little time and patience. Slice the cabbage into strips, roughly 1/4" thin, and the strips into smaller pieces. If you want it smaller, but still crunchy, then grate the cabbage on the largest hole of your vegetable grater. If you want it "minced" in a hurry – cut the cabbage into marshmallow-sized chunks, fill a blender half full of water and drop the cabbage chunks in until the water is displaced within an inch of the top of the blender container. Use an on/off agitation, on high speed, about 8-10 times to mince the cabbage. Don't over-do it on the speed or you'll have "mushed" instead of "minced." You can always put the cabbage and water back into the blender to make smaller; but once you have over-minced it, you can't fix it. Dump the whole thing into a fine mesh sieve or colander to drain.

Prepare the cabbage to your liking; then, soak it in milk (just enough to cover sufficiently) and add about ¼ cup sugar and ½ teaspoon salt for every 6 cups of cabbage (or about half a head.) When the sugar and salt mixes with the cabbage and milk, it softens it just enough that in an hour or so you can drain the liquid off, add your favorite dressing and the texture is perfect!

Years ago, the Chef at the Port-O-Call restaurant in Algonac, MI suggested to me that, if you make coleslaw often, you should reserve about a cup of the prepared coleslaw each day and add it to the 6 cups of a newly prepared batch the next day, using it like a starter.

COLESLAW RECIPE – *Like Port-O-Call*

6 cups prepared cabbage (minced, shredded, grated, or chopped)
1 cup milk (or as much as is needed to drench the cabbage thoroughly)
¼ cup granulated sugar
1 cup finely-shredded carrots
½ teaspoon salt
¼ teaspoon pepper
3 tablespoons dry, minced onions
1 cup each: mayonnaise and Marzetti's Slaw Dressing (or my version of it in this chapter)
½ cup buttermilk
½ teaspoon celery seed

Combine cabbage, milk, and sugar; then cover and refrigerate for an hour. Drain in a colander and combine with remaining ingredients. Re-cover and refrigerate for at least an hour before serving. Additional dressing may be added, to taste. Serves 6 sufficiently. If you're going to make more in the next two days, reserve 1 cup of this batch to add to the next prepared batch.

MUER SLAW - This dressing is delightfully Italian; made by combining 6-cups prepared cabbage (see above), 1 cup shredded carrots & 3 tablespoons dry minced-onion with 8-ounce bottle Italian dressing, ½ cup corn oil, 2 tablespoons lemon juice, a dash of garlic salt & ½ teaspoon sugar. Cover and refrigerate several hours before serving. Serves 6 to 8.

HEN'S REACH SLAW DRESSING

¼ cup Miracle Whip
½ cup mayonnaise
2 tablespoons horseradish cream sauce
¼ cup sugar
1/3 cup light vinegar
¼ cup light corn syrup
2 teaspoons salt

Mix everything with a spoon, then put in blender on lowest speed. Add ¼ cup corn oil, almost a drop at a time, and 2 raw egg yolks, one at a time. Blend on high-speed for 1 minute, using an on/off agitation. Refrigerate in covered container for 24 hours before serving to allow it to stabilize. Makes 1 pint. Do NOT freeze this!

POTATO SALAD – *Like The Voyageur – this is how I tried to come close to the original, at home!*

¼ cup Miracle Whip
½ cup mayonnaise
1 teaspoon prepared mustard
1 tablespoon sugar
½ teaspoon salt
¼ teaspoon pepper
1/8 teaspoon turmeric
4 to 6 cups cubed potatoes (that have been cooked in their skins, chilled & peeled)
1 cup diced celery
1 cup diced sweet pickle or watermelon-rind pickles
½ cup scissor-snipped green onions

Combine everything, one at a time, as listed, stirring well with each addition. Refrigerate in a covered container for an hour or so before serving. Serves 4 to 6. Left-overs keep well refrigerated up to 3 days.

COLESLAW, PANTRY-STYLE

The Pantry Restaurant in Los Angeles, CA served more meals in its lifetime than any other restaurant like it! Here's my version of their wonderful coleslaw.

Combine, with mixer on medium speed, 1 ½ cup mayonnaise, 6 tablespoons sugar, 3 tablespoons wine vinegar, ¾ cup corn oil, 4 teaspoons lemon juice, ¾ cup Half & Half liquid creamer, ½ teaspoon salt and a few shakes, each, of – garlic powder, onion powder, dry mustard, celery salt and black pepper. Add in 1 reasonably-sized cabbage head, sliced into spaghetti-like thin strips.

Something Better

Frankenmuth Bavarian Inn 713 SOUTH MAIN ST FRANKENMUTH, MICHIGAN

FRANKENMUTH, MI *is well-known for 2 very fine German restaurants – The Bavarian Inn and Zender's. One of their specialties used to be this very good, hot potato salad. It keeps warm nicely in a slow-cooker, up to 7-hrs, when you need to put dinner on hold for a little while. It tastes even better the second day, re-warmed.*

FRANKENMUTH HOT GERMAN POTATO SALAD – *Like Zender's*

1-pound sliced bacon, cut in 1" pieces
5 ribs celery, sliced thin
¼ cup dry, minced onion
1 ½ cups water
½ cup light vinegar
½ cup sugar
8 cups cold, cubed potatoes (cooked in their skins, chilled & peeled)

Fry the bacon until crispy, then remove the slices from the drippings to cool on paper towels, leaving the drippings in the pan on lowest heat. Add the celery to the drippings and sauté for a few minutes; then, add the remaining ingredients and crumble the bacon into the mixture, keeping it on low-to-medium heat and stirring well with each addition. When you get to the potatoes, stir lightly so not to break up the pieces. Stir often until piping hot and time to serve it. Serves 6-8. Leftovers keep beautifully up to a week if well-covered and refrigerated. Do NOT freeze this! It turns out to be mush! Freezing cooked potatoes gives them a rubbery texture when thawed.

HOT SPINACH SALAD DRESSING – *LIKE HUDSON'S*

Prepare the Hot German Potato Salad recipe (above) minus the potatoes, and pour the warm dressing over 1 pound of well-rinsed and torn fresh spinach leaves. Add a few fresh chopped tomatoes (with most of the seeds removed), plus some red or Spanish onions in thin rings. Garnish with a few hard-cooked eggs crumbled on top for a salad equal to one once served in the J. L. Hudson's dining room.

FAT-FREE GERMAN POTATO SALAD

2 cups water
2/3 cup light vinegar
1 cup granulated sugar (or to taste)
1/3 cup cornstarch
1 tablespoon dry, minced onion
1 teaspoon hickory flavored salt
½ cup sweet pickles, cut up
2 Ball Park style, all-beef hot dogs, diced fine
½ teaspoon dry marjoram leaves, crushed fine

Put the first 4 ingredients through a blender until smooth. Pour in a sauce pan on med-high heat, stirring constantly until thick, smooth and almost transparent. Turn heat to low and stir in the remaining ingredients. Pour over 6 cups of cubed potatoes that have been boiled and drained. Keep warm in a Pam-sprayed, 2-quart baking dish in a 325°F oven for about 15 minutes. Serve hot to 4 to 6 people.

GERMAN POTATO SALAD – PENNSYLVANIA DUTCH-STYLE

This combination of ingredients is different from the Zender's version in this chapter, but the flavor is almost identical.

1-pound sliced bacon
6 ribs celery, chopped fine
1 white onion (the size of an orange), chopped
¾ cup packed brown sugar
¼ cup lemon juice
¼ cup light vinegar
1 cup water
¼ cup prepared mustard
½ cup honey
8 cups cold, cubed potatoes (cooked in their skins, chilled & peeled)

Fry the bacon until crispy, then remove the slices from the drippings to cool on paper towels, leaving the drippings in the pan on low heat. Add the remaining ingredients as listed, stirring well with each addition. Crumble the bacon fine and add it to the mixture. Cover and keep warm until time to serve. Serves 6 sensibly.

BLEU CHEESE - FRENCH DRESSING

Stir together: 8-ounce bottle creamy French dressing, ¼ cup mayonnaise and ½ cup crumbled bleu cheese; plus, salt & pepper to taste. Keep refrigerated in covered container. Makes 1 ¾ cup dressing.

YOGURT PANTRY DRESSING

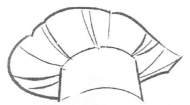

The Pantry Restaurant in Los Angeles was a side-street gourmet gallery of unusual dishes, home-baked sourdough bread interesting salads and sandwiches and a full dinner menu that included this "house dressing"...

1 cup plain yogurt
1 cup mayonnaise
2 tablespoons dry minced onion
½ teaspoon dry marjoram leaves
½ teaspoon dry rosemary leaves
½ teaspoon garlic salt
½ teaspoon onion powder
¼ teaspoon pepper

Beat the yogurt and mayonnaise together until smooth, or put through a blender on medium speed for 30 seconds. Stir in remaining ingredients. Refrigerate in a covered container for at least 4 hours before using to permit flavors to blend and mellow. Makes about 2 cups of dressing.

BEAN SALAD – *Like Houllahan's*

I had this at Houllahan's in Torrance, CA where the salad bar was quite creative, and the assortment was more than I had seen anywhere else.

2 cans (15 ounces each) Northern beans, un-drained
10-ounce can Campbell's Bean & Bacon Soup
½ cup sugar
¼ cup light vinegar
½ teaspoons hickory-flavored salt

Simmer all ingredients, very gently, for 10 minutes on the lowest heat possible. Stir to blend the soup, which will be quite thick right from the can, trying not to break up the beans themselves. When smooth, refrigerate it thoroughly before serving. Makes 4 to 6 servings.

HERBAL DRESSING, LIKE SHOT OF CLASS – Sacramento, CA

Mix together with a spoon: ½ cup mayonnaise, ½ cup yogurt, 2 tablespoons minced-onion flakes, 2 tablespoons fresh-chopped parsley leaves and ¼ teaspoon each: cider vinegar, lemon juice, season salt and Worcestershire. Makes about 1 cup dressing to use as a hamburger sauce or on a salad.

BOB OVEN'S COLONIAL DRESSING

When you visit the restaurant chain that is well-known for its hospitality and good breakfast menu, you can purchase a bottle of their own special salad dressing, which accompanies their equally good lunch and dinner menu selections. It appears to be a basic celery seed dressing, but unlike anything you'll try elsewhere. The challenge of re-creating it at home, with only the bottled product to go by, was no simple assignment; but, my readers and radio listeners had requested it over, and over again. So, I felt it was worth a try!

1 cup water
1/8 cup cornstarch
½ cup vinegar (light or dark)
1 cup sugar
1 teaspoon onion powder
1 tablespoon salt
¼ cup butter or margarine
½ teaspoon pepper
1 teaspoon celery salt
1 tablespoon celery seed

Put water and cornstarch through a blender on high speed for 1 minute or until smooth. Transfer to a 2 ½-quart sauce pan and cook over med-high heat, stirring constantly as you begin to add each of the remaining ingredients, one at a time, as listed. Continue stirring and cooking until mixture thickens and becomes smooth. Let it cool completely before transferring it into a container for the refrigerator, capping it tightly. It will keep nicely for about 6 weeks. Do NOT freeze this dressing!

CREAMY ITALIAN COLONIAL DRESSING – To one recipe of the Colonial Dressing (above), add 1 tablespoon each: prepared mustard, light corn syrup and dry oregano leaves; plus, 1/2-tsp garlic powder and ½ cup mayonnaise. Stir thoroughly and keep refrigerated. Makes about 3 cups dressing. Again, do NOT freeze it!

CATALINA COLONIAL DRESSING – To one recipe of the Colonial Dressing (above), stir in 1 cup ketchup and ½ cup sweet pickle relish. Makes about 3 ½ cups dressing. Do NOT freeze!

CREAMY ONION COLONIAL DRESSING – To one recipe of the Colonial Dressing (above), stir in one 8-ounce tub onion chip/vegetable dip. Makes 3 cups dressing. Do NOT freeze!

COLESLAW COLONIAL DRESSING – To one recipe of the Colonial Dressing (above), stir in ½ cup each of sour cream and mayonnaise. Use this one within a week. Makes about 3 cups of dressing. Do NOT freeze!

MAKING VINEGAR AT HOME

Vinegar, like bread or yogurt, requires a "starter", which can be used repeatedly. The "starter" can be vinegar, itself, cider or even wine that's beginning to turn sour from having been open too long (yes, believe it or not, it can happen!) The best container in which to make your vinegar is a plastic-lined thermos jug with a spigot. You must extract the liquid from the lower portion of the container without disturbing the fermentation at the top. Wood is the best material to use for this container, but it's extremely hard to find; so, the next best thing is plastic.

The "mother" (starter) for making apple cider vinegar begins with the foam that forms when you cover bruised-but-not-rotten apples (including peels and cores) with warm water and let it stand (loosely-covered) in a warm place for three days. Scoop the foam off carefully and add it to apple cider or juice, letting it float on that until it works and begins to ferment.

Or you can follow the simple, kitchen counter-top recipe for a quick home-made vinegar that can be perpetuated with commercial vinegar and flavored with old wine or herbs and other flavorings. Then it should be (as directed below) carefully strained and bottled.

AN EASY WAY!

VINEGAR – HOME-MADE

You should use well-bruised, but never spoiled, apples. Those that look soft or a bit aged with withered skins work well for home-made vinegar. Cut them up – cores, peels and all – and put them into a blender with enough water to cover them, within 2-inches of the rim of the pitcher. Put the lid on and blend on high-speed for 2 minutes or until the mixture is smooth.

Pour the apple-water mixture into a large, glass pitcher or container (do NOT use metal) and measure it. Add an equal amount of store-bought vinegar – or, for a good wine vinegar, you can use half store-bought vinegar and half dry, white wine (in a total amount equal to the apple-water mixture.) Use apple cider instead of the water, when processing apples for a strong cider vinegar.

Allow your mixture to stand at room temperature, with a loose-fitting lid, for 21 days. Then, strain it well, using a linen napkin or paper coffee filters in a fine-mesh strainer. Bottle it and keep it refrigerated forever and ever!

NOTE: The separation you'll see at the top of the apple/water mixture is called "the mother" and should be carefully spooned off and reserved to be added to your next batch of home-made vinegar. You can reserve it in a container in the refrigerator until it's needed. Then, simply put it in the blender with your cut-up apples and water and repeat the recipe as described above.

RANCH-STYLE DRESSING MIX

When the creators of this unusual and very tasty, dressing-mix powder came up with the idea, it required only the addition of buttermilk and mayonnaise to make the dressing. Since then, everybody has been trying their creative hands at duplicating the recipe. All the recipes sent to me to test required buttermilk. I made this version a little different than those, and even still-different than the one I previously published in my monthly newsletter [no longer in publication.]

6 tablespoons Creamora powder
4 tablespoons lemonade drink mix, powder
1 tablespoon onion salt
1 tablespoon onion powder
1 tablespoon beef gravy mix, powder
1 tablespoon salt spice
1 tablespoon dry, minced parsley
½ teaspoon each – garlic salt and dry dill weed

Combine well, using a fork to blend. Store in covered container at room temperature up to a year. Makes 1 cup of powdered mix, which is adequate to make 16 cups of prepared dressing.

TO USE THE RANCH-STYLE DRESSING MIX: Combine ¼ cup milk with 1 teaspoon lemon juice and let it stand for 2-3 minutes to thoroughly sour. Meanwhile, blend ½ cup mayonnaise and 2 tablespoons Ranch-Style Dressing Mix, using a good mixing spoon. Then, stir the soured milk into the dressing mixture. Makes 1 cup of prepared dressing.

THOUSAND ISLAND RANCH DRESSING

Into 1 cup of prepared Ranch-Style Dressing (above), blend ¼ cup bottled chili sauce and 2 tablespoons relish. Makes 1 1/3 cup of dressing.

CUCMBER RANCH DRESSING

Peel and grate, or put through a blender, 1 medium cucumber (with seeds removed) and puree on high-speed. Combine this pulp with 1 teaspoon celery seed and blend into 1 cup prepared Ranch-Style Dressing (above). Makes 1 ¾ cups dressing.

ITALIAN CREAMY RANCH DRESSING

Into 1 cup prepared Ranch-Style Dressing (above), blend with fork 1 teaspoon dry minced oregano leaves, ½ teaspoon basil leaves, 2 tablespoons chopped dill pickle, 3 tablespoons dill pickle juice and 4 tablespoons oil. Makes 1 ¾ cups of dressing.

CATALINA RANCH DRESSING

Into 1 cup prepared Ranch-Style Dressing (above), blend with fork 1 teaspoon chili powder, ½ teaspoon paprika, 3 tablespoons ketchup, ¼ teaspoon cumin powder, 2 tablespoons sugar and 1 tablespoon vinegar. Makes 1 ¾ cups of dressing.

CUKES AND SOUR CREAM – MARIE CALIBER'S

Most of the time, restaurant salad bar cukes are too "soupy" and I think I know why, now that I've experimented with this simple combination. While talking to the people who worked on the ingredients for the Marie Callender's Restaurant salad bar in California, I found that it is all in the way you prepare the cucumbers – NOT the dressing!

First, you need to peel and slice the cukes and arrange them in a single layer on a cookie sheet. Allow 1 cup sliced cukes per serving. Sprinkle them lightly with salt and cover them with plastic wrap, letting them stand for 30 minutes – set your timer! Next, dump them in a colander and rinse them in COLD water; then lay them out on paper towels to absorb as much water as possible. Next, place them into an accommodating bowl.

For the dressing, combine for every 4-cups cucumber: 1 ½ cups mayonnaise, 1-pound tub sour cream, 2 tablespoons sugar (or artificial sweetener equivalent), 1 teaspoon season salt, ¼ teaspoon pepper and 1 teaspoon horseradish cream sauce (for my homemade sauce, see Index.) When it's well-mixed and tastes right to you, add the dressing to the cucumbers, gently mixing them together. Cover and chill them thoroughly before serving them garnished with parsley and a dusting of paprika.

CUKES IN VINEGAR & OIL

Prepare the cucumbers as directed above. For the dressing, combine for every 4 cups cucumbers: 8-ounce bottle Italian dressing and ¼ cup corn oil with 1 tablespoon sugar (or artificial sweetener equivalent.) Add sliced Spanish onions to taste. Cover and refrigerate these for several hours before serving. Allow 1 cup peeled and sliced cukes per serving.

GREEK OLIVE SALAD

The Michigan Inn (Southfield, MI) must use the same salad bar format as Michael's Inn in Niagara Falls, Ontario, for I sampled this very same salad at both places – and never any place else!

6-ounce can ripe, pitted olives, drained
7-ounce jar stuffed green olives, drained
8-ounce can of mushrooms – drained
4 green onions, scissor-snipped fine
2 ribs celery, sliced fine
1 large fresh, ripe tomato – seeds removed and chopped well
1/3 cup corn oil
2/3 cup bottled Italian dressing-mix
1 tablespoon each: dry, minced parsley and granulated sugar

In a 9" Pyrex loaf dish, combine all ingredients. Cover and refrigerate at least 4 hours before serving. Keeps well refrigerated up to a week. Serves 6 to 8.

CAESAR SALAD

The Caesar Salad, which has been attributed to Caesar's Palace, rather than "Caesar's P-l-a-c-e", has unfairly allowed credit to be given when it is not due. Caesar Cardini concocted this zesty salad in the early 1900's, at his Tijuana, Mexico restaurant. Here is the true story from Cardini's daughter, Rosa. One weekend, when a holiday brought Cardini unexpected tourist business, all he had on hand was a little romaine, some eggs, a wheel of Italian cheese, some lemons and dry bread. Wondering how he would handle the unusual crowd without sufficient food to serve them, he created a marriage of his various ingredients – and the salad that was a culinary accident, became a legend of gourmet fare!

Break 3 medium heads of romaine lettuce (chilled, dried and crisp) into pieces of 2- or 3-inch lengths. At the last minute, before serving, place these in a chilled salad bowl and drizzle with garlic-flavored corn oil (or olive oil), a few tablespoons of wine vinegar and the juice of 1 lemon. Break two 2-minute coddled eggs (barely soft-boiled) over this with a grind of pepper and salt and a dash of Worcestershire sauce. Sprinkle liberally with grated Parmesan and toss lightly with 2 cups toasted croutons (see Index for my homemade recipe.) If it is to your liking, add a few anchovy fillets to the salad. Serves 4.

BIG PLOY'S PICKLE JUICE ITALIAN DRESSING

When you're in a pinch for a quick salad dressing, do what I saw them do at a Big Boy restaurant, when they ran out of their standard dressing… Mix 2/3 cup dill pickle juice with 2 teaspoons sugar, 1/8 teaspoon garlic salt, ¼ teaspoon oregano leaves and ¼ cup corn oil. Shake vigorously in a tightly covered jar. Serve it cold. Makes 1 cup.

PEAS AND PEANUTS SALAD – *Like that served on The Voyageur restaurant's salad bar – in St. Clair, MI – I found this very good and a refreshingly different change from the green salad.*

Open a 10-oz package of frozen peas and let them thaw in a nice glass salad bowl. You don't cook these peas; but, don't worry – once they marinate with the dressing, they'll be fine. Combine the peas with 2 cups dry, roasted peanuts, 1 ½ cups mayonnaise, 2/3 cup sour cream and 3 green onions – finely scissor-snipped. Cover tightly and refrigerate several hours before serving. Makes 6 to 8 servings. Left-overs keep refrigerated for 3 to 4 days. Do not freeze this.

DELI-STYLE PISTACHIO PUDDING SALAD

Prepare 2 small boxes of instant pistachio pudding per package directions. Into it, stir a 9-oz tub Cool Whip, 10-oz jar maraschino cherries (well-drained), 4-cups miniature marshmallows, a 7-oz package flaked coconut, 2 cups broken pecans and a 1-lb can pineapple chunks or tidbits (well-drained.) Chill well before serving. Serves 6 to 8 nicely.

CARROT & RAISIN SLAW

I've tried this at the Sweden House, as well as many smaller "fine" restaurants. At home, I combined the best ideas from each of them.

Grate 1 carrot for each serving you plan to have, using the largest hole of your vegetable grater. Measure out the grated carrots – for every 2 cups of grated carrots, add an 8 ½-oz can crushed pineapple, un-drained, and a 7-oz pkg. of flaked coconut. Mix it well in a nice bowl, adding 1 cup raisins.

The dressing is made by mixing together ½ cup each: Marzetti's slaw dressing (or my "Marzesty's" version, see Index), mayonnaise and sour cream. Repeat this combination as often as you find it necessary, to keep the carrot mixture well-moistened. Cover the salad and refrigerate it several hours before serving. Allow ½ cup mixture for each serving.

MARSHMALLOW AMBROSIA SALAD

1-pound bag miniature marshmallows
2 cups broken pecans
10-ounce jar maraschino cherries, well-drained & halved
1 pound can pineapple chunks, well-drained
7-ounce pkg. flaked coconut
10-ounce can Mandarin orange sections, well-drained
1-pound tub sour cream
2/3 cup mayonnaise
¼ teaspoon nutmeg

Combine all the ingredients as listed; cover and refrigerate at least 4 to 6 hours. Over-night is better. Serves 8 to 10. Left-overs will keep up to a week in the refrigerator. Do NOT freeze!

BUTTERMILK POWDER MIX

You'll find so many reasons to use this homemade version of the commercial product. Not only is it a great ingredient in salad dressings, but also in baked goods and other recipes.

Combine 2 boxes (3 ounces each) instant vanilla pudding powder with 2 cups dry milk powder. Add the finely grated rind of 2 lemons and ½ cup powdered creamer, such as *Creamora* or *Coffeemate*. Sift it well, about 6 times, and store it in a covered container up to 6 months in a cool, dry place or refrigerate it even longer. You can also freeze this powder up to a year.

TO USE THE BUTTERMILK POWDER: combine ¼ cup of the powder with 2/3 cup cold water in a blender for 1 minute on high-speed (or use an electric mixer on medium-speed for 4 to 5 minutes, or until thoroughly combined.) Then, add 3 tablespoons butter or margarine chopped into tiny bits and beat/blend until smooth. Use in place of any required buttermilk or sour milk. Makes about 1 cup.

CHILI & MEXICAN FOODS

THE INFLUENCE OF MEXICAN COOKING TRADITIONS on the American restaurant industry is not as confined to the Southwest as most people would believe. While living in Southern California for a short while, I realized that the Mexican influence in food choices and restaurant decor was much stronger there than in the Midwest and Eastern parts of this country. Nonetheless, it was an intricate part of our heritage as a growing nation comprised of many ethnic and geographical persuasions.

CHILI IS JUST A KISSING COUSIN OF THE GREEK CONEY SAUCE and a second cousin, twice removed of the Italian pasta sauce. It's probably related, as well, to the Hungarian goulash sauce. With or without beans, chili has become very Americanized! Chili is more popular in Cincinnati than it is in San Diego. In fact, chili is to Cinci what beans are to Boston! It is served in many ways in the various "chili parlors" and is regarded as the only place in the United States where it is "properly" prepared and served. The fast food industry launched a new frontier devoted to expanding on the idea of Mexican cuisine with American-touches that makes it appeal to those who want a change from hamburgers.

Among some of the restaurants that will be with us for a long time to come are Taco Bell, Del Taco, The Red Onion, Casa Maria, Taco John's, Taco Patio, Zantigo's, Taco Time International, Taco-Tico Pub 'N' Taco Drive-Ins, Taco Bueno, El Taco, Pedro's Fine Mexican Food, Taco Casa, Taco Gringo, Taco Hut and many, many more. KFC patterned their own Zantigo concept after the Taco Bell, giving the building the slump stone and cream stucco look, topped off with the authentic Spanish-style roof, offering about 15 different Mexican dishes on their menu. Del Taco offers alternatives, however, to their Mexican menu by including the usual hamburgers and fries, etc.

With my make-at-home versions of these famous dishes from famous places, I try to keep to one basic combination, from which you can make several other interesting dishes, sauces and accomplishments for your Gringo-style south-of-the-border family menu.

WHEN A VERY SUCCESSFUL HAMBURGER FRANCHISE decided to give the "Golden Arches" a little nudge in the marketplace, it won the public's approval by adding a velvety-textured, mildly-seasoned chili to its menu, which has not been duplicated by any other food chain. Today, it's the leading lady of Wendy's fast food menu. Here's my version.

WEDNESDAY'S CHILI

1 ½ to 2 pounds ground round
2 tablespoons corn oil
½ teaspoon seasoned salt
10-ounce can Campbell's Onion Soup, undiluted
1 tablespoon chili powder
2 teaspoons cumin powder
½ teaspoon pepper
21-ounce can kidney beans, un-drained
6-ounce can tomato paste
8-ounce can tomato sauce

Brown the beef in the oil and crumble it with the back of a fork until it resembles rice; then, sprinkle on the seasoned salt and turn the heat to low, covering the pan to let it simmer gently in its own juices. Put the onion soup through a blender on high-speed until it's smooth; then, add it to the beef mixture and mash it thoroughly again with the fork. Stir in the remaining ingredients and simmer gently for about 15 minutes or until the flavors are well-blended and the chili is piping hot! Makes about 6 servings. Leftovers keep well in a covered container in refrigerator for a week, or freeze up to 6 months, but it should be thawed/re-heated in the top of a double boiler over gently simmering water. NEVER thaw frozen meat and tomato sauce over direct heat or it may scorch. Oven-thawing tends to dry it out quicker, evaporating the natural juices more than steaming it will do.

SPAGHETTI SAUCE can be made from my Wednesday's Chili recipe, simply by omitting the beans and using only ½ teaspoon of the cumin powder and replacing the chili powder with 1 envelope dry Italian dressing mix powder. To this, add a 28-ounce can diced tomatoes (un-drained.) This sauce can be a close relative of the spaghetti sauce served at another famous restaurant chain in the Northeast.

BAKING SODA IS THE SECRET ingredient that most restaurant chefs use to cut the acidity in tomato sauce. If you're making chili or spaghetti sauce, as a final ingredient, about 5 minutes before removing the sauce from the heat, stir in ¼ teaspoon baking soda per 18 cups prepared sauce. Stir constantly for those last few minutes on the heat to ensure the soda has penetrated the sauce completely. It will foam a little, then you can adjust the seasonings, to taste, with a bit of sugar or artificial sweetener or with a spoonful of molasses or honey, depending on the recipe you're using.

One of the versatile features of my Wednesday's Chili recipe (see Index), as I've attempted to duplicate it, is that you can omit the beans and thicken it a little with wheat germ or finely-grated fresh carrots and you have a nutritious Coney Island sauce. I experimented for several weeks with the recipe until I was convinced that the secret of the franchise chili was more meat than beans.

CONEY ISLAND SAUCE, from the famous Greek chain, is not exactly like the other restaurant's chili recipe, but it can be modified to make a fair duplication of it by simply browning the ground beef in a skillet until tender and all the pink has disappeared, then placing half of it into a blender with just enough water to cover the blender's blades. Using an on/off agitation on high speed, the meat should be blended until it resembles cement mortar and then returned to the remaining beef in the skillet. Omit the beans from my chili recipe and add ¼ teaspoon garlic salt, 2 tablespoons dark molasses, ½ teaspoon dry minced-oregano leaves and ¼ cup of either bottled wheat germ or finely-grated carrots. Simmer on low until thoroughly heated, then serve over grilled hot dogs on buns; or serve on hamburger buns as a Sloppy-Joe-style sauce.

KITCHEN SINK CONEY

Make up one batch of my "Wednesday's Chili", but leave out the beans! Then, make one batch of my "O'Nasty's Coney Sauce" (see Index for both recipes.) Combine the two of these in the same kettle. The marriage of the two compatible mixtures will be beautiful. If you want a thinner sauce, dilute it with Coca-Cola or Tab. If you want it thicker, stir in Grapenuts or crushed Special K cereal, a few tablespoons at a time until you achieve the desired consistency. Sufficient for 16 sensible servings or 6 to 8 silly servings! Left-overs freeze well for up to 6 months.

CHILI POWDER, HOT

This home-made version is hotter than the store-bought product!

1 tablespoon each: cayenne pepper, black pepper and powdered oregano
6 tablespoons cumin powder
4 tablespoons paprika
1 teaspoon each: garlic powder, onion powder, dry mustard and MSG (optional)
¼ teaspoon curry powder

Combine all ingredients in a small flour sifter over a small bowl. Sift these 6 to 8 times. Store mix in a covered container and refrigerate, to be used within a year or so. Makes about ¾ cup powder.

ONION SOUP SEASONING MIX

This can be used as a seasoning in any recipes calling for bouillon powder. It's also a good soup mix with the addition of boiling water, per directions below.

1 cup dry, minced onions
¼ cup scissor-snipped, fresh parsley
    (or 1/3 cup dry parsley flakes)
1 teaspoon pepper
½ teaspoon finely-grated lemon peel
    (or 1 teaspoon bottled lemon zest)
2 jars (3 ½ ounces each) beef bouillon powder
¼ cup onion powder
2 tablespoons onion salt
1 teaspoon paprika
2 envelopes beef gravy mix
    (or ¼ cup home-made gravy mix, beef-flavored)
½ teaspoon dry Summer Savory leaves
½ teaspoon dry Thyme leaves

Combine all ingredients well. Force mixture through sieve with the back of a spoon, or put it through a blender on high-speed, using an on/off agitation for about 30 seconds or until well-combined. Store at room temperature in a tightly covered container to use within 6 months. Makes 3 cups of mix; ¼ cup is equal to 1 envelope of the store-bought product.

TO USE THE MIX FOR INSTANT SOUP: Dissolve 1 tablespoon of mix in 6 ounces of boiling water.

SLOW-COOKER CHILI

You can take the best from each of your favorite restaurant dishes, when it comes to making a good pot of chili, and combine it all into one lovely recipe. Chili is one dish that you can put on hold for a long time, providing the temperature is either hot or cold – but never left in between. If you're going to serve it within a 3- to 4-hour period, keep it hot in a slow cooker. Otherwise, keep it refrigerated.

Prepare the chili in a large pot on top of the stove first; then, transfer it to a slow-cooker set on high for a little while then turned to low for up to 6 hours.

1 ½ pounds ground round or chuck
2 tablespoons corn or vegetable oil
15 ½-ounce jar Ragu Spaghetti Sauce, meat or traditional flavor
   (or 2 scant cups of home-made spaghetti sauce)
10-ounce can onion soup
15-ounce can red kidney beans, un-drained
2 cans (11-oz each) chili beef soup
1-pound can stewed-tomatoes, un-drained
1 tablespoon each: chili powder and brown sugar
½ cup bottled apple butter

Brown the ground beef in the oil, using a 10-inch skillet, on medium heat, mashing it with the back of a fork until the pink has disappeared. Transfer meat to a 4-quart saucepan or kettle and add remaining ingredients, mixing each one in well. Cover and cook very gently on a very low heat, stirring occasionally to combine everything thoroughly. I like to stick the blades of two knives between the pot and the burner, breaking that direct contact with the heat, which can cause scorching. A round wire pie-cooling rack also works well for this type of pan protection. Cook the chili about 30 minutes or until piping hot; then, transfer it to a slow-cooker. Set the heat to "HI" for 30 minutes and then on "LOW" for up to 6 hours. Keep it covered, but still stir it about once every hour until it's served. If it thickens too much while heating, dilute it with V-8 juice or canned beef broth (or beer for a truly hearty flavor) until it is to your liking. Serves 6 to 8. Left-overs freeze well to be used within 6 months.

MARGUERITAS

If you can't find ice that is crushed so well it almost resembles snow, you might as well forget the whole thing. The ice makes the drink! To crush regular cubes at home, I hammer them into chips first, then put them through my blender in small portions with just a little water to make it snow-like. I fill a pitcher half-full of the "snow". Next, into the blender I put 1 cup tequila, 1/3 cup Triple Sec and enough "snow" to absorb all the liquor. Then I add 2 cups bottled Margarita mix (non-alcoholic) and turn on the blender until it's well-combined. Wipe the rim of your Margarita (or wine) glasses with a slice of fresh lime and dip the wet rim into a saucer of coarse salt. Put the piece of lime into the glass and add enough "snow" to fill it half-way, then add the Margarita mixture up to the rim!

STEAK AND SHAKE RESTAURANTS

In the Mid-West (especially in the St. Louis, MO area), one of the most-often requested recipe secrets from my visits with KMOX-RADIO was for Steak and Shake's chili. On my way to Los Angeles in March of 1982, I had to change planes in St. Louis and had some lay-over time in which to visit some of the area and get a good bowl of chili! The trip was well worth it!

STAY IN SHAPE CHILI

2 cups hot, black coffee
3 cans (6 ounces each) V-8 juice
1 envelope onion soup mix
10-ounce can beef broth
2 teaspoons chili powder
1 teaspoon paprika
2 teaspoons Hershey's Chocolate Syrup (don't faint!)
2/3 cup of my home-made "Cup of Thoup" tomato-flavored powder (see Index)
    (or use 4 envelopes of the commercial product)
2 tablespoons corn oil
1 ½-pounds ground round
2 cans (1 pound each) DRAINED red kidney beans

Combine coffee, juice, soup mix, broth, chili powder, paprika and syrup in a tuna half quart sauce pan. Stir in the home-made "Cup of Thoup" powder (or the commercial product) and turn the heat to medium, stirring often until piping hot and it begins to thicken into a smooth sauce. [NOTE: I found that if the liquid gets too hot, the "Cup of Thoup" powder will "lump"; use a wire whisk or an electric mixer to smooth it out in the pan.]

Place the oil in a 10-inch skillet and brown the beef, breaking it up with a fork until all of the pink disappears. Transfer the beef and drippings to the sauce mixture and stir. Drain the cans of beans well and stir those into the mixture as well. Heat it all until it's piping hot. Serves 6 sensibly! If you plan to freeze the chili for future servings, do not add the beans until you're ready to thaw and re-heat it or the beans may become "mushy".

MEXICAN SEASONING MIX - *Use to season tomato sauce or your favorite Mexican dishes.*

2 tablespoons chili powder
1 tablespoon each: cumin powder and paprika
1 teaspoon onion powder
½ teaspoon each: celery salt, garlic powder, black pepper and Salt-Spice (see Index for my version)

Mix it all together and store in a covered container at room temperature for ages. Makes 1/3 cup.

COMPATIBLE SAUCE BASE FOR CHILI OR SPAGHETTI

1 ½ pounds ground round
3 tablespoons oil
2 tablespoons beef bouillon powder
¼ cup dry, minced onion
2/3 cup bottled Wish Bone Italian Dressing
½ cup raspberry jam
2 tablespoons sugar
½ teaspoon garlic salt
2 tablespoons Cream of Wheat instant cereal mix, uncooked
1 ½ cups hot black coffee-maker
1 envelope tomato-flavored Cup-a-Soup powder (or use my "Cup-of-Thoup" mix - see Index)
26-ounce can tomato soup (or three 10-ounce cans)
1 tablespoon dry, minced oregano leaves
¼ teaspoon pepper

Brown the ground beef in the oil until the pink has disappeared. Transfer it to a 2 ½-quart sauce pan, drippings and all! Turn the heat to medium-high and stir in, well, each ingredient as listed. Let it heat without boiling until hot. Refrigerate it, well-covered, for up to a week or freeze it for up to 6 months.

AS A BASE FOR CHILI, when you thaw this sauce to re-heat it, add 1 tablespoon chili powder, 2 teaspoons cumin powder and 3 cans (1-lb each) un-drained, red kidney beans. Serves 6 to 8.

AS A BASE FOR SPAGHETTI SAUCE - add an additional 1 to 1 ½ pounds of browned ground beef and another 1/3 cup of the Italian dressing, plus an 8-oz can of un-drained mushrooms.

REFRIED BEANS

Cook 2 ½ cups dry pinto beans in 6 cups simmering, slightly salted water (covered) for about 3 hours or until fork-tender. Drain, rinse and place in a large heavy skillet – containing enough melted butter, Crisco, or lard to ½-inch deep. Stir and fry the beans about 4 to 6 minutes. Drain off excess fat and refrigerate until time to use in other recipes. Salt and pepper to taste. Makes about 6 cups cooked beans.

HOT PEPPER SAUCE

Combine, as listed: 1 teaspoon cayenne pepper, 1 tablespoon each – paprika and chili powder, ¼ teaspoon curry powder, 1 tablespoon vinegar, 1-ounce vodka and ¼ cup hot water. Blend until smooth with an electric mixer or in a blender, using medium to high speed. Store at room temperature, preferably near a fire extinguisher. This is really H-O-T! One drop is equal to the commercial brand. Keeps for ages in the refrigerator in a covered container. Makes 6 ounces.

JOHNNIE LEGA'S CHILI

"The Working Man's Palace" was the name Pearl Beach had given to Johnnie Lega's Bar when we lived near there for nearly 12 years. It was known around the world. Once, when Julia Lega was traveling in Europe, she was sitting in a train station in Spain where she struck up a conversation with another American who asked her what part of "The States" was she from. Julia assured him that he had probably never heard of it – the town was so small; but, when she said, "Pearl Beach, Michigan," the American replied, "Johnnie Lega's Bar!" He was from the East Coast, but had never forgotten his one visit through Pearl Beach area and a memorable bowl of chili at Lega's! We were all so saddened when Johnnie passed away from cancer. But, everyone can still enjoy his unique chili recipe. You have no idea how long it took me to duplicate this recipe. Johnnie never used a measuring utensil and it came out perfect every day! I observed him making his famous dish, jotting down everything he put in the kettle – it was months later and many failures before even HE had to admit, I had it right on target!

2 pounds ground beef (chuck preferred)
1 small onion, the size of an egg
1 green bell pepper, seeds removed
5 ribs celery, sliced paper thin
1-quart water
6-ounces tomato paste
½ teaspoon garlic powder
2 tablespoons chili powder
1 teaspoon oregano powder
2 tablespoons vinegar
2-pound can red kidney beans, un-drained
12-ounce can of light beer

Brown the beef in a large hot skillet without adding any oil or shortening. Chuck ground beef has enough fat in it. Chop the onion and pepper and add to the beef, stirring and cooking until the onions get transparent. Add celery, water, tomato paste, garlic, chili and oregano powders. Stir well, cover and turn heat to low. Simmer gently for 20 minutes. Then, add Johnnie's "secret" ingredient – the vinegar – followed by the un-drained can of beans and the beer. Cover and simmer gently for about 1 hour. Leftovers taste even better the second day! Unfortunately, it doesn't freeze well. Makes 8 servings.

I'M VERY GRATEFUL TO CHILI!

ONE OF THE NICEST THINGS ABOUT MAKING CHILI is that it goes so far! After I had walked out of the newspaper editor's office, telling him to "mail me my check," I didn't know if he had fired me or if I had quit! But to go home and start my own paper was an impulsive reaction, if not foolish. It was a nice job for a housewife with 5 kids. The money wasn't "good", but it did buy the kids a few things we couldn't otherwise afford. Paul was working as a draftsman for a sign company in Mt. Clemens and that weekly paycheck was spent on house payments, utilities and insurance even before it was cashed. The money I earned from writing helped and I gave it up because of pride and integrity.

The first thing I did with my writing, at that time, was to take all the recipes I had published in my newspaper column and all of the articles on recipes that I had sold to "Lady's Circle" and "Home Life Magazine", and secured permission to re-print my own material in a small cookbook. With Free Press columnist, Bob Talbert, to "plug" the little book, I sold all 1,000 copies in a month! Rather than re-print it at the "Quickie-While-You-Wait" printer shop, I decided I would put those recipes into a monthly publication – not exactly my own newspaper, but certainly worth the opportunity to try it and see if it would pay. We lived on a lot of chili in those days. And this chapter seems like a good place to bring this all up to you, because I am very grateful to chili! It fed our family of seven nicely – night after night – when there was no money for much else but hamburger and beans! And because I only owned 4 cooking pots – small, medium, large, and the no-life-guard-on-duty size, making chili and any of its spin-offs was substantial fare for us for the time being.

It was a good thing that I kept a complete list of names and addresses of those who wrote to me at the newspaper, requesting recipes, and all of those who purchased my first little cookbook, "The Better Cooker's Cookbook", for I invited each one by post card to subscribe to my monthly newsletter. The response was sufficiently enthusiastic to cause me to take on the commitment – but, without Paul knowing anything about it, for he surely would have put his foot down and said, "NO!"

Until the newsletter could pay for itself, Paul thought what I was earning was coming from the ironing I did each week for other people at $5 a basket. Since Paul worked late many nights and bowled two nights a week, he couldn't keep an accurate account of how much ironing I really did. What I scraped together from the ironing money, I used as a down payment on a hand-cranked mimeograph machine so that I could print my own newsletter. For nine months, I kept this from Paul; and, with our daughter Debbie's help, put out the publication, paid off the mimeograph and saw my subscriptions reach 100 readers. That is when I was invited to appear on Dennis Wholley's television program, "AM Detroit" on WXYZ-TV. I had to tell Paul! He took it rather calmly, I thought; but now, in retrospect, I believe he was suffering from a mild case of shock from it all.

FOOD FOR THOUGHT

HUITLACOCHE *is corn smut eaten in Mexico. The large swollen growths are chopped & cooked in oil with lightly sautéed onion and garlic for about 15 minutes. For a more Mexican touch, include pieces of chili pepper and oregano. - N. Chalotta of Taco Bell, New Mexico*

CINCINNATI CHILI – *is a serious seminar of culinary creativity. The hallmark of Ohio's chili is a pinch of clove and a dash of allspice!*

To my Wednesday's Chili recipe (see Index), omit the beans and, when required to add the chili powder, also add: 1/4-tsp powdered cloves and 1/8-tsp powdered allspice for this Cincinnati version.

You have one of five options for serving the sauce: (1) over the omitted beans [gently heated in a saucepan along with the liquid in which they're canned, a dab of butter and salt & pepper to taste until piping hot, but never boiled or the beans turn to mush] or (2) over prepared spaghetti or (3) with grated cheese or (4) with fresh-chopped onions or (5) over hot dogs in buns with or without mustard & onions.

SHY LION CHILI PARLOR CHILI

When our good friend, Sherry Ellis, was helping me with my recipes, she returned from a weekend trip to her hometown in Cincinnati, bringing me a container of her favorite chili to see if I could tell how to make it at home. This is my version.

3 pounds ground chuck
2 tablespoons corn oil
1 cup minced fresh onion
2 cans (10 ounces each) beef broth
2 teaspoons cumin powder
1 teaspoon allspice
½ teaspoon powdered clove
1 ½ teaspoons onion salt
1 teaspoon each: garlic salt and black pepper
2 tablespoons chili powder
1/8 teaspoon cayenne pepper
½ cup molasses
½ ounce bitter chocolate (or a half square)
1 teaspoon paprika
6-ounce can tomato paste
1 tablespoon *Postum* instant drink powder, OR 4 teaspoons instant tea powder

Brown the chuck and onions in the oil on medium heat, mashing the beef with the back of a fork until all the pink disappears and the onions become transparent. Add the broth and cover and simmer for 15 minutes. Remove about half of this mixture to a blender, using high-speed until it's about the consistency of cement mortar and then return it to the remaining beef & onion mixture. Then, transfer all of it to a 6-qt kettle that has a tight-fitting lid. Also, add all the remaining ingredients and stir well. Cover and cook on very low heat for about an hour, stirring often. If you wish to give it a snappier flavor, add in a whole dry bay leaf, crumbled fine; as well as, a teaspoonful of Worcestershire and about half of a green bell pepper, seeded and finely-grated. If you wish to dilute the chili, do so with hot, black, strong tea. You may keep it refrigerated up to a week or freeze it up to 6 months. Serves 10.

CHILI SEASONING MIX

You can buy this mix in an envelope at your local supermarket or put this recipe together in less than 20 minutes and have a bowl of benevolent chili that's so good, you'd bet your Gringo sombrero it came straight from Tijuana by burro! This makes about 1 ½ cups of mix.

12 Ritz Crackers, crushed or blended to a fine powder
4 envelopes Tomato-flavored soup powder
    (or 1-cup of my "Cup of Thoup" – see Index)
¼ cup dry, minced onions
4 teaspoons instant tea powder
2 teaspoons each: beef bouillon and chili powders
½ teaspoon each: hickory-flavored salt, garlic salt, cumin powder and dry minced parsley

Combine cracker powder with the soup powder and remaining ingredients, stirring thoroughly. Store at room temperature in a 2-cup container with a tight-fitting lid. Keeps for weeks and weeks.

To use the mix: Brown 1-lb ground chuck in 2 tablespoons corn oil in a 3 ½- to 4-quart sauce pan or Dutch oven-type kettle, mashing the beef down with the back of a fork until all the pink color disappears. Turn heat to lowest setting and stir in 4 cups boiling water and a 15-ounce can of un-drained, red kidney beans. Then, add all the chili seasoning mix (from one batch), stirring until well-combined and it begins to thicken slightly. Serves 4 to 5.

If you like more beans, add another can, but drain it first. If you like it hotter, stir in a little dehydrated chili pepper flakes, to taste, for individual servings.

V-ACHE JUICE

16 chopped tomatoes
½ cup each: carrots, onions and celery – all chopped
2 tablespoons each: salt and lemon juice
1 teaspoon Worcestershire sauce

Combine everything and boil rapidly for 25 minutes in a roomy saucepan or kettle, until all the ingredients are very tender. Press this mixture through a fine-mesh strainer to remove the tomato seeds and skins. Take a small portion of this mixture at a time and run it through a blender until it's as smooth as the commercial product. Ladle the mixture into hot, sterilized jars, allowing 1-inch head-space. Seal and process in a hot water bath for 15 minutes. If you don't want to go with the hot-water-bath-canning route, ladle the juice into plastic, freezer containers with tight-fitting lids; still, allowing 1-inch head-space. Makes 2 quarts of juice. Freezes well up to a year!

SOPAIPILLAS

Mario Leal settled in Texas when he came from Mexico. He wanted, very much, to show people that good Mexican food meant more than enchiladas. He wanted to remove the image of Mexican food being mostly spicy and greasy. His restaurant, Mario's Chiquita (in the Dallas area), is where these delicate little fried pillow-pastries were a treat for me!

4 cups flour
3 teaspoons baking powder
1 ½ teaspoons salt
1 tablespoon sugar
1 tablespoon butter
1 envelope dry yeast
¼ cup warm water
1 teaspoon sugar (yes – more sugar)
1 ¼ cups scalded milk
about 1 ½ pints corn oil
cinnamon-sugar mix (1/2 cup sugar to 1 tablespoon Cinnamon powder)

Combine the flour, baking powder and salt with the 1 tablespoon sugar; then, cut-in the butter and set aside while you soften the yeast in the warm water with the 1 teaspoon sugar. Let stand 4 to 5 minutes, or until bubbly. Meanwhile, scald the milk and let it cool to lukewarm; then, add the yeast mixture to it. Make a well in the center of the dry ingredients and pour in the liquid mixture. Work into a smooth dough, kneading for about 5 minutes with lightly floured hands until dough is elastic in texture, but not dry. Roll dough out to ¼-inch thickness and cut into 3-inch triangles. In a heavy sauce pan, fry a few at a time in the oil, keeping it about 3 inches deep and about 425°F. When golden brown and puffed like little pillows, lift out with a slotted spoon to drain on paper towels. Dust with the cinnamon-sugar mix. Makes about 4 dozen. They keep well in a covered container at room temperature up to a week.

TOMATOES FOR FREEZING

I want to detour here long enough to tell you about putting tomatoes away for future use, since most Italian and Mexican recipes call for tomato sauce or paste, or even stewed tomatoes. Here's a little trick to take care of that end-of-summer bounty of tomatoes: take your whole, ripe tomatoes (intact and ripe from the vine) one at a time, being careful not to puncture their skins, and dip them into a pan of HOT (but not boiling) water for 30 seconds. Remove each with a slotted spoon and place individually in lightly-greased cupcake tins. Set these in the freezer, unwrapped, just until they're frozen solid – about 4 to 5 hours. Working quickly, remove them and place carefully in food-storage, plastic, freezer bags; seal and return to freezer to be used within 6 months. I like to put the bags of tomatoes into plastic containers in the freezer to protect the tomatoes from getting damaged from heavier foods. When you use the tomatoes from the freezer, let them thaw only long enough so you can insert the tip of a sharp, thin-bladed knife around the core to remove it. Then place the tomatoes upside down on paper towels to let all the liquids that accumulated in the freezing process drain out. The removal of all the excess liquids will leave the tomatoes nicely firm and the skins should slip off easily by splitting each one carefully around their "equator". You can, then, slice them up for salads or use them in cooking. The complete draining is the "secret" to a fresh-as-just-picked texture!

PASTA PERFORMANCE TOMATO SAUCE MIX

This is a pantry-shelf friend if ever you had one! It makes up almost like my "Chili Seasoning Mix" (see Index) and is just as versatile!

12 Ritz Crackers, finely crushed to a powder
4 envelopes Tomato-flavored soup powder
    (or 1 cup of my "Cup of Thoup" – see Index)
¼ cup dry, minced onions
4 teaspoons instant tea powder
2 teaspoons each: beef bouillon powder and paprika
1 teaspoon each: dry, oregano leaves and parsley flakes
½ teaspoon each: garlic salt and cumin powder

Combine cracker powder with the soup powder and remaining ingredients, stirring thoroughly. Store at room temperature in a 3-cup container with a tight-fitting lid. Keeps for weeks. Makes about 2 cups.

To use the sauce mix: Brown 1-pound ground chuck in 2 tablespoons corn oil in a 4-quart sauce pan or Dutch oven, mashing the beef down with the back of a fork until all the pink color disappears. Turn heat to medium and stir in 4 cups boiling water and a 6-oz can of V-8 Juice (and one 8-ounce can drained mushrooms - optional). Then, add all the tomato sauce mix (from one batch), stirring until smooth. Turn heat to low and cover pan with a tight-fitting lid. When piping hot, pour over your favorite prepared pasta, allowing 1 cup uncooked pasta per batch of this recipe. Serves 4 to 6 sensibly!

CONEY SAUCE MIX

As in the "Tomato Sauce Mix" recipe (above), brown the beef and put half of it in a blender with enough water to cover the blades. Blend to the consistency of cement mortar, then return to the remaining browned beef. Continue as otherwise directed (above), omitting the V-8 Juice and adding ½ cup pickle relish along with the boiling water. Also, add ½ cup Grapenuts cereal to the sauce ingredients while simmering. When piping hot, spoon sauce into split, toasted hot dog buns.

HOSTILITY SAUCE

For either tacos or burritos – this is one quick, "nasty" sauce that's guaranteed to remove the lint from your naval, open your sinus passages and make a liar out of Rolaids!

Mix together thoroughly, 1 cup Thousand Island dressing, ¼ cup well-chopped green pepper, ½ teaspoon Tabasco sauce and 1 tablespoon each: my Mexican Seasoning Mix powder and Horseradish Cream Sauce (see Index for both.) Store in covered container in refrigerator. Makes about 1 1/3 cups.

BURRITO SAUCE

1-cup ketchup
2-TB each: horseradish cream sauce and honey
1/4-cup pickle relish
2-TB chopped green pepper
1/4-tsp Tabasco sauce (or to taste)
1-tsp onion powder

Combine all ingredients well and keep refrigerated until ready to serve over hot burritos! Makes 1 1/2-cups of sauce. Do not freeze it. Keeps 30 days if tightly covered and refrigerated.

CHILI SAUCE, LIKE BLUNTS

In a pinch, you can create your own quick chili sauce, using 1 cup ketchup (any commercial brand or use my homemade version – see Index), plus ½ cup pickle relish & ¼ cup bottled apple butter. Stir it all together thoroughly. Makes 1 ¾ cup of sauce.

CHILI MIGNON, *Like Chasen's Chili*

This is a favorite of my family! It's so close to Chasen's Chili, which Liz Taylor & Richard Burton would always have flown to them, wherever they were in the world! From my "Better Cooker's Crock Book" (out of print now), this was one of my most-often requested recipes!

3 pounds ground beef
1 small onion (the size of an egg), chopped
5 ribs celery, sliced paper thin
4 tablespoons corn oil
½ teaspoon season salt
10-ounce can beef broth
4 cups strong, black, hot tea
6-ounce can tomato paste
4 teaspoons chili powder
2 teaspoons cumin powder
½ teaspoon pepper
1 teaspoon each: garlic salt and oregano powder
3 tablespoons vinegar
16-ounce can stewed-tomatoes
4 cans (1-lb each) red kidney beans, un-drained
2 cans (10-oz each) Campbell's Chili Beef Soup

Brown the beef with the onions and celery in the oil, crumbling the beef to the consistency of rice. When the onions are transparent and the beef is no longer pink, put it in a Dutch-oven or slow-cooker and add everything else to it. Simmer it, covered, on low heat for about 2 hours – or until all flavors have blended to your taste and it's piping hot, but never let it boil!

TEXAS STYLE: Dilute the finished chili with two 12-ounce cans Busch Light beer! Ed McMahon never had it so good! Left-overs freeze well in family- or individual-sized containers. Serves 10 to 12.

TOMATO PASTE

4-quarts ripe tomatoes, peeled and sliced ¼ inch thick
2 tablespoons table salt
1-quart oil – corn, vegetable, or safflower

Place tomatoes in a shallow pan and sprinkle with the salt. Let them stand for 4 hours; then, put them in a 4-quart kettle (without adding any other liquids) and bring them to a slow and easy boil. The heat will force the tomatoes and salt to draw their own juice. Stir constantly until soft. Press this mixture through a fine-mesh strainer to remove seeds and skins. Return to kettle to cook gently (or into a slow-cooker to prevent scorching) until it's reduced to a puree, thick enough to spread with a knife over the surface of a lightly-greased roasting pan or jelly roll pan. Score the paste in several places with the knife. Oven-dry it at the lowest heat setting, leaving the oven door open an inch, until the paste is thick enough to shape into 1-inch balls. Place the balls in a container with a loose-fitting lid and let them stand at room temperature for 4 days (mark the time down so that you give the balls at least 72 hours of drying time), at which time, knead the tomato balls into a smooth mixture. Shape the mixture, again, into smaller balls, ½ inch in diameter. Dip each ball into the oil (important to cover them completely in oil) and then drop them back into the container, keeping the container covered with wax paper or cheese cloth that's secured with a rubber band (or use a Mason jar with a Snap-On-type of sealing top.) Aunt Angela preferred Olive Oil when she made these; but, with cholesterol of such concern these days, I try to stick with the lighter oils...it's up to you.

To reconstitute the balls, mash the tomato paste into a measuring cup and measure out an equal amount of warm tap water, stirring it into the paste until smooth. Then use it in place of any commercial-type tomato paste. It keeps at room temperature for months. If you plan to use the ½-inch tomato paste balls for specific recipes you can season the oil to your liking with garlic powder, or onion powder, or finely-crushed oregano leaves (however you like) before dipping the balls into it. If the balls seem to dry too quickly, you can drizzle a little more oil over them while in the storage jar after a week or two, depending on the amount of humidity in the room. You can freeze them to keep for years too. This recipe makes about 50 balls, ½ inch in diameter.

SALSA – MILD SAUCE

1 pound can stewed-tomatoes
6-ounce can tomato paste
¼ cup raspberry jam
1 tablespoon my Mexican Seasoning Mix (see Index)
¼ teaspoon hot pepper sauce
1 teaspoon chili powder
½ teaspoon garlic powder
3 tablespoons butter or margarine, softened

Put everything in a blender on high-speed until smooth. Keep refrigerated in a covered container until time to serve with your favorite corn chips or other dipping items. If you like it "5-alarm" style, add more hot seasonings, to taste. This will keep refrigerated up to 6 weeks. Makes about 2 cups of sauce.

TACO BEEF SAUCE

1 ½ pounds ground round
3 tablespoons oil
8-ounce can pizza sauce
1 teaspoon each: onion powder and dry oregano leaves
½ teaspoon each: chili powder, onion salt, season salt, pepper and cumin powder
2 teaspoons sugar

Brown the beef in the oil, crumbling it with the back of a fork until it resembles rice. When all the pink is gone from the meat, turn heat to low and add remaining ingredients as listed, stirring thoroughly as you go. Cover and simmer 20 minutes. Refrigerate left-overs in a covered container up to a week. Freezes well, up to 6 months. Use as needed to fill taco shells. Serves 4 to 6.

TACO LAYERED SALAD

Prepare the taco beef sauce (above) as directed. To the finished sauce, add 2 cans (1 pound each) red kidney beans, drained. Let this chill in the refrigerator while you grease a 9 x 12 x 2" baking dish well with corn oil. Slice half a head of lettuce into shreds and spread evenly over the bottom of the oiled dish. Over the lettuce, arrange about 2 cups fresh diced tomatoes (with some of the seeds and juicy parts removed.) Over the tomato-layer, sprinkle the finely-sliced stems and tips of 4 green onions. Drizzle 1 ½ cups Thousand Island dressing over that layer; then, sprinkle that with 2 cups shredded Cheddar or Monterrey Jack cheese. Now, spoon on chilled Taco Beef Sauce, with added beans. Arrange 3 cups crushed corn chips over the beef-layer. Spoon one batch of my Guacamole recipe (see Index) over the chips. Chill thoroughly before serving to six!

TOSTADO SALAD – Shape tortillas to fit an oiled salad bowl. Add the same fillings as in the Taco Salad (above); but, rather than Thousand Island dressing, use an equal amount of your favorite taco sauce. Serve it well-chilled to 6.

GUACAMOLE – Authentic Mexican-Style

Peel 2 ripe avocados and remove their pits – reserve these. Place avocados in a bowl and mash to a chunky consistency; then, add the following: 4 teaspoons lime juice, 1 large fresh tomato (seeded & chopped), 2 tablespoons dry minced onions, 2 tablespoons finely-chopped fresh red onion, 1 well-chopped (bottled) chili pepper with 1 tablespoon of the liquid in which it's bottled, as well as 1 teaspoon powdered coriander. Beat it all together with an electric mixer on high-speed – or run the mixture through a blender – until pureed. Press the reserved pits into the mixture and refrigerate for 1 hour before serving. Remove the pits and discard when ready to serve. Makes 2 cups.

THE SECRET TO A GOOD CONEY SAUCE is simple – brown and crumble the beef; then put half of it through the blender with just enough water to cover the blades until it's the consistency of cement mortar, mixing back in to the other half. Jack McCarthy of Detroit's Channel 7 (WXYZ-TV) confessed to me that this was the secret to good, authentic Greek Coney Sauce, when he came to our home on Christmas Eve [1977] to do a film about us. Apparently, Jack's a gourmet cook! When he traveled, he'd take a lot of kidding about carrying, with him…a crepe pan in a tennis racket cover.

O'NASTY CONEY SAUCE – *Don't be over-whelmed by the number of ingredients! It's an everything-in-one-kettle dish, that can't go wrong!*

2 ½ to 3 pounds ground chuck
2 teaspoons cumin powder
a few grains of cayenne pepper
½ teaspoon black pepper
1 teaspoon crushed oregano leaves
3 tablespoons beef bouillon powder
6-ounce can tomato paste
3 cups hot, strong black tea
1 envelope onion soup mix
1 tablespoon chili powder
1 teaspoon paprika
½ teaspoon garlic salt
3 tablespoons packed brown sugar
1 cup ketchup
6-ounce can V-8 Juice
½ teaspoon Kitchen Bouquet

Brown the chuck in a large skillet (when using lean beef, brown in a few tablespoons of oil), mashing it with the back of a fork over medium-high heat until all the pink disappears. Cover the blades of your blender with about 1/3 cup water, then put half of the browned beef in and blend on high speed with an on/off agitation until smooth. Return this to the skillet to mix with the rest of the browned beef. Stir in cumin powder, peppers, oregano, bouillon, tomato paste and hot tea. Turn off heat and transfer everything to a 2 ½-quart saucepan, then add remaining ingredients. Cook and stir frequently over medium heat until piping hot. Spoon mixture over grilled hot dogs in buns – or just into plain buns with plenty of diced onions on each serving. Leftovers will keep up to 2 weeks in refrigerator. Freeze mixture up to 6 months. Makes 8 to 10 servings.

FOR A GREAT CHILI – to the above recipe, add 3 cans (1 pound each) red chili beans in chili gravy and double the amount of chili powder.

LOOSE HAMBURGER

In Kansas City, this is a close kissing-cousin to a Sloppy Joe, but referred to merely as "loose hamburger."

2 pounds ground chuck
1 envelope onion soup mix
2 envelopes Tomato Cup-A-Soup
    (or use my "Cup of Thoup" - see Index)
½ cup chopped onion
¼ cup ketchup
¼ cup pickle relish
2 tablespoons dry, minced green pepper
1 teaspoon paprika
½ teaspoon garlic salt
½ teaspoon pepper
¼ teaspoon Anise extract
1 tablespoon dry parsley flakes
1 tablespoon Worcestershire
¼ cup all-purpose flour

Press ground chuck into a non-greased 10-inch skillet to cover pan evenly. No additional oil is needed since the chuck has enough of its own fat to grease the pan as it cooks. Cover with a tight-fitting lid and simmer slowly for 15 minutes to bring out the natural juices in the beef. Remove the lid and break up the meat with the back of a fork and stir it around, adding each of the remaining ingredients as listed EXCEPT the flour! Pack the mixture back over the bottom of the pan, keeping heat on low to medium. Now, add the flour; but, dust it evenly over the meat mixture, allowing it to absorb the flour. Stir it gently just to incorporate the flour. Pack it down again with the back of a large spoon and cover the pan tightly again. Simmer it very slowly for 10 minutes. If you like a thicker sauce, stir in 1/3 cup Grapenuts cereal during the 10-minute-simmer time! Spoon the mixture into split, toasted hot dog buns for 8. Left-overs can be refrigerated for up to a week if tightly covered. Frozen left-overs should be used within 3 months.

MAN-WITCH SLOPPY JOES

Prepare the Loose Hamburger exactly as directed above except, after stirring in the flour and just before the last simmering period, you should also add a 1-pound can stewed-tomatoes, ¼ cup bottled Italian salad dressing, 8-ounce can tomato sauce, 8-oz can jellied cranberry sauce (mashed well with the back of a fork), 6-ounce can V-8 Juice and 10-ounce can tomato soup. Stir well. If the skillet in which you prepared the hamburger doesn't look like it will accommodate all the additional ingredients, transfer the meat mixture to a pan that will, then add the Man-Witch ingredients. Spoon the mixture into split and broiler-toasted hamburger buns. Sufficient for serving 8 with leftovers, which can be refrigerated up to a week if tightly covered. Freezes well up to 3 months.

LEADING-PARENTS' WORCESTERSHIRE SAUCE

2 tablespoons ketchup
3 green onions, minced
2 anchovies, finely chopped (or 1 teaspoon anchovy paste)
½ teaspoon powdered cloves
1-quart dark vinegar

Combine ingredients in top of a double boiler over simmering water, stirring until thoroughly heated. Never let it boil, nor put it on direct heat. When thoroughly heated, remove from double boiler and let it stand in a covered container at room temperature for 48 hours. Strain it several times and then bottle it. Keep it tightly-capped and refrigerate. It will keep for many months. Makes almost a quart of sauce.

TORTILLA SHELLS

It's amazing how this Mexican form of bread could be a 2ⁿᵈ-cousin-twice-removed (probably on its mother's side of the family) to the Jewish Matzah; and on its father's side of the family, it could be a cousin-by-marriage to the Arabian flat bread, or the Far-East pita bread.

Mix 2 cups Quaker Masa Harina (or see Index for my version) and 1 cup cold water into a smooth dough, adding just enough more water to keep it moist and smooth. Divide the dough into 12 equal-sized balls. Work with one at a time, keeping the rest in plastic bags so they won't dry out. Roll each portion into a paper-thin circle between two sheets of waxed paper and stack (with wax paper between layers) and then – just as if you're making pancakes – brown them very lightly on a slightly oiled, hot griddle. Keep them soft, not crisp. You can, then, freeze them to be used in other recipes within 6 months – or refrigerate to use within a week. Makes 12 tortillas.

TACO SHELLS – Heat 1-pint corn oil in a 12" skillet. Fry your prepared tortilla shells (above), one at a time in hot oil, using a pair of tongs to fold each, loosely, in half while it's frying to a crispy, golden brown. Remove from hot oil and let it drain on paper towels until all have been fried. *It's all in the way you shape the tortilla!*

FLOUR TORTILLAS – Prepare these easily with 2 cups self-rising flour, 1 tablespoon Crisco and ½ to ¾ cup lukewarm water. Follow the same method in my Tortilla Shells recipe (above) as it directs for rolling out and browning them.

CORN CHIPS – Prepare the corn or flour tortillas, but shape and roll out into paper-thin circles, 3" in diameter. Brown on a lightly greased griddle as in the tortilla recipe (above); but, while still hot, dust with your favorite butter-flavored popcorn salt.

TOSTADOS – Just like the tacos method (above); but, deep-fry the tortilla flat. Layer each tortilla with beef-filling, shredded lettuce, chopped tomatoes and shredded cheese. Add taco or burrito sauce on the side or drizzle it over the top.

NACHOS CON CARNE

Stewart Anderson's Black Angus Restaurant (Lakewood, CA) served an appetizer in the lounge that consisted of a platter of corn chips, arranged in a single layer over the bottom of the plate, with a little taco beef filling spooned between the chips and a side dish of melted cheese. To re-enact the dish, pour an 8-ounce jar of Cheez Whiz into the top of a double boiler (over simmering water) with 3-ounces cream cheese, stirring until melted and smooth – or use an electric beater on low speed as it is melting. Then stir into this: ¼ teaspoon hot pepper sauce, 1 teaspoon chili powder and 1 tablespoon of the liquid in which yellow peppers are bottled, plus 1 pepper – finely chopped. Serve the sauce warm on the side of corn chips and beef. Serves 4 nicely.

TACOS

The Mexican answer to the Big Mac – its beef mixture, lettuce, cheese, onions and "special sauce" are piled artistically into a crisp (or soft) taco shell!

1 to 1 ½ pounds ground chuck
2 tablespoons oil
2 cups V-8 Juice
12 Ritz crackers, crushed to a powder
1 tablespoon chili powder-for1/2-tsp paprika
½ teaspoon each: garlic salt, season salt and pepper
½ teaspoon Tabasco Sauce (or to taste)
¼ cup finely-grated green pepper
¼ cup dry, minced onions
2 teaspoons beef bouillon powder

Brown the beef in the oil until the "pink" disappears. Stir constantly and mash with a fork until it's the consistency of rice. Turn heat to low and add remaining ingredients, stirring frequently. Keep meat mixture warm as you fill 12 taco shells with it. Top each one off with shredded lettuce, shredded Monterey-Jack or sharp cheddar cheese, chopped fresh onions & taco sauce. Makes 1 dozen tacos.

FIVE-ALARM TACO SAUCE

Prepare 1 recipe of my "Big Match Special Sauce" (see Index) and add to it: 1 teaspoon paprika, 1 teaspoon chili powder and ¼ teaspoon Tabasco sauce (or to taste). Sufficient to top-off a dozen tacos.

MASA HARINA IMITATION

Combine 1 cup all-purpose flour with ¼ cup yellow or white cornmeal and ¼ cup finely-crushed cornflakes cereal. Sift the mixture together 3 times and store in a covered container at room temperature for up to 60 days. Multiply the ingredients as needed. Makes a good understudy for the commercial corn flour.

ENCHILADAS

These are like burritos, but they are filled and rolled up with two ends open. After browning your tortillas, dip them in hot oil for 10 seconds or just until limp. Fill them with my Burrito Mixture and Re-Fried Beans (see Index.) Roll up and arrange in a shallow baking pan at 425°F for 12 minutes or until crispy. Top with shredded cheddar cheese, chopped green peppers and either my Hostility Sauce or Burrito Sauce.

SMORGASBORD – FREEDOM OF CHOICE

It's a mistake to think of the fast food industry as being confined to hamburgers and fries and buckets of chicken or fish. It is really a more versatile banquet of menu selections than the critics give us time to consider. The public is fickle and very easily swayed by the aggressive opinions of self-styled experts who preach the evils of fast food with all the charisma of a revival tent evangelism; and we, the believing public, will go in whatever direction the wind blows the strongest!

Nobody dreamed that the step-child of the food industry would ever have endured this long – for, to everybody's surprise, "fast food" has, indeed, become the "Liza Doolittle" of the restaurant industry. The humble streetcar diner of the 50's and 60's has blossomed into the Cinderella of the commercial dining division of the food industry. It has soared in sales while all other major enterprises have suffered set-backs in the shadow of the recent economic gloom! [NOTE: That was originally written in 1982, showing that history does repeat itself.]

The reason the fast food industry has become a virtual smorgasbord of appealing menu selections is that it is affordable! People who work hard for their money and have little of it left after essentials have been paid for, look for leisure and escape hatches by which they can derive a little pleasure for the money they have left to spend on such luxuries. Fast food chains cater to crowds with very little fuss, but surroundings that reflect informality. The costs of eating out, however, have increased along with everything else. Now it's becoming less and less appealing to spend the same money on one fast food meal that would also buy a bag of groceries that could make several meals at home!

So, we can have our cake and eat it too! We can dine in as if we're eating out – whether we choose to be catered to by wine stewards and parking valets or whether we wish to impersonate the plastic palaces of the fast food kingdom – eating out at home can be a pleasant experience.

SECOND THOUGHTS

FAST FOODS HAVE ARRIVED IN OUR CULTURE at a point in our growth as a society, when "time" is of the essence... held cheaply, spent foolishly, and made to be one of the most aggressive influences in our lives.

The calendar and the clock have given a sense of order to civilization. Our lives are, both, governed by and regulated by the limitations of these two man-made inventions. In a world created and perpetuated by an infinite Spirit, man has adjusted to the divisions of time. The records of one's birth and death are accounted for by date and moment; and all the time in between is categorized by years, months, weeks, days, hours, moments—even seconds. We are hardly conscious of the limitations to which we submit ourselves by confining our lives to the measurements of calendar and clock divisions.

Without even realizing it, we are constantly meeting deadlines in our lives. We catch a bus, a train, a plane in accordance with the hour and minute scheduled. We compete in and watch sports that honor seconds by which winning and losing and records are determined.

It is, with some frustration, that man attempts to occasionally free himself of the obligation to live within the framework of the deadline. Our work is subject to how much we can accomplish within a repeating allotment of time. Our leisure is limited by the number of hours and minutes that remain.

Even the successful results of the foods we prepare is completely dependent on the timing we employ. From this, we have derived "instant coffee", "the 3-minute egg", "day-old bread", "Minute Rice", "Hour-by-Hour" deodorant soap, "the 5-minute phone call", "the 12 Days of Christmas", and on and on. We can have a "good time", a "great time", a "bad time". About the only thing not governed by, nor subject to, time is love. So, "Fast Foods" arrived when it could be most appreciated and most recognized. "Fast" indicates – or, at least, implies – that there will be time left over one would not ordinarily have with food that was NOT "fast". Most food preparations require a lot of time. But "Fast Food" was capitalized on by the promotional people as being something the on-the-go generation could enjoy and would buy, because they had better things to do than sit around restaurants waiting to be waited on; when, instead, they could run in and out with a meal and be on their way to the fun things in life – or on the way to the more time-consuming things in their life, such as work or business of one kind or another.

But with the extensive research into the effects of stress, pressure put upon many people from having too little "time" to be relaxed, to enjoy leisure, freedom from worries, there has been a turn-around in the fast food promotional field. Now they are gradually – without you hardly even being aware of it – changing to a "family" restaurant theme. They want to bring back the old-fashioned, close-knit, solid family unit. Back and forth, like the pendulum of a clock, the gimmicks are given a new face and flavor. The public will eventually become conditioned to the new theme and "fast food" will take on a cosmetic change that we will hardly even notice.

PIZZA AND PASTA DISHES

ITALIAN CUISINE has been a part of our American restaurant industry since the early days of its discovery – if you recall – by an Italian, Columbus! If Christopher Columbus had never tasted pizza or spaghetti with meatballs, then he surely didn't know what he was missing! But the influence of good Italian cooking in our American "Melting-Pot" cuisine has had a long life of appealing dishes that have influenced, still, other food creations. The pizza, as we know it in this country, was the creation of an Italian baker in New York's East side during the late 1800's. Dock-workers and sailors frequented the bakery for their lunch food, requesting a slice of cheese with their bread and glass of "Vino". The enterprising baker dreamed up what was probably the very first delicatessen in the restaurant industry.

WHEN THE CUSTOMERS REQUESTED bread and cheese, he also added some spicy tomato sauce to it, like an open-face sandwich; and, as the popularity of the dish grew, he topped it off with sausage and other condiments until someone asked him what he called his dish. He thought a moment and replied, "Pizza!" It came from the same word as the musical term, pizzicato, to pinch or pluck a stringed instrument, such as a violin or guitar. So, pizza may have been so-named from the fact that the dough, being rounded at first, is pinched and plucked outward until circular and flat. For whatever reasons, the Italian baker went without recognition for his creation until we were informed by a woman, in her 80's, that her father and his before him worked the docks in New York where the legend of the beginning of the pizza was a well-known story, handed down from generation to generation, that the dish was, indeed, created in this country and preserved with Italian traditions for all of us to enjoy.

The pasta dishes of our American restaurant cuisine have been expanded to include some very interesting creations, employing imagination when combining compatible ingredients. Although there are probably as many recipes for good sauces as there are cooks to prepare them and restaurants to serve them, I chose only a few for this book that would offer a good, basic dish.

THE PRACTICAL ART

MORE THAN BEING A GOOD COOK, it's having a good feeling about yourself in the kitchen! Some folks think of themselves as being a complete klutz when it comes to cooking. The simple requisite for being a good cook is to have a good attitude about what you're doing! The enthusiasm with which the interested cook works in the kitchen makes the difference between the success and the failure of a truly reliable recipe. You should "think" about what you're doing, what you want it to be like when you're finished with it and know that you completely understand the recipe you are following, having read it from beginning to end BEFORE you even touch the first ingredient! You should be enthusiastic; but, you should also be careful!

BE CAREFUL because, in cooking, there are no guarantees! Even with the most precise instructions and the most carefully measured ingredients, something can alter the results. It might be the size of the eggs in a cake or the lack of humidity in the room with yeast breads not rising properly. It can be the quality of dry milk powder in any given recipe, including my home-made version of sweetened condensed milk. Sometimes the difference between success and failure with a recipe is timing! Other times, it depends on the products. Even products from the same food company can vary in quality. Be careful, also, about the choice of cookbooks you use. Be certain that the recipes have been tested by the authors. Every single recipe in my book has not only been tested many times, but has also been developed from the very first ingredient to the final product!

CHIEF BOY HARDLY ITALIAN DINNER SAUCE - *Herb & Spice Mix*

1 packet Mix & Eat Cream of Wheat
   or 3 tablespoons quick-cooking Cream of Wheat
½ teaspoon black pepper
2 tablespoons seasoned salt
2 teaspoons each: onion powder, garlic salt and granulated sugar
1 tablespoon each: dry - celery leaves, oregano leaves and minced onions

As listed, put all ingredients except the dry, minced onions into a blender, agitating with an on/off high speed for 2 minutes or until well-powdered, but still having a slight trace of celery leaves in it. Add the minced onions and blend for a few seconds, to break them up, but not powder them. Empty the mixture into a container with a tight-fitting lid and store at room temperature to use within 3 months.

FOR MEATLESS SAUCE: combine a 6-ounce can of tomato paste with 2 paste cans full of water, 2 tablespoons Herb & Spice Mix (above) and 2 tablespoons margarine in a 1 ½-quart sauce pan over medium heat, stirring constantly until piping hot. Makes a little more than 2 cups of sauce to serve 4.

FOR MEAT SAUCE: brown 1 ½ to 2-lbs ground beef in 2-TB oil in a medium skillet until the pink color disappears, crumbling it with the back of a fork. While the meat is browning, put into a blender a 14-oz can stewed-tomatoes, an 8-oz can tomato sauce and 2-TB Herb & Spice Mix (above.) Blend on high-speed until smooth. Pour into the skillet with the meat and stir over medium heat until piping hot. Makes a little more than 2 ½ cups of sauce to serve 4 to 6.

CHIEF BOY HARDLY SPAGHETTI SAUCE

The nice thing about this is that the sauce is ready when the spaghetti is! It takes about 8-10 minutes to prepare it!

6 ounces each: V-8 Juice, canned tomato paste and water
2 cans (10 ounces each) tomato soup
1 envelope dry onion soup mix
¼ cup bottled Italian Salad Dressing
1 tablespoon each: soy sauce and sugar (or artificial sweetener equivalent)

Put it all into your blender, as listed, on high speed for 20 seconds or until well-blended. You can also use an electric mixer. Put 2 tablespoons oil & 1-pound ground chuck in a 10-inch skillet on medium-high heat, stirring the beef until the pink color disappears and mashing it with the back of a fork until it resembles rice. Pour the blender mixture into the pan, keeping heat at medium and stirring frequently until ready to ladle over hot, drained (but NEVER rinsed) spaghetti. Sufficient to accommodate a 1-lb box thin spaghetti or Vermicelli. Serves 4.

MARIO'S SPAGHETTI SAUCE

I once argued with Tish Meyers, the then-food-editor of The Detroit News, about the tomato soup in this recipe, for she insisted that Mario would NEVER use tomato soup! I don't personally care WHAT any of the famous food companies or restaurants use in their dishes. The result is the important thing to be concerned about and, to equal a sauce like the famous Mario's Restaurant in Detroit, this is what I do to re-create it at home… Double my recipe for Chief Boy Hardly Spaghetti Sauce (see Index). To the finished sauce, stir in ¼-tsp Anise Extract, which is the chief flavoring (in seed form) in Italian sausage and pepperoni. Then, 10 minutes before putting the sauce on the table, stir in ¼-tsp baking soda, which really smooths out the acidity in the sauce, from the tomato-based ingredients. Next, add ¼-cup sweet pickle relish, 1-TB Kitchen Bouquet and salt and pepper to taste. It makes enough to accommodate 2-lbs spaghetti, cooked for 8 servings!

LASAGNA – *With Ricotta Substitute*

At "Two Guys from Italy" (Palos Verdes, CA), there was a baked lasagna on the menu that was as good as any I have tried in my many visits to Italian specialty restaurants. It was like the Roma Cafe version, which I attempted to duplicate [around 1975.] There is nothing worse than a passive pasta sauce, and this pasta does well with a pleasing presentation of crisscrossed strips of Mozzarella, barely melted across the top of the finished dish.

10 large lasagna noodles, cooked & drained (buttered and kept warm in a covered dish)
1 recipe of my Chief Boy Hardly (Meatless) Sauce (see Index)
8 ounces Mozzarella cheese, in slices; plus, 4-5 extra slices cut into strips for garnishing
½ cup grated Parmesan
12-ounce tub cottage cheese
2 eggs, beaten
8-ounce can of mushrooms, drained

Butter a 9 x 12 x 2" baking dish. Cut each of the cooked noodles into 3 equal pieces and set aside. Assemble the ingredients in the dish in this order: 1/3 cup sauce, 1/3 of the cut-up noodles, 1/3 of the first 8-oz of Mozzarella slices and 1/3 of the Parmesan. Let it stand a few minutes.

Next, put the cottage cheese and eggs through your blender until smooth. (This makes a super substitute for the absent **RICOTTA** ingredient.) Divide this mixture in half, spreading half of it over the Parmesan layer in the baking dish. Repeat the layers as listed above, topping it with the remaining cottage cheese mixture. Repeat the layers of ingredients above once more, topping it with the drained mushrooms. Bake, uncovered, at 375°F for 35-40 minutes, or until cheese is golden and bubbly and the sauce appears to be piping hot. Crisscross the remaining strips of Mozzarella over the top of the dish in an artistic fashion and return the dish to the oven only long enough to slightly melt the cheese strips. Let it stand about 10 minutes before cutting into squares to serve. This keeps it from getting too "runny" when you serve it up! Serves 6-8 adequately!

RICOTTA – HOMEMADE

Making cheese at home – like making wine – can be an involved and elaborate undertaking or it can be a simple, economic shortcut! Whenever a recipe calls for "Farmer's Cheese" or "Ricotta", I use my homemade version, which took me several months of continuous tests to finally develop to my own satisfaction.

1 cup each: whole milk and buttermilk
13-ounce can Pet Evaporated Milk
Juice of half a lemon
½ teaspoon salt (optional)
1 teaspoon paprika
½ teaspoon powdered turmeric
¼ teaspoon dry mustard

Put the first 4 ingredients in top of a double boiler over HOT – not boiling – water. Put a lid on it and set your timer for 1 hour. At that time, stir in the remaining ingredients. Check the water to be sure it's still hot and on the lowest heat setting for the burner without being turned "off". Add more water if necessary to keep it just touching the bottom of the top pan of the double boiler. Let it keep warm that way for another 40 minutes. Then, pour into a coffee-filter-lined colander, which should be sitting in a larger bowl or container (non-metal) to catch the dripping liquid. *[NOTE: That liquid is called "whey" and will be the "starter" for use in many other recipes. Freeze it in an accommodating container. Well-sealed and dated to be used within 1 year.]* Let the cheese drain this way for about 4 or 5 hours or until you can no longer see any liquids dripping into the reserve container. Transfer the cheese to an accommodating container. Cover it tightly and keep it refrigerated to use within 2 weeks. It will freeze well up to 6 months. Makes 1 ½ cups cheese.

POTATO WHEY SOUP – *Before you put that "whey" away, in the above recipe, consider this:*

The scooped-out pulp of 2 cold baked potatoes
1 ¼ cups reserved "whey"
10-ounce can each: Campbell's Onion and Cream of Chicken Soups

Combine all ingredients, stirring constantly over low heat until smooth. Never let it come to a boil or it will curdle! You can also prepare this in the top of a double boiler over barely-simmering water, stirring frequently until piping hot. Serves 4 favorably!

OPEN PITZER BBQ SAUCE

Mix together, 1 cup each: bottled apple butter, ketchup and Catalina dressing. Refrigerate in covered container up to 3 months. Makes 3 cups sauce. Recipe may be cut in half or into thirds. To add zest, stir in Tabasco or Worcestershire sauce, to taste.

SKILLET PIZZA

In the supermarket, there is a boxed mix for making pizza in a skillet that, for some time now, has enjoyed a rather nice applause from people who want to avoid the bother of a from-scratch creation. First, you should have a large 12" skillet with, preferably, "rounded" sides rather than straight and, also, Stoneware-lined or Teflon-coated. If it doesn't have an oven-proof handle on it – because the last step of this recipe calls for putting the skillet under the broiler – wrap the handle in aluminum foil, triple thick!

2-cups biscuit mix (I used Bisquick)
2/3-cup milk
4-tsp oil
4-oz can pizza sauce
    OR 4-oz can tomato sauce, plus 1-TB dry Italian dressing mix OR 2-TB bottled Italian dressing
1-cup shredded Mozzarella
½-cup grated parmesan
8-oz can of mushrooms, drained*
1-cup diced boiled ham*
2/3-cup pepperoni slices*
½-lb bacon, fried "limp" and chopped*

Blend the biscuit mix and milk into a smooth dough. Place oil in 12" skillet and spread dough evenly over the bottom. Then spread pizza sauce over the dough. Mix the 2 cheeses together and sprinkle over the sauce. Of the remaining ingredients, with the * following them, add one of them or all of them.

Turn the heat on your large stove-top burner to medium and keep a watch on the bottom of the crust, using a spatula to lift and peek, until it's golden brown. At once, remove from top of stove, turning off the burner and placing the skillet under the broiler, 3 inches from the heat for about 3-4 minutes or until the cheese and toppings are bubbly. Serves 4 reasonable adults or one ridiculous adolescent!

FOR A 10-INCH SKILLET: Use 1 ½-cups biscuit mix and ½-cup milk and only 2 ½-tsp oil in the skillet. Proceed as directed above, reducing the other ingredients to taste.

FOR A 7-INCH SKILLET: Use 1-cup biscuit mix and 1/3-cup milk and only 1 ½-tsp oil in the skillet. Proceed as directed above, reducing the other ingredients in half or to taste.

TO PREPARE THE PIZZA FOR FREEZING: Follow the recipe as directed, but do not place it under the broiler. Slip the pizza out of the skillet and onto a greased foil pan of an accommodating size. Wrap and freeze to use within 6 weeks. Thaw for 30 minutes at room temperature, then place under broiler as directed above.

IN-A-PINCH PIZZA SAUCE

Whenever you're out of your favorite store-bought pizza sauce, rely on a good substitute I made by combining a 10-oz can of Campbell's Tomato Soup with ¼-tsp Anise Extract, ½-tsp garlic salt, 1-TB dry oregano leaves, pinch of sugar or dash of artificial sweetener and 1-tsp onion powder.

PIZZA HAT CRUST MIX

Put this together ahead of when you plan to use it, adding liquid and yeast as you get ready to bake it. Work the following ingredients together thoroughly: 6-cups all-purpose flour, 1/8-tsp baking soda, 2-tsp sugar, 1-tsp garlic salt and ½-tsp oregano leaves, crushed. Cut in 3-TB Crisco and then store it on your pantry shelf in a covered container for up to 6 months.

TO USE THE MIX: Soften 1 envelope dry yeast in ½-cup warm water. Stir in 1-tsp sugar and let it stand for 5 minutes, until bubbly. To the crust mix, beat in 1 ½-cups warm water, then the yeast mixture. Knead the dough until it's like elastic. Shape it to fit a greased 15-inch round pizza pan lightly dusted in cornmeal. Add toppings to taste and bake at 450°F for about 18-20 minutes or until the cheese and toppings are bubbly and the crust is golden brown.

TACO PIZZA

This great at-home version is best served as a skillet pizza. [To prepare the crust per pan-size diameter, use my Skillet Pizza recipe – see Index.] The only difference between this recipe and my Skillet Pizza version is that, in this version, you spread the crust with only the sauce and seasonings, then remove it from the burner when browned. The rest of the ingredients of this taco version (see below) must wait to be added just before you want to serve it – that's when to place it under the broiler, 3 inches from the heat, for a minute or two to let the cheddar on top melt – but not bubble!

FOR A YEAST DOUGH CRUST: Use the recipe for my Pizza Hat Crust Mix (above) – begin with the crust patted out on a greased & cornmeal-dusted 15-inch pizza pan. Add sauce to your liking. Sprinkle with any additional seasonings you enjoy, such as oregano, garlic, etc. Bake the crust as the Pizza Hat recipe suggests. Remove from oven and add the toppings to either crust version (quantity to taste and pizza size) in the following layers: 1st, my Coney Beef Sauce OR my Taco Beef recipe (see Index); 2nd, chopped fresh onions, sprinkled evenly over the beef; 3rd, my Refried Beans recipe (see Index), scattered here and there; 4th, shredded lettuce and fresh chopped tomatoes; then, top it all with shredded cheddar cheese. Place under the broiler, as directed above, just to melt the cheese. A 15-inch pizza should serve 5. A 12-inch pizza serves 4 reasonable adults and so on.

SPAGHETTI SAUCE MIX – CHIEF BOY HARDLY

This is one of those pantry shelf powdered foods to which you add only a few ingredients when it's time to prepare the principle dish from it. Chief Boy Hardly is the name I have given to this recipe, and I wouldn't be without it! It comes in handy for last-minute company, like when my mother-in-law would drop in unexpectedly and our youngest child would come running to tell me grandma had arrived. Then I could hear her telling her grandma how mommy was going to do her special trick for everyone. When I asked her, "What special trick?" - Cheryl replied, "You said the next time she came for dinner you were going to climb the walls! Remember?"

3 boxes (12 – envelopes, 1 serving each) Lipton Cup-A-Soup – Tomato
    (or my version – See Index for "Cup-of-Thoup Powder")
2 envelopes (4 serving sizes each) Onion Soup Mix
0.31-oz can dehydrated celery flakes
3 ½-oz jar beef bouillon powder
3-TB dehydrated diced green pepper flakes (optional)
1-TB sweet basil leaves
1-tsp black pepper
2-TB oregano leaves
2-TB dry minced onions
2-TB dry minced parsley
¼-Cup grated Parmesan cheese
1 ½-tsp cumin powder
1-TB Marjoram leaves

Combine all ingredients as listed and stored at room temperature and covered container. Keep up to six months. Make enough to fill a 2-quart container or jar. 1/3-cup of this homemade mix equals one envelope of store-bought mix.

TO USE THE MIX FOR SPAGHETTI SAUCE:

Remove 3 tablespoons of above mix and add it to ½-cup boiling water, stirring until smooth. Add a 4-oz can tomato sauce. Heat over medium, stirring constantly for five minutes or until piping hot. Do NOT let it boil! Spoon over 2 ½-cups cooked, well-drained (but not rinsed) spaghetti. Serves 2.

MEAT SAUCE:

Brown 1-pound ground chuck in 2-TB oil until all the pink is gone. Mash beef with the back of a fork until the consistency of rice. While spaghetti is cooking in another pot, per box directions, bring 1 cup water to boil in a 1 ½ quart saucepan. Add 1/3 cup of spaghetti sauce mix powder. Stir well. Add a 10 ounce can of tomato soup. Heat until piping hot, but do not let it boil! Mix in the browned chuck and spoon over 5 cups of cooked, drained spaghetti. Serves 4.

The American fast food frontier has many superstar food chains; but the one that inspired my own version of their product, is probably the most successful of them all!

LITTLE SEIZURE PIZZA

To prepare the crust: sprinkle 2 packages dry yeast over 2/3-cup warm water and stir in 2 teaspoons sugar. Let it stand about 5 minutes or until very bubbly. Combine the following ingredients: 3 tablespoons corn oil, 2 tablespoons sugar, 1 teaspoon salt, ¼ teaspoon garlic salt, ½ teaspoon dry oregano leaves and about 3 ½ cups all-purpose flour, beating to a smooth batter.

Beat in the yeast mixture, then, with a sturdy spoon, work in 3 to 3 ½ cups MORE flour until you can toss it lightly on a floured surface and knead it until it feels elastic in texture. The kneading may require about 2/3-cup additional flour just for coating your hands as you knead the dough. Don't let the dough become too stiff; yet, you don't want it to stick to your hands.

The sauce and toppings:

10 ½ ounce can of tomato soup
1 tablespoon dry oregano leaves
½ teaspoon garlic salt
8 ounces each: Mozzarella and Muenster cheese, shredded
1/3 cup grated Parmesan
8-ounce thinly-sliced pepperoni
8-ounce can of mushrooms, drained

Spray the inside of a large plastic food bag with Pam, or wipe the inside of it with oil, and place the ball of kneaded dough in this to rise until doubled in bulk. Be sure the plastic bag is large enough that it will permit the dough to double without splitting the bag. You can place the bag of dough on a warm, sunny spot on the table or kitchen counter, which helps it to raise quickly – and, if it's summer time, place the bag of dough (with the open-end sealed tightly with tape or a wire twist) in your car with the windows up! When it has doubled in size, punch it down and shape it to fit two 15-inch round pizza pans that have been greased and dusted in cornmeal. Onto the dough, add the sauce and topping ingredients exactly in the order listed above, spreading each ingredient evenly over the dough. Let this rise for about 20 minutes in a warm place and then bake at 450°F for about 20 to 25 minutes, putting one pizza at a time on center rack of the preheated oven. If you can only handle eating one pizza at a time, wrap the second pizza in foil or plastic and seal it with tape to lock out all air BEFORE it rises for a second time and freeze it. After letting it thaw for 30 minutes, you can bake it as directed above.

UPSIDE-DOWN PIZZA

One of the best pizza recipes I've come across was the result of an accident in my test kitchen, when I put out the ingredients for imitating a franchise product, only to find our youngest daughter had put the sauce into the pan first, and then the cheese and other toppings. I was not about to waste the ingredients at the price of groceries! When she called my attention to the fact that she had forgotten the crust, I was at another counter in the kitchen trying to duplicate the giant popovers served at Bullock's Department Store in Lakewood, California. To salvage the pizza, I thought it would be an interesting experiment to pour the popover batter over the pizza fillings and see what would happen! The popover batter baked up high, puffy and golden brown; and when we served it to our panel of critics (the family), they all agreed, relatively speaking of course, "It's a print!"

2 tablespoons oil
10-ounce can of tomato soup
½ teaspoon garlic salt
1 teaspoon each: dry oregano leaves and onion powder
2/3 cup grated Parmesan
4 ounces shredded mozzarella
8-ounce can drained mushrooms
1 cup pepperoni, sliced paper-thin
4 ounces shredded provolone cheese (or additional mozzarella)
1 cup milk
1 cup flour
2 eggs
1 teaspoon onion salt
¼ cup grated Parmesan

Grease a 10 x 13 x 2" pan or Pyrex baking dish with the 2 tablespoons of oil. Spread the soup evenly over the bottom of the pan or dish. Sprinkle on the garlic salt, oregano leaves, onion powder, Parmesan and mozzarella. If you don't like pepperoni, you can substitute 1 pound browned hamburger or ground sausage, well-drained and crumbled. Then sprinkle on the provolone or additional mozzarella and set it aside. Put the milk in your blender and then the flour, eggs and onion salt, blending on high speed for 2 minutes. If you don't have a blender, use an electric mixer to combine. Pour mixture gently over the top of the cheese layer, but don't try to cover it completely. It will spread during baking. Sprinkle the remaining Parmesan over the batter and slide it gently into a preheated 450°F oven for 10 minutes. Then reduce the temperature to 400°F and continue baking another 10 minutes or until the top is golden brown. Let stand 5 minutes before cutting into squares and sliding them carefully onto plates! Serves 6.

CLAM SAUCE FOR PASTA, *Like J. L. Hudson's (Detroit, MI)*

In 1982, J. L. Hudson's served this type of sauce with linguine. As soon as the manager spotted me there, she brought me a sample of it and asked for my opinion. Of course, one of the most identifying things about me when I'm restaurant-sleuthing is the Sherlock Holmes hat that I often wear, and the magnifying glass on a gold chain around my neck. It has reminded several restaurant people that I am concerned about the industry and that my readers do mention, to the restaurants they patronize, that it was recommended in one of my publications.

1-pound box of linguine
2 large cloves garlic, mashed
    or use ½ teaspoon garlic powder
2 tablespoons fresh chopped parsley
1 teaspoon dry oregano leaves
½ cup Crisco oil
16-ounce can mince clam, undrained
2 to 4 tablespoons starch water from the linguine (above)
1 packet Herb Ox Chicken Broth Powder
    or use 1 ½-teaspoon chicken bouillon powder
a dash of hot pepper sauce
2 teaspoons dry minced onions
1 teaspoon bottled onion juice

Prepare a 1-pound box of linguine; cooked until tender, per box directions. Drain, reserving ¼ cup of the starchy water, but don't rinse (or you'll wash away all the protein and vitamins.) I like to use the Mueller's brand of pasta myself!

Place garlic, parsley and oregano in the oil in a 10-inch skillet and stir over medium-high heat until soft and hot, but do not brown! Stir in the clams and the liquid in which it was canned – also, about 2 tablespoons of the starchy water, the broth or bullion powder, hot pepper sauce, onions and onion juice. Stir over medium heat, adding another tablespoon or so of the starchy water as necessary to make the sauce of medium consistency. Serve it piping hot over the linguine. Serves 4 to 6.

RED CLAM SAUCE FOR PASTA

Prepare the clam sauce (above) and stir in a 1-pound can stewed-tomatoes, cutting the tomatoes up quite fine. Serve piping hot over 1 pound of cooked and drained linguine. Serves 4 to 6.

MARINARA SAUCE FOR PASTA – *Like Denny's offered on their Torrance-Carson, CA menu!*

Gently heat together a 1-pound can stewed-tomatoes, cut up fine, with a 1-pound jar of Ragu meat-flavored spaghetti sauce, a 10-ounce can of tomato soup and a 6-ounce can of V-8 juice. Serve it piping hot over 1 pound of cooked and drained pasta.

BUDDY'S PIZZA – *a Detroit-based operation that has, for years, enjoyed a singular success for its unusual crust. While their recipe remains a closely guarded secret, I couldn't help but try to imitate it at home. After all, it's a 100-mile round trip for me to have the real thing.*

However, because I also like to avoid making yeast crust, it gave me a chance to experiment with a no-yeast recipe that can be mixed with a spoon and patted into a prepared pan - which, in this case, is made in a 10 x 15 x 1" jellyroll pan, Sicilian style. Our 16-year-old daughter could whip one up in no time, so surely the experienced cook can too!

THE CRUST:

½ cup mayonnaise
1 cup milk
½ teaspoon sugar
¼ teaspoon salt
1 teaspoon dry dill weed (optional)
1 teaspoon dried oregano leaves
¼ teaspoon garlic salt
2 ¼ cups self-rising flour (no substitute)

Combine all ingredients just as listed, using a sturdy spoon to mix well. Be sure every dry particle is completely moistened. Let the dough rest while you prepare the pan. Here is the secret of the crust – first, grease a jellyroll pan, applying a generous coating of Crisco over the entire pan and, then, spray it with a coating of Baker's Joy or Pam. This will give the bottom of the crust a rich, almost buttery texture without affecting the top part of the crust, which is what Buddy's Pizza is all about! The top of the crust, should bake up just like bread if you do this. Preheat the oven to 350°F while you assemble the other layers for the pizza.

After preparing the pan, wash your hands with cold water and pat the dough evenly over the bottom of the pan. If the dough begins to stick the least bit to your fingers, wet your hands again, continuing to do so until the dough has been evenly patted over the bottom of the pan. Now, add the toppings, as listed below:

- Spread two 8-ounce cans pizza sauce over the crust – OR use this homemade version:

    One 10-ounce can of tomato soup mixed well with ¼ teaspoon anise extract, ¼ teaspoon dry oregano leaves, ½ teaspoon garlic salt, ½ teaspoon onion salt and a dash of pepper.

- Sprinkle ½ cup grated Parmesan over the sauce in an even layer.
- Spread 8 ounces of shredded mozzarella over the Parmesan.
- Spread 8 ounces of sliced pepperoni over the mozzarella.
- Spread 8 ounces of canned mushrooms, drained, over that.
- You also have the option of adding four slices of boiled ham, cut into matchstick pieces.

Bake at 350°F for 15 minutes, then increase the heat to 400°F for another 10 minutes or until toppings begin to bubble and cheese is well-melted. Let it stand for about five minutes before you attempt to cut it into serving pieces. Serves 4 to 6 – OR one "starving" teenager!

WIND SHOOTERS MEATBALLS

Win Schuler's was a restaurant of fine dining, based in Marshall, Michigan. They once served a delectable Swedish meatball appetizer in a smooth barbecue sauce. The appealing aspect of this dish is how the meatballs are shaped, as well as the flavor of the sauce.

The meatball mixture:

1 ½ to 2 pounds ground round
5 ½ ounce can of Pet milk (small can)
2 eggs, beaten
3 cups bottled wheat germ OR crushed Wheaties flakes
¼ cup each: sweet pickle relish and ketchup (see Index for my homemade version)
one envelope each: onion soup mix and spaghetti sauce mix
    (or see Index for my homemade versions)

Combine all ingredients thoroughly. When you make these, be sure to keep them small! Make them bite-sized – and I don't mean the Jolly Green Giant's bite either – a bit bigger than a cherry and smaller than a walnut. These will swell during baking to about twice their original size. Brown the shaped meatballs in a single layer on a lightly oiled jellyroll pan (rather than browning in a skillet) at 450°F for about 6 minutes without turning them. Transfer them carefully to a Pyrex glass baking dish in a single layer, inserting a wooden toothpick into each one for appetizer servings; or put them into a deep baking dish if you're going to spoon them out and serve them as part of the main course. Then smother them in the barbecue sauce (below.)

The sauce:

1-pound can jelly cranberry sauce
¼ cup packed brown sugar
12-ounce bottle chili sauce
12-ounce can V-8 juice
hot black tea, just enough to dilute
    and keep meatballs submerged

Combine sauce ingredients, breaking up cranberry sauce with the back of a fork. Heat in a medium-size saucepan until sugar dissolves and cranberry sauce melts, but, do not let it boil! Pour over meatballs. Loosely cover the dish with a sheet of foil, baking them quite slowly. The round wooden toothpicks inserted before you bake them in the sauce, in no way will affect the food! Serves 6 to 8 as appetizers or 4 to 6 as a main course.

TO SEASON AN IRON SKILLET – Coat it in corn or vegetable oil, so that it's about 1/8-inch deep in the bottom. Set it on a high-temperature burner on top of the stove, wiping the oil into the pan and replacing it as the pan becomes hot. Then wipe it again liberally with another even-coating of oil and place it in a 400°F oven for about 5 minutes. Let the oil bake into it! Every time you remove something from the oven and you turn the oven off, place the oiled skillet in the oven as the oven cools down. NEVER wash an iron skillet in soapy water. Always clean it with additional oil and salt - wiping it out with a clean rag or paper towels. Building up the oiled surface, filling the pores of the skillet with oil and applying intense heat is the way you "season" it.

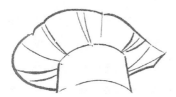

PAN PIZZA

Using an oven-proof skillet that is about 12 inches in diameter and well-seasoned (as described above) with baked-in oils, you can imitate one of the more recently popular pizza parlor preferences.

For the crust:

½ cup each – lukewarm: water and milk
1 tablespoon sugar
1 teaspoon salt
¼ teaspoon baking soda
1 package dry yeast

In a mixing bowl, combine all ingredients as listed with a sturdy spoon, stirring until you have a smooth dough. Let it stand about 5 minutes. Then beat into this, in the following order:

2 cups flour
2 tablespoons oil
3 more cups flour

Work each addition in thoroughly before adding the next addition. *(Dividing the flour in those portions, adding the oil between, seemed to be the best technique of all the tests I made.)* Batter will be sticky and even a bit lumpy. Grease a seasoned 12-inch iron skillet, Stoneware or Teflon coated, with about 4 tablespoons of oil. *(A 10 x 15 x 1" well-greased jellyroll pan can be used instead of the skillet.)* Wipe out excess oil. Dump the dough into the prepared pan of choice. Dip your fingers in oil and spread the dough out to fit the pan. Let it rise, uncovered, in a warmish place for about 10 minutes and then add sauce - use my "In-a-Pinch Pizza Sauce" (see Index) or your own, plus assorted cheeses and toppings, as desired. Let it rise again, uncovered, in a warmish place for about 30 minutes. Bake at 400°F for about 20 to 25 minutes or until the toppings are bubbly and you can peek at the underside of the crust to see that it is golden brown. Serve it while it is still piping hot, right from the skillet or pan. Serves 4 to 6.

YOU'LL NOTICE, as you continue through my recipes, that I use several flavoring techniques to achieve a finished dish that hopefully will duplicate one of the famous name products of the food industry. What they use in their products is anybody's guess! We have no way of knowing the exact amounts of any single ingredient, even if they are listed on the packaging. Of course, restaurant foods do not come to the customer's table with an accompanying list of ingredients - so we have to suppose that our taste buds will tell us if it is appealing or not. In one of the seasoned salt recipes I've given you, I use curry powder and not much of it - but, just enough that it sets it apart from other recipes. Curry powder is one seasoning that must be treated with respect! It is readily available in most supermarkets but I like to make my own - it's five-alarm-flavored!

HURRY CURRY POWDER

2 tablespoons coriander powder
1 tablespoon turmeric
1 teaspoon each: cumin powder, powdered ginger, allspice and mace
1 teaspoon (or to taste) canned, minced hot chili peppers; crushed
½ teaspoon dry mustard

Mix all ingredients together thoroughly. Store in a tightly-capped bottle out of direct sunlight. Keeps indefinitely. Makes about ¼ cup powder.

IN SEASONING HAMBURGERS: a dash of curry, a dash of soy sauce and a dash of Worcestershire adds just enough zip that no one could ever accuse "fast foods" of being less than dignified. To add more personality to your meal – whether you serve the burgers on grilled or toasted buns or as the main dish meat selection – add a good barbecue sauce on the side, passed in a condiment dish or served from a beer goblet with a small bouillon spoon, giving the impression that the All-American hamburger has class!

CHICKEN & OTHER RELATED DISHES

FRIED CHICKEN has always been a basic American favorite, even before it was a restaurant offering. It was "down-home" and wholesome and has never lost its popularity. When Colonel Harland Sanders, in his retirement years, took a can of his favorite secret spices & herbs and his precious fryer and traveled across the country demonstrating his technique for preparing chicken. No one dreamed it would someday become one of the most successful corporations of the American restaurant industry, much less of the American free enterprise system, itself!

There are names that will be identified with fried chicken for a long time to come that include Church's Fried Chicken, Brown's, Popeye's, Original Recipe, Banquet Fried Chicken, Pioneer Fried Chicken, Southern Fried Chicken and, of course, the leader of the industry, Kentucky Fried Chicken, which will be familiar to us with an affectionate regard, as we recall the big bucket at the top of the pole revolving above the Colonel's restaurants across the country - and now across the world!

There are very minute differences between these popular restaurants in the way that their individual recipes are prepared. At home, when you want definite inspiration in preparing your own fried chicken, I have given you only a few of the great versions. There are many more, but the side dishes that accompanied the chicken in these various restaurants deserve some attention as well. I have included some of these in this section. My own favorite is still the original recipe that we sampled when we were traveling in Ontario many, many years ago, and stopped at the White Horse Inn, where the Colonel, himself, was preparing his chicken and passing samples around to the customers. If the owners of the restaurant liked the response, Harland Sanders would provide them with the spices and the technique for preparing it under his name, which he eventually did - growing to the largest in the business.

The Significant Difference –
WITH THE COLONEL'S HELP

I look back now to 1976 and 1977 and realize how fortunate I was to have had my life touched by so many helpful people - so many famous people! It's almost incredible that what started out to be merely the frosting on the cake, of my monthly newsletter, soon became the whole cake! While duplicating the secrets of the food and restaurant industry was only going to be a part of the publication I was writing, it was a surprise to me that the interest and the response from the public led to my specializing in the fast food division entirely! I thought my first book was going to be my "only" book on that subject, but - six books later – I was still seriously, but lovingly, engaged in the pursuit of new information and challenging recipe imitations. I've been asked by restaurants to give them permission to use my recipes and say so on their menus. I've been asked by "People Magazine", at least once a month for six months - even before the Donahue show appearance - to grant them an interview. The fact that I had declined the invitation because I couldn't handle any additional mail, made the columns of the Detroit Free Press, when their "Tip-Off" columnist said it was "classy" to turn down People Magazine - refusing publicity in a national magazine because I did not want to "get big"! It was just good business sense to me. For like Maurice and Dick McDonald, I like what I'm doing and having somebody else do it for me, as Ray Kroc did it for the two brothers, would be like Liberace having somebody play the piano for him. However, one of the most important turning points in the events of my recipe work was the influence that Col. Harland Sanders had over me and his direct suggestions on how to make my fried chicken recipe more like the one he originally developed!

With the tests for COUNTERFEITING FRIED CHICKEN AT HOME that was as good as what you could buy out – but for less – I felt I HAD to have a pressure fryer. This meant I had to have a place to also put it in my kitchen, which was already bursting at the seams with appliances and gadgets and utensils I really didn't get enough use from, as it was. Then one summer, while visiting relatives in West Virginia, we sampled some pan-fried home-style chicken that was every bit as good as the chicken produced in a pressure fryer. Paul's 82-year-old-and blamed why the chicken always came out just right every time she made it, which was religiously every Sunday! It was the pan! She used 800-year-old wrought iron skillet that had never been washed in soap and water. She "seasoned" it was shortening – lard, mostly. She kept it in the oven of her wood-burning, porcelain enamel dough, where it was always warm.

THE FRIED CHICKEN RECIPE that first called attention to my recipes nationally – through the "National Enquirer", "Money Magazine", "Catholic Digest", "The Christian Science Monitor", "Campus Life Magazine" and, yes, even "Playboy Magazine" – was this following combination of ingredients. The method is quite unorthodox and the original idea for developing it in this manner, came from a conversation I had with "Col. Sanders" over the air with radio station WFAA in Dallas when I was a regular guest on a talk show with them for several months. We discussed the secrets of the food industry with listeners by phone from our homes. The Colonel was fascinated by the publicity I had received for my "Big Bucket in the Sky" fried chicken recipe and agreed that I was on the right track if I'd add more pepper. He loved pepper! He also suggested browning the chicken in a skillet and, then, oven-baking it until tender to achieve a likeness more to the original recipe he had created in 1964. He told me to look around the grocery store for 1 packaged product to replace the 11 spices – which I did diligently – and discovered that powdered Italian salad dressing mix was the secret!

So, I set to work to revamp the recipe. My original recipe was quite close to the famous Colonel's product, but the coating kept falling off – because, as he explained, I couldn't get the oil hot enough. He liked peanut oil, himself, but suggested that I could achieve a similar result by using corn or Crisco oil – with 1 cup solid Crisco for every 4 cups of oil. He talked about the quality in his product changing after turning the business over to new owners.

When Heublein Conglomerate bought out the franchise, they paid a few million dollars for "The Colonel's" recipe and technique. It seemed unlikely that a home-kitchen-rendition of such a famous product could be had for the price of my book. But the letters came in – "best chicken we ever had"; "l-o-v-e-d that fried chicken recipe"; "our favorite chicken recipe – so, please don't change it"; and "maybe 'The Colonel' should have YOUR recipe!"

BIG BUCKET IN THE SKY! CHICKEN

3 pounds of chicken fryer parts – cut small
2 packages Good Season's Italian Salad Dressing mix
3 tablespoons flour
2 teaspoons salt
¼ cup lemon juice
2 tablespoons butter or margarine
1 ½ pints of corn oil
2/3 cup Crisco solid shortening
1 cup milk
1 ½ cups boxed pancake mix combined with: 1 tsp paprika, 1/2 tsp powdered sage and 1/4 tsp pepper

Rinse chicken and wipe pieces dry. Make a paste out of the first five ingredients. Brush to coat chicken evenly with the paste…the underside as well. Stack pieces in a large refrigerator container, seal in foil and refrigerate several hours or, better yet, overnight. 1 ½ hours before serving, heat oil and Crisco, until melted, in a heavy saucepan. Put just enough of this into two large heavy skillets so that it covers the bottom of each 1-inch deep and just set the rest aside, as the oil will have to be replaced as you remove fried pieces and continue to fry more. Dip each pasty chicken piece, 1st in milk and then in pancake mixture (having combined it as directed above with the last three ingredients.) Dust off excess mix and place skin-side down in the very hot oil mixture. Brown the chicken on each side until golden. Then, place browned pieces in shallow baking pans, single-layered with skin-side up. Spoon remaining milk over pieces. Seal with foil on only 3 sides of the pan. Bake for 40 minutes at 375°F or until chicken is fork-tender, basting with milk and pan drippings every few minutes. Remove foil and bake another 8-10 minutes or until crispy. Serves 6-8. Leftovers keep up to a week refrigerated.

DONAHUE

THIS RECIPE was created on-the-spot when I discovered that my usual ingredients and my most familiar utensils were not ready for me to use on The Donahue Show (when I appeared on it – July 7, 1981.) I could only hope and pray that what I, then, suspected would be a second–best method of preparing my "Big Bucket in the Sky" fried chicken – and would not discredit me entirely. I had to adlib the experience, calling upon every possible thing I could remember about good cooking. It was luck! And luck – of course – is when preparation and experience meet opportunity!

There was a toaster oven on the table the staff had set up for me to use during the live–telecast of the show. At 8 o'clock in the morning, the producer of the show was driving around Chicago, trying to find a Kentucky Fried Chicken restaurant that was open, so that the audience could later compare what I had prepared to what the restaurant prepared. So, I looked at the ingredients I had on hand and tried to improvise with what was there. The on-the-spot recipe was every bit as good as what Paul & I had been publishing and was so much easier, that again we could prove that there will always be more than one way to arrive at a given result!

OVEN-FRIED KENTUCKY-STYLE CHICKEN

In doubled plastic food bags, combine well: 3 cups self-rising flour, 1 tablespoon paprika, 2 envelopes Lipton Tomato Cup-a-Soup powder (see Index for my "Cup-of-Thoup" recipe), 2 packages Good Seasons' Italian dressing mix powder and 1 teaspoon season salt. Twist the end of the bags tightly, creating an inflated balloon affect. Then shake the mixture well to combine.

Spray a jellyroll pan (10 x 15 x 3/4-inch) with Pam, or wipe it well with oil. Run a cut-up chicken fryer under cold water and let excess water drip off, putting all the pieces into a colander to drain a few minutes. Dredge pieces one at a time in the flour mixture, by placing each piece in the bag of seasoned flour and shaking to coat. Arrange the coated pieces, skin-side up on prepared pan. Melt ¼ pound margarine or butter and, using a 1-inch-wide, soft-bristled, pastry brush (or one from a paint store with soft hair bristles – NOT plastic bristles,) dab the melted butter or margarine over the floured surface (skin-side only) of each chicken piece. When all the melted butter or margarine has been divided between the pieces, bake it in a 350°F oven, uncovered, for 1 hour or until golden brown and tender.

FOR CRISPY COATING: After applying melted butter or margarine, dust pieces with a few additional tablespoons of seasoned flour and drizzle with more melted butter or margarine before baking. Serves 4 to 6.

IMPROVISATION!

DEEP-FRIED CHICKEN

This is not my favorite at-home method of preparing chicken because (1) it's messy, (2) its troublesome, (3) it's not always fool-proof and (4) … How much time do you have? The list, for me, is quite long… But for those who have asked and almost insisted upon knowing how to prepare it at home, I will recommend this technique…

Par boil the chicken until tender, but not falling apart. Chill it thoroughly. Remove skin and all bones of white meat pieces only. Cut into pieces no larger than a matchbook cover. Moisten and coat pieces in all-purpose flour, then dip into one prepared recipe of either of my "secret fish batters" – the Archer Treacher version or the Lone John Sliver recipe (see Index.) Deep fry a few pieces at a time in 425°F oil for a few minutes on each side or until golden brown. Drain on paper towel. Keep pieces warm in a 300°F oven on a cookie sheet, uncovered, until all the pieces have been fried.

ELEVEN SECRET SPICES - *Make your own seasoned chicken coating using this combination:*

(1) 2 tablespoons paprika
(2) 1 tablespoon onion salt
(3) 1 teaspoon celery salt
(4) 1 teaspoon rubbed sage
(5) 1 teaspoon garlic powder
(6) 1 teaspoon allspice powder
(7) 1 teaspoon powdered oregano
(8) 1 teaspoon chili powder
(9) 1 teaspoon black pepper
(10) 1 teaspoon sweet basil leaves
(11) 1 teaspoon marjoram leaves, crushed fine

Combine all the ingredients as listed in a small jar with a tight-fitting lid, such as a baby food jar. Shake the mixture to combine it all and then store it out of direct sunlight, and away from heat or humidity. Lasts for months and months. Makes about 1/3 cup mixture.

TO USE THE SPICES:

Mix together – 4 teaspoons of the 11 Secret Spices (above), 1 cup flour, 2 tablespoons brown sugar, 1 teaspoon season salt. Repeat the mixture as necessary per amount of chicken you will be coating and place in a doubled, plastic food bag to use to coat chicken - as instructed in the "Oven-Fried Kentucky Chicken" recipe (see Index.)

When preparing "Big Bucket in the Sky!", omit the 2 packages of Italian dressing mix and replace them with 3 tablespoons of the 11 Secret Spices (above), plus 3 tablespoons cornstarch. Also omit the last 3 ingredients that you combine with the pancake mix and, instead, use 2 teaspoons of the 11 Secret Spices (above) with the pancake mix. Follow the recipe as it otherwise directs.

ABOUT SWEET MARJORAM LEAVES – a tender herb grown in most parts of the U.S. It's a close cousin to oregano, but has a milder, sweeter flavor with a cool aftertaste. Marjoram was a mystery ingredient in love potions concocted by the ancient Greeks and Romans. I like to use a pinch of it when scrambling a couple eggs, in cream soups and especially in clam chowder. It goes well in pasta sauces, chili, baked beans and stuffing; as well as, with ground beef. When you use the powdered marjoram, keep in mind that the substitution for the leaves is not equal – 1 teaspoon dry marjoram leaves (crushed), as you would purchase them in a bottle or a small can from the spice rack of the supermarket is approximately equal to ½ teaspoon of the powdered marjoram.

BARBECUED BABY CHICKEN LEGS

These are chicken wings, split at the joints, with the boney wing-tips discarded. Arrange them side-by-side in a single layer in a greased, shallow baking pan. Coat liberally in any barbecue sauce. Bake at 375°F, uncovered, for 20 minutes per pound of chicken (3 pounds will serve 6 to 8.) About every 10 minutes or so, apply additional barbecue sauce to the pieces as they're baking, without turning them.

HUNCH PDQ – BBQ SAUCE

Blend until smooth – 1 cup Coca-Cola, 1 cup A-1 steak sauce, 2 cups ketchup and ¼ cup bottled Italian salad dressing. Keep it refrigerated in a covered container for up to 2 weeks. Sufficient to cover about 2 ½ to 3 pounds of chicken wings, prepared as directed in recipe above.

DIPPING SAUCE FOR CHICKEN NUGGETS

This is my personal favorite! Combine ¼ cup each: Catalina salad dressing, ketchup and bottled apple butter. Mix this with ½ cup cold, strong black tea. Makes 1 ¼ cup of sauce. Keep refrigerated in a covered container to be used within 30 days.

CRACKLIN' GOOD GRAVY

Blend until smooth – 1 cup water and ¼ cup cornstarch (using blender or jar in which to Shake mixture, with Secured tightly). In a 1 ½ quart sauce pan, over medium heat, combine this with a 10-ounce can of chicken broth (or homemade equivalent), 2 teaspoons chicken bouillon powder (or two cubes, mashed) and two cans (10 ounces each) of Franco-American Beef Gravy. Stir until thick and clear. Serve over chicken, thoroughly heated – but NEVER let the gravy boil! Serves 4 to 6.

HIGH ENDS GRAVY

Blend until smooth: 10-ounce can beef broth, 10-ounce can chicken broth and ¼ cup cornstarch. Pour mixture into medium sauce pan, stirring over medium-high heat until it begins to thicken and become transparent. Turn heat to lowest point and, at once, stir in ½ teaspoon Kitchen Bouquet, a pinch of sugar and a few flecks of cinnamon. Heat gently and keep warm until time to serve – 4 to 6 servings.

KENTUCKY SPOON GRAVY

In a sauce pan on medium-low heat combine one can Franco-American Beef Gravy and one can of their Chicken Gravy, stirring constantly until nicely warmed. Add a dab of butter or margarine and a fleck or two of powdered sage, plus a dash of light red wine, such as a rose. Add the wine a tablespoon at a time and taste it to see if you think it should be stronger. And by hack – if it's been one of those days… Throw out the meat and drink the gravy!

CHICKEN PAPRIKASH GRAVY

After you have browned your chicken, using any of the skillet type recipes, and have removed the pieces to a roasting pan or oven-proof platter, loosen the drippings in the skillet by stirring in a 10-ounce can of chicken broth. Turn the heat to its lowest setting. Then, like my Meaningful Maryland Gravy method (see Index), beat 1½ cups thick sour cream with 1/3 cup flour, using an electric mixer on high-speed. Beat until smooth. Beat in 1 to 2 tablespoons paprika (to taste) and 1 to 2 teaspoons season salt (to taste). Stir the sour cream mixture into the broth and drippings, adding it a little at a time. It will appear to curdle at first, but don't worry, as you continue to stir it, the mixture does smooth out. Keep it warm – but don't let it boil – and spoon it over the chicken as you serve it. The gravy is sufficient to accommodate a 3-pound cut-up chicken fryer.

ITALIAN SEASONED COATING MIX – *Good for chicken as well as fish and veal.*

4 cups fine bread crumbs
   (put toasted pieces through blender until finely powdered to yield 4 cups full)
½ cup grated Parmesan
½ cup corn oil
3 small cloves garlic, sliced very fine
1 cup fresh chopped parsley
1 teaspoon season salt
1 teaspoon black pepper
½ teaspoon powdered oregano
½ teaspoon sweet basil leaves, crushed

Combine all ingredients in a large mixing bowl and mix well. Sift the mixture several times through a sieve, rubbing the larger pieces of the ingredients through the holes of the sieve with the back of a spoon – OR put it all through your blender on high-speed, a little at a time, until powdered. Store in a refrigerator in a covered container to use within a week, but you can also freeze it up to one year.

TO USE THE COATING MIX: Put approximately 1½ cups of mix in a food bag. Moistened chicken pieces in water. Coat by dropping pieces into the bag of mix and shaking them until covered. Place pieces in a single layer in a greased baking pan. Drizzle with melted butter, about 1 tablespoon per piece. Bake uncovered at 400°F, without turning the pieces, for about 40 minutes or until tender.

CHURCH'S FRIED CHICKEN

Another of the leading fried chicken chains to give KFC some worthy competition, is the Church's chain, which served it crispy and delicious – always golden and never over-fried. The mixture I selected for imitating this at home was a bit different than in my other chicken recipes, but it works!

CLERGYMAN'S FRIED CHICKEN – *The dry mix:*

1½ cups self-rising flour
½ cup cornstarch
4 teaspoon season salt
2 teaspoons paprika
½ teaspoon baking soda
½ cup biscuit mix
1 envelope Italian dressing mix
    (or equivalent in my homemade version – see Index)
1½ ounce package dry onion soup mix
    (or equivalent in my homemade version – see Index)
1 tablespoon sugar

Mix all ingredients thoroughly and store in a tightly-covered container at room temperature for up to 3 months. Makes 3 cups of mix.

TO USE THE MIX: Beat 2 eggs with ¼ cup cold water. Dip fryer pieces, first, in egg mixture; then, in dry mix and back into egg; then, finally, back into dry mix. Have 1 cup of corn oil piping hot in a heavy skillet on medium-high heat. Brown the pieces, skin-side down, for 4-6 minutes. Then brown underside a few minutes. Transfer to a Pam-sprayed 9 x 12 x 2" baking pan. Cover in foil, sealing it on 3 sides. Bake at 350°F for 45-50 minutes. Remove foil. Bake 5 more minutes or until crispy. Serves 4 to 6.

MARYLAND-STYLE FRIED CHICKEN

This is not only the name of a national chain of chicken restaurants, but a method by which the dish has been served traditionally in this country for over 100 years. Prepare the Clergyman's Fried Chicken mix (above.) Then consult the Index for my Blender White Sauce, which you'll combine, in equal parts, with a prepared chicken gravy, and warm the mixture in the top of a double-boiler until piping hot. Spoon it over the fried chicken when you serve it – along with fluffy, whipped potatoes.

MEANINGFUL MARYLAND GRAVY

Into the chicken drippings in the skillet, stir in a 10-ounce can of chicken broth and let it simmer gently for two or three minutes, loosening any particles as you stir it up. Beat ¼ cup flour into 1 cup thick sour cream. Turn heat to lowest setting and gradually stir the sour cream/flour mixture into the chicken broth and drippings. Keep it warm and serve it spooned over fried chicken.

FRANKENMUTH FRIED CHICKEN

The German community of Frankenmuth, Michigan, which for decades has celebrated the art of fried chicken (served family-style) has had thousands of customers lined up every weekend and holiday, waiting to be seated in one of their 2 large restaurants. Their fried chicken is like "Grandma used to make" – richly flavored, moist inside and never greasy. The family-style dinner provides the table with large bowls of homemade mashed potatoes and gravy, moist and spicy dressing (called "stuffing" in other parts of the country), a fresh-from-scratch cranberry-orange relish, hot breads and beverages.

The fried chicken method: Begin by setting your electric skillet at 400°F and melting ¼ pound margarine and ½ cup corn oil in it. Blend only until the margarine bubbles, without letting it change color. Don't let it brown, please!

Run the pieces of a cut-up chicken fryer under cold water. Shake off the excess water but don't let it get too dry. Dredge each piece evenly in flour, turning it over and over about 3 or 4 times to let the moisture of the chicken absorb the flour as you turn it and form a coating. Place the floured pieces skin-side down in the oil/margarine mixture and, as it brown's, sprinkle each piece with the following: 1/8 teaspoon onion salt, 1/8 teaspoon pepper, ¼ teaspoon paprika and a dash of sage.

When the skin-side of each piece is golden brown, turn and let the bone-side that you just seasoned, brown as well. Dust the browned side with the same 4 ingredients given above. Also sprinkle each piece, skin-side up and nicely browned, with 1 tablespoon flour per piece and then about 2 teaspoons of the drippings in which the chicken is being fried.

Rinse a baking pan in hot water and shake it off, but don't dry it. Transfer chicken pieces to the moist pan, skin-side up, in a single layer. Put it in a 400°F oven to bake, uncovered, for about 30 minutes – for a moister coating cover the pan with foil as the chicken is baking. Serves 4.

FRANKENMUTH FRESH CRANBERRY RELISH

Fill your blender half-full of cold water. Add enough whole, raw cranberries that it displaces the water to within an inch of the top of the container and cap it securely. Use an on/off agitation, on high speed, for half a minute – or until you can see that the cranberries are evenly and coarsely chopped, but not mushy. Dump it into a colander to let the water drain. Repeat the blender process with an UNPEELED seedless orange, cut in pieces no larger than a marshmallow, until the size of confetti. Measure out the cranberries and then dump the orange pieces into the colander to drain. Repeat until you have half as much oranges, as cranberries. Mix together, lightly, in a large bowl. Measure enough sugar that you have half as much sugar as you have cranberry/orange mixture. Combine the sugar with the fruit mixture. Cover and let stand at room temperature for about 2-3 hours, stirring it occasionally. When juice has formed in the mixture, taste it for tartness. Adjust the sugar to taste – if it is too sweet, add another chopped orange, or part of an orange, until the flavor tastes right to you. It's not easy to give specific measurements because not all oranges have the same flavor and sweetness. Since the orange peel is included in this recipe, the sugar amount may vary.

FRANKENMUTH STUFFING

6 cups finely crumbled cinnamon raisin bran cereal or dry cinnamon rolls (with icing)
2 cups boiling water, with ¼ teaspoon season salt
3 tablespoons dry minced onion
4 teaspoons chicken bouillon powder
1 teaspoon rubbed sage
7 ½ ounce jar baby food (Junior) apples and apricot strained dessert
2 tablespoons butter or margarine

Put it all in a pan, stirring lightly just to blend. Cover and cook on low heat until time to serve, but don't let it dry out. Additional liquid may be added if too much evaporates while it's kept "on-hold" –no longer than 1 hour – or put it in the top of a double boiler over simmering water if you must hold it longer OR – grease a 2-quart casserole and bake the dressing, covered, at 350°F for about 40 minutes or until piping hot. Freezes well up to 3 months. Serves 4 to 6.

Something Better

Frankenmuth Bavarian Inn 713 SOUTH MAIN ST. FRANKENMUTH, MICHIGAN

POPEYE'S FRIED CHICKEN

If there really is a "gourmet" fast food, then Popeye's fried chicken food chain has capitalized on this compliment. One would say, in the refined culinary circles, that gourmet food is not found in chain restaurants – but a "chain" is any division…that operates more than 2 establishments in different locations. This would make the Hyatt a "chain." It would also include several ethnic eateries where linen table cloths, wine stewards, valet parking and menus without prices are as much a part of the syndicated restaurant division of the food industry as is McDonald's.

However, the compliment to fried chicken belongs to Popeye's, a spicy New Orleans-style chicken coating that is without competition. Popeye's, which is a growing New Orleans-based franchise, has gone from being almost plucked out of existence, to the third-largest chicken chain in the industry. The introduction of KFC into the New Orleans area was originally what prompted Al Copeland, a franchisee in his brother's Tastee Donuts operation, to think about initiating a competing chicken franchise operation. Copeland worked and reworked his recipe until he devised one that was truly unique in consistency and flavor. I searched for a sample of this product to determine if it was as good as the reputation awarded it. I must agree, it was deserving, and then some. The recipe procedure is wrought with pitfalls, as it is not the kind of dish you can "throw together." But anything worth having is worth working for – and, really, this recipe is not as difficult as it looks!

SAILORMAN'S FRIED CHICKEN

3 cups self-rising flour
1 cup cornstarch
3 tablespoons each: season salt and sugar
2 tablespoons paprika
1 teaspoon baking soda
1 small package Italian salad dressing mix powder
1½ ounce package each: onion soup mix and spaghetti sauce mix
    (or use equivalents of my homemade versions – see Index)

3 cups corn flakes, slightly crushed
2 eggs, well-beaten with ¼ cup cold water
3- to 4-pound cut-up chicken fryer

Combine the first 9 ingredients in a large bowl. Put the cornflakes into another bowl. Put eggs and water in a third bowl. Put enough corn oil into a heavy, roomy skillet to fill it 1-inch deep. Get it HOT! Grease a 9 x 12 x 2" baking pan and set it aside. Preheat oven to 350°F.

Dip chicken pieces, one at a time, as follows: (1st) into dry coating mix, (2nd) into egg mix, (3rd) into the corn flakes and (4th) briskly, but briefly, back into the dry mix. Next, drop each piece into the hot oil, skin-side down, to brown for 3-4 minutes on medium-high heat. Then brown the other side. Don't crowd the pieces during frying. Next, place the pieces in the prepared baking pan, single-layered with skin-sides up. Seal pan in foil, on 3 sides, so steam can escape. Bake at 350°F for about 35-40 minutes. Remove foil to test for tenderness. Allow it to bake, uncovered, 5 minutes longer to crisp the coating. Serves 4 to 6. Leftovers refrigerate well for up to 4 days. Do not freeze these. Left-over dry coating mix (the 1st 9 ingredients) can be stored at room temperature in a covered container for up to 2 months.

SHOOK & COOK COATING MIX – *FOR CHICKEN* – *When I once published a recipe for "Shape & Bake", I received a letter from the General Foods lawyer, who insisted that I find another name for my recipe. I immediately took offense, reading more into the directive then was there. Having been threatened so many times by so many hard-core food company people, I was ready to put up a defense. However, General Foods was persistent in having me understand why it was important that I change the name of my recipe and why it was only the fair thing for me to do. Their explanation was one of information rather than threats, as were the aggressive letters I received from Stouffer's and Orange Julius. General Foods explained how "thermos", "aspirin" and "escalator" were abandoned by their inventors when their trademarks were not protected and the terms became commonly used in our vocabulary, rather than trademark names protected by copyright. When I submitted the alternative name to General Foods' lawyer, it was agreed that my new recipe title would in no way infringe upon their trademark name.*

Combine in a blender, using an on/off speed on high until thoroughly mixed: ½ cup fine, dry bread crumbs and 1 envelope each (1½-ounce, dry mix) – spaghetti sauce and onion soup. Pour into a 1½-quart mixing bowl and stir in 2 cups self-rising flour. Mix well and place in a container with a tight-fitting lid. You can store it at this point until ready to use.

OVEN BAKED METHOD: run 1 piece of chicken at a time from a 3-pound cut-up fryer, under cold water. Shake off excess water. Place one piece at a time into bowl containing the coding mixture. Secure the lid in place. Shake the bowl a few times to coat the piece. Arrange pieces after coding them on a Pam sprayed, or well-greased, 10 x 15 by three-quarter inch jelly roll pan, about 1 inch apart. Set aside. Melt ¼ pound butter or margarine in a small skillet or saucepan. "Lap" it on the top-side of each piece of coated chicken, arranged on the prepared pans with skin-side up. Use only enough of the melted margarine or butter to evenly and lightly caress each piece. Then place ½ cup of the coating mixture in a small flour-sifter. Sift it all over the margarine-covered chicken pieces. Bake uncovered, without turning the pieces, at 400°F for about 1 hour.

SKILLET METHOD: melt equal parts margarine and oil, sufficient to cover the bottom of a roomy skillet, keeping the oil mixture at least ¼ inch deep. Coat the pieces of chicken as directed above for the other method. Brown for about 2 minutes on each side on medium-high heat. Do not over-brown these or the meat will be tough. Transfer browned pieces to a greased baking pan and continue heating in the oven at 400°F for about 10 to 15 minutes or until desired doneness.

FOR PORK CHOPS: Allow 4 center-cut pork chops for coating mix given above, but add to the mixture: 1 teaspoon chili powder, ½ teaspoon paprika and 1 teaspoon cumin powder. Proceed as recipe otherwise directs for coating and baking per method of choice.

FOR CUBE STEAKS *(or Chicken Fried Steaks, like Denny's restaurant once offered on their menu):* to the coating mix (above), add 1 teaspoon brown sugar and ½ teaspoon bottled lemon peel or finely grated lemon rind. Follow as recipe otherwise directs for coating and baking per method of choice.

FOR FISH FILLETS: to the coating mix (above), add 1 teaspoon paprika and 1 teaspoon bottled lemon peel or finely grated lemon rind. Proceed as the chosen method/recipe otherwise directs.

FOR VEAL CUTLETS: add 1 teaspoon dry marjoram leaves to the coating mix (above), and follow the recipe instructions, as given for preparing the chicken.

GRUNDY'S GARAGE MICRO POTATOES

In Kalamazoo, MI there was once a Grundy's Garage Restaurant that served a white-coated baked potato. It was pretty on the plates and it tasted as good as it looked – but nobody would even give a clue on how it was prepared! The only way you can really prepare them is in a microwave, because when I tested baking them in a conventional oven, the coating turned brown. Microwaving doesn't change the color of food.

Begin by cutting an "X" in the center of 6 long, unpeeled, well-scrubbed baking potatoes – which prevents the potato from bursting while baking. Wipe each potato well in about 1 tablespoonful of oil per potato. Into a small paper sack put 2 cups all-purpose flour and 2 tablespoons salt; then, one at a time, shake the potatoes in the sack of flour and salt to coat the outside of the potato evenly. Place the potatoes in the microwave without letting them touch each other, or the coating will be marred. Allow about 4 minutes on high power for each potato – or until the potatoes yield to a slight pressing when you pinch them in the middle. Serve at once.

FLOUR AND HOW TO STORE IT

One of the best tips I ever had from Bob Allison's "Ask Your Neighbor" show, was how to keep flour (and other wheat-based products, such as noodles, cereal, barley, etc.) from having any pesky little insects set-up housekeeping in them. For most of the products, simply tape a dry bay leaf or 2 to the inside of the lid of the container or in the box in which the wheat products are stored. If you want to keep the pests away from the cupboard altogether, you can unwrap several sticks of spearmint chewing gum and place them here and there within the storage pantry or cupboards. Depending on the contents, I would use the chewing gum, unwrapped and taped to the inside lid if the product was more apt to be used for a dessert than anything else, such as cake flour – but bay leaf has a stronger flavor, and would be detected in the flour if you were using it for a delicately flavored recipe.

Finger-lickin' yummy!

HONEY-BAKED CHICKEN

¼ cup dark corn syrup
1-pound honey
2/3 cup butter or margarine

Combine the ingredients in a small sauce pan and bring to a boil. Stir constantly over just enough heat to keep the mixture at a very gentle boil for about 15 minutes. Remove from heat and apply liberally to skin-side-up chicken pieces, as prepared in my Broasted Chicken recipe (see Index) – using the honey mixture instead of oil or barbecue sauce and following the directions for simmering, chilling and arranging in the pan. Bake, without turning the pieces, at 350°F for 20 to 30 minutes or until the skin and honey coating is to your liking. Just before you remove the chicken from the oven, turn on the broiler heat, placing the chicken about 6 inches from the broiler and watch it, just long enough to see the honey coding bubble of little bit, which will "candy" the coating nicely. Allow 2 pieces of chicken per serving. Honey mixture may be doubled to accommodate the desired amount of chicken pieces.

PEPPER-ITCH ARM SEASONED STUFFING BREAD

This is a heavy, well-seasoned bread that is not meant to be eaten with butter like ordinary bread.

1/3 cup sugar
2 cups bottled wheat germ
3 cups self-rising flour
1 egg, well-beaten
12-ounce can light beer
1 cup each, finely diced: celery and fresh white onion
1 tablespoon each: rubbed sage and dill seeds

Mix each ingredient in a small bowl, as listed, until a smooth batter. Pour into a greased and floured 9-inch loaf pan (NOT Pyrex) and bake for 80 minutes at 375°F. After an hour of baking, loosely cover the top of the bread with foil to keep the crust from over-browning. When the bread comes out of the oven, wipe the top crust in 1 tablespoon of soft margarine or butter. Cool for 1 hour. Cut into ½-inch slices and dry in single layers on cookie sheets in a 200°F oven, turning the slices often, until the bread is brittle enough that you can crumble it between your fingers. Store it like bread crumbs, in a container with a tight-fitting lid…at room temperature to use within 2 months. Freeze up to a year.

TO USE STUFFING BREAD: mix 8 cups of bread crumbs with 1 envelope dry onion soup mix, 1 cup raisins and 1 cup chopped walnuts. Add 1 cup applesauce, ½ cup melted butter or margarine and ½ cup chicken broth or water. Bake in a greased 2½ quart baking dish, covered, at 350°F for 30 minutes.

OR – combine 1 loaf of crumbled bread with a 21-ounce can apple pie filling, 2 well-beaten eggs and a 10-ounce can cream of celery soup. Spread in a well-greased 9 x 12 x 2" baking dish. Spray a sheet of foil with Pam and place it Pam-side down ceiling the edges around the baking dish. Bake at 375°F for 30 to 35 minutes. Cool for 10 minutes before cutting into squares to serve it once with meat or poultry. Serves 6 to 8 adequately. Leftovers freeze well up to 6 months.

OR – brown 1-pound breakfast-style bulk pork sausage in a skillet, crumbling it with the back of a fork until well cooked. Stir both sausage and drippings into the stuffing mixture before baking it. You can also add 1 cup diced celery or peeled and chopped apples to the stuffing mixture before baking it.

CHICKEN IN THE ROUGH

The successful franchising of fried chicken was originally the creation of Mr. Beverly Osborne, who pyramided a pioneering idea into "Chicken in the Rough" – a network that introduced the restaurant industry to multiple-unit operations. He began in the 30's with a 6-stool counter lunchroom that served sandwiches, pancakes, waffles and eggs in Oklahoma. In 1936, he opened his 1ˢᵗ drive-in restaurant, close to the state capital building – and it was there that he first served his "Chicken and the Rough".

Even today, the chicken with the golf club is the most easily recognized trademark of the food industry. Beverly Osborne and his wife coined the phrase when they were picnicking with a basket of chicken while driving through Texas. They hit a series of bumps in the road, upsetting the basket of food. When his wife picked up the lunch basket and its contents, they began what she called "roughing it" – and her husband had a flash of genius, commenting that "Chicken in the Rough" would make a terrific menu selection in the restaurant, serving it without silverware. The logo-trademark of the chicken with the golf club must have been the inspiration of an advertising person who appreciated the fact that "the rough" is that part of the golf course that is to either side of the fairway. The fairway is a well-manicured lawn, cut specifically to a regulation height, while the rough is exactly what it sounds to be – a rough area of taller grass and uneven ground levels. To be sure that nobody could use the same method of serving his chicken, Mr. Osborne had the "served-without-silverware" slogan patented. By the time, Col. Sanders came around in the 50's, the Chicken in the Rough success had already influenced the "finger-licking-good" advertising campaign to sell the Kentucky Fried Chicken and the concept was apparent that KFC's promotional people were hopefully capitalizing on Osborne's idea, but with a different approach! Osborne, however, instructed the waitresses in his restaurants that, if anyone asked for silverware, they would be charged extra and very few people asked – finding that the picnic-style eating was fun. [Below is my version of their famous dish.]

By the beginning of WWII, there were 385 franchise holders of Chicken in the Rough in the US and Canada, plus one in South Africa. Before Mr. Osborne would hire an employee for any of his restaurants, he once remarked in an interview that he would be sure they knew he was not asking them to do anything for him that he had not already done himself – including cleaning the restrooms, washing the dishes and polishing the floors.

CHICKEN IN THE GRUFF

Run the cut-up fryer pieces of 3 pounds of chicken under cold water. Drain off excess water. Coat each piece in flour. Heat enough oil and Crisco in equal parts that, when melted, it fills a large heavy skillet to about 1-inch deep. Brown the floured pieces a few at a time, with the skin-side down first, for about 4 or 5 minutes or until golden brown, sprinkling liberally with season salt. Brown both sides of the chicken pieces and arrange them in a shallow roasting pan with the skin-side up, in a single layer. Do not heap the pieces in the pan. Drizzle each piece with about 2 tablespoons chicken broth – homemade or canned. Bake uncovered at 375°F for about 30 minutes, basting the pieces every 5 minutes with a spoonful of drippings. Do not turn the pieces while baking them. When the meat of the chicken appears fork-tender and the coating is golden and crispy, it's ready to serve to 4-6 people.

STOVE STOCK STUFFING

You can make this ahead or on the spot! While I was living in California briefly, and without my personal recipe files, I had to improvise in preparing this stuffing for a rolled steak dish I was attempting to duplicate from one of the better hotel menus. From what I had on hand, evolved the following combination.

8 cups very dry crumbled bread, biscuits or coffeecake
1 envelope dry onion soup mix
1 teaspoon each: dry oregano leaves and rubbed sage
½ teaspoon celery salt
¼ teaspoon garlic powder
1 tablespoon chicken bouillon powder
1 cup each: raisins and chopped pecans – both optional

Combine first 9 ingredients and store in a covered container at room temperature, at this point, up to 6 weeks – or whenever ready to prepare with the next 3 ingredients.

1 cup applesauce
½ cup butter or margarine, melted
½ cup water

In a bowl, stir to combine thoroughly, the prepared dry mix with the butter or margarine and water. Transfer to a lightly greased 2-quart baking dish. Bake it, covered, at 350°F for 35 to 40 minutes or until piping hot, but not over-baked, which may make it dry. *If it dries out due to whatever interruption may occur in your house, then you can reconstitute it quickly with the addition of heated chicken broth.* Serve it as a side dish with poultry. OR – rather than putting the mixture into the baking dish – stuff a bird, up to 5 pounds in weight, and roast the stuffed bird per that poultry recipe.

OR – you can spread the prepared mixture evenly over the bottom of a greased 9 x 12 x 2" baking dish and arrange skillet-browned chicken (any recipe) over the stuffing mixture in a single layer and loosely cover with foil. Bake for about 35 minutes or until the chicken is tender and the stuffing is piping hot. You may drizzle heated chicken broth over the chicken and the dressing if you like a moister consistency. The stuffing mixture is sufficient to serve 6. Left-over stuffing may be refrigerated if tightly covered for up to a week, reheating it at 350°F in the oven or covered in the microwave on a "roast" setting for about 3 minutes per cupful of mixture. You may also rewarm it in the top of a double boiler over simmering water until piping hot. It freezes well for up to 3 months.

BROASTED CHICKEN

This is another of my favorite restaurant dishes that I don't find too often these days. But, back in the days of what I loosely refer to as "my youth" – when favorite places to "dine" were Greenfield's, Hedge's Wigwam, Northwood Inn and Devon Gables – you were certain to find broasted chicken on the menu. This chicken was, first, boiled and, while barely tender, refrigerated; then, it was roasted at a very high oven temperature for "prompt" service to the dining customer who would order and enjoy it.

Simmer cut-up chicken pieces in a shallow, roomy skillet – with just enough water in it to cover the bottom of the pan about 1-inch deep. Simmer, covered, for 10 minutes per pound of chicken. Drain and reserve the chicken broth, salting and peppering it to taste, to be used in other recipes. Cover and refrigerate the chicken pieces to be used within 2 days. About 30 minutes before serving arrange the chicken pieces, skin-side up and side-by-side, in a shallow greased baking pan (not Pyrex). Brush each piece of chicken with melted butter or margarine (or half butter/margarine and half corn oil.) Sprinkle each piece liberally with season salt. Bake in a preheated 425°F oven for 20 minutes or until the skin of the chicken is crispy and golden, basting with additional oil every few minutes or so as you like.

BARBECUED BROASTED CHICKEN: for a barbecued flavor – instead of the melted butter, margarine or oil, brush the pieces of chicken in the baking pan with a mixture of half barbecue sauce and half creamy style French dressing. Repeat the application of the barbecue/French dressing mix every few minutes as you wish, continuing with the recipe above as it otherwise directs.

CHICKEN CROQUETTES

Devon Gables was a "fine" restaurant located in Bloomfield Hills, Michigan and a favorite place for enjoyable dining. One "dined" at Devon Gables, but one "ate" at McDonald's. It was an unreasonable luxury when my dad insisted that Paul and I have our wedding supper there and, while I felt it was an unnecessary extravagance at the time, now that dad is gone, it's been one of our most cherished memories. Among their many excellent menu choices, when they were in business, was a chicken croquette that I spent a good deal of time trying to re-create. I'm glad I did! I hope you will be also!

Put 2 to 2 ½ cups of left-over, cooked and shredded, white and dark meat chicken (skin and bones removed) into a 10-inch skillet with just enough water to cover. Put a lid on the skillet and simmer about 10 minutes. Drain and reserve the liquid, adding enough water to it to give you 2 cups. Combine liquid with chicken in a large bowl. Add 1 envelope dry onion soup mix, 2 beaten eggs, 1 teaspoon poultry seasoning or sage and enough dry, fine bread crumbs (about 2 ½ cups) to be able to form the mixture between your palms into 3-inch-high cones. Dredge lightly in plain flour. Dip in additional beaten eggs. Coat evenly in fine bread crumbs – OR use crushed, seasoned croutons for a better flavor. Brown these in a skillet with a half-and-half margarine/oil mixture, keeping it about ½ inch deep in the pan. Turn cones carefully to brown all sides, arranging them side-by-side, widest end down, in a greased 9-inch baking dish. Bake uncovered at 350°F for about 15 to 20 minutes, just to warm. Spoon one recipe of my 'Blender White Sauce" (see Index) on top of these before you serve them along with cranberry sauce on the side. Add some red skin potatoes, boiled in their jackets, and broccoli spears with my "Hollandaise in a Hurry" (see Index) over that. Allow 2 per serving. They freeze well.

For pork croquettes, use left-over pork roast instead of chicken, following recipe as it otherwise directs.

HOT STUFF!

SPICY CHICKEN RICE – try this spicy, Cajun-type rice that is not only a break from potatoes, but an interesting experience in creative common-sense cookery! The packaged mixes for spicy rice dishes, to which you need add only liquid and 1 or 2 other ingredients, come under various names. When all is said-and-done, you can imitate the famous dish from this famous place, simply by making up your own – created by combining tiny egg noodles and instant rice. Since the other seasonings are so much like those used in Lipton's Noodle Soup Mix, it was a cinch to omit all the from-scratch-ingredients and hop right in to the boxed product.

RICE ERRONEOUS

Put 2 cups Minute Rice, right from the box, into a dry skillet. Turn the heat on under the skillet to medium and stir the dry rice in the ungreased, dry skillet, until rice begins to turn light brown. Remove the pan from the heat and, at once, stir in 3 ½ cups boiling water. Also, stir in 1 envelope (4-serving size) Lipton Noodle Soup Mix (which contains, besides the noodles, a patty of chicken seasoning and bullion powder.)

Blend these 3 ingredients and cover the skillet with a tight-fitting lid. (No heat under the skillet.) Stir it occasionally until rice fluffs, replacing lid between stirs. Finally, add to the mixture, when rice is light and fluffy, the following ingredients:

½ cup scissor snipped green onion stems
½ cup well-diced fresh tomato, with most of the seeds removed
1 teaspoon dry minced parsley, rub to a fine dust between fingers
5 tablespoons butter or margarine, melted

Keep mixture warm in lightly greased 1 ½ quart baking dish, covered, in a 200°F oven for up to 30 minutes before serving. Serves 4 to 6.

CHICKEN SPICED RICE

Prepare the "Rice Erroneous" recipe (above); but, before you put it into the casserole to keep it warm until time to serve, also add to it:

1 teaspoon paprika
½ cup well-chopped celery (about half a rib)
½ teaspoon chili powder
¼ teaspoon each: garlic and onion powders
a few flecks each: cayenne and black peppers

Stir well to combine ingredients and spoon into greased 1 ½ quart casserole. Cover tightly. Keep warm in a 200°F oven up to 30 minutes. Serves 6.

SPATZELS – *This is a good substitute for potatoes or noodles, and is served in most traditional German restaurants. I like the way that Eberhardt's Inn (Richmond, MI) prepared it.*

2 cups flour
2 eggs, plus 2 raw egg yolks
2/3 cup milk
1 tablespoon minced parsley
1 ¼ teaspoon salt
1 dash each: pepper and nutmeg
¼ cup butter or margarine
½ cup soft bread crumbs

With an electric mixer on medium speed, combine the flour, eggs, yolks and milk in a medium-sized bowl, to a smooth dough – adding parsley, salt, pepper and nutmeg. Place the mixture in a colander and force it through the holes into 4 quarts of gently simmering chicken broth or water. When all the mix has been pressed through the colander's holes, cook for 5 minutes, stirring often. Strain the spatzel and catch the broth in another container (for serving later or freezing for other recipes – or, if you prepared it in the simmering water, drain it well and discard the water.) Melt the butter in a 10-inch skillet on medium heat. Stir in bread crumbs, lightly browning them; then stir in the spatzel and continue browning lightly. Put in a serving bowl and dust with parsley and paprika. Serves 6 to 8 adequately.

A LASTING IMPRESSION

The recipes in this book are all my favorite – those I trust – those I've tested and re-tested during the many years I've investigated the secrets of the food industry. Every one of the recipes have been originally inspired by a famous dish from a restaurant or food chain or grocery product that I have purchased and enjoyed.

I have no idea in the world what the food companies really use in their recipes. Furthermore, I don't really want to know. However, I DO know, that with a compatible combination of ingredients in a positive mental picture of how the finished product should taste and look, we can imitate these famous foods in our own kitchens. We can, in almost every case, prepare our versions for much less than the price we would pay to purchase it off the grocer's shelves! We have the added advantage of knowing exactly what we are putting into our product, while we cannot know exactly what others put in theirs.

A PURE FOOD GUIDELINE

If you wish to know exactly what purely good food should taste like and contain, there is one recipe book on the market that you really should have at finger-tip-reach. The recipes are not necessarily from famous food inspirations, as are these in my collection; but, they are wholesome, nourishing and tasty dishes that were created by one of the authoritative voices in the field of food and nutrition, Marian Burros – "Pure and Simple" (1978.) She gives the average cook an interesting and practical approach to buying and using ingredients that do not contain the unwanted substances in so many of the foods marketed to the public today. Get it! Trust it! Use it! I do!

FISH AND CHIPS AND OTHER RELATED DISHES

THE ENGLISH inspired the fish and chips contribution to the American menu offerings of our restaurant industry. But it was probably Arthur Treacher, an English-born, American movie star and celebrated actor, who pioneered fish and chips into the fast food frontier. He took the simple, crisp, delicate coating of English popularity and the wide-ridged crisp potatoes and added quick service at affordable prices in pleasing surroundings; thus, creating a legend in his own time. When he passed away, the restaurant concept he fathered continue to grow and become one of the most recognized and respected members of the American food industry.

Fish and chips have become most popular with family franchise restaurants because the batter can be prepared by a parent-company and, with very little experience, even the youngest member of the restaurant staff can be taught how to prepare it to perfection. It is an inexpensive dish to offer and a popular choice with people who want a break from the hamburger or fried chicken habits. Some other concepts in the fish and chips fast food arena include H. Salt and Long John Silver. The preferences are individual. Their menus' prices are similar and the success of each is without dispute.

At home, when you imitate the famous foods of these famous places, there is only one way to prepare battered foods so that the coating is never greasy and it doesn't break apart while frying. Keep the oil mixture adequately hot – between 400°F and 425°F – to prevent the finished product from becoming greasy. Flour the moistened food, allowing it to dry a few minutes before coating it in the wet batter. Another tip in frying any batter-coated food is to not crowd the pieces in the frying mixture. Allow room for them to "bob" around without bumping into each other. Too many pieces in the hot oil mixture, cuts down the degree of heat drastically, which causes a soggy product.

The few basic recipes I give you in this section are truly my favorites and I hope yours too.

SCRUMPTIOUS!

YORKSHIRE FISH BATTER

This was my first attempt to imitate "the meal you cannot make at home", as the ads insisted. Some of my charter subscribers to my monthly newsletter continued to write to me that they still prefer this batter to the version I came up with later (that tasted most like the famous batter of Arthur Treacher's restaurants), because this one puffs up so nicely and makes the fish look dignified!

2 eggs, beaten
2/3 cup beer
2 tablespoons oil
½ cup each: whole wheat and all-purpose flours (or use 1 cup of either)
½ teaspoon season salt
enough corn/vegetable oil to be 1-inch deep in a heavy skillet
1-quart buttermilk, with 1 fresh lemon sliced thin (OR see my notes below)
3 pounds of perch, pickerel, and/or cod fillets (fresh or frozen)

Combine eggs, beer and oil. Slowly beat in the flour(s) and salt until batter is thick and smooth like a biscuit dough. Cover and refrigerate 1 hour before using. Cut fish fillets into triangle shapes. In a covered container, submerge fish in buttermilk with lemon slices on top. Refrigerate this for an hour also (to tenderize the fillets and remove any strong fishy tastes.) *If you prefer the strong fishy taste, forget about the buttermilk and lemon step, rinse the pieces off under cold water and go directly to the next step.* If you have marinated the fillets in the buttermilk and lemon juice, drain the pieces well. Coat each piece evenly in the batter and drop a few pieces at a time in very hot oil (at 425°F) for about 4 to 6 minutes or until beautifully browned and puffy, which makes a little bit of fish look like a lot more! Keep the pieces warm in the oven, on an ungreased cookie sheet, at 250°F to 300°F, until all the pieces have been fried. Serve at once to 4 to 6 people.

NOTE: I've been advised by some chefs that they prefer to soak fish fillets in beer, which removes the fishy odors and flavors that are sometimes overwhelming – depending on where they're caught and how long they're stored before preparing. Also, if you have trouble with the batter breaking apart while frying, or not adhering to the fillets as you'd like, it could be that the pieces are over-battered. To be certain this doesn't happen, moisten the fillets in water and dredge them LIGHTLY in plain flour before coating them in batter – just as I've done with my "Archer Teacher" batter recipe (see Index.) Also, if the oil in which the fish are fried is not hot enough, the fish will be greasy when you serve them!

ARTHUR TREACHER

As an actor, we remember him best from his frequent roles in the Shirley Temple movies, where he most often played a Butler. When the famous English actor, Arthur Treacher, went into the fish and chip franchising, many wondered how long his success would last! Fish and chip franchising was a new idea to the restaurant industry. Fried chicken, as well as hamburgers and fries, had already been widely accepted by the public as an affordable eating-out experience. Fish and chips, however, had not yet been a proven success. But, the public loved the idea. The advertising promotion was unique in the idea of a "secret batter" – "you cannot make at home" – was enough to arouse the curiosity of the most particular critics of fast foods. The name of Arthur Treacher gave a genuine English touch to a traditionally English dish. It was a success! The basic menu of his famous fish and chip restaurant chain was not altered much after his death.

This recipe is the result of nearly a year of testing and re-testing a basic batter combination. The type of fish fillets you use is not as important as the batter, itself! The combination of club soda and pancake mix was a lucky accident, for I was out of the ingredients I would normally have used in the batter and found that club soda would contain probably most of the ingredients I required, if used in combination with a boxed pancake mix – and it worked!

The batter should only be made when you plan to prepare the fish. If there is any batter left-over, it can only be refrigerated for 24 hours, if tightly covered.

JUST A SUGGESTION – you can turn the extra batter into great Hush Puppies (see Index for my recipe), or use it for coating onion rings or cauliflower buds, as in my "Secret Shrimp" recipe (see Index.)

WE HAVE THE COMBINATION WORTH PROTECTING!

ARCHER TEACHER'S FISH BATTER

2 to 3 pounds of fish fillets (I've used Walleye, Pike, Pickerel, Cod, Perch and Snapper)
about 1 quart of milk
1 fresh lemon, sliced thin
about 2 cups of all-purpose flour
1 ½ pints of corn or vegetable oil
2 cups Crisco or Spry – do NOT use lard
1 teaspoon sweet basil powder
1/8 teaspoon each: oregano powder and sage powder
1 teaspoon pepper
½ teaspoon garlic salt
about 3 cups of boxed pancake mix
2 to 3 cups of bottled club soda

Cut each fish fillet in half to resemble triangles, like the original famous dish. Place these in a bowl or refrigerator container, submerging them in milk with the sliced lemon over-top. This tenderizes the fish nicely. Cover and refrigerate 3 to 4 hours. Drain the fish thoroughly and then dip each piece, to coat evenly but lightly, in the flour. Set them – without touching each other, which breaks up the coating – on waxed paper to dry a few minutes. The floured-coating acts as an adhesive with the wet batter that prevents the coating from falling apart during deep drying. Meanwhile, put the oil and Crisco (or Spry) in a 2 ½-quart heavy sauce pan. Heat it to 425°F. Combine the remaining ingredients to give you a batter that has the consistency of buttermilk…not too thick and not too thin, but still pourable! Dip the floured fillets, one piece at a time, into the batter, coating each lightly and letting the excess batter drip back in the bowl. Fry a few pieces at a time in the hot oil mixture, allowing about 3 minutes each side or until golden brown and crispy. Do not use tongs to remove the fish from the oil or the coating will break apart. Spear the pieces as you remove it with the tip of a thin-bladed sharp knife. Place carefully on cookie sheet and keep warm in a 300°F oven until all the fillets have been fried. Serve them at once! Sufficient to serve 4 to 6.

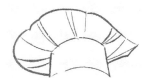

BERVILLE HOTEL SECRET SHRIMP

Just outside of Muttonville, MI there used to be a turn-of-the-century hotel that served imitation "popcorn shrimp" – however, there wasn't a lick of shrimp in the recipe; yet, you'd swear there was! This is the way I have selected to purport it.

4 cups of cauliflower buds, no larger than the tip of your little finger
10-ounce can Campbell's Shrimp Soup, plus 1 soup can of water
plain flour, for dredging
1 recipe Archer Teacher's Fish Batter (see Index)
1 ½ pints corn oil
2 cups Crisco

Combine the cauliflower buds with the shrimp soup and water. Cover and refrigerate at least 4 hours – the longer, the stronger the shrimp flavor. Drain the soup liquids into a bowl and reserve this, while you flour the cauliflower pieces lightly and spread them out in a single layer on dry paper towels. Put the reserved shrimp liquid into the prepared fish batter. Heat oil and Crisco to 425°F in a deep and heavy 2 ½-quart saucepan. Dip floured pieces into the batter, using a French-frying basket to hold them in a single layer, and fry them 4 to 6 minutes until golden and crispy. Keep warm on a brown-paper-lined cookie sheet in a 300°F oven until all have been fried. Serve with 1 prepared recipe of my Shrimp Cocktail Sauce (see Index.) Serves 4 to 6 people.

HUSH PUPPIES – *from fish batter*

2 cups prepared fish batter (either, my "Archer Teacher" or "Lone John Sliver" recipe – see Index)
¼ cup each: chopped onions and boxed biscuit mix
½ cup yellow cornmeal

Remove 1 cup of prepared batter and set it aside. Mix remaining cup of batter with rest of ingredients until it's a thick dough. Drop dough by tablespoonful into the reserved cup of batter, to coat evenly. Then drop it into a 400°F oil/Crisco mixture, as given in the fish batter recipe. Fry a few at a time until golden brown and crispy. They will drop to the bottom of the pan at first and then "bob-up" to the top of the oil mixture when they begin to brown. Keep them warm on a paper-lined cookie sheet in a 300°F oven until all of them have been fried. Serve with my Shrimp Cocktail Sauce (see Index.) Serves 4 to 6. Leftovers do not keep well, nor do they freeze well; therefore, prepare only as much as needed.

CHICKEN LIVERS, DEEP FRIED

Run 1-pound chicken livers under cold water. Strain in colander to remove excess water. Dredge each piece lightly in all-purpose flour. (Rice flour is better if you can find it!) Let pieces dry 1 to 2 minutes; then, dip them, one at a time, in 1 recipe of prepared fish batter (either, my "Archer Teacher" or "Lone John Sliver," see Index) fry a few at a time in 400°F oil/Crisco mixture as directed in the fish batter recipe. When brown and crispy, keep them warm on a paper-lined cookie sheet in a 300°F oven until all the pieces have been fried. Serve with shrimp cocktail sauce. Serves 4 fabulously – or 2 foolishly! Left-overs do not keep well! However, the batter will keep refrigerated for 3-4 days, well-covered!

HUSH PUPPIES, SOUTHERN STYLE

12-ounce can whole kernel corn, drained
1 ½ cups biscuit mix
1/3 cup self-rising flour
2 green onions, stems only, scissor-snipped
1 teaspoon each: season salt and onion salt
½ cup club soda

In a small, deep, but narrow mixing bowl – combine the corn, biscuit mix, self-rising flour, onions and salts. Mix well with a fork until thoroughly combined. Pour in soda and mix with a spoon until you have a moist, thick, biscuit-like dough. Drop dough by rounded-teaspoonfuls into 425°F oil, deep-frying until golden brown and crispy. Remove from hot oil with a slotted spoon and let drain on paper towels. Serve piping hot with my Shrimp Cocktail Sauce (below.) Serves 4 to 6 subtly, but surely!

SHRIMP COCKTAIL SAUCE

Stir together vigorously with a fork: 1 cup bottled chili sauce, 1 tablespoon bottled horseradish, 1 tablespoon sugar, 1 teaspoon lemon juice, ¼ cup ketchup and 1 tablespoon sweet pickle relish. Keep tightly covered and refrigerate up to 2 weeks. Makes 1 ½ cups of sauce.

CORN DOGS

Cut ballpark-type hot dogs, each into 3 pieces. Insert rounded wooden toothpicks into the cut and half-way through the center of each piece and use this as a handle later when serving and eating them. Moisten pieces in water. Coat in plain flour and then coat in a recipe of prepared fish batter (either, my "Archer Teacher" or "Lone John Sliver," see Index.) Drop a few at a time in 425°F oil/Crisco mix as given in the batter recipe. Fry for 4 to 5 minutes, or until golden brown and crispy. Remove them from the oil, using a pair of plyers or tongs with which to grasp the toothpicks. Let them drain on paper towels, and keep them warm on a paper-lined cookie sheet in a 300°F oven until all have been fried. Serve them piping hot with my mild homemade mustard (see Index!)

SOUTHERN CORN DOG BATTER

Even though Arthur Treacher's may be a national fast food chain, you'll find that regional influences play a big part in the style of preparations for these foods. In the South, the corn dog batter was a bit different than in the northern states. To one recipe of my prepared "Archer Teachers Fish Batter" (see Index), stir in ¼ cup chopped onions and ½ cup yellow or white cornmeal. After you have moistened and floured the hotdog pieces as directed in the Corn Dog recipe (above), then coat them each evenly in the prepared batter and fry as the above recipe otherwise directs. One recipe of fish batter is sufficient to prepare 1 pound of hotdogs. And don't worry about the wooden toothpicks being inserted before frying the corndogs! They don't hurt the food a bit!

FISH BATTER SEASONING

1 teaspoon each: sweet basil powder and garlic powder
½ teaspoon each: powdered oregano and powdered sage
1 tablespoon each: paprika, finely-grated lemon peel, chicken bouillon powder and season salt

Combine all ingredients, sifting them 2 or 3 times through a small sieve or flour sifter. Store at room temperature in a covered container out of direct sunlight and away from humidity or heat. Keeps up to 6 months. Makes about 1/3 cup seasoning.

LONE JOHN SLIVER FISH BATTER

Similar in texture and flavoring to my "Archer Teacher Batter", but made a bit differently. You can pirate your way through a seaworthy voyage of vittles with this crispy fish coating!

½ cup each: flour and biscuit mix
1 teaspoon season salt
½ teaspoon sugar
1 egg
2 tablespoons corn oil
about 1 cup club soda, or Busch light beer
grated rind of half a lemon
¼ teaspoon onion salt

Combine flour, biscuit mix, season salt and sugar. Set aside. Beat egg and oil, adding to half of the club soda or beer. Stir in flour mixture, plus enough more club soda or beer to make it the consistency of buttermilk (as in my "Archer Teacher Batter" recipe.) Stir in lemon rind and onion salt. Tenderize fish fillets in buttermilk as directed in my *Treacher* recipe (see Index.) Drain fillets and dredge in plain flour. Allow them to dry a few minutes. Dip to coat in prepared batter and fry, a few pieces at a time, in 425°F oil/Crisco mix as directed in my *Treacher* recipe. When golden brown, remove and keep warm on a paper-lined cookie sheet in a 300°F oven until all pieces have been fried. Serve with my Tartar Sauce (see Index.) Serves 4 to 6 sensibly!

DEEP-FRIED MUSHROOMS

Use the fish batter and the same method (above) – with fresh, whole mushrooms as you did with the fish. Simply, rinse the mushrooms under cold water and dredge them lightly in plain flour, allowing them to dry a few minutes. Then dip them into prepared fish batter and drop into 425°F oil/Crisco mix. Keep them warm on a paper-lined cookie sheet in a 300°F oven until they have all been fried. Allow 1-pound fresh mushrooms for one recipe of batter – to serve 4 well!

DEEP-FRIED CORN-ON-THE-COB

There is a restaurant in Marine City, MI that excels in this selection. Again, treat the corn as you do the fish fillets in any of my fish batter recipes. Slice the cobs into 2 or 3 inch lengths. Simmer them until tender in slightly salted water. Drain each piece and dredge lightly in plain flour. Dip each in a recipe of prepared fish batter (either, my "Archer Teacher" or "Lone John Sliver," see Index.) Drop a few at a time into 425°F oil/Crisco mixture, as instructed in the fish batter recipe. Fry a few minutes on each side until golden brown and crispy. Keep warm on a paper-lined cookie sheet in a 300°F oven until all pieces have been fried. Allow one recipe of fish batter for 6 ears of corn, which serves 3 to 6.

CHICKEN McNIBBLERS

Simmer 6 chicken breasts until tender. Remove skin and bones. Chill each piece of chicken thoroughly to make it easier to cut into bite-sized chunks. Moisten each piece in water, drain and then dredge lightly in plain flour. Let pieces dry a few minutes on paper towels. Dip into prepared fish batter and drop into 425°F oil/Crisco mixture as instructed in my fish batter recipe, frying for a few minutes on each side until golden brown and crispy. Allow 1 split chicken breast per serving and 1 recipe fish batter for every 6 chicken breasts. See Index for barbecue and other sauce recipes for dipping.

ONION RINGS, *Like B.K. Used to Serve*

There was a time when Burger King spent a good deal of money advertising their onion rings. At that time, no other chain in their fast food industry division had this selection. It was a good side-dish, but for some reason, the rings have changed and Burger King no longer emphasizes the selection. To imitate the old-style rings, I use my Archer Teacher's recipe, treating the onions the same as the fish.

Use firm white onions, about the size of an orange. Peel off the paper-like coating. Remove ¼ inch thick slice from each end and cut into ¼-inch-thick slices. Separate the rings of each slice. Arrange them lightly in layers in a refrigerator container. Salt them liberally to draw out the natural juices. *You need this juice – rather than adding water – to hold the floured coating in place and form a paste-like adhesive, which in turn, holds the batter-coating on the food.* Allow the onions to remain covered and refrigerated for an hour or so, before you lightly and evenly coat the rings, one at a time, in plain flour. Let them dry a bit and cover each completely in one prepared recipe of my Archer Teacher's Fish Batter (see Index.) Use the oil/Crisco combination at 425°F – allowing 1 cup Crisco for every quart of oil. Fry a few at a time, 1 to 2 minutes, until golden brown. Lift out carefully with a knife blade and place them on paper towels to drain. Keep warm on a paper-lined cookie sheet in a 300°F oven until all have been fried. One large, sliced onion will serve 2 nicely! Left-overs do NOT keep well!

CORNSTARCH BATTER (Tempura)

When you order Oriental batter-coated foods in a restaurant, the crispy, light coating is quite different than either of the popular fish batters in this book; but, it's a more versatile combination that is neither bulky nor heavy and can be used on practically any food.

1 ½ cups cornstarch
½ cup flour
2 teaspoons baking powder
1 teaspoon season salt
½ teaspoon lemon-pepper
1 cup club soda
1 egg, beaten lightly

In a medium-size bowl, stir together the first 5 ingredients. Add the club soda to the egg in a small bowl, whipping it well. Stir egg mixture into the cornstarch mixture. Let batter stand for 5 minutes before using. Moisten food and dredge lightly in plain flour. Shake off excess flour. Allow to dry a few minutes on waxed paper. Dip pieces into batter, coating evenly, letting excess drip back into the bowl. Fry a few pieces at a time in 425°F oil/Crisco mixture (allowing 1 cup Crisco for every quart of vegetable or corn oil). Fry the batter-coated food on all sides until golden brown. Remove with the tip of a sharp knife – as tongs will break the coating – or use a French-frying basket to lower the food into the oil mixture and lift it out when browned. Drain the fried food on paper towels. Salt to taste.

SUGGESTED FOODS TO USE WITH TEMPURA:

- *Cauliflower buds*
- *uncooked shrimp*
- *mushrooms – whole, uncooked; or canned and drained*
- *unpeeled, sliced zucchini*
- *chunks of Eggplant*
- *onions, sliced and separated into rings*
- *whole fresh strawberries*
- *frozen and un-thawed cheese balls, the size of marbles*
- *chunks of cooked, skinless, boneless chicken*

NOTE: You may adjust the recipe by substituting ¾-cup beer for the club soda. The consistency of the prepared batter should be equal to buttermilk – pourable, but not too thin, nor too thick. Adjust the amount of liquid, adding as necessary to achieve this consistency when you prepare the batter.

BEER BATTER RECIPE

Boxed pancake mix and beer is probably the most reliable recipe for preparing a good batter, whether you're frying fish or any other foods. The only trick is to, first, moisten the food and then dredge it lightly in flour before coating it lightly, but evenly, in the wet batter. It works with cauliflower buds (as in my Secret Shrimp recipe – see Index), mushrooms, onion rings, apple slices (which can be used for fritters), etc. The list of possibilities is endless. Be inventive! Make your cooking experience interesting!

BEER BATTER PANCAKES can be made by mixing 2 cups boxed biscuit mix with 1 ¼ to 1 ½ cups beer, or just enough that the batter is the consistency of buttermilk. Even **BEER DUMPLINGS** add something to a bubbling stew or thick soup by combining 2 cups boxed biscuit mix with about 2/3 cup beer, or enough that you have a stiff dough that you can spoon into the bubbling broth. Cover the pot with a tight-fitting lid for gentle simmering, 12 to 15 minutes, to produce an interesting and different dinner!

Because the element of yeast is already in the beer, the coating produced with the pancake mix and beer, is almost equal to that of the patiently prepared Oriental Tempura, using perhaps a dozen ingredients and 3 times the effort! The alcohol content of the beer evaporates with the cooking process, so you are left with only the remaining ingredients compatibly working together to create a light, crisp and flaky crust over the food you are batter-frying. The moistening and flouring of the foods before dipping into the batter, acts as an adhesive, keeping the coating from breaking apart during frying. If you can possibly flour the moistened foods in "rice flour" – all the better! The end-product will be much improved with that one substitute! One other reminder – when frying battered foods – keep the oil mixture hot enough! Not too hot that the coating browns before the food inside is cooked, but not too low that the food inside cooks to slowly while the coating becomes greasy!

BATTER-COATED CHEESE SANDWICH

Prepare one recipe of my Archer Teacher Fish Batter (see Index) – but instead of the club soda, use beer. Melt ½ cup Crisco oil and ¼ cup margarine in a 12-inch round skillet and get it hot without letting the margarine turn brown. Prepare a cheese sandwich, buttering one side of each of 2 slices of bread; then applying mayonnaise and mustard, if you like, and 2 or 3 thin slices of Monterey Jack cheese and one slice Swiss cheese, plus a few thin slices tomato – if you wish. Put the sandwich together securing it in 3 or 4 places with wooden toothpicks. Dip it in the prepared beer batter on both sides to coat it evenly and lift it with a pancake turner into the hot oil mixture. Fry until golden brown and crispy on both sides. Replenish the oil and margarine as needed to maintain at least a 1-inch depth of melted oil mixture in the skillet. Serve it at once with a side of my shrimp cocktail or tartar sauce (see Index!) This is a favorite fast food of the Texas–Oklahoma area!

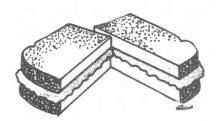

CHICKEN CUTLET SANDWICH

To imitate the chicken patty that is now a big best-seller on most restaurants' lunch menus – flatten 6 boneless chicken breasts with a meat hammer until very thin. Dip pieces in water and let excess drip off, then dust in plain flour and dip into a bowl of any of the fish batter recipes given in this chapter. Brown in about 1 inch of hot oil, in a skillet. Transfer to cookie sheet and bake, uncovered, at 375°F for 15 to 20 minutes or until tender and nicely browned. Serve on split and toasted buns or onion rolls.

BATTER-COATED, CHEESE-STUFFED PEPPERS

While we're on the subject, let me tell you about a good semi-Mexican "Gringo"-type luncheon specialty in the Texas, Oklahoma and Southern California area. Hollow out the pulp and seeds of 4 medium-size green peppers. Remove about a ½ inch slice, including the stem, from the top of each pepper. Fill hollows with piping hot prepared Coney Sauce (see Index for my recipe.) But, to 1 cup of prepared Coney Sauce, mix in 1 cup of shredded Monterey Jack or cheddar cheese. Moisten the stuffed peppers in a little water and dust them in plain flour – even the top portion, containing the Coney-cheese mixture. Then coat each, nicely, in one recipe of my prepared Archer Teacher's Fish Batter (see Index – preparing it with Beer in place of the club soda, as called for in that recipe.) Drop the peppers carefully, one at a time, in a French-frying basket into 425°F oil until puffy and golden. Takes about 4 to 6 minutes. Remove at once. Drain on paper towels and keep them warm on a paper-lined cookie sheet in a 300°F oven until all have been fried. Serve piping hot. One recipe Coney Sauce is sufficient to fill 4 medium-size peppers, allowing 1 pepper per serving.

TARTAR SAUCE

¼ cup each: mayonnaise, Miracle Whip and sweet pickle relish
1 teaspoon sugar
½ teaspoon onion powder
1 teaspoon dry minced onions (optional)

Put all ingredients together in a small bowl, using a spoon to stir until well blended. Refrigerate any left-over sauce to be used within 2 weeks. Makes about 1 cup of sauce.

FOR **BIG PLOY'S TARTAR SAUCE** VARIATION: Add a pinch of dry dill weed to above recipe. Substitute Miracle Whip with sour cream and use chopped, dill pickles in place of sweet relish for a sauce more like that served at the Big Boy Restaurants.

SOUPS, SAUCES AND SIDE-DISHES

ABOUT SOUP

Soup is either an accompaniment or an appetizer, but seldom the main course! By itself, soup can be the center of attraction on any table. There are many secret restaurant recipes for good, memorable soups. Fast food places that serve soup, do so as an afterthought! In Toronto, however, I visited a soup-specialty restaurant in one of the underground malls, where fast foods flourished in grand array. Soup was the leading lady in this restaurant, rather than a member of the supporting cast. They served as many kinds of soups as Howard Johnson does ice cream flavors.

You can pack a lot of nourishment into a pot of soup. It can be filling or light. It can be plain or fancy. It can be inexpensive or extravagant, with ingredients that range from cabbage to crabmeat. It depends upon the cook, the appetites to be appeased and the limitations of your budget. In the "old days," soup meant there were bills to be paid – meat and potatoes would have to wait until the next paycheck. Soup was one way in which one could use up all the leftovers in the refrigerator. It's probably the way that we have been accustomed to presenting soup, that we don't make a fuss over it. We don't go out of our way to enjoy it in a restaurant like we do a steak or broiled fish. "Soup" conjures up thoughts of cans in red and white labels, school cafeteria kitchens and recovering from the flu! I'm going to draw you a new picture of soup! It will be a lovely landscape of incredible ingredients – inexpensive, but elegant. You'll relish in the aroma that fills the kitchen with curious, inquisitive visitors, sniffing the air and asking, "What are you're cooking?" – and when you reply, "Soup!", they'll look surprised – but they'll want to try it! You'll use unlikely, but becoming, receptacles and, when you present it to those who share your table, they'll be even more surprised and remark that you are not serving it in the common, uninteresting bowls, we've all been accustomed to.

MAKING SOUP is like making music! The secret ingredient is harmony. The ingredients must be as compatible in soup as do the chords in a melody! Restaurants try to give their soups a little "uummph", but seldom do they make soup the leading lady! Personally, cookbooks don't even treat soup with much fanfare! They're apt to treat them more like a side dish you hadn't ordered, lacking in imagination when it comes to good flavoring and ideas for serving them in something other than a dumb bowl!

One of the restaurants I visited in Southern California had a neat idea for serving their soup and accompanying hot bread in matching China. They used small Blue Willow tureens for the soup and the bread was baked and served in Blue Willow coffee mugs. The Croc & Block in Sarnia, Ontario (Canada) also uses this idea and it is most-appealing to the customers. The Voyageur Restaurant (St. Clair, MI) has very creative soups on their menu, varying the flavor of the soup each day – with their famous Creamy Clam Chowder and French Onion soups always on the menu as well. The Reef restaurant (Marysville, MI) has been well-applauded for their clam chowder. The Fog Cutter penthouse restaurant (Port Huron, MI) has been well-liked for their onion soup. But, Win Schuler's is absolutely the "untouchable" when it comes to onion soup! No matter what restaurant inspires you to create your own versions of their products, use imagination when it comes to serving the soup.

CREAM SOUP BASE – *BASIC RECIPE*

1 ½ cups milk
½ cup flour
2 tablespoons butter or margarine
¼ teaspoon season salt
dash of pepper

Put all 5 ingredients through the blender for a minute or so, until smooth, and transfer to a 2 ½-quart saucepan. Stir the mixture constantly over medium-high heat for 3 to 4 minutes, until it thickens and becomes smooth. Remove from heat as soon as you see the very first bubble of a boil so that it won't be apt to scorch. To this mixture, you can add any of the following seasonings and ingredients for making homemade creamed soups – just as the restaurants do!

CREAM OF CAULIFLOWER: To the above mixture, as soon as you remove it from the heat, stir in 1 ½ cups cooked, drained and still-hot cauliflower buds, a pinch of sugar (or a dash of artificial sweetener), 2 tablespoons dry minced onion, ½ teaspoon dry minced parsley flakes, ½ teaspoon onion powder, 2 tablespoons chicken bouillon powder and 2 tablespoons extra-dry (white) vermouth – optional, however, the vermouth DOES make the soup! Serves 4.

CREAM OF CELERY: Just as in the Cauliflower Soup (above), to the basic cream soup base, as soon as you remove it from the heat, stir in 1 cup of cooked, diced and still-hot celery plus 1/2 cup of the liquid in which it was cooked. Continue as the Cauliflower Soup otherwise directs.

CREAM OF BROCCOLI: Again, to the basic cream soup base (above), as soon as you remove it from the heat, add in 1 ½ cups cooked, drained and still-hot chopped broccoli. Follow the Cauliflower Soup recipe (above) as it otherwise directs.

CREAM OF CABBAGE: Again, to the basic cream soup base (above), as soon as you remove it from the heat, add 1 ½ cups chopped cabbage (cooked, drained and still-hot), keeping the pieces about the size of a dime. Follow the Cauliflower Soup recipe (above) as it otherwise directs.

CREAM OF POTATO: Again, instead of the cauliflower (above), use the scooped-out pulp of 3 cold baked potatoes. Also, add ½ cup crispy-fried and crumbled bacon with 2 tablespoons of the bacon drippings, if you wish. Continue as the recipe otherwise directs.

CREAM OF CLAM CHOWDER – New England-Style: make the Cream of Potato version from the Cauliflower Soup (above), with the bacon and drippings as suggested; and using only 2 potatoes instead of 3. However, when you add the vermouth [as directed above, in the Cauliflower Soup recipe], use 1 tablespoon dry sweet vermouth and 1 tablespoon of the extra dry white vermouth. Also, add a 10-ounce can of Fancy Whole Baby Clams, drained. Continue as otherwise directed.

QUICK BEER CHEESE SOUP

In top of a double boiler, over simmering water, combine a 10-ounce can of each: cream of celery and cream of chicken soups, with ½ cup Cheez Whiz and 4 to 6 ounces of light beer. Heat gently. Serves 4.

BIG PLOY'S CREAM OF BROCCOLI SOUP

If you like Big Boy's Broccoli Soup, this should please you – because it's fast and practically "on target" in imitating theirs! You can cook your heart out if you like, making the smooth white sauce from scratch, seasoning it appropriately as the gourmet chefs would – or be a pantry-shelf chef and, in half the time, produce a smooth, rich, creamy soup that's BETTER than theirs and as good as Big Boy's!

10-ounce can each: cream of celery soup and cream of chicken soup
one half of a soup can full of mayonnaise
8-ounce can mushrooms, undrained
14 ½ ounce can clear chicken broth
10-ounce package frozen chopped broccoli, thawed
2 tablespoons dry minced onion
4 slices of packaged boiled ham (lunch meat)

In top of a large double boiler, over simmering water, combine both soups with mayonnaise, stirring until very smooth. Put remaining ingredients in a 10- or 12-inch skillet and simmer about 10 minutes, until broccoli is tender. Don't cover it while cooking. Stir the broccoli mixture occasionally. When tender, stir it all into the creamed mixture. When piping hot, serve to 6. Leftovers can be refrigerated, if covered tightly, to be rewarmed within 3 days. Don't freeze this because of the mayonnaise in it!

THE BEAUMONT INN (Harrodsburg, KY) has, for 4 generations of the Dedman family, been a favorite for their southern hospitality and cooking techniques. Prepared as it might have been in the days of the Civil War, their broccoli soup is quite like the Big Ploy version (above) with a few exceptions… Omit the mushrooms and ham. Cut up 4 slices of Kraft's American Cheese (the kind that comes individually wrapped) while you let the broccoli simmer until tender in the clear chicken broth, along with the dried minced onions. Stir the cheese into the mayonnaise mixture, then, stir in the broccoli mixture and continue to cook, stirring often until it is piping hot!

NOTE: If the soup is too thick, dilute it with Half-and-Half coffee cream – or another liquid, non-dairy creamer product – a few tablespoons at a time to please you. The soup thins out quite a bit the longer it sits over the hot water. You can keep it warm over the hot water for up to an hour before serving it – but cover it to keep the surface of the soup from drying out.

CREAM OF CORN SOUP – *For those days when you are not up to a from-scratch endeavor…*

In top of a double boiler, over simmering water, combine 1-pound can cream-style corn, 10-ounce can cream of celery soup, 10-ounce can cream of chicken soup, half a soup can of liquid non-dairy creamer (the frozen product) and 4 tablespoons butter or margarine. Add a pinch each: sugar, salt and pepper – to taste. Serve it with small pretzels or cheese crackers floating on top. Serves 6.

GREENFIELD-STYLE SPANISH BEAN SOUP

Ever since Greenfield's restaurant (Detroit, MI) went out of business, I've been asked if I remember some of their more outstanding dishes – among which was always the request for their Spanish Bean Soup! To make the procedure as simple as I can, I used canned products to achieve the same result I had with from-scratch ingredients.

1-pound can pork and beans
2 cans (10 ounces each) beef broth
14-ounce can stewed-tomatoes
4 tablespoons dry minced onion
½ teaspoon hickory smoked salt
¼ cup minced green pepper
a scant teaspoon season salt (optional)
1 rib of celery, chopped fine
½ teaspoon pepper
¼ teaspoon garlic powder

Combine everything, as listed in a 2 ½-quart sauce pan, stirring occasionally, on medium heat until piping hot. Serves 6 sensibly!

MARIE CALIBER'S CREAM OF MUSHROOM SOUP

Here is one version of my own favorite restaurant soup that's like Marie Callender's offering in the Los Angeles (Lakewood and Torrance) area. Begin with my Cream Soup Basic Recipe (see Index), which can be used for several other cream soups as well. When thick and smooth turn heat to lowest point and add the following ingredients as listed: 4-ounce can of mushrooms (undrained), 1 cup milk, 1 tablespoon chicken bouillon powder, ½ teaspoon onion powder, ¼ teaspoon dried marjoram leaves, 2 tablespoons extra dry vermouth and ¼ teaspoon sugar (or artificial sweetener equivalent.)

Stir ingredients just to blend. Keep soup warm until time to serve, but don't allow it to boil. For an extra mushroom flavor, add one more 4-ounce can of mushrooms – but, drain this one or the soup will be too thin! The dry vermouth really makes this soup special! If you do not cook with alcoholic beverages, I cannot really suggest anything to take its place. I'd simply leave it out – but, do not be disappointed if the flavor is not all you expected. Vermouth is one of the most frequently used restaurant ingredients when making all flavors of soup – either the dry white or the sweet red vermouth. The alcohol in the vermouth evaporates in the heating process, so all that remains is the flavor of the fruit from which the vermouth was originally prepared and fermented.

POTATO SOUP

To two 10-ounce cans cream of celery soup and one 10-ounce can chicken broth, add 4 potatoes that have been baked, cooled, peeled and mashed. Stir in 2 tablespoons each: dry minced onion and butter or margarine, heating it very gently over low heat – or putting it in top of a double boiler over simmering water – until piping hot. Serves 4 nicely. Using left-over baked potatoes in a basic cream soup seems to be a favorite technique of many restaurants. Reserve the peels and cut them into 1-inch squares. Fry them in bacon drippings until crispy, to serve along with the soup.

CREAM OF CAULIFLOWER – *Faster than the usual from-scratch method, but every bit as good!*

13 ¾-ounce can chicken broth (or 1 2/3 cups homemade)
½ cup non-fat dry milk powder
1/3 cup flour
1 teaspoon onion salt
¼ teaspoon pepper

Put all ingredients in your blender as listed. Blend until smooth using high-speed for about 30 seconds. Pour this white sauce mixture into a 1 ½-quart saucepan, over medium to high heat, stirring constantly until mixture thickens and resembles a pudding. Remove from heat and stir in:

3 tablespoons butter or margarine
½ cup liquid non-dairy creamer (not powdered)
10-ounce package frozen chopped cauliflower – thawed and broken into small buds
1 tablespoon grated Parmesan

Cook over lowest possible heat, so the mixture will not scorch – or put in top of a double boiler over simmering water – until piping hot and cauliflower is tender. Serves 4 to 6.

CREAM OF ASPARAGUS SOUP

If you don't want to be bothered with the white sauce procedure in the above recipe, then try it with these canned products.

10-ounce can cream of chicken soup
10-ounce can cream of celery soup
10-ounce can cream of onion soup
half a soup can of liquid nondairy creamer that powdered
10-ounce package frozen cut up asparagus, slightly thawed
3 tablespoons butter or margarine
salt and pepper to taste

In top of double boiler, over simmering water, combine all ingredients and stir gently just to mix. When piping hot, serve with a sprinkling of grated Parmesan and a dusting of paprika. Serves 4 to 6.

CHICKEN SOUP

We called this "Jewish penicillin" when I was growing up. What my mother couldn't cure with chicken soup, she would cure with guilt! But it kept us all in line and, now, I wish I had used the same philosophy on my own 5 children! There are very strong family loyalties in the Jewish home, which my Gentile father reluctantly succumbed to, as most Englishmen do in their strong, silent and stubborn way! At least he gave in to the family circle, and with each holiday came the chicken soup, rich and potent with schmaltz that we would skim off the top of the chilled left-over soup and spread over Challah bread and sprinkle with salt when we wanted a snack. Imagine the table we would sit down to – with Yorkshire pudding and beef and kidney pie at one end; while bagels, lax, cream cheese and matzah balls in chicken soup graced the other end. There was a hearty echo of conversation and smiles that you could "hear" coming from the next room, even though you didn't see their faces. And if we could steer the uncles away from political discussions and credit versus cash-and-carry, we were in good shape for another meaningful holiday get-together. I think my children will someday remember that the home they wanted so desperately to get away from, will be again, the one they'll enjoy returning to, when they have children of their own! It happens that way in families.

5 pounds cut-up chicken fryer parts
3-quarts water
3 large carrots – scraped, but not peeled, and cut in 1" pieces
1 large white onion, peeled and quartered
3 dry bay leaves
1 stalk celery – core, leaves, ribs and all – cut up small
12 whole peppercorns
1 tablespoon season salt
1 teaspoon sugar

In a large kettle, bring it all to a hard boil. Cover and simmer gently for 3 hours. Cool to lukewarm. Remove chicken and cover the pieces with just enough broth to keep it moist while you refrigerate it to use later in other recipes. Remove all the large pieces of vegetables from the broth. Poor soup through a fine sieve, straining it 2 or 3 times. Discard remaining ingredients that you catch in the sieve. Return broth to a gentle simmer. Break 3 raw eggs into the broth – shells and all – then cover and simmer for 15 minutes; which makes the soup crystal clear when you pour it, once more, through a sieve to remove the eggs and shells and any other particles. The calcium in both, the shells and eggs, is an added virtue of nutrition! Chill the broth. When the fat (schmaltz) rises to the top and becomes solid, lift it off with a slotted spoon and return soup to top of stove to bring back to a brief boil for only half a minute. Serve with cooked, drained, hot noodles or rice. Don't add these to the soup! Add the soup to the noodles or rice, in the serving bowls – as the starch will only cloud the soup all over again, making it look less appetizing! You may also use a few carrots (grated in the large hole of a vegetable grater) in the simmering broth, plus a pinch of parsley. Left-over soup freezes well up to 6 months. Serves 8 to 10.

BEAN SOUP

When you ordered bean soup at The Voyageur (St. Clair, MI), you could be sure it was a "from-scratch" recipe, prepared just as Grandma would have made it, but Chef Frank added a little more artistry than Grandma. Chef Frank Krzywiecki made his soup creations such that you looked forward to each one of them. And, as well as he knows me, nothing would prompt him to give me his recipes! I have come close, but I still do not know for certain if Chef Frank uses the same ingredients that I do!

Put 1 pound of dry, uncooked Northern beans in a shallow, ungreased pie tin and bake at 375°F for 20 minutes. Transfer the beans to a 2 ½-quart sauce pan, adding 10 cups of water, 1 teaspoon of my Salt Spice (see Index), ½ teaspoon pepper, ½ teaspoon onion powder, 2 tablespoons chicken bouillon powder, ¾ teaspoon hickory flavored salt and ¼ cup of my homemade Onion Soup Mix (see Index) – or use one envelope of store-bought version – and allow the mixture to come to a full, rolling boil for 1 minute. Then turn heat to lowest point. Continue cooking on low, letting it simmer for 2 ½ hours – set your timer! Stir it frequently and keep the pot covered.

To be certain the soup will not scorch, I placed the blades of 2 table knives, crisscrossed, between the burner and the bottom of the pan. Test beans for complete tenderness after the 2 ½ hours are up. If they aren't quite soft, continue cooking until they are. Then remove 1 cup of the beans and ½ cup of the broth to put in your blender and purée it for 30 seconds on high-speed. Return this mixture to the remaining soup, which then acts as a thickening agent.

Stir in a 6-ounce can tomato juice, 1 tablespoon dry minced parsley and 4 tablespoons butter or margarine. Heat thoroughly and serve. Makes 2 quarts. Serves 6 to 8. Leftovers freeze well up to 6 months.

BEAN WITH HAM SOUP: when you place the oven-baked dry beans in the pie tin, also set a hambone in the soup pan to cook for those 20 minutes that the beans are baking – allowing the required 10 cups of water as directed in the recipe above, and bringing it to a boil. Keep the pan covered. The bone can remain in the soup right up until the time you serve it, adding each of the other ingredients as directed above. Chunks of diced ham can also be stirred in (to taste), if you so wish.

SPLIT PEA SOUP: The recipe is the same as for the bean soup (above) – but, substitute 1 pound of dried split peas for the Northern beans, and follow the recipe as given – using either the 1st Bean Soup recipe or the "Bean with Ham" version that follows.

LENTIL SOUP: Here again, the recipe is the same as for the bean soup (above) – but, substitute 1 pound of dried lentils for the Northern beans. Continue as the recipe otherwise directs – using either the 1st recipe or the "Bean with Ham" version that follows.

SCORCHED SAUCEPAN TIP – if, and when, you let something like thick soup overcook and scorch or burn to the bottom of a pan – especially, a stainless-steel sauce pan like Revere ware – you can loosen and remove the burned-on food by covering the bottom of the inside of the pan with Comet cleanser powder, ½ inch deep, and water, 2 inches deep. Simmer it gently for an hour. Rinse out and use a Brillo pad to remove whatever particles are left. Repeat process as needed to remove all burned-on particles.

PEANUT SOUP

THE WAYSIDE INN (Middletown, VA) was established in 1797 and, since the time of George Washington, has offered "bed and board." The architecture and decor is colonial, and the menus feature regional dishes that include mountain-cured ham, pan-fried chicken and Shenandoah apple pie. Most of their meals begin with their famous Peanut Soup. This is my version.

3 cups chicken broth
1 cup smooth & creamy peanut butter
1/8 teaspoon each: celery salt and onion salt
pinch of sugar
13-ounce can Pet Evaporated Milk

Heat broth to boiling and stir in peanut butter until smooth and completely dissolved. Turn heat to low at once. Add seasonings and sugar. Taste to adjust the seasonings, adding more if you wish. I started with a delicate offering of the spices, from memory of the original flavor; but, you can certainly increase these if you wish. Finally, slowly stir in the canned evaporated milk, keeping heat on lowest setting. Do not let the soup boil or it will curdle. Serves 6. Top each serving with a few tablespoons of chopped, dry-roasted peanuts. Left-overs refrigerate well for 3 or 4 days. Do not freeze.

BLACK BEAN SOUP – *Like the Bird & Bottle Inn (Garrison, NY) – built in 1761, it became an inn in 1940. This is one of their grand menu delights!*

12-ounce package black "turtle beans"
10 cups cold water
1 cup chopped celery
2 cups chopped white onions
4 tablespoons butter or margarine
4 teaspoons flour
¼ cup chopped parsley
rind and bone of smoked ham
¾ cup chopped green onion
2 bay leaves
1 ½ teaspoons salt
¼ teaspoon pepper
½ cup dry sherry wine

Wash and pick through beans. Cover with boiling water. Soak overnight. Drain and put into large accommodating kettle. Add 10 cups cold water. Bring to boil, then turn heat to low for 1 ½ hours. In skillet, sauté celery and onion in the butter or margarine. Stir in flour and parsley, plus 2 cups of beans and liquid from the kettle. Return this to remaining bean mixture and stir to blend. Add ham rind and bone, green onions, bay leaves, salt and pepper. Cover and simmer for 2 ½ hours or until beans are tender. Discard rind, bone and bay leaves. Drain beans, reserving broth, and put through a sieve or blender until smooth. Return this to the broth and stir in wine. Serve it in small cups with a paper-thin wheel of fresh lemon floating atop each serving. Makes 8 to 10 servings. Left-overs refrigerated well up to a week – OR freeze in family-sized portions to be used within 6 months.

CLAM CHOWDER, PDQ – *Creamy New England style*

Recently, I was asked to recommend a good creamy clam chowder that required very little effort in preparation. Off the top of my head, I took a guess at the likely combination of fast ingredients, that I thought would taste a good deal like The Voyageur's and like Noah's Ark Chowder. Since this was a friend who had asked, and she knew everything there was to know about me, and still liked me, I felt she would forgive me if I guessed incorrectly. How delighted she was with the combination that she couldn't wait to tell me how many people she had given the recipe to, since the 1st time she served it to company and was thrilled with their complements.

10-ounce can New England Clam Chowder (Snow's brand preferred)
10-ounce can cream of celery soup
10-ounce can cream of potato soup
10-ounce can minced-clams, undrained
half a soup can liquid (frozen) non-dairy creamer (such as Coffee Rich – but not the powdered type)
3 tablespoons butter or margarine
a pinch each: thyme leaves and parsley leaves, both rubbed to fine dust between your fingers
a dash each: garlic powder and pepper

Heat very gently, stirring constantly over medium to medium low, until smooth and piping hot. If chowder must be put "on hold" for an hour or so, prepare it in top of a double boiler over simmering water until piping hot and then keep it over "hot" water until time to serve. NEVER let it boil! Leftovers will keep refrigerated up to 3 days. Do not freeze. Will serve 4 to 6 sensibly!

NOAH'S ARK CHOWDER, may of course, be imitated, by taking the above recipe and using 2 of everything! This will serve 8 adequately.

NOTE: whenever you're working with a flour-thickened base, remember that continued heat will thin it out. If you keep it just warm enough to be suitable to the taste, you will retain the proper thickening.

Some chefs have confessed, that in thickening their chowders and gravies and even some sauces, they will put soda crackers through a blender until finely powdered, stirring this into their hot mixture a little at a time and allowing about 5 minutes between additions, until they are satisfied with the thickness. With gravies or red sauces, you may use, instead of soda crackers, Ritz crackers or other butter-flavored, hard and dry crackers – even Zweibach or Holland Rusks. As in my Blender White Sauce recipe (see Index), bread products will make a very compatible thickening agent.

ICED STRAWBERRY SOUP

Another delightful dish that I discovered in several of the Los Angeles area restaurants is year-round fresh strawberries in every conceivable dish you can imagine, but especially good in a cold soup.

2 pints of fresh whole strawberries (or frozen and thawed)
½ cup each: cold water and orange juice
½ cup sugar (or to taste)
a pinch of powdered cardamom
a dash each: nutmeg and salt
2 cups plain yogurt

Put half of the strawberries into your blender with the cold water and blend until smooth. Combine this with the remaining berries and other ingredients, stirring gently, just to combine. Serve in small soup cups with a dusting of nutmeg added to the top of each serving. Serves 4 to 6.

CALIFORNIA FRIJOLES SOUP

2 cans (10 ½ ounces each) beef consommé
1 ¼ cups tomato juice
2/3 cup can stewed-tomatoes, mashed well
1 teaspoon each: Worcestershire sauce and lemon juice
a few drops of Tabasco
1-pound can re-fried beans
¼ teaspoon season salt
1/8 teaspoon lemon pepper
2 cups crumbled tortilla chips

Combine everything but the chips in a 2 ½-quart sauce pan. Heat gently, but do NOT let it boil. Serve piping hot with crushed tortilla chips to garnish each of 6 (possibly 8) servings.

SHRIMP BISQUE

Heat a 10-ounce can cream of tomato soup with half of a soup can of milk on low heat, stirring until smooth. Do not let it boil! Stir in 2 tablespoons butter or margarine, one 10-ounce can chicken broth, ½ teaspoon dry Summer savory leaves (Spice Island brand preferred) – or use parsley instead. Add a 6 ½-ounce can of baby shrimp, undrained. Adding a dash of light dry vermouth to this is very good too! Divide the bisque between 4 serving bowls (possibly 6), adding a dollop of sour cream to the top of each and sprinkling them with a few chopped chives.

WIN SCHULER RESTAURANTS believed in good 1ˢᵗ impressions. Mine, of them, was of hospitality. Their onion soup was a tradition. Sweet vermouth was, to this soup, what a bow is to a violin. Without it, the soup just sits there and looks good, but it doesn't make music until you've added the vermouth!

HONEST ONION SOUP *– Like Win Schuler's*

2 tablespoons each: margarine and corn oil
1 white onion, the size of an orange, peeled and sliced thin
2 cans (10 ounces each) chicken broth
2 cans (10 ounces each) beef broth
½ cup strong, black hot tea
2/3 cup Sweet vermouth
sliced dark rye bread
½ cup each: shredded mozzarella, grated Parmesan and mayonnaise

Combine margarine and oil in a roomy skillet on medium-high until margarine melts. At sliced onions, stirring frequently until onions become transparent. Transfer to a 2 ½ quart saucepan. Add chicken and beef broths, plus the tea. Bring mixture to a boil. Remove from heat. Stir in vermouth. Divide between 6 oven-proof bowls or crocs – or between 8 to 10 oven-proof mugs. Cut the slices of bread into a shape that fits the top of the serving bowls or mugs neatly and artistically. A biscuit cutter or a cookie-cutter will do. Combine the cheeses with the mayonnaise to a paste and spread over the sliced bread. Float one slice atop each serving in place 4 inches from the broiler heat for a minute or 2 or until cheese mixture bubbles. Serve at once. Leftovers may be refrigerated, if tightly covered, up to 3 days. It also freezes well up to 6 months – without the added vermouth!

GOODY-GOODY CREAMY ONION SOUP

Prepare the Honest Onion Soup (above), as directed – but don't use the vermouth. Instead, put 1 cup of the hot soup through your blender with 2 slices almost-stale bread, in small bits, and ¼ cup non-dairy creamer powder. Return to remaining soup. Serve it with a sliced rye or French bread floating on top of each serving and sprinkle the bread with shredded mozzarella instead of the mixture in the Honest Onion Soup recipe. Place servings, in heat-proof bowls or mugs, about 4 inches from broiler heat for about a minute or until the cheese melts – or put in your microwave on high for half a minute or until cheese melts. Makes about 6 to 10 servings – depending on the bowl's size!

BEAN SOUP – PDQ

Purée half of a 1-pound can, undrained, Northern beans in a blender. Add purée to remaining half of beans in a 1 ½-quart sauce pan and stir in one 10-ounce can chicken broth, 2 scissor-snipped green onions, ½ teaspoon sugar (or the equivalent in artificial sweetener) and 2 tablespoons bacon drippings (or butter with a dash of hickory-flavored salt). Add ¼ teaspoon pepper and 1 tablespoon ketchup. Keep it piping hot, but do not let it come to a boil or it may scorch! Serves 4 famously!

GOOD SOUP – *SIMPLE, but to the point! Made from pantry-put-togethers!*

13 ¾-ounce can chicken broth
16-ounce can stewed-tomatoes
10-ounce can beef broth
12-ounce can V-8 juice
1 pound can green beans, undrained
1 cup strong, black, hot tea
1 teaspoon onion powder
¼ teaspoon pepper
½ teaspoon season salt
1 teaspoon sugar
2 tablespoons dry barley, uncooked
¼ teaspoon Summer savory leaves (or parsley flakes, crushed fine)

As listed, put everything into a 2 ½ quart saucepan. Bring JUST to a boil. At once, turn heat to low. Cover and let it cook gently without boiling, about 45 minutes or until barley is tender. Serves 4 to 6. Leftovers refrigerate well up to a week. Freeze soup to use within 6 months.

CINNAMON CONSOMMÉ

One of the menu attractions of the Sheraton Brock penthouse dining room in Niagara Falls, Ontario, was their crystal-clear consommé. It had a striking resemblance to what I had developed at home as a Mock Turtle Soup, so beginning with that recipe, this is how I re-created the gourmet broth...

4 cups of my Mock Turtle Soup (see Index)
13 ¾-ounce can College Inn chicken broth
½ cup water
1 raw egg, shell and all
6 pieces of stick-cinnamon, ½ inch long each
6 paper-thin slices fresh, unpeeled lemon

Bring the Mock Turtle Soup, chicken broth and water JUST to a boil. At once, turn heat down to a gentle simmer. Break the egg into the soup, adding the broken shell also. Cover the pan. Turn off the heat. Let it stand 10 minutes. Set your timer! Line a colander with a fine linen napkin or handkerchief. Strain soup through this, catching broth in another saucepan. When completely strained, discard the egg and such that you caught in the lined-colander. Return the broth to a gentle heat, adding cinnamon sticks and lemon slices. Do not try to use the powdered cinnamon in this. If you can't get the cinnamon sticks, better forget the whole thing! Let the cinnamon stick and lemon float nicely in the soup until piping hot, but do not let it boil! When you serve the soup, ladle it into glass punch cups, pre-rinsed in hot water so the soup won't crack the glass. Add one slice of lemon and one piece of cinnamon stick to each serving. Serves 6 adequately. Refrigerate leftovers to use within a week. Freeze to use within 6 months.

When you serve the consommé, do as they do at The Sheraton and add a dash of Sweet vermouth – about a cap-full of the wine bottle. It will make a big difference!

MULIGAWTAWNY SOUP, *Like Sanders*

When I told Jack Sanders, then chairman of the board of the company founded by his grandfather, Fred Sanders, that this was one of my favorite memories of lunch at Sanders in the early 50s, he put out a call for the recipe from his staff. When they moved their kitchen facilities into new quarters, some of the old recipes from earlier years of operations, were lost. This was one of them. But as I remember it, this was a soup that could stand up and walk away with flavor!

2 cans (10 ounces each) beef broth
2 soup cans of water
3 cups strong black tea
1-pound can stewed-tomatoes, cut-up
2 ribs celery, chopped fine
4 green onions, scissor-snipped
¼ teaspoon each: chili powder, paprika, season salt, pepper
1-pound can okra, sliced and undrained
   (or 10-oz pkg. of frozen okra, thawed and cooked per package directions – not drained)
3 tablespoons old-fashioned rolled oats, uncooked
1 teaspoon each: chicken bouillon powder and onion powder
3 tablespoons uncooked barley
3 cups cooked, diced, left-over roast beef or steak (with absolutely NO gristle or fat)

Bring all ingredients to a boil, uncovered in an accommodating kettle, for only 3 minutes. At once, turn heat to low. Cover the pan and let it simmer about 45 minutes – very gently! Serve piping hot. Freeze in family-sized containers to use within 6 months. Refrigerate leftovers up to a week. Makes about 8 to 10 servings.

SIDEDISHES AND SUCH

Edy Meader, Executive Chef for the Fred Sanders company in Detroit, was the originator of the "Butter Sauce" and frozen vegetable product that is now processed and packaged by one of the leading frozen food companies. Green Giant does a good job with Edy's idea and you can too, at home, if you make good use of your freezer and either a reliable produce supplier – or the benefits of your own backyard garden.

When working with vegetables and even fruits in creating interesting side dishes, remember that the side dish should never appear to be an "after-thought" to the rest of the meal. It should not, of course, steal any applause from the main course or dish; but, it certainly should have its rightful place on a table of otherwise stunning dishes, all stars in their own rights. Children will learn to develop an appetite and an appreciation, also, for side dishes – if they are prepared properly at home.

MINESTRONE

When you say Lili's or Mario's – both fine-dining restaurants – you, at once, think of their minestrone soups. So much alike, yet so different, that I wonder if the real difference isn't in the decor, atmosphere and China in which it is served – and not in the recipe. At home, I duplicate it this way…

10-ounce can beef broth
10-ounce can chicken broth
1 (10-ounce) soup can of hot black tea
10-ounce can chili beef soup
10-ounce can bean and Bacon soup
6-ounce can V-8 juice
½ cup broken-pieces of spaghetti, uncooked
½ cups sliced and diced pepperoni
1-pound can stewed-tomatoes, cut up and undrained
2 tablespoons dry minced onions
¼ cup Sweet vermouth or Chianti wine

Put everything, just as listed, into a 4-quart kettle. Bring JUST to a boil. At once, turn to a gentle simmer for 20 minutes. Serves 8 to 10. Leftovers freeze well up to 6 months or refrigerate up to a week.

BAKED BEANS, KENTUCKY-STYLE – *Like the original Colonel's*

I could never find another good recipe for baked beans like the Col. offered when he first began his chain of fried chicken restaurants. Unfortunately, when KFC was purchased from Harland Sanders by Jack C Massey in 1974 (who sold it to Heublein Inc. 7 years later), the recipe changed over the years. This is my version of the original…

1 cup packed brown sugar
¼ cup light vinegar
1 tablespoon soy sauce
4 tablespoons butter or margarine
3 tablespoons light molasses
5 cups cooked, drained Navy beans
3 tablespoons granulated sugar
2 tablespoons sweet pickle juice
3 tablespoons bacon drippings
6 strips bacon, fried crispy and crumbled
4 tablespoons Grape-Nuts cereal

In a sauce pan over medium heat, combine brown sugar, vinegar and soy sauce. Bring to boil for 1 minute, stirring constantly. Reduce heat and add butter and molasses, stirring just to blend. Place beans in an 8-cup baking dish. Pour cooked mixture over them and stir to blend. Combine remaining ingredients and stir into bean mixture. Cover and bake just to heat thoroughly in a 350°F oven, about 20 to 25 minutes. Serves 6. Very good reheated the 2nd day!

MOCK TURTLE SOUP

INSPIRED BY one of the late Elsie Masterton's creations, which she called her 'consommé with cinnamon stick' (like that served at the Sheraton Brock), from her book, "Nothing Whatever to Do", about her successful Blueberry Hill Inn, located in Vermont, during the early 50s... Here's my re-creation!

2 cans (13 ¾-ounce each) chicken broth (College Inn brand preferred)
3¼-ounce can light tuna (Star Kist brand preferred)
1 rib celery, cut in 1-inch lengths
1 onion the size of an egg, cut in half
1 whole clove
6 peppercorns
1 dry bay leaf
1 teaspoon beef bouillon powder
1 tablespoon lemon juice
1 stick cinnamon, 2 inches long (do not use the powder, please)
¼ teaspoon garlic salt
2 cans (1 pound each) stewed-tomatoes, cut up a bit
½ cup Chianti wine
1 tablespoon dry, minced parsley flakes

Combine chicken broth and tuna in a 2 ½ quart sauce pan. Add celery, onion, clove, peppercorns, bay leaf, bullion powder and lemon juice; then drop in the cinnamon stick. If you can't find the cinnamon in stick-form, forget the whole thing! Add garlic salt and bring to a gentle simmer with barely a bubble showing, but sufficient to "cook" the ingredients, rather than just "heat" them. Leave it this way for about 45 minutes, or until celery is tender. Pour it through a fine-mesh sieve. Discard the ingredients and spices left in the sieve. Return broth to sauce pan. Now, simply, "heat" it – rather than "cook" it, which prevents any unnecessary evaporation of the broth. Add the tomatoes, with their own liquid of course, in the wine. When it is piping hot, without boiling, ladle it into 6 serving cups. Rub the parsley between your fingers to a fine dust on top and serve. Keeps refrigerated up to 2 weeks. Do not freeze.

SPINACH SIDEDISH

Joe Muer's Seafood House in downtown Detroit always pleased us with this simple side dish.

1 recipe of my Blender White Sauce (see Index)
¼ teaspoon nutmeg
10-ounce package (frozen) chopped spinach, cooked and drained
pinch of sugar
salt and pepper to taste

Prepare my Blender White Sauce as directed and, while it is still warm, combine it gently with the cooked, drained spinach. Stir in nutmeg, sugar, salt and pepper to taste. Spoon into small dishes to serve 4 to 6 people.

CHUCK'S CHOWDER – *Like Chuck Muer's restaurants*

Chowder was the magic word at Muer's restaurants across the country. It was red, "tomatoey", spicy and prepared-from-scratch in their kitchens with the guidance of their executive Chef, Larry Pagliara, who created the many unusual dishes that accompanied their fresh fish and seafood menu selections. In taking some shortcuts to imitate this favorite soup at home, I encountered some good-natured ribbing from Chuck Muer, who was also one of our neighbors here in St. Clair. He didn't think that I could "sleuth-out" the secret of their famous chowder – but, I did come close – hook, line and sinker!

2 cans (10 ounces each) beef broth
2 cups bottled Clamato juice
3 cups strong, black tea
2 cans (1 pound each) stewed tomatoes, cut-up quite small
2 long ribs celery, chopped fine
2/3 cup green onions, scissor-snipped
¼ teaspoon each: chili powder, paprika, season salt, pepper
1 teaspoon onion powder
½ cup bottled Bloody Mary Mix (non-alcoholic)
6 ½-ounce can fancy packed white meat tuna in Springwater,
    flaked to separate tuna meat with a fork
8-ounce can fancy packed salmon, bones removed and flaked

Put it all in a 3-quart sauce pan, just as listed. Cover and simmer 30 minutes on lowest heat or until mixture is reduced in volume to a thick "sauce-like" mixture. A dash or two of dry red wine, Chianti or burgundy, is also good in this soup. Serves 6 to 8.

SPINACH SOUFFLÉ – *Better-Than-Frozen*

Some restaurants do this so elegantly that you're convinced there is a mystery surrounding the creation of the dish, when in layman's language, what it really amounts to is chopped spinach, a baked custard combination and some grated cheese – and you can call it a soufflé! There is one on the market in the frozen food section, which, in the picture on the box, looks like it was made in heaven; but when it comes out of my oven, I am convinced that the food company either needs a new photographer – or a new chef. What goes into the box, NEVER looks as good as it does in the picture of what you are expected to find inside. Sometimes, it just doesn't pay to complain! Therefore, I devised a recipe for my own side dish, which I once adored when I was apt to buy the frozen food product or to order when dining in one of their restaurants.

3 whole eggs, plus 2 raw egg yolks
1 tablespoon sugar, or artificial sweetener equivalent
¼ teaspoon salt
a few flecks of pepper
½ teaspoon each: nutmeg and vanilla
2 ½ cups scalded milk
¼ cup each – shredded cheese: cheddar and Swiss
2 tablespoons grated Parmesan cheese
10-ounce package frozen chopped spinach, thawed

Put the eggs and egg yolks through your blender with the sugar (or artificial sweetener), salt, pepper, nutmeg and vanilla, blending on low speed about 2 minutes. While continuing to blend, add scalded milk in slow steady stream. Pour into a mixing bowl and stir in the cheeses. Pat the thawed spinach very dry with paper towels and stir into cheese and egg mixture. Pour into a greased 3-quart baking dish – or a 9 x 12 x 2" baking dish and place it inside a slightly larger pan or baking dish that contains enough water to come half-way up the sides of the dish containing the spinach mixture. Bake at 350°F for about 50 to 55 minutes or until a knife inserted in the center comes out clean and the soufflé appears to be "set." Serve it while quite warm. Serves 6 satisfactorily.

GREENFIELD'S-STYLE SPINACH SOUFFLÉ

Prepare a good basic "medium" White Sauce (see Index for my recipe) – to 3 cups of white sauce, add ½ cup shredded Swiss cheese, ¼ cup grated Parmesan, a thawed and well-drained frozen package of chopped spinach and ½ teaspoon nutmeg. Bake it in a greased 9 x 12 x 2" pan on the center rack of a 350°F oven for almost an hour, or until "set"; which is the way it was served at Greenfield's restaurant back in the 50s. This will also serve 6 sensibly.

SOLID DAY INN STUFFED ROLLED STEAK

When you wish to make a good impression, then offer this dish as a side or main – and you'll never be scandalized again as a klutz in the kitchen!

I love to use my Frankenmuth stuffing recipe (see Index) prepared (uncooked) and served in thin, rolled-up round steak pieces. To make this sensational dish, get a large cut of round steak about ½ inch thick, about 12 inches long and, about 6 to 7 inches wide. Use a meat hammer to pound the steak paper-thin and almost twice its original size, turning it often to pound each side. Wipe both sides with corn oil and dust lightly with season salt. Spread the prepared, uncooked stuffing mixture over the steak and roll it up length-wise, in a jellyroll-fashion. Cut it into 4- to 6-inch lengths. Place rolls seam-side down in a greased 7 x 10 x 2" metal baking pan, keeping them close together. Wipe the tops with 1 tablespoon of oil and place them about 3 inches from the broiler heat, just to sear their surfaces. In about 10 to 15 minutes they should appear crispy. Don't turn them! Keep them seam-side down and cover with 3 cans (10 ounces each) Franco-American mushroom gravy, one 8-ounce can sliced mushrooms (drained) and ½ cup Burgundy or Lambrusco wine. Cover and seal tightly in foil. Bake at 325°F for about 1 hour and 45 minutes. Serves 4 to 6 nicely.

GRAPE-NUTS PUDDING

Here is a very good stuffing casserole dish that is a threat to any would-be gourmet at your table!

2 cups Post Grape-Nuts (pebbles)
13-ounce can (1 2/3 cup) chicken broth
4-ounce can of mushrooms, undrained
1 teaspoon rubbed sage
2 tablespoons dry minced onion
¼ cup bottled apple butter
1 tablespoon chicken bouillon powder
2 eggs, beaten
½ cup each: raisins and chopped walnuts

Place Grape-Nuts in a 1-quart bowl. Heat soup just to boiling and, at once, pour over cereal. Let it stand 10 minutes, stirring occasionally to soften cereal. Add liquid from canned mushrooms and cut mushrooms up small. Stir these into the cereal mixture. Add remaining ingredients, stirring just to incorporate. Pour into greased and floured 8 ½-inch Pyrex loaf baking dish (or spray with Baker's Joy or Pam.) Place this dish in a larger pan containing enough water that it comes half-way up the sides of the dish containing the cereal mixture and bake at 350°F for 1 hour. Let it cool slightly before serving in place of stuffing, sliced as you would a loaf of bread. Rewarm in a 400°F oven for about 8 to 10 minutes if you refrigerate the leftovers to be used within a week. Serves 4 to 6 nicely.

BATTER-FRIED CHEESE BALLS

One of the best recipes for making this unusual side dish was originally from Northwood Inn (in the old Royal Oak area, where I grew up.) Years later, it was one of the fast food menu selections, and often found at carnivals and amusement parks – I once had them at Cedar Point in Sandusky, Ohio.

The way I have prepared these is to mix 2 cups shredded cheddar cheese with a softened 3-ounce package of cream cheese, working it all together well in my hands, like I would a meatloaf mixture. Then I shape them into balls about the size of a whole walnut shell – and freeze them a day or two, until they are very, very solid. I don't let them thaw at all when preparing them – which keeps the cheese from running all over the place. I heat 1 ½ pints corn oil to 425°F in a deep 2 ½-quart heavy saucepan. Have a French-frying basket handy and 1 recipe of my Archer Teacher Fish Batter (see Index), prepared and ready to use. Then coat the frozen cheese balls in plain all-purpose flour, dropping each into the batter until they are evenly coated and then lowering them in a single layer – without crowding them – in the French-frying basket, into the hot oil. Let them fry a few minutes only. They brown quite quickly. When golden brown and puffy, I lift them out to drain on paper towels and serve them while they're hot. This mixture would likely serve 4 to 6.

BATTER-FRIED ZUCCHINI

At Muer's restaurants, where this was a side-dish specialty, it appeared that the unpeeled zucchini was sliced about ½ inch thick, moistened and coated in plain, all-purpose flour – probably allowing the slices to dry a few minutes before coating in a batter like my Archer Teacher's Fish Batter (see Index) and deep-frying in 425°F vegetable oil for just a few minutes or until puffy and golden-brown.

STUFFED BAKED POTATOES

When I had these at the Golden Lion (Detroit, MI), I would've guessed that the baked potatoes had been scooped out of all the potato pulp while still warm from the oven, but without disturbing the shell of the potato. At home, I removed a slice, about the size of a 50-cent piece, from the tops of 6 baked potatoes and used a small spoon to remove the pulp. Then I mixed all the pulp from the baked potatoes with 1 cup (8-ounce tub) of onion chip dip and whipped it until smooth. Next, I spooned the mixture carefully back into the shells and added 1 tablespoon of grated Parmesan to the opening of each potato. I re-baked them on a cookie sheet at 350°F for 20 to 25 minutes until golden-brown and piping hot.

PRINCE CHARLES' SKILLET STRATA

When WJR Radio, Detroit, sent Warren Pierce to cover the wedding of Lady Diana and Prince Charles, Warren saved a very special recipe for me. It was created by the chef of the country inn where Prince Charles and his royal party dined on the way to the theater. His favorite dish there was an egg creation, quite like strata, but without the bread. When Warren returned from his assignment in Great Britain, he phoned me for a radio conversation with the chef from England. The chef was on one phone, I on the other and Warren bringing us together on the air for his afternoon program. It was, indeed, an honor to talk with someone of his stature. The recipe he shared with us was not in exact measurements, but rather in technique – and it works beautifully... A true Royal dish!

Separate 2 eggs. Beat the whites until stiff, but not dry, and set aside. Beat the 2 yolks with 2 more whole eggs, using an electric mixer on medium speed for about 5 minutes, or until thick and lemon-colored. Slowly beat in ¼ cup un-whipped whipping cream (heavy cream) and then fold in the stiffly beaten whites. Melt ¼ pound butter in a heavy 10-inch skillet, but do not let it change color. Regulate the heat under the skillet so that the butter remains golden yellow, but hot and melted. Pour in the egg mixture. Do not stir it. Over the top of the egg mixture – sprinkle ¼ cup shredded cheddar cheese, ½ cup well-chopped boiled ham, ¼ cup minced or finely-diced green pepper, 2 green onions (finally snipped with kitchen scissors, whites and the green stems), ¼ teaspoon pepper and ½ teaspoon season salt. Let it cook about 3 minutes on medium to low heat or until the edge of the egg begins to thicken. Then fold it over so that the uncooked part with the ham, etc., is enclosed in the middle. Turn it carefully to cook the top part about 2 minutes and serve it promptly while piping hot with a hollandaise or béarnaise sauce on the side. Serves 2 royally!

MEDIUM WHITE SAUCE – *a quick sauce that's a very good base for both soups and sauces.*

3 cups cold water
1 cup nonfat dry milk powder
2/3 cup flour

Put these ingredients into a blender on high speed for about 1 minute, or until very smooth. Transfer mixture to a 1 ½-quart sauce pan and, over medium to high heat, stir constantly until it begins to thicken like a pudding. This should take about 4 to 5 minutes. As soon as you see the very first bubble of a boil, remove from heat and stir in:

3 tablespoons butter or margarine
¼ teaspoon pepper
½ teaspoon onion salt
pinch of celery salt

Stir until the butter melts. Combine ingredients thoroughly, stirring well. This may now be refrigerated to use within one week, reheating it in the top of a double boiler over simmering water; or it can be frozen until needed, to be used within 3 months. You can also use it at once for any recipe calling for about 3 ½ cups medium white sauce. You can omit the seasonings altogether if you are working with a "sweet" recipe, such as a dessert, but for most soups and sauces or side dishes, the seasonings I suggest above, are adequate.

TAKE THE JUNK OUT OF JUNK FOODS

EATING OUT AT HOME: Going to a restaurant is like going to a movie, a way of escaping your day-to-day environment in the office or at home or at most functional places. Restaurants should be places that make you feel separated from your daily environment. Many restaurants are successful because their design is theatrical, suggesting another time, or a more environmental experience that makes you feel far away from your problems. McDonald's has been successfully employing the theme of total decorating concept into their units for many years with the family as the center of their attention; whatever appeals to family groups, children, parents, grandparents. Their concept is warm, functional, attractive and wholesome. They have set the trend in the fast food industry for this type of the core, always emphasizing their immaculacy concept.

SCRAMBLED EGGS, *For a Crowd*

In trying to determine the best way to prepare scrambled eggs for a large group – that may not be eating all at the same time – I watched them work magic at McDonald's with their eggs – which were never tough or rubbery or over-cooked, which sometimes happens when you make them ahead. This is the "secret" recipe for soft delicately cooked "on-hold" scrambled eggs!

Beat 8 eggs with an electric mixer until thick and lemony colored – about 6 minutes. Add ½ teaspoon salt and ½ cup milk, beating for 2 to 3 minutes more. Slowly add ¼ cup melted and cooled butter (or margarine) a little at a time, beating until combined. Lightly butter the bottom and sides inside a double boiler's top pan and place it over simmering water. Add the egg mixture, cover and allow to cook at lowest temperature possible for about 15 minutes. After that, turn the congealed portions of the egg toward the middle of the pan and cover it again, continuing to cook for another 5 minutes or until all the eggs are in large congealed pieces. Serves 4 to 6. Recipe may be multiplied as you wish.

EGGS BENEDICT – *Like Brennan's (New Orleans – circa 1960s)*

Unlike the usual fast-food-like Eggs Benedict that we are now use to at either McDonald's – where it is lovingly called Egg McMuffin – or at Big Boy, where it is also prepared with an English muffin and a sausage patty… Here is the most memorable way of serving it, the way Ella Brennan Martin prepared it years ago, when Paul Blange was her head chef.

Top crisp rusks, such as packaged Holland Rusk or homemade rounds of Zwieback, with sliced and grilled Canadian bacon. Add a soft poached egg to each and ladle hollandaise sauce over the eggs, sprinkling each with a bit of paprika.

BRENNAN-STYLE HOLLANDAISE: In top of a double boiler, beat 4 egg yolks just to combine and whip in 2 tablespoons lemon juice. Place over hot, but not boiling, water and do not allow the water in the bottom pan to touch the top pan. Add ½ pound melted butter or margarine, stirring constantly with a sturdy spoon, until mixture thickens – or use portable electric mixer on lowest speed to blend until thickened. Serve sauce warm with salt and pepper added to taste if you wish.

BILL KNAPP'S AU GRATIN POTATOES

This is a unique side dish offered at the Midwestern restaurant chain that was one of our family's favorites, having originated in Battle Creek, Michigan in 1948. Every selection on their menu was a masterpiece and at very reasonable prices. But, I am absolutely in love with their potato side dish. At home, I attempt to duplicate it this way…

GLORIOUS AU GRATINS

Into your blender put 1 ½ cups cold water, ½ cup nonfat dry milk powder and 1/3 cup flour. Blend for 30 seconds on high or until smooth. Pour into a 2-quart sauce pan. Cook and stir constantly over medium-high heat until thickened and smooth like a pudding. Remove from heat and add 2 tablespoons margarine, pinch of pepper, ½ teaspoon onion salt, dash of celery salt, 1 tablespoon dry minced onion, 1 packet Herb Ox Chicken Broth Powder or 1 ½ teaspoons chicken bouillon powder. Stir in an 8-ounce jar of Cheez Whiz, 2 slices of Kraft "Singles" American cheese (torn in bits) and 3 cups cooked, peeled and cubed potatoes. Pour mixture into a 2-quart greased baking dish. Dust top of it liberally in paprika. Bake uncovered in a 350°F oven – about 30 minutes or until bubbly and piping hot. Serves 4 nicely. (Recipe may be doubled for 8 to 10.) Leftovers refrigerate well, to be used within 3 days.

BLENDER WHITE SAUCE

1 ½ cups very hot milk
¼ cup butter or margarine
4 slices stale white bread, in small bits
2 tablespoons chicken bouillon powder
dash of pepper

As listed, place all ingredients in a blender. Cover and blend on high-speed with an on/off motion until smooth. (About 30 seconds should do it!) Keep the sauce hot in top of a double boiler over simmering water until time to serve – or put it in the microwave on lowest possible setting for a minute or so just before serving. Spoon the sauce over steamed vegetables, or whatever pleases you. Makes about 3 cups of sauce. Refrigerate leftovers to rewarm in, either, top of double boiler or microwave as suggested above.

HOLLANDAISE IN A HURRY

1 cup mayonnaise
1 tablespoon chicken bouillon powder
½ teaspoon bottled lemon peel
½ teaspoon Summer savory leaves or parsley
1/3 cup grated Parmesan cheese
½ teaspoon onion powder

Combine all ingredients with a fork or spoon. Refrigerate until time to serve it on the side with steamed vegetables. Makes a little more than 1 cup of sauce.

GRAVY MIX POWDER

3 tablespoons instant tea powder
1 tablespoon onion salt
2 tablespoons onion powder
1 teaspoon dried marjoram leaves, crushed
4 tablespoons beef bouillon powder
2/3 cup cornstarch
1 teaspoon paprika
8 gingersnap cookies (about 2 ½ inches)

Place all ingredients, just as listed, into your blender, blending on high-speed until it becomes a very fine powder. Use on/off speed on high and turn off the motor 3 or 4 times to clear the mixture away from the blades during the blending. Store at room temperature for weeks and weeks. Makes 2 cups of dry mix.

TO USE THE GRAVY MIX: place 2 cups cold water in your blender. Add 3 tablespoons of "Gravy Mix" and blend 30 seconds on high-speed or until smooth. Transfer to small sauce pan and cook on medium, stirring constantly until thick and smooth. Adjust seasoning with salt and pepper to taste. Then stir in 2 tablespoons butter or margarine until blended. Remove from heat and serve. Makes a little over 2 cups prepared gravy. *Add a dash of dry red wine to the gravy as you serve it! Very cosmopolitan and uncommonly good!*

NOTE: if you do not use a blender, combine the 2 cups of water and the 3 tablespoons gravy mix (above), in a jar with a tight-fitting lid, shaking the mixture vigorously until smooth – or beat briskly, using an electric hand-mixer or a wire whisk. Strain the gravy through a fine mesh sieve to remove any annoying lumps.

CHICKEN GRAVY

Prepare the basic "Gravy Mix" (above), using chicken bouillon powder instead of beef. Mix the prepared gravy with a 10-ounce can cream of chicken soup. Heat gently until piping hot. Serves 4 to 6.

MUSHROOM GRAVY

Prepare the basic "Gravy Mix" (above), but blend the finished hot gravy with a 10-ounce can cream of mushroom soup, using a spoon to stir and blend, rather than a blender or mixer. Use medium-high heat to continue cooking, without ever once letting it come to a boil! When the gravy boils, it thins out. So, do be careful about the heat. Makes 1 quart. Serves 4 to 6.

PORK GRAVY

Combine 2 ¼ cups prepared gravy from the basic "Gravy Mix" (above) – give or take a spoonful or so – with a 10-ounce can cream of celery soup and add ¼ teaspoon hickory-flavored salt, heating thoroughly and stirring constantly until smooth. Do not let it boil! Then, at serving time, stir in about 2 tablespoons of reserved bacon drippings to serve 4 to 6!

CARCASS SOUP

Every time the turkey is stripped from its frame, a bundle of nutrition is discarded with the carcass. In the days of my grandmother's cooking adventures, one never threw out the turkey carcass until a pot of good, rich, wholesome soup had been sapped from the bones of the bird. Even to this day, I find it a must to simmer a soup from the bones and – after straining it and clarifying it with egg shells and raw eggs, and straining it again – have several quarts for the freezer, from which I could later make many other dishes, other than soup.

To make this soup, take every bit of the turkey carcass, with some meat on the bones yet, and about 1 cup of the drippings from the pan in which you roasted the turkey and put it all into an accommodating kettle. Submerge it in enough water to cover it an inch above the frame of the carcass. You don't have to break up the bones, unless your kettle isn't big enough to hold the carcass as is. Put a lid on the kettle and let it simmer very slowly for 2 hours. Set your timer! Then remove as many of the bones as you can, using a pair of tongs. Add 3 white, peeled and quartered onions – each about the size of an orange. Cut up a stalk of celery, core, leaves and all. (NOTE: a "stalk" of celery is comprised of several "ribs" of celery, so do keep the difference between a "stalk" and a "rib" in mind.) Put the lid back on the kettle and bring the broth back to a gentle simmer once again – allowing it to simmer for 1 hour, or until the onions are limp and the celery is quite soft.

Now, allow it to cool rather quickly, if you can, by removing the lid and placing the kettle in a cool place – like near an open window. If it's during the winter, place the kettle, covered of course, in the snow and once it is lukewarm, you can refrigerate it. Check the soup between 4 to 5 hours to see if the fats have risen to the top and solidified. Lift the solid fats off with a spatula. Heat the soup just so that it is pourable and, then, run it through a colander, catching the broth in another kettle. Discard the onion and celery pieces, in as much as you've reaped all the flavor from them – later, you'll add some other ingredients to the finished broth that will make it far more attractive when you serve it.

Next, place a linen handkerchief or paper coffee filters in the colander and drain the soup again. Return it to the burner to bring just to a boil, turning the heat down at once to low, so that you don't let the flavor boil away. Now, break 2 raw eggs, shells and all, into the broth and cover. Allow the eggs and shells to cook very gently with the broth, which gives the calcium in the eggs a chance to clarify the broth. It will be as clear as a mountain stream when it's properly cooked. Strain it once more through the cloth-lined colander. Divide it up into family-sized containers for the freezer. Depending on the size of the turkey you start with – which averages from 12 to 18 pounds – you should be able to obtain about 4 to 5 quarts of broth from one carcass, 3 onions and a stalk of celery. Allow a 1-inch headspace when you cap and seal the containers for freezing. Triple seal the lids in masking tape and date each one to be used within 6 months. When you use the frozen broth – defrost the solid chunk on low and then add the vegetables of your choice, adjusting salt and pepper, etc., to taste at that time.

* * * * * *

Food for Thought:
I love to watch the same man who criticized his wife for the way she parked the car in the garage, trying to thread a needle.

* * * * * *

DIME STORE-STYLE MACARONI AND CHEESE

In the days when lunch counters in large dimestores, like Woolworths or Montgomery Ward, were the only "fast food" eateries, the menu was simplified and usually, for the price we paid, very good! This was one of my favorites when I was a regular lunch-counter-customer in the early 50s.

7-ounce package elbow macaroni
8-ounce package (½ pound) Velveeta cheese
½ cup milk
¼ pound (one stick) butter or margarine
1 tablespoon dry minced onion
¼ pound grated cheddar cheese
10-ounce can cream of celery soup
1 cup mayonnaise, not salad dressing
¼ teaspoon pepper
½ teaspoon season salt

Cook macaroni per package directions until tender. Drain. Meanwhile, in a medium saucepan over medium heat, melt cheese, milk and butter or margarine, adding the onion and cheddar. Stir until smooth. Do not let it boil! Add remaining ingredients, keeping mixture on lowest heat, add drained macaroni. Pour into 2 ½-quart greased casserole dish. May be served at once or kept in a warm oven at 275°F for up to an hour before serving. Leftovers refrigerate well up to a week. Serves 4 to 6.

VARIATIONS: You may top the casserole, before baking it, with 1 cup finely crushed potato chips or buttered bread crumbs and a light dusting of paprika. You can also stir in a 6 ½ ounce can of tuna fish to the finished sauce mixture and proceed as recipe otherwise directs. Crispy-fried and crumbled bacon (6 to 8 ounces) may be added to the top in place of, or in addition to, the crushed chips.

CHEESE STRATA

Cut 6 slices of buttered bread into triangle halves. Place overlapping slices, point up, in a buttered 7 x 10 x 1.5" baking dish. Beat together 4 eggs and 2/3 cup milk with 1 teaspoon onion salt, ¼ teaspoon pepper and 1 packet Herb Ox chicken broth powder (or 1 ½ teaspoons chicken bouillon powder.) Stir in 8 ounces of shredded cheddar cheese. Pour over bread. Cover and refrigerate 2 to 3 hours (or overnight if you wish.) Bake uncovered in a 325°F oven for almost an hour, or until puffy and cheese mixture is bubbly and slightly browned. Dust in paprika and dry parsley leaves, first, rubbed to a fine dust between your fingers. Serves 4 nicely. Leftovers do not keep well, nor do they freeze well.

BREADS, PANCAKES… AND OTHER BAKED-GOODS

THE FAST FOOD INDUSTRY has been one of the largest consumers of bakery products in the nation. As a mainstay of the fast food menu, buns, biscuits, roles, breads and crackers have been incorporated into the restaurant menu, on their tables and in their kitchens. At home, we also use many bread products in our family meal preparations. In Great-Grandma's day, baking bread was as much a part of a woman's household routine as was the laundry or the dusting. In colonial days, bread was often the main dish, used like a sponge to soak up whatever broth or gravy might accompany a meager meal, which most of colonial cuisine consisted of on the frontier.

BREAD RECIPES have attracted cooks to new recipe collections for a long time, but there has been a revival to the interest in baking your own bread, as most of what is available on the market shelves becomes more and more like angel food cake then it does bread!

Biscuits and rolls and coffee cakes are offered, along with donuts and some sweet items, with great success in even the smallest restaurant operation. The shelf-life of a loaf of bread at room temperature is about 3 days – refrigerated, about a week; but in the freezer, up to 6 months. The savings are terrific when you make your own – and the pure pleasure of letting the house fill up with the wonderful aroma of yeast is enough to whet the appetite of even the most critical audience.

Hardtack, which comprised a good deal of the early settlers' meals, has become popular again in restaurant bread baskets, as well as homemade crackers and sweet rolls. When the Danish invented "dunking" their rolls and bread into hot beverages, they knew a good thing – and we apparently do also, for it is considered quite permissible to dunk a donut in your coffee…or a bread stick or whatever your preference might be.

BREAD-BAKING has filled my house with the most delicious aromas – on those occasions when I have ventured into the catacombs of conscious cookery. I was taught by a grandmother who believed that the way to a man's heart was through his stomach; and, if you kept your man well-fed and loved and listened-to, everything else would fall into its proper place in perspective. Well, we can't all be right all the time. Grandma tried. Bread-baking was not the Elmer's "Glue-All" of my marital bliss and stability. In fact, on occasion, it might have threatened our harmony – considering that, before I learned a few chosen shortcuts to better baking, I could (at the drop of a hat) clutter the countertops with every bowl, dish, spoon, pan and ingredient possible! This, of course, necessitated having to "eat out" on those nights when there was no place to prepare a deserving dinner at home. It reminded me that somewhere there should be a clause in every cookbook warning young wives with old-fashioned morals about marriage that there are some things Mother never told us… Or if she did, I just wasn't paying attention! In any case, I recommend cooking as being thoroughly therapeutic! Bread-baking includes the energetic kneading of the dough – which enables one to work off pent-up emotions that one cannot otherwise rid themselves of verbally.

Whenever I had problems to work out (which was like every other minute or so) I would either be in the kitchen, cooking something, or at the typewriter, writing about cooking something! Kneading a large batch of yeast dough is a great way to unwind and relieve tensions. Of course, it didn't always solve my problems, since most of them were directly related to my finding my utensils, which I had to locate before I could start relieving myself of unwanted tensions. I'll bet I was the only woman on the block who had to sift through the kids' sandbox before I could set the table, or bake a loaf of bread!

Step-by-Step Yeast Bread

THE SECRET OF GOOD BREAD is in the kneading and rising. If given enough time, bread will rise anywhere - in the refrigerator, on the sink top, in a dark closet! The more you allow the dough to rise, until it is doubled in bulk, and the more you punch it back down again to let it rise once more, the better the texture. Not enough salt in the dough will make it course. Too much shortening will make it heavy. Not enough shortening will make it dry. Eggs will make it soft like a coffee cake. No eggs at all will make it spongy like old-fashioned bread. Homemade bread can be anything you want it to be, depending on the amount of time and effort you put into it. The ingredients are simple for a good white bread. In fact, the first time I worked with this recipe, making notes of what I put in the batch, I thought I had left something out when I discovered that the final product was light and lovely and evenly textured. But after 3 or 4 more tests, I was perfectly satisfied that this was going to be my favorite white bread recipe for lack of a better name I called mine…

THUNDER BREAD – *Homemade White Bread*

1 cup warm water
1 tablespoon sugar
1 package dry yeast
¾ teaspoon salt
2 tablespoons Crisco
2 ½ to 3 cups all-purpose flour

Grease a 9-inch loaf pan. Remove ¼ cup of the warm water and stir in 1 teaspoon of the sugar and all the yeast. Do not use a metal bowl, nor a metal spoon to stir! Metal and yeast are not compatible and using metal utensils or bowls with yeast could keep the yeast from working as well as it should. I usually use plastic or Pyrex bowls and only wooden or plastic spoons for stirring or mixing this bread. Set the yeast aside for a few minutes to allow it to double in bulk. In the meantime, mix the remaining ingredients with only half of the flour, beating it vigorously until you have a smooth batter. Beat in the yeast mixture and then work in the remaining flour. Have some additional flour nearby in a shallow dish so that you can dip your knuckles in, working it into the dough on a floured surface until the dough was no longer sticky. Toss the dough lightly and repeatedly, working in just enough more flour with your knuckles that it has a smooth elastic-like consistency. Place it in an accommodating, greased or Pam-sprayed bowl or plastic bag, turning the dough once so that all sides are greased. Let it rise in a warm place, like a sunny spot on the kitchen table or counter. After an hour, when doubled in size, punch it down and let it rise once more. Then shape the dough to fit the pan in a nice smooth loaf. Let it rise in the pan until doubled in size. Place it in a cold oven, because sudden temperature changes may cause it to deflate and then you'll lose all that lovely air texture. Set the temperature to 450°F for 7 minutes then reduce the oven heat to 350°F and let the bread continue to bake 20 minutes more, or until golden brown and makes a hollow sound when you tap the crust with your fingers. Remove the loaf pan and let it cool on its side for 10 minutes. Then remove the loaf from the pan and let it continue to cool on its side about 2 hours longer. Don't attempt to slice freshly baked bread for at least 4 hours after it is out of the oven! Makes 1 loaf. Recipe can be doubled or tripled as you wish! Freeze up to one year.

HOME-BAKED BREAD

Nothing gives the awesome aroma to a kitchen like homemade bread in the oven! In fact, whenever Nancy Hughes had problems on "As the World Turns", she baked bread. Of course, Nancy was not an average person. She wore an apron that dated her to the 40s, and put bread in the oven on Tuesday that wasn't ready to come out until you tuned into the show on Friday - just in time for her husband, Chris, to bring another homeless, un-wed mother in to occupy their daughter Penny's room, who was off doing summer stock (but we weren't supposed to know that!) Penny, as you remember, was married to Jeff and then she was married to Neil and from that point, everyone forgot because they were still waiting to see Nancy take the bread out of the oven. I became very nervous about it as I watched the show day after day. Had Nancy forgotten the bread? No! Of course, not! It always emerged like a beautiful mahogany finished model from the slick pages of Better Homes & Gardens!

IT WAS THE PRACTICAL-MINDED ROMANS who developed the circular millstone and enlarged the baking oven to mass production capacity. The commercial baker, in business by 168 BC, carefully put his mark on each loaf. The ruins of Pompeii revealed beehive-shaped ovens, as well as the remains of bread baked in those ovens. Pliny states that bread "sine pondere" (without heaviness) is best, revealing an early preference for light, white bread.

ROAMIN' MILE WHEAT BREAD

4 to 5 cups all-purpose flour
2 teaspoon salt
2 packages dry yeast
1 cup lukewarm water
½ cup honey
¼ cup butter or margarine
1 cup small curd cottage cheese
2 eggs
2 cups Graham or whole wheat flour
½ cup quick Mother's oats uncooked

Combine flour and salt in a roomy bowl. Place yeast and ½ cup of the water with 1 teaspoon of the honey in a smaller bowl and stir it once or twice. Let it stand for 5 or 6 minutes or until bubbly. Heat remaining water with remaining honey and butter to lukewarm and beat into flour and salt mixture until you have a smooth batter. Beat in the eggs and then the yeast mixture. Switch to a sturdy spoon to work in the Graham flour and oatmeal. Add only enough additional all-purpose flour that you have a smooth dough that is no longer sticky. Knead in the bowl for about 10 minutes. When dough is elastic in texture, place in a plastic bag that is lightly greased inside and large enough to permit the dough to triple in bulk without breaking the bag open. Let it rise for about 90 minutes in a warm place or until doubled in bulk. Punch it down and let it rise once more, until it doubles again. Now, divide dough into 2 equal portions, shaping to fit two 9-inch greased loaf pans. Wipe the top of each loaf with about a teaspoon of soft margarine or butter and let it rise until doubled. Place loaves at least 2 inches apart on center rack of a COLD oven. Set temperature at 450°F for 5 minutes and then reduce heat to 350°F, letting loaves bake about 35 to 40 minutes more or until golden brown and crust makes a hollow sound when you tap it lightly with a finger. Remove at once from pans and let loaves cool on their sides on a towel. Do not slice the bread for at least 4 hours after baking. Makes 2 loaves. Freezes up to 6 months.

BREAD HISTORY

The bread of primitive man was unleavened and perhaps, as the story goes, the discovery of a leavening agent by a cook of ancient Egypt was purely by chance. However, it came about that the Egyptians baked some of the finest bread in the ancient world in cone-shaped ovens. Flattened, and perhaps coarse to present-day taste, the ancient round or triangular loaves unearthed at Deir-el-Bahari were a great improvement over the open-air baking of earlier times. Bread, the symbol of the bounty of the Nile, was cast upon its waters as a tribute to the gods. It was, also, placed in tombs to feed the departed spirits of the deceased. Egyptians literally earned their daily bread as workers, as they were given bread at the end of the day as wages for their labor. The Egyptians, who discovered the principle of baking raised bread, didn't fool around. They just left some dough around in the hot weather until it went bad, and then they baked it. And - lo - it puffed up in old clay ovens and tasted great! The leavened loaf was launched, with no questions asked. The Egyptians regarded "yeast-ification" as an occult, not subject to the whim of man.

WHITE BREAD – *The Leavened Loaf*

4 cups warm water
¼ cup sugar
3 packages dry yeast
2 teaspoon salt
3 tablespoons each: butter (or margarine) and Crisco (or use 6 tablespoons butter/margarine)
10 to 12 cups all-purpose flour (almost all a 5-pound bag)

Grease four 9-inch bread loaf pans. Remove 1 ½ cups from the 4 cups of the warm water and stir it into 3 tablespoons of the sugar. Dissolve yeast in this, stirring once or twice and letting it stand for 5 minutes, or until bubbly. Mix remaining ingredients with 4 cups of the flour, blending well with electric mixer on medium speed. Add yeast mixture and, 1 cup at a time, the remaining flour until you have a soft, smooth, firm dough that can be kneaded in the bowl. *So as not to tear the bread texture, shape your hand in this way: stretch your hand out in front of you palm side up and place your thumb across the middle of the palm, closing your fingers over your thumb.* Knead the dough with your hand in this position, dipping your knuckles in the flour, periodically, to keep the dough from sticking, until elastic in texture (about 5 minutes) – with tiny dough bubbles just beneath the surface, bursting as you knead.

Place the dough in a greased bowl or plastic food storage bag that will permit it to triple in bulk without bursting the bag open or pouring out of the bowl. Place in a warm spot (about 90 minutes) until dough has tripled. Punch it down. Let it rise again for another 90 minutes. Shape into 4 loaves to fit the prepared pans. Brush the top of each with a slightly beaten egg yolk mixed with a teaspoon of cold water for a rich, brown crust. Omit egg wash if you want a pale-color bread crust. Let each loaf triple in bulk (about 1 hour) in a warm place. Put loaves in a COLD oven, allowing about 1 inch of space between the pans for heat to circulate. Turn oven heat to 450°F for 8 minutes and, then, turn down to 350°F. Continue baking for 20 to 25 more minutes or until golden brown and crust makes a "hollow sound" when you tap it with your finger. As soon as you remove the pans from the oven, turn them on their sides and let them cool this way for about 10 minutes. Remove the loaves from the pans and let them continue cooling on their sides for another hour. Don't attempt to slice the bread for at least 4 hours. Makes four 9-inch loaves. Recipe may be cut in half. Freeze baked bread up to 6 months.

NO-FAULT PEANUT BREAD

From a happily married baker who has enjoyed success in both baking and marriage, here is a fast, simple recipe for dinner bread!

1 ¾ cup all-purpose flour
2 teaspoon baking powder
1 teaspoon salt
1/3 cup sugar
2 tablespoons butter or margarine
1 egg
1 ¼ cup milk
1 cup chopped, dry-roasted peanuts

Stir dry ingredients together and, with a fork, cut in butter. Beat egg with milk and stir into flour mixture. Add peanuts and pour into a lightly greased, 9-inch bread loaf pan. Bake in a preheated 350°F oven for about 1 hour or until it tests done – when a toothpick inserted in center comes out clean. Turn out onto cake rack to cool completely. The bread will slice much better the 2nd day. Makes 1 loaf.

GREENFIELD'S-STYLE CLOVER-LEAF ROLLS

6 to 7 cups all-purpose flour
¼ cup sugar
2 teaspoon salt
2 packages dry yeast
1 cup lukewarm water
1 cup lukewarm milk
1/2 cup butter, very soft
1 egg

Combine the flour, 1 teaspoon of the sugar and the salt in a roomy bowl. Combine the yeast in ½ cup of the warm water with the other teaspoon of sugar, stirring once or twice. Let this stand 5 to 6 minutes or until bubbly. Combine the remaining warm water with the warm milk and butter, beating it into half of the flour until it's a smooth batter. Beat in egg in yeast mixture. Work in remaining flour until dough is no longer sticky. Knead in the bowl, with floured hands, for about 10 minutes or until elastic in texture. Place dough in plastic bag that has been greased inside and is big enough to permit dough to triple in bulk without breaking the bag. Twist ends of bag tightly to seal out air. Let dough rise in a warm place for 90 minutes or until double in bulk. Punch it down and let it rise again. Then punch it down and divide it into 36 ping-pong-sized balls. Using a large muffin pan, drop these 3 at a time into one greased muffin cup or well, brushing them in a bit of oil (1/2 teaspoon per cup or well of dough balls.) Cover pan loosely with plastic kitchen wrap that has been sprayed with Pam on the side that goes down on the dough so it won't stick to the plastic when it rises. Refrigerate these roles for 24 hours - do not freeze. Remove from refrigerator and let rise until doubled in size. Bake (one tin at a time) at 375°F for about 20 minutes or until golden brown. Freeze roles if not using within 2 days. Makes 3 dozen clover-shaped rolls.

CROUTETTS

Croutons are an essential ingredient, not only for stuffing mix, but also for Caesar salad (see Index for mine.) Begin by removing the crust from slightly stale bread. Reserve the crust to, later, make your bread crumbs. Cut the sliced bread into little cubes about ½-inch square. Arrange them in a single layer on an ungreased cookie sheet and place in the oven, leaving the door ajar about an inch and turning the heat to lowest possible temperature. Some ovens register 150°F and others 200°F, so adjust the time accordingly to thoroughly dry the bread crumbs to the point that they're very brittle – perhaps about 2 hours. This is a good job for one of those chilly days when the kitchen could use a little additional heat. Let the dried cubes cool completely on the cookie sheet and then transfer to a container with a tight-fitting lid. Store at room temperature, to use within 2 months. Freeze them, to use within 6 months.

SEASONED CROUTONS

After you have trimmed away the crust of the bread slices, as in the recipe above, melt some margarine in a small pan (don't let it change color) and brush it lightly and evenly over one side of each slice. Then dust the slices, very lightly, in a mixture of a little onion powder, a bit of garlic powder, a bit of season salt, a dash of paprika and just a pinch of powdered sage. Now cut the slices into cubes and arrange in a single layer on cookie sheets to oven-dry, just as directed above for the "Croutetts". The seasoned croutons, however, may take a little longer to dry, so make allowances for the time. If you are skeptical about trusting your own "to taste" judgment for the seasonings, you can do it this way:

For every 8 slices of bread – allow ¼ pound (1 stick) margarine. Melt it, remove from heat and stir in:

½ teaspoon onion powder
½ teaspoon garlic powder
1 teaspoon paprika
2 teaspoon season salt
¼ teaspoon powdered sage

If you want an even heartier flavor for your croutons, also add 1 teaspoon each: A-1 steak sauce and Worcestershire sauce to the melted margarine, before applying to sliced bread, continuing as recipe above otherwise directs.

BREAD CRUMBS

Put the trimmed crusts, as from the above recipes' cast-offs, plus seasoned or unseasoned stale or dried bread (broken into pieces) into your blender. Use on/off speed until finely powdered. Store in covered container at room temperature for up to 2 months. Freeze them to be used within 6 months.

POTATO BREAD

1 ½ cups warm mashed potatoes
1 cup of the starchy-water from the cooked potatoes
2 packages dry yeast
¼ cup sugar
1 teaspoon salt
1/3 cup corn oil or vegetable oil
2 eggs
5 to 6 cups flour

Place mashed potatoes in a large mixing bowl and set aside. Put the "potato water" in a small bowl, adding the yeast to it and stirring in the sugar. Let it stand 10 minutes, uncovered – but, in a warm place so that it can triple in bulk. Add the salt and oil to the potatoes, beating in the eggs and only 1 cup of the flour with an electric mixer. When yeast mixture is puffy and bubbly, beat this into the flour mixture until you have a smooth batter. Remove the beaters and switch to a sturdy spoon, working in about half of the remaining flour. Let dough stand for 15 minutes. This is important, as it gives the yeast mixture time to become intimately acquainted with the other ingredients – on a small scale. Then, add the remaining flour and you'll have a soft dough that's no longer sticky and a bit elastic to the touch.

Spray a clean, large, mixing bowl with Pam and drop the dough into this. Also, spray one side of a sheet of wax paper with Pam and place it greased-side-down over the dough. Now, place the bowl away from any drafts and leave it alone for about an hour or until twice its original size. Then punch it down. Cut the dough in half with a knife sprayed with Pam. Put each half of the dough into separate, greased, 9-inch loaf pans. Cover loosely with sheets of plastic wrap that have been Pam-sprayed on the face-down sides. Let loaves rise 1 hour or until doubled in bulk. Place both loaves in a COLD oven so that the shock of direct heat won't threaten the yeast-rising process, causing it to fall. Turn the oven temperature to 450°F for about 6 minutes and then turn it down to 350°F, letting the loaves bake, then, for about 30 minutes or until the crust is a deep brown color and there is a hollow sound when you tap the crust lightly with your finger. Don't under-bake it! Even if the crust is browned at 25 minutes, cover the top loosely with a sheet of foil and continue the baking time to be sure the bread is baked all the way through. Cool the bread in the pans for 1 hour, placing them on a wire rack on their sides. Remove bread from pans by loosening the sides with the tip of a sharp knife. Let bread cool on its side another hour before wrapping for storage or slicing to serve. Freeze up to 3 months.

POCKET BREAD

Prepare my Pita Bread (see Index) – but, to ensure you have a good-sized pocket in the pita bread, grease the bottom sides of layer cake pans and dust in cornmeal, placing the circles of rolled out dough on these to bake. The pan is then placed on the floor of the oven, rather than on the rack; and the oven is preheated to 450°F with the baking time at about 10 to 12 minutes. As soon as bread has puffed up, place the pan of bread on the middle rack of the oven and turn on the broiler for about 1 minute, just to brown the tops. Another suggestion, if you like, is to brush the top of each unbaked circle of dough with a little raw egg you've beaten with a few drops of water before you set the pan on the floor of the oven, and just leave it there to bake completely until evenly browned and puffy, thus omitting the need to turn on the broiler.

DARK & MOIST, RAISIN-OATMEAL BATTER BREAD

If you're ever visiting the Cape Cod area, be sure to stop at a little restaurant in Orleans, MA, called Rags & Roses – where, for breakfast, you might be served sliced and toasted, homemade oatmeal bread, covered generously in softened cream cheese! Ooooh-h-h!

DON'T BE ALARMED about the amount of soda and baking powder in this recipe. It does sound like too much, but trust me - it isn't! The recipe does not contain shortening, as you will notice. It doesn't need it! The finished bread is light and moist. You might even suppose it had molasses in it, which is the thing that really threw me off when I began to test various combinations of ingredients to duplicate it. The bread keeps well if you refrigerate it, sealing it tightly in a plastic bag, for up to a week. It should freeze well for up to a year! Of course, you can increase the number of raisins to your liking. Another cupful might be sufficient if you like raisins. Without any raisins, the bread was lacking something. If you don't like raisins, however, you could probably substitute chopped walnuts or pecans. Be creative!

2 cups each: whole wheat flour and quick-cooking Quaker Oats
2 tablespoons each: baking soda and baking powder
2 cups buttermilk
3 eggs
1 cup packed brown sugar
½ cups raisins

Combine flour and oats and mixing bowl. Set it aside. Stir the baking soda and baking powder into the buttermilk. Let it stand a few minutes. Beat the eggs until foamy, about 2 minutes on medium speed of an electric mixer. Add brown sugar a little at a time, then beat in the buttermilk. Make a well in the center of the flour mixture and pour in the liquid mixture. Stir to moisten all the dry particles. Run the raisins under water in a fine sieve. Drain and toss them lightly in a little all-purpose flour, just to coat them so that they won't sink to the bottom of the batter during baking. Fold floured raisins into batter. Pour into two 9 x 5" greased loaf pans. Bake at 350°F for about an hour or until a toothpick inserted in center comes out clean. Cool 10 minutes in pan on a wire rack. Remove from pan and cool bread on rack about an hour before slicing to serve. Makes 2 loaves.

UNBELIEVABLE!

BUTTERSCOTCH BISCUITS, LIKE HUDSON'S

I used to stand in line for hours, waiting for these at the Detroit Hudson's Pantry Counter. Can you imagine how many people were disappointed when the store closed in 1982? Now, the only time you can probably enjoy the sweet rolls is with my kissing-cousin version...

2 cups biscuit mix
½ cup dry milk powder
¼ cup each: sugar and butter or margarine, melted
1 egg
½ cup cold water
1 teaspoon vanilla
2 ½ cups additional biscuit mix

With electric mixer on low speed, beat first 4 ingredients until crumbly. Combine next 3 ingredients – also, until crumbly – and beat into other crumbly mixture. Set timer to beat for 5 more minutes. Beat in 1 cup of remaining biscuit mix, and work in last of it by hand until smooth enough to knead in the bowl with lightly floured hands (about 5 minutes) until smooth and elastic in texture.

1 tablespoon cinnamon
½ cup packed brown sugar
2 tablespoons melted butter
1 tablespoon water
½ cup chopped nuts

Pat out dough on ungreased, waxed paper to a 9 x 15" rectangle of even thickness. Dust with the cinnamon. Spread the brown sugar evenly over that. Drizzle the melted butter over the sugar and then the water over that. Sprinkle on nuts and roll-up like a jellyroll, length-wise. Seal seam by pinching it. Let it "proof" for about 10 minutes (in sunlight helps.)

12 teaspoons each: butter and cold water
12 tablespoons packed brown sugar
1 prepared recipe of my Vanilla Glaze (see Index)

Meanwhile, divide remaining butter, brown sugar and water equally between 12 Pam-sprayed muffin wells. Cut the rolled-up dough into 12 equal-size slices. Place slices cut-side-down in the muffin wells. Bake 30 minutes at 350°F. Remove at once, to a buttered plate, using the tip of a sharp knife. Scrape out excess sugar from the wells and add to each roll, drizzling with glaze at once. Cool 10 minutes before serving. They freeze well up to 3 months.

3-INGREDIENT APPLE BREAD

Beat together an 18-ounce package Pillsbury Plus Applesauce Spice Cake mix, a 21-ounce can apple pie filling and 3 eggs, using an electric mixer on medium speed for about 3 minutes. Divide batter, equally, between 2 greased and floured 8 ½-inch Pyrex bread loaf dishes. Bake at 350°F for 45 to 50 minutes or until a toothpick inserted through the centers comes out clean. While these are still warm out of the oven, drizzle them in my Vanilla Glaze (see Index). They freeze well for 3 months.

OLD-FASHIONED BATTER BREAD – *Like Sanders once made*

In the old days, you could buy a loaf of the best, and most delicately textured, coffeecake-type bread at Fred Sanders' bakery in the Detroit area. But, as all the food industry changes or tries to improve upon their selections, this bread is no longer available. With some diligent sleuthing and testing of various combinations, I finally developed what I suspect is as close to the original as one can get!

2 cups all-purpose flour
1 cup granulated sugar
4 teaspoons baking powder
1 teaspoon salt
1 cup buttermilk
1/3 cup corn oil
½ teaspoon vanilla
2 eggs

Preheat oven to 350°F and grease and flour a 9 x 5" bread loaf pan. In an accommodating bowl, combine the ingredients just as I have listed them and beat with an electric mixer on medium high speed for about 4 minutes. Pour batter into prepared pan and bake for about 50 minutes or until a toothpick inserted in the center comes out clean. The bread will develop a deep crack down the middle of the top as it bakes and even though it appears to be browning well, be sure it is thoroughly baked inside or it will fall! Ker-plop! So, the best test to see if it is done is to insert a long paper-covered, wire twist tie or thin wooden skewer through the center. Be certain it touches the bottom of the pan when you insert it. If it comes out clean of any wet batter, it is done! Remove from oven and it once remove the loaf from the pan. Let it cool completely on a wire rack before slicing it to serve.

COFFEECAKE BATTER BREAD

Another version of this batter bread (above) is to turn it into a coffeecake or streusel bread by preparing the batter, just as directed above, and pouring it into the pan. Set that aside while you combine in a small bowl: 2 tablespoons sugar, 1 teaspoon cinnamon and 1 teaspoon butter or margarine. Mix together until crumbly and sprinkle over the top of the prepared batter, swirling it into the batter a bit with the tip of a table knife. Bake as directed above (350°F for about 50 minutes or until it tests done.) It's also good with 1 cup finely-chopped pecans added to the batter-top before baking.

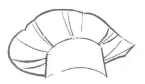

BLUEBERRY MUFFINS, PDQ

2 eggs
2 cups firmly-packed vanilla ice cream, melted into a mushy cream
2 cups self-rising flour
1-pound can blueberries, drained and rinsed

Beat the eggs, then, beat in the mushy ice cream. Put self-rising flour in an accommodating mixing bowl, creating a well in which to add the creamy egg mixture. Mix only until flour particles are completely moistened. Do not over-beat. Batter may be a bit lumpy, but that's okay. Dredge the blueberries lightly in flour, shaking off as much excess as you can by putting them in a strainer and tossing carefully. Stir the coated berries gently into the muffin batter. Fill paper-lined muffin tins 2/3 full and bake at 400°F for 10 to 12 minutes or until golden brown and they test done. Makes 1 dozen.

HUNGARIAN-JACK-STYLE BONGO BISCUITS

This is a quick, muffin-like biscuit that never fails! They should be served warm but can be prepared ahead of time, refrigerated in plastic food bags and then warmed in the microwave just before serving, if used within a week. They can be frozen up to 6 months.

2 cups self-rising flour
2 tablespoons sugar
1 cup milk
¼ cup mayonnaise

Mix the flour and sugar together thoroughly in a medium mixing bowl. Stir the milk and mayonnaise together well and pour over dry mixture. Do not over beat, as with a muffin batter, but do stir well to moisten every single dry particle. Spoon batter into greased or paper-lined muffin tins, filling them half full. Bake at 350°F for about 30 minutes or until golden brown. Makes 1 dozen.

BLUEBERRIES may be added to the batter (above) - drain a 1 pound can of blueberries of all juice and then toss them lightly in flour (so they won't sink to the bottom of the biscuit while baking.) Fold the floured berries gently into the batter in a clockwise motion using a rubber scraper, rather then stir them in, which often breaks the flour away from the berries, streaking the batter in an unattractive wash. With the addition of the blueberries you should yield about 14 to 16 biscuits.

RAISED BISCUITS

1 package dry yeast
½ cup warm water
1 teaspoon sugar
4 ½ cups flour
1 cup water
1 tablespoon sugar
2 tablespoons salt
1 cup butter, melted and cooled
1 egg yolk, beaten with 1 tablespoon water

Dissolve yeast in warm water. Stir in sugar and set aside for 5 minutes or until bubbly. Meanwhile, beat 2 cups of the flour with the water, sugar, salt and ½ cup of the butter. Set the other ½ cup of melted butter aside until later. Beat yeast mixture into flour mixture, working in as much of the rest of the flour, as is necessary to make the dough smooth and elastic in texture and kneading it about 5 minutes with floured hands. Roll out on a lightly floured surface to about ½-inch thick. Cut with a 2-inch floured biscuit cutter. Brush half of the biscuits with the remaining ½ cup melted butter. Place the other half of the biscuits on top of these and brush them with one egg yolk, that has been beaten with 1 tablespoon water. Let rise 1 hour or until doubled in size. Bake at 425°F for 10 to 12 minutes or until golden brown. Makes 3 dozen biscuits.

BEER BREAD

2 cups self-rising flour
3 tablespoons sugar
1 egg, beaten
12-ounce can Busch Light beer

Mix the flour and sugar together with a fork and set aside. Beat the egg and beer together in an accommodating cup. Make a well in the center of the flour mixture and add the liquid. Mix it only until all dry particles have been moistened, like a muffin batter should be mixed. Do not over-beat! Pour into a greased and floured 9-inch loaf pan. Bake at 350°F for about 30 to 35 minutes or until you can insert a thin wooden skewer through the center to the bottom of the pan and remove it without any traces of wet batter. Cool in pan 15 minutes. Wipe top of loaf with melted butter and dust lightly with sugar. Slice when cooled. If the bread appears to fall or sink while cooling, it means you didn't bake it long enough. If it's heavy and moist, it means you over-beat it. If it turns out dry and crumbly, it means you didn't beat it enough - so don't be fooled into thinking that just because the recipe has only 4 ingredients that you can slap it together and have it turn out beautifully. Combine ingredients with care.

SHARE-A-LEASE DANISH COFFEECAKE

2 packages dry yeast
½ cup warm water
1 teaspoon sugar
1 cup warm milk
½ cup butter or margarine (butter preferred)
2/3 cup sugar
4 ½ to 5 cups flour
1 tablespoon vanilla
½ teaspoon salt
2 eggs

Soften yeast in warm water, stirring in the teaspoon of sugar. Let it stand for about 5 minutes or until it begins to triple in bulk. Put the warm milk, butter and remaining sugar in a medium-size mixing bowl. Beat in 2 cups of the flour to a smooth batter. Add vanilla, salt and eggs. Beat 2 minutes with electric mixer on medium speed. Remove beaters. Work-in remaining flour until you have a smooth dough that can be kneaded on a floured surface until elastic in texture. Place dough in a greased bowl that will permit it to triple in size without climbing out of the bowl. Cover and let dough rise in warm place about 1 hour. Punch it down. Let it rise once more. Shape into rolls of desired size as noted below or bake as bread for those directions. Let rise per that recipe and bake - rolls at 350°F for 30 minutes; bread, in a 9-inch prepared loaf pan, at 350°F for 45 to 50 minutes. Makes 14 3-inch rolls or 2 loaves.

CINNAMON ROLLS

After the Danish-dough has risen twice, pat it out on a floured surface to about 8 x 12". Spread 4 tablespoons soft margarine on surface of dough. Dust lightly in a mixture of ½ cup packed brown sugar, 1 teaspoon cinnamon and ½ cup chopped pecans or raisins. Beginning with the wide side, roll up jelly-roll-style. Keep roll seam-side down. Cut into 12 slices, 1-inch thick, placing cut-side down in greased 9 x 12 x 2" baking pan. Let rise until doubled in size. Bake at 350°F for 30 minutes or until golden brown. As soon as they're out of the oven, drizzle with Thin Vanilla Glaze (see below.)

THIN VANILLA GLAZE

Into a blender, put 3 tablespoons milk, 2 tablespoons margarine, 1 teaspoon vanilla, a dash salt and 2 cups powdered sugar. Blend on high-speed until smooth. Drizzle over hot cinnamon rolls.

DANISH BREAD

Just as you would prepare the cinnamon rolls (above), pat out the dough, spreading it with the margarine, sugar, cinnamon and nuts or raisins. Roll up jelly-roll-style. Divide the roll in half. Place each half in buttered 9-inch bread pans. Let rise until doubled in size. Bake at 350°F for about 45 to 50 minutes or until golden brown and crust makes a hollow sound when tapped with a finger. As soon as it's out of the oven, drizzle it with the Thin Vanilla Glaze (above.) Makes 2 loaves.

CHEESE BREAD

There was something special about lunch at the Eastland Hudson's Basement Store lunch counter, when you were shopping there. They turned it into a locker room; and gone were those special sandwiches on that very special cheese bread they baked in their own kitchens!

1 cup warm water
1 package dry yeast
½ teaspoon sugar
3 ½ to 4 cups flour
1 ½ cups shredded cheddar cheese
3 eggs
2 teaspoons unsalted butter
2 tablespoons milk

Place water, yeast and sugar in a small bowl. Stir once or twice; let stand 5 or 6 minutes until bubbly. Combine 3 ½ cups flour, cheese and 2 of the eggs in a bowl. Add yeast mixture and stir with a spoon until all the liquid has been absorbed. Gather dough into a ball. On floured surface, knead for about 10 minutes, dipping your hands into the remaining flour, if necessary, to keep dough soft and elastic, but no longer sticky. With 1 teaspoon of the butter, grease a bowl 3 times the size of the ball of dough. Let the dough rise until doubled in bulk (for about 90 minutes.) Punch down and let it rise again. Punch down, again, and shape into a 9-inch loaf pan, which has been greased with the last teaspoon of butter. Brush the top of loaf with remaining egg, beaten with the 2 tablespoons of milk. Bake at 375°F for about 45 to 50 minutes or until golden. If you double the recipe, please add another extra package of yeast, giving you a total of 3 packages in a doubled recipe.

CHEESE CRACKER ROUNDS

1-pound Cracker Barrel sharp cheddar cheese, grated well
½ pound (2 sticks) butter, not margarine
3 cups flour
1 teaspoon each: paprika and Accent
½ teaspoon salt
1/16 teaspoon cayenne pepper

Cream grated cheddar with the butter until light and fluffy, using an electric mixer about 15 minutes. It should be so light, it looks as if it will just float out of the mixing bowl. If you begrudge the creaming time even 1 minute, you'll have a disappointment! Work in remaining ingredients one at a time, beating well after each addition. Using a Spritz Cookie Press and the "star" insert for the applicator, force the dough through the press forming donut shapes with it, rather than "drops." Keep circles about 2 inches apart on ungreased cookie sheets. Bake at 400°F for 9 to 10 minutes. Remove at once from cookie sheets. Cool on paper towels. Makes about 7 dozen. They freeze well up to 6 months.

DANISH PASTRY DOUGH

This is the basic recipe for dough that can become coffeecake, Hawaiian bread, sweet rolls and other good things with just a twist of the wrist, some peace and quiet in the kitchen and a little know-how!

2 envelopes dry yeast
½ cup lukewarm water
1 teaspoon sugar
1 cup warm milk
½ cup butter (1/4 pound or one stick)
2/3 cup sugar
5 cups flour
1 tablespoon vanilla or almond extract
½ teaspoon salt
2 eggs

Soften yeast in the half cup warm water. Stir in the 1 teaspoon sugar and let it stand for 5 or 6 minutes until quite bubbly. Place the warm milk and remaining sugar with only 2 cups of the flour in a bowl, beating to a smooth batter. Beat in the vanilla, salt and eggs; and, then, the yeast mixture. Gradually, work in remaining flour until you have a soft dough. Knead it in the bowl with lightly floured hands until dough is no longer sticky, adding only that much flour as is necessary to make the dough nice and smooth and elastic in texture. Transfer dough to a greased bowl, turning the dough once to grease what is the top of it. Cover it loosely in a sheet of plastic kitchen rap with one side sprayed in Pam and placed that-side-down over the dough, letting it rise for 90 minutes or until doubled in bulk. Punch it down and let it rise again. Then you are free to shape it and bake it accordingly.

You can bake it up as 2 loaves of bread by splitting it in half and shaping the halves to fit neatly into 2 greased 9-inch bread loaf pans. Let them rise until doubled in size and bake, putting them into a COLD oven and setting the temperature at 450°F for 8 minutes. At once, turn temperature down to 350°F and allow it to bake for 40 minutes or until golden brown and crust makes a hollow sound when you tap it with your finger. Remove from pans at once and let bread cool on their sides. This bread slices best the 2nd day - or, at least, after several hours of cooling! Makes 2 small loaves. You can use disposable foil bread pans for baking, placing these on a cookie sheet. Wrap and freeze, to be used within 3 months.

HAWAIIAN BREAD

After the second rising (in the above recipe), shape the dough into a large round ball. Place it in a greased 10-inch Pyrex pie plate or a metal pie tin larger than the standard 8- or 9-inch size – or use a 10-inch greased, oven-proof skillet. Let bread rise until doubled in bulk and place in a cold oven, setting the temperature at 450°F for 8 minutes and reducing it at once to 350°F. Allow bread to bake for about 15 minutes more or until crust is firm, golden brown and makes a hollow sound when you cap it with your finger. Brush hot bread with a little honey. Let it cool in the pan and slice it when completely cold. Serve it from the pan, cutting in pie-shaped wedges! Makes 1 large round loaf.

PORTUGUESE SWEET BREAD

A kissing cousin of Hawaiian Bread, and just as light and rich - this round loaf bread, baked in a greased, 10-inch pie/cake pan or spring-form pan. If you want to use an 8-inch pie/cake pan, better divide the dough between 2 of these for smaller loaves, or the dough baked as one loaf might just climb right out of the smaller pan and make a mess in the oven!

½ cup warm water
2 packages dry yeast
1 tablespoon sugar
¼ pound butter (one stick)
2/3 cup warm milk
2/3 cup sugar
3 eggs, beaten well with a fork
5 cups flour
1 teaspoon salt
1 teaspoon vanilla

Dissolve water, yeast in the 1 tablespoon sugar in a small bowl. Stir it once or twice and let it stand 5 or 6 minutes. Meanwhile, melt the butter just enough that it does NOT change color or foam while melting. Combine the melted butter, warm milk, sugar, eggs, 2 cups of the flour, salt and vanilla; beating it to a smooth batter. Beat in the yeast mixture and then work in remaining flour to a smooth and soft, but not sticky, dough. Knead it in the bowl with lightly floured hands, until dough feels elastic in texture (about 10 minutes.) Transfer to a greased bowl. Turn dough once so top becomes greased. Spray one side of a sheet of plastic wrap in Pam and place it Pam-side-down over dough. Let it rise about 90 minutes or until it's doubled in bulk. Punch it down and let it rise again. Shape dough to fit a greased 10-inch pie/cake pan or spring-form pan. Let bread rise once more until doubled in size. Place in COLD oven, setting temperature to 450°F for 8 minutes, then reducing it at once to 350°F and continue baking about 35 to 40 minutes or until crust is golden brown and makes a hollow sound when you tap it with your fingers. Drizzle the bread, while still warm in the pan, with one recipe of my Karo Icing (below.) Cut bread into pie shaped wedges when completely cooled. Makes 1 large round loaf.

KARO ICING

4 tablespoons each: butter (or margarine) and Karo light corn syrup
dash of salt
1 teaspoon almond or vanilla extract
1 cup on sifted powdered sugar

Bring butter and corn syrup to a gentle boil in a small sauce pan. Stir constantly and let it simmer for 5 minutes. Keep heat low, but so that mixture continues to boil very gently. Remove from heat and beat in salt and extract. Beat in the cup of powdered sugar. Drizzle over warm baked coffee cake or rolls. Makes 1 ½ cups icing.

IMITATION BUTTER VERSUS REAL MARGARINE

Man-made food has always been the subject of much controversy, but more knowledgeable food technicians realize that it is the best answer to solving world hunger problems. Contrary to popular belief, margarine is not a substitute for butter. It's an alternative; and, for many years, since its discovery as a man-made food, has been an economical alternative. Today the blessings of the spread are many. For people who must watch their cholesterol intake and those who simply watch their food budgets, margarine has been a great replacement for the more expensive spread. However, with food prices rising all the time, even margarine is becoming as much a luxury item as butter.

During World War II, when butter was rationed, my mother used a recipe that was popular across the country, or whipping canned milk with butter and increasing its volume. It led me to consider the possibility of developing margarine into a more economical spread which I call "Park Cake Whipped Margarine," to avoid infringing on a popular trademark name. You can watch this margarine "grow," right in the mixing bowl.

I don't recommend it for frying or baking ingredients, but as a plain spread for the dinner table, breakfast toast, sandwiches, potatoes, vegetables, it does save a good deal of money. It freezes indefinitely and gives you about 30% more per pound for the price.

PARK CAKE WHIPPED MARGARINE

8-ounce tub soft Parkay Margarine
1 pound or 4 sticks solid inexpensive margarine
2 cups Crisco
2 cups Creamora Non-dairy Creamer (powder)
    (or use an inexpensive brand)
1 cup corn or vegetable oil, not peanut oil
2 teaspoon salt (optional)
Few drops yellow food coloring (optional)

Using a large mixing bowl, beat first 2 ingredients together until light and fluffy. Add Crisco and creamer powder, continuing to beat on high-speed and rotating the bowl in the direction opposite of what the beaters are turning. Beat about 2 minutes. Then add remaining ingredients, one at a time. It's best to use the manual type countertop mixer for this job, as the secret is in beating the mixture exactly 30 minutes after last ingredient has been added. Pack into four 1-pound tubs. Freeze up to a year or more. Refrigerated, keeps well for 2 or 3 months.

The addition of the yellow food coloring is only to make it look like the store-bought products, but is purely up to you. A pinch of powdered turmeric may also be added to give it a deep yellow color, but the flavor will be altered a bit with this addition. Altered, but interesting! Makes 4 pounds.

PUMPKIN BREAD

I started to test several recipes for what truly talented cooks insisted was THE perfect pumpkin bread. Test after test, the loaves went out to the birdfeeder – as they were either too heavy, too spicy, too dry, didn't raise enough or had so many ingredients in the recipe I had to "let out" the kitchen just to make room for the groceries. I wanted the bread to be as light as cake, with a minimum of ingredients and delicately spiced so even an ulcer-sufferer could enjoy it. I started with a spice cake and computed the amount of liquid necessary to give it a bread-like texture. I bought several loaves of pumpkin bread from various bakeries, none of which would give me their secrets, of course, and discovered this beautifully light, delicately spiced, wonderful bread!

1 pound can pumpkin
3 large eggs
½ cup vanilla ice cream – firmly pressed into a measuring cup and softened to a mushy cream
1 envelope Dream Whip powder
18-ounce package Pillsbury Plus Applesauce Spice Cake mix – or any good, moist, spice cake mix

Use a large mixing bowl and electric mixer to combine the pumpkin and eggs until smooth. Beat in ice cream and Dream Whip powder and then dump the cake mix into it. Beat for 6 minutes on medium-high speed, dividing batter equally between 2 greased and floured 8 ½-inch Pyrex loaf dishes or 9-inch metal bread pans. Bake the glass dishes at 350° for 40 to 45 minutes or until bread appears to be cracked on top and beginning to brown nicely around the edges. The metal pans should be baked 5 minutes longer or until a toothpick inserted in the center comes out clean. As soon as the loaves are out of the oven drizzle with my Vanilla Glaze (below.)

VANILLA GLAZE – *for bread*

2 tablespoons milk
1 teaspoon vanilla
10 tablespoons firmly packed powdered sugar

Whip ingredients together, with a fork, until smooth. Makes about ½ cup of glaze, which will harden nicely if applied while the loaves are still hot from the oven. Bread will freeze well up to 3 months.

PITA BREAD

Prepare my Thunder Bread (see Index) and divide the dough after the last rising into 14 equal portions, shaping into balls. Roll each ball out to a 7- or 8-inch circle, about 1/8 inch thick. Arrange them about 3 or 4 inches apart on a greased and cornmeal-dusted cookie sheet. Let them raise for 30 minutes and bake at 475°F for 5 minutes (set timer), reducing heat to 450°F and allowing them to bake another 5 minutes or until golden brown and puffy. Let cool on wire racks and then cut in half from top to bottom, like you would a hamburger bun. You'll note a little pocket in the middle. You can fill this with any desired sandwich filling or salad. The pitas will freeze nicely up to 6 months.

SCONES

Restaurant bread baskets are becoming more and more interesting. At the Chicago Airport Hotel, I had a sampling of these at dinner; and the next morning they were served warm in the breakfast bread basket. The waitress, at my request for information on these, returned from the kitchen to explain that they prepared these in their kitchen and, basically, used a biscuit mix. This is my version.

3 cups biscuit mix
2 tablespoons sugar
¼ cup each: melted margarine and milk
1 tablespoon lemon juice
1/3 cup Club Soda
¼ teaspoon vanilla

Stir the biscuit mix and sugar together with a fork. Stir in the melted margarine, also, with a fork until mixture is crumbly. Put the milk and lemon juice into a small cup and let it stand a minute or so to thicken. Combine it with the Club Soda and vanilla. Make a well in the center of the biscuit mix and poor in the liquid mixture. Stir until a smooth dough forms. Dip your hands into a little biscuit mix from the box and knead the dough in the bowl about a dozen times, or until smooth and elastic. Don't skimp on the kneading! Grease a 10-inch, oven-proof skillet and pat the dough out to cover the bottom of it evenly. With the straight edge of a pancake turner, score it into 8 pie-shaped wedges. Wipe the tops with a just little bit of soft margarine. Then, very lightly, dust the tops with, at most, ½ teaspoon sugar. Bake at 450°F for about 18 to 20 minutes or until golden brown. Don't under bake it, or it will be brown on the outside and doughy near the bottom. Cut through the scored lines with a knife to separate the pieces. Split them carefully, horizontally, and spread with softened butter and jam. Makes 8 scones. (Rewarm them in the microwave the next day, by wrapping each piece individually in a plastic food bag and setting temp at high for 30 seconds or less.)

FRENCH TOAST BREAD

Prepare my Danish Pastry Dough recipe (see Index), but cut the sugar in half. Shape the Danish dough to fit a greased 9-inch bread loaf pan and bake per that recipe, cooling bread completely before slicing it at least 1 ½ inch thick. Let bread slices air dry about an hour on each side. Then use in the French toast batter as follows:

For each slice of air-dried bread, combine in a shallow bowl: 1 egg, 1/8 cup milk, ¼ teaspoon vanilla, dash of salt and ½ teaspoon sugar. Soak bread on both sides until almost all the mixture has been absorbed into the bread. In a Teflon-lined skillet, melt 2 tablespoons Crisco and 1 tablespoon margarine on medium-high heat, and get it HOT! Slide the bread into the hot shortening and while it browns on the 1st side, spoon the remaining egg mixture into center of the top of the bread so bread can absorb it while the underside is browning. Brown the other side. It'll puff up beautifully. Place on a serving plate with a pat of butter and a lavish sprinkling of powdered sugar, sufficient to create its own glaze.

Scrumptious!

ALL BUTTER COFFEECAKE – *Almond-Flavored*

Here is where shrewd advertising puts a phrase before the public and we automatically think one thing while the reality is another. The "all butter" claim to fame, means that it contains all butter in the shortening department – that you do not use half butter and half margarine or Crisco or some other form of shortening – and, by the way, to clear up any misunderstanding about what shortening really is, remember it is another word for "fats or oils." Some people think of only Crisco as a "shortening" while it can also mean "butter" or "oil"! It is a fat – so, Crisco is just fat in a can!

¼ cup warm water
1 envelope dry yeast
1½ teaspoon sugar

¼ pound butter, melted and very cool
1/3 cup granulated sugar
2 eggs
2 teaspoons almond extract
½ teaspoon salt
1 ½ teaspoon cornstarch
"The Yeast Mixture" (see above)
¼ cup thick buttermilk or sour cream
¼ teaspoon baking soda
2 cups all-purpose flour

Combine the first 3 ingredients and set aside for 5 minutes or until bubbly. For the batter, work in these ingredients exactly as listed, using a roomy bowl and an electric mixer on medium speed. Beat well, allowing about 1 minute with EACH addition. Beat 3 minutes after the addition of the last ingredient, adding that flour a little at a time. Spread dough into greased and floured 9-inch round cake pan. Streak it with one recipe of my "Streusel Mixture" (to follow). Use a rubber scraper to incorporate mixture into dough. Cover and let rise 1 hour, using Pam sprayed sheet of plastic kitchen wrap, Pam-side-down over rising dough. Place in preheated 400°F oven to bake for 25 to 30 minutes. Drizzle with one recipe of my Karo Icing (see Index) as soon as you remove it from the oven. Then, quickly, before icing has a chance to "set", sprinkle top with about ½ cup thinly sliced almonds. Let coffeecake cool several hours before cutting into pie-shaped wedges. Serves 6 sweetly.

STREUSEL MIXTURE – *for Coffeecake*

Mix thoroughly with a fork to a crumbly consistency: 1/3 cup flour, 1/3 cup packed brown sugar, 4 tablespoons butter (melted) and 1 teaspoon almond or vanilla extract. Makes ¾ cup.

WHOLE WHEAT LOAF – *There's a bakery and café called "The Windows" in Victoria, Texas that has a very good loaf – moist and light in texture. I do this for 1 loaf:*

1 ¼ cups warm water
2 teaspoon sugar
1 envelope plus 1 teaspoon dry yeast
2 tablespoons butter or margarine
1 tablespoon honey
1 teaspoon salt
1 cup all-purpose flour
3 cups whole wheat or Graham flour
¼ cup butter or margarine, melted and cooled (optional, for soft-crust loaf)

In a small bowl, stir once or twice ½ cup of the warm water with the sugar and yeast. Let it stand 5 minutes or until bubbly. Put remaining water in large mixing bowl with the butter, honey, salt and all-purpose flour. Beat with electric mixer on medium speed until smooth. Add the yeast mixture. Beat 2 minutes. Add the whole-wheat flour a little at a time, working it in with a sturdy mixing spoon and then your hands, until dough is no longer sticky. Add only enough more whole wheat flour to the dough that it becomes smooth and elastic as you knead it, per the same directions as in my "Thunder Bread" recipe (see Index.) Let it rise in a warm place until doubled in size. Punch it down and let it rise again. Now shape it to fit a greased 9 x 5 x 3" loaf pan. Let it rise until doubled (about 90 minutes.) Place in a COLD oven and set temperature at 450°F for 5 minutes, at once turn oven heat down to 375°F and bake about 30 minutes or until you can tap the crust with your finger and it makes a "hollow" sound. Remove the bread pan to cool on its side on a wire rack. For a soft crust, brush loaf-top, immediately, with the melted butter or margarine. If you want a crisp crust, omit this. Turn the bread out of the pan after 10 minutes, letting it cool on its side. Don't attempt to slice the bread for at least 4 hours.

BIG PLOY'S GARLIC BREAD

When you eat at Big Boy restaurants, at least those in Michigan (operated by Elias Brothers), you can enjoy their special garlic bread with most of the dinner selections. At home, it is a trick to imitate; but, in the sincerest form of flattery, I try to this way…

In a small skillet melt ¼ pound butter or margarine, but do not let it turn brown nor change color. Keep the heat properly adjusted at medium to control the melting. Stir in ½ cup oil and a tablespoon each of Worcestershire, Soy sauce and A-1 steak sauce. Add 1 teaspoon of garlic salt. Stir it well and, at once, remove from heat before garlic has a chance to overwhelm you - and it will - even in salt-form, when too much heat is applied too quickly. Dip, quickly, just to coat the cut surfaces of 6 hard rolls (or hot dog buns) and transfer to a lightly greased skillet to brown on the coated sides slowly, until crispy. Sufficient to coat 6 cut rolls or buns.

QUICK, SUNDAY BRUNCH CAKE

This is the kind of cake you can whip up in a hurry, whether it's Sunday or not and whether it's for brunch or not. It's ready to serve in 30 minutes, including mixing time… Unless, that is, you have unforeseen interruptions or you are very, very slow.

¼ cup corn oil
1 tablespoon margarine
1 egg
½ cup milk
1 teaspoon vanilla or other flavoring

2 teaspoons baking powder
½ teaspoon salt
dash of nutmeg
1 cup granulated sugar
1 ½ cups all-purpose flour

1 prepared recipe each: "Streusel Crumb Mix" and "Vanilla Glaze for Breakfast Pie" (see Index for each of these)

Into a 1 ½ quart mixing bowl, combine first 5 ingredients with electric mixer on medium speed. Beat until smooth and then beat in the next 5 ingredients, one at a time. Beat for 5 more minutes on low to medium speed with the last addition. Pour into greased and floured 9-inch round or square baking pan or Pyrex baking dish and sprinkle top of batter with the prepared "Streusel Crumb Mix", cutting it into the batter with a table knife to slightly marble it. Bake in a 375°F, preheated oven for 25 minutes or until toothpick inserted in center comes out clean. At once, out of the oven, drizzle top of cake with the Vanilla Glaze. Let cake cool 5 minutes after glazing, then cut into 4 to 6 serving pieces.

TONIC BREAD

Mix together 2 cups biscuit mix and ¾ cup bottled "Tonic Water" to a rather thick, but smooth, paste. Add enough more biscuit mix just so it's not pouring consistency; but thick, like a biscuit dough. Spread it evenly over the bottom of a greased, round, 9-inch layer-cake dish – Pyrex preferred to metal pans, because you can see when the bottom and sides of the bread begin to bake properly to a golden brown. Sprinkle the top of the batter with 1 ½ teaspoon sugar and bake in a preheated, 450°F oven for 12 to 14 minutes or until nicely golden. Cut into pie shaped wedges and serve it right away, while it's still warm, with plenty of butter and warmed honey or thick preserves.

I've tried other liquids in this recipe, but it was never as light or flavorful as with Tonic Water. You can also add ½ teaspoon cinnamon to the batter, if you wish – or, for an Italian dinner, add a little onion powder. It's wonderful!

ICE CREAM BREAD

If you like Pepperidge Farm products and their pound cake and coffeecake textures, you may enjoy trying this recipe – which, seemed to me, would make a grand combination and possibly a good, slightly sweet, coffeecake loaf. The recipe may look simple, but it took several tests and many discouraging failures before the proportions were just right and the baking-time accurately set. I found that you cannot use a metal loaf pan – for each time I did, the loaf fell or baked too quickly on top and not enough in the center. You must combine the ingredients in order, exactly as listed, instead of dumping it all in a bowl. It should come out perfectly, if you follow the recipe!

1 egg
½ teaspoon vanilla
2 ¼ cups mushy vanilla ice cream
2 cups self-rising flour

Beat the egg and vanilla with an electric mixer on medium speed, adding the ice cream and continuing to beat until very thoroughly for 4 minutes. Work-in the flour, in 4 equal portions, using medium speed – just enough to moisten all the dry particles, much like a muffin batter. Do not over-beat this or the bread will be heavy and coarse. When well moistened, spread the batter into a Pam-sprayed or well-greased, 8 ½-inch, Pyrex loaf-baking dish. Let it "proof" for 5 minutes. Bake on center rack in a preheated, 325°F oven for exactly one hour. Remove and let it cool in the dish about 15 minutes; then, remove it to cool on a rack for 2 or 3 more hours, before slicing it. Makes 1 loaf.

ICE CREAM MUFFINS

You can drop the prepared bread batter (above) into greased muffin tin wells, filling them about two-thirds full and baking them at 325°F for about 30 minutes or until golden brown.

TO ADD BLUEBERRIES: pour a 1-pound can blueberries into a strainer and rinse in cold water. Drain well and toss lightly in a little flour. After completing the beating process, fold the flour-dusted blueberries, very gently, into the prepared batter. Spoon the batter into greased, muffin tin wells, filling each two-thirds full. Bake at 325°F for about 30 minutes. Makes about 1 dozen muffins.

SOUR CREAM INTO SWEET CREAM

My old-fashioned "in-a-pinch" method for turning sour cream into sweet cream, if needed for hot bread toppings or desserts, is to put 1-pound sour cream (about 2 cups) into a small mixing bowl and thoroughly beat in 1/8 teaspoon baking soda for about 5 minutes on medium speed. A pinch more may be necessary as you beat it and taste for decreased sourness. The topping has a very pleasant flavor, which you can sweeten with a bit of sugar and a dash of nutmeg, if you wish.

ROLLING-PIN BREAD

Using very fresh, sliced, white bread, flatten the slices with a rolling pin until paper thin. Brush each, on one side, with a little melted butter or margarine. Cut into finger-shapes and toast on a cookie sheet, buttered side up, about 6 inches from broiler heat until golden brown. Cool completely before adding to your dinner bread basket assortment.

BUTTERMILK DONUTS

When you stop at the donut shop that offers you 638 varieties, be sure to look for the Buttermilk Fry Cakes – made with applesauce, which keeps them light and moist!

4 ½ cups flour
1 cup sugar
1 tablespoon baking powder
1 teaspoon each: soda and salt
½ teaspoon nutmeg
pinch of cinnamon
2/3 cup buttermilk
½ cup applesauce
¼ cup corn oil
1 teaspoon vanilla
2 eggs

In a large mixing bowl, mix together well, the first 7, dry ingredients. Put everything else in your blender on high-speed for 30 seconds or until well-combined. Make a well in the center of the dry stuff and pour in the liquid stuff. Stir as you would a muffin batter, just until all dry particles are thoroughly moistened. Don't over-beat. Chill dough 2 hours to make it easier to work with. Then, toss the dough on a lightly floured surface. The secret of keeping donuts light is when you toss it on the lightly floured surface and work with that so that is no longer sticky. Don't get carried away with the flouring of the dough. Add only smidgens of flour at a time until dough no longer sticks to your hands. Then roll it out, a small portion at a time, to about 1-inch thick – VERY lightly, please. Cut with a floured donut-cutter. Fry a few at a time in about 3 inches of 400°F oil. When donuts are lightly browned on both sides, remove and dust in powdered or granulated sugar. Makes about 2 dozen.

QUICK, BISCUIT MIX DONUTS – *Another way to make donuts, using boxed biscuit mix!*

Preheat enough oil, in a 2 ½-quart heavy saucepan, so that it's at least 3 inches deep and 400°F. Combine 2 cups Bisquick-brand biscuit mix, ¼ cup sugar, 1/3 cup milk, 1 teaspoon vanilla and 1 egg – adding a pinch of nutmeg, if you like. Turn dough onto floured surface and knead lightly about 12 times with floured fingers. Roll dough out about ½ inch thick. Cut with floured donut-cutter. Fry a few at a time in the hot oil until golden brown on both sides – about 1 minute per side. Remove from oil and drain on paper towels. Dust in powdered or granulated sugar. Makes about 1 dozen.

STRAWBERRY NUT BREAD

The Wine Country Inn located in St. Helena, California, has been a Napa Valley landmark for years. It was originally designed to look like a well-aged vintage tavern with modern lines. One nice thing, that I personally liked about the Inn while I was in California, was a long table of displayed menus from restaurants that the Smiths, who operate the Wine Country Inn, would recommend. On the same table was a serving of juice and fruits in homemade breads like this particularly different quick bread.

2 packages (10 ounces each) frozen, sliced strawberries
4 eggs
1 cup corn oil
2 cups granulated sugar
3 cups flour
1 tablespoon cinnamon
1 teaspoon baking soda
1 teaspoon salt
1 ½ cups chopped pecans or walnuts

Thaw strawberries and set aside. Beat eggs until light and fluffy, adding oil and sugar a little at a time. Beat in the thawed strawberries and any liquid with these. Set aside as soon as it is thoroughly blended. In a medium-sized bowl combine the remaining ingredients, except for the nuts. Make a well in the center of the flour mixture and pour in the strawberry mixture. Combine only until all dry particles are thoroughly moistened. Do not over beat. This should be treated as you would a muffin batter. Stir in the nuts. Pour into 2 greased and floured 9 x 5 x 3" bread loaf pans. (I sprayed my pans with Baker's Joy.) Bake loaves, spaced 2 inches apart on center rack, centering the 2 pans as best you can for an even rotation of the heat during baking, and bake at 350°F for almost an hour or until a toothpick inserted into the center of each loaf comes out clean. Cool in pans about 15 minutes, placing pans on wire racks for this time. Then turn out of pans to allow loaves to completely cool. Bread should be chilled before slicing to serve. May be rewarmed in microwave oven on defrost a few minutes or wrapped in foil in a 350°F oven for about 8 to 10 minutes. Then slice and serve with cream cheese.

STREUSEL CRUMB MIX

This is a good mix to use with, both, coffeecakes AND quick breads, or even cupcakes…

1 cup each: biscuit mix and packed brown sugar
2 tablespoons of my Cinnamon and Sugar Mix (see Index)
6 tablespoons butter or margarine, in bits

Combine everything with a fork, stirring it to the consistency of gravel. Store in a covered container and keep refrigerated until time to use in recipes calling for the streusel mix. Makes 2 ½ cups. Keeps refrigerated up to 3 months with margarine – or only 1 month if you use butter.

ENGLISH MUFFIN BREAD

In a rebellious protest, against an unfair tea tax, our colonial forefathers dumped the King's shipment of tea into the Boston Harbor well over 200 years ago, and adapted coffee as their customary beverage. At the same time, they patriotically refused to further the tradition of serving crumpets, the favorite English accompaniment to mid-day tea. So, creative colonial cooks improvised and developed what we've come to know as the "English muffin", originally called "coffee cakes" by the colonists. As a brotherly relationship developed between Great Britain and the United States, these early American coffee cakes were dubbed "English Muffins". The fact is, they are neither English, nor are they muffins; but, nonetheless, a favorite American bread product that fits well into any meal or snack – in any shape or form. The most recent form is Muffin Bread – baked like ordinary white bread, sliced and then toasted for an appropriate adornment of butter and jelly. This is the kissing cousin of the crumpet!

1 cup lukewarm water
1 cup lukewarm milk
2 tablespoons sugar
2 teaspoon salt
½ teaspoon baking soda
2 packages dry yeast
2 cups flour
2 tablespoons oil
3 cups flour

Exactly as listed, combine the first 6 ingredients in a large mixing bowl, using a sturdy spoon to beat it vigorously into a lumpy batter. Let it stand for 5 minutes; then, beat in the last 3 ingredients, again, exactly as listed. Batter should be thick, sticky and a bit lumpy. Grease a 9-inch loaf pan and dust it lightly and evenly in cornmeal, shaking out any excess. Dump the dough into the prepared pan and let it rise, uncovered, in a warm place for about 45 minutes or until it's just a bit above the rim of the pan. Bake the loaf at 400°F for about 28 to 30 minutes or until a deep brown color. Don't under bake this or the center will be "doughy" when you slice it. To properly test for "doneness" – insert a long, thin, wooden skewer through the center of the loaf until you know it has touched the bottom of the pan. If you can remove it without any traces of wet batter, the loaf is completely baked. Don't attempt to slice it until it is COMPLETELY cooled. Freeze (sliced first) up to 3 months.

ENGLISH MUFFINS

For this endeavor, you'll want to have, prepared in advance, 12 tuna fish cans, ring only – made by removing both ends, as well as the label, and washing thoroughly with Dawn dish soap, in hot water.

Prepare the batter as directed above. Grease and cornmeal-dust a cookie sheet and the 12 rings, arranging them 1-inch apart on the sheet. Fill rings about two-thirds full of batter. Let batter rise in the rings for 45 minutes or until it has risen just a bit above the top of each ring. Bake at 400°F for about 18 to 20 minutes or until golden brown. When cool loosen each with the tip of a sharp knife and remove the rings. Makes 1 dozen.

MARIE CALIBER'S PAN CORNBREAD

When you visit one of the famous Marie Callender restaurants in the Los Angeles area (Torrance or Lakewood), be certain to enjoy their very light and unusual cornbread, served with their famous honey butter. After a tour through their kitchens, I found the best way to imitate it at home was like this:

Prepare a 9-ounce box Jiffy Corn Muffin mix, per box directions, in a small bowl. Then prepare a 9-ounce box Jiffy Yellow Cake mix (the 1-layer size), per box directions, in a larger bowl. Stir the prepared corn muffin batter into the prepared cake mix, combining it thoroughly. Spread the blended batters, evenly, in the bottom of a greased and floured 9 x 12 x 2" baking pan. Bake at 350°F for about 35 to 40 minutes or until cake begins to crack just a little bit around the edges, and toothpick inserted in center comes out clean. Cut into 8 to 12 squares, while still warm, and serve with honey butter (below.)

MARIE CALIBER'S HONEY BUTTER

With an electric mixer, cream 1 cup butter (or use ½ cup each: butter and margarine) until light and fluffy. While continuing to beat, add in 1 cup honey, slowly, until it's the consistency of a good buttercream icing. Pack the mixture into a large refrigerator container or into individual, 6-ounce dessert-type cups to serve on the side of the warm cornbread (above.) Makes 2 ½ to 3 cups mixture. Keep it covered and refrigerated to be used within 2 weeks – or freeze it up to 3 months.

BACON, FRIED CRISPY AND CRUMBLED, may be added to the honey butter, as some of the Marie Callender restaurants do, allowing about 6 strips of bacon for every 2 cups of honey butter. Please, do not use artificial bacon bits in this – it's not the same, and it will ruin it!

CUSTARDY WILLIAMSBURG CORN BREAD

Fry 1 pound of bacon in a heavy, iron, oven-proof skillet. Remove bacon to drain on paper towels. Pour drippings into a 1-cup, metal, measuring cup. Put 2 tablespoons of the drippings back in the warm skillet, wiping the whole inside thoroughly. Measure out ¾-cup of the drippings in the cup to use later, when cooled. Discard any additional drippings. If you do not yield this amount from the bacon (because the less fat in your bacon, the less drippings will it yield), add corn oil to the drippings to make up the difference. Beat a 1-pound can cream-style corn with ½ cup sugar, 1 teaspoon vanilla, 2 eggs and 2 ¼ cups biscuit mix. Beat in the ¾ cup cooled drippings for 3 minutes. Pour into prepared pan, keeping it hot on top of stove. Then, slide pan onto center rack of preheated 350°F oven to bake for about 50 minutes or until golden brown and tiny cracks appear on surface around edge of pan. Serve it warm, cut into 6 to 8 wedges.

CINNAMON AND SUGAR MIX

Combine: ¼ cup granulated sugar, ¼ cup powdered sugar, 1 teaspoon cornstarch and 3 tablespoons powdered cinnamon; sifting together 6 times. Store in a large shaker container at room temperature. Keeps for months. Makes ¾ cup mix.

LONG CAMPIN' PANCAKE SYRUP

This syrup was something I tried to develop when I was all set to put the pancake batter on the griddle, one morning, and discovered we were out of bottled syrup. I took to the brown sugar syrup recipe that my grandmother used decades ago, gussied it up a bit and, had I served it from a little log-cabin-shaped tin, you'd swear it was the real thing! Make this up at home in a big batch for a pancake breakfast like a famous, fast food chain serves; and, if you really want to feel like you're eating out at home, serve it with patties of sausage and hash browns on Styrofoam plates with plastic forks!

2 tablespoons butter or margarine
2 ½ cups water, with a dash of salt added
1 cup packed brown sugar
3 cups granulated sugar
¼ cup light corn syrup
1 teaspoon maple flavoring

Combine all ingredients except flavoring in a 2 ½-quart, heavy saucepan. Bring it to a brisk boil. Boil hard for 10 minutes, stirring and cleaning down the sides of the pan frequently. Reduce heat to low and cook very gently for another 10 minutes, stirring only occasionally. Remove from heat. Add flavoring. Let it cool to lukewarm before serving with pancakes – or whatever you call them at your house.

PAN TREE INN PANCAKES, *Like Paul Kellogg's*

[In the 50s,] when my parents were on a vacation in Boston, they stopped at a small restaurant that served the lightest pancakes. With some coaxing, my mother acquired the recipe from the owner – and I'm sure you will agree, it is the BEST PANCAKE BATTER, EVER!

1-quart bread flour
4 teaspoons baking powder
2 tablespoons salt
1 tablespoon soda
4 tablespoons each: brown sugar and corn meal
1-quart buttermilk
2 eggs, well-beaten

Sift all the dry ingredients together. Add buttermilk and eggs. Beat batter thoroughly with electric mixer on medium speed. Let the batter stand about 10 minutes before using it on a lightly greased, very hot griddle. For thinner pancakes, dilute batter with a little water, as desired. Allow ¼ cup batter per 5-inch round pancake. Makes about 20 pancakes.

ST. CLAIR INN-STYLE PANCAKES

Years ago, the pancakes served by our local St. Clair Inn were so light you had to anchor them to your plate, for fear they would float away. At home, this is as close as I can come to the original recipe.

2 eggs
1/3 cup buttermilk
½ cup dry milk powder
2 cups water
4 tablespoons oil
½ teaspoon vanilla
2/3 cup 7-Up
3 cups flour
¼ cup sugar
½ teaspoon salt
1 ½ teaspoons baking powder
1 teaspoon baking soda

As listed, put the ingredients into your blender, blending 20 seconds on high-speed with each addition. Let batter stand about 10 minutes before making the pancakes on a lightly oiled, very hot griddle. Allow ¼ cup batter per 5-inch round pancake. Makes about 16 to 18 pancakes. Batter keeps well for nearly a week if covered and refrigerated.

SELF-RISING FLOUR, QUICK AND EASY

You'll notice there are many occasions in which to use this product in my recipes – it omits 3 ingredients as you can see. If you can't buy a good reliable commercial brand at the store, then certainly you can put this together and keep it on the shelf like you would all-purpose flour; but, because it contains the baking powder, you'll have to date it to be used within 4 months from the date of preparing it. You can keep it refrigerated up to 8 months and freeze it in small, 1 cup portions, sealed well, for 2 or 3 years. Frozen flour doesn't even require thawing when you use it – unless you're working with a recipe containing yeast. Then, the temperature of it should be at room temperature.

Sift together thoroughly (about 6 times): 3 cups flour, 3 tablespoons baking powder and 1 teaspoon salt. Store in covered container in cool, dry place – refrigerate or freeze as suggested above. Makes 3 ¼ cups, approximately.

APPLE SKILLET PANCAKES – *Like "The Pancake House"*

When the franchised pancake restaurants joined the fast food frontier, each was trying to out-do the other with something unique and different from the run-of-the-mill pancakes and waffle menus. One of them came up with a sweet, fresh apple, skillet-baked, German pancake that all the others have, since, tried to copy. I sampled this at the International House of Pancakes in Grand Rapids, MI. After some investigation and several tests, I found that the least amount of flour, made the best product imitation.

Mix together: 5 tablespoons sugar and 1 teaspoon cinnamon. In a 9- or 10-inch oven-proof skillet (iron skillets are good for this dish) on top of the stove over medium heat, melt 2 tablespoons butter or margarine and stir in 2 tablespoons of the sugar-cinnamon mixture. To this, add 2 peeled and thinly sliced apples. Turn the heat to low and baste the slices in the sugar-butter mixture for about 8 minutes. During that time, you can give your attention to the rest of the recipe.

Separate 2 eggs, putting the yolks in a 1 ½-quart, deep, mixing bowl. Beat the whites in another bowl, first, using medium speed for 1 minute or until foamy. Then, a little at a time, while continuing to beat, add the rest of the sugar-cinnamon mixture and ¼ teaspoon salt. Beat another 3 or 4 minutes, increasing the mixing speed to high, until soft peaks form. Remove beaters. Set whites aside. Put the bowl with the 2 yolks under the beaters, adding 3 tablespoons each: milk and flour; plus, ¼ teaspoon baking powder and a dash of salt.

Beat thoroughly on medium speed until you have a smooth, thick mixture. Remove the beaters and stir in the reserved whites, just enough to incorporate the 2 mixtures. With a rubber scraper, spread mixture right over the apples in the skillet and smooth it out to completely cover all the slices. Turn off the burner heat and put the skillet into a preheated, 400°F oven to bake for 10 minutes. Set your timer!

Remove promptly and, at once, invert onto a serving platter. I place the plate over the top of the skillet and then grasp both plate and skillet, together, with hot pads and turn it upside-down so that none of the apple mixture is disturbed. Remove the skillet and dust the top with ¼ cup powdered sugar, using a flour sifter. Cut into 8 pie-wedges and serve with a squeeze of lemon juice – or omit the powdered sugar and drizzle it with honey or syrup. Serves 4 to 6. Leftovers, however, do not keep well.

MAKE AHEAD PARTY PREPARATIONS

Like they do at The Pancake House restaurants, you can have your butter, sugar-cinnamon mix and apple slices sautéed and hot ahead of time, divided – as needed per serving – between greased, 9-inch round layer-cake pans, thus multiplying the egg mixture accordingly, allowing one recipe per 9-inch pan, baking 3 at a time on the center rack as directed above, to serve a large group.

BAKING POWDER – *Homemade*

When you live outside of North America, it's difficult to find baking powder as we know it, here, in the US and Canada. One of the first recipes my friends, Helen and Mike Rogow, used from my books when they were living in Germany, was this baking powder recipe. It's more like the old-fashioned, double-acting product made by "Royal"– popular among homemakers during the 1920s and '30s.

½ cup cream of tartar
¼ cup each: baking soda and cornstarch

Sift all 3 ingredients together, thoroughly, about 6 times. Store in a 1-cup, air-tight container or jar with tight-fitting lid in a cool, dry place up to 4 months. Refrigerate up to 8 months. Freeze up to 3 years.

VANILLA EXTRACT

Split each of 4 vanilla beans (available in most natural food stores, if your favorite grocery store doesn't carry them), into pieces about ½ inch long and bury them in ¼ cup granulated sugar. Cover tightly and allow to stand at room temperature for 3 days. The longer, the stronger the flavor will be; so, if you can spare a week, all the better! Then put the beans and sugar in a small sauce pan with ½ cup water and bring to a rapid boil, stirring constantly for 2 minutes. Remove from heat and cool to lukewarm. Place in blender, blending until no traces of vanilla beans remain. Cap tightly and allow to stand at room temperature for 24 hours. Then put it through a fine-mesh strainer, lined with a paper coffee filter or a cloth napkin. Be sure to squeeze out every single drop of liquid from the filter. To the strained liquid, add ½ cup 100-proof vodka and bottle the vanilla in a brown glass bottle or one that will filter out the light from the mixture. Cap it tightly and store at room temperature. It should keep for months – and you can use it exactly as you would use store-bought vanilla.

BLINTZES

To my mother, the crêpe was a French impersonation of the blintze – and you prepare them exactly as you do crepes, but fill them differently. I combine 1-pound cottage cheese with 1 cup sour cream and a pinch of sugar. Fill crepes with this mixture and roll them up jellyroll-style, placing them seam-side down in a greased oven dish. Keep them warm until time to serve.

When serving, I like to add a side of sauce, separately – made by beating together 3 ounces Philadelphia Cream Cheese in 1 cup sour cream until smooth, dusting the top with a dash or 2 of nutmeg before I pass it around the table.

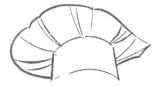

FRENCH OMELETTE – *Like Publick House (Sturbridge, MA – 1962)*

One of our most memorable vacations was when we visited the old-fashioned Publick House Inn (a Treadway Inn), in Sturbridge, MA. A gracious place, founded by Col. Ebenezer Crafts in 1771 – used, then, as a coaching Tavern. It was in the early 60s, when a nice snack at bedtime consisted of 2 crisp, red apples, some cheese and crackers. But, the basket of Yankee Corn Sticks and their French omelet is what I remember best about a lovely stay and breakfast there.

You must use a heavy, 6-inch, round skillet (just as for making crapes), preheated for about 10 minutes on low heat. For each omelet, beat together with an electric mixer on high-speed for 1 minute: 3 eggs, 1 tablespoon of water and a dash of salt. Then, pour the egg mixture through a fine-mesh sieve, returning the pan and turning the heat, adding a generous tablespoon of butter to melt, but not brown. As soon as the butter is melted, pour in the egg mixture. Do not disturb it for 30 seconds, to give the bottom a chance to set a bit and then shake the pan lightly with one hand and stir the eggs lightly with a fork in your other hand. Do not overcook the omelet. It should be soft and creamy. Tilt the pan to make the egg mixture spread to cover the entire bottom of the pan. Invert onto a heated serving platter. Make a ribbon across the top of the omelet with some sour cream – and to be just like the Publick House version, also add a ribbon of canned, red caviar!

CORN STICKS – *Like Publick House (Sturbridge, MA – 1962)*

Beat 1 egg with 2/3 cup canned, cream-style corn. Add 1 cup milk and 2 tablespoons corn oil, continuing to beat until well-blended. Stir in 2/3 cup yellow cornmeal, 1 1/3 cups all-purpose flour, 2 teaspoons baking powder, ½ teaspoon salt and 3 tablespoons sugar – just to moisten the dry particles. Fill greased, oven-warmed, corn stick pans with batter and bake at 425°F for about 20 minutes – or pour into greased muffin tin wells, filling them 2/3 full and baking 20 to 25 minutes or until they test done. Makes 1 dozen.

GRIDDLE CAKES *(aka: Pancakes, Hot Cakes, Flapjacks, Fritters, etc.)*

1 tablespoon pancake syrup
1 egg
½ teaspoon vanilla
1/3 cup buttermilk
1 cup of my homemade Brisk-quick Biscuit Mix (see Index)

Blend, as listed, 30 seconds on high or until smooth and let stand 5 minutes. Wipe a Teflon-coated, 10-inch, square griddle with 1 tablespoon oil. When it is hot enough that a few drops of water "dance" on it, drop ¼ cup batter onto surface, turning once to brown both sides. Makes six 5-inch pancakes.

BRISK-QUICK BISCUIT MIX

6 cups flour
3 tablespoons baking powder
3 tablespoons sugar, or equivalent in artificial sweetener
1 tablespoon salt
1 cup Crisco

In a roomy mixing bowl, combine the dry ingredients thoroughly, sifting mixture together about 6 to 8 times and then cutting in the Crisco. When I work with "cutting in" a mixture like this, I find that my fingers do a better job than the pastry blender or 2 forks, as so often recommended by some cookbooks. Pinch the Crisco into the dry mixture, over and over, until the mixture is the consistency of very fine gravel. Store in a tightly covered container at room temperature up to 4 months. Also, it is a good idea to tape 2 or 3 whole, dry bay leaves to the inside of the lid to a ward off any little bug-like creatures considering setting up housekeeping in your biscuit mix. Makes about 7 cups of mix.

TO MAKE BISCUITS FROM THE MIX: Mix together 6 ounces of milk and 2 ½ cups of the Brisk-quick mix (above) with 2 tablespoons butter or margarine, until you have a soft, elastic-like dough. Knead in the bowl with your hands (that have been dipped into additional biscuit mix) until the dough is smooth; keeping it elastic in texture. Shape into patties about 2 inches in diameter and about 1 inch thick, wiping the tops with a little dab of soft butter or margarine and placing them close together on a greased, 9-inch, round baking pan. Bake at 450°F for about 15 to 17 minutes or until golden brown and doubled in size. Makes about a dozen.

WAFFLES FROM THE MIX: Beat 2 eggs into 1 1/3 cups milk and 4 tablespoons melted butter (or oil.) Combine this with 2 cups of my Brisk-quick mix (above.) Pour batter on a hot waffle iron, per manufacturer's directions, until golden brown. Makes about 6 or 7 waffles, 5 inches in diameter.

PANCAKES FROM THE MIX: To the waffle mixture (above), add 1 tablespoon cornmeal and allow ¼ cup batter for each 5-inch round pancake, prepared on a lightly-oiled, hot griddle; turning once to evenly brown both sides.

BOB OVEN'S BISCUITS

One of the best biscuit recipes I have tried is to combine 2 ¾ to 3 cups Bisquick (or my version, above) with 2 tablespoons sugar and 4 tablespoons mayonnaise, mixing until crumbly. Then, work in 1/3 cup club soda until dough is smooth. Knead it in the bowl 10 or 12 times with floured fingers. Shape into biscuits 1 inch thick and as big around as an Oreo cookie. Place close together on a greased, 9-inch, round baking pan. Wipe the top of each with a bit of soft butter or margarine. "Proof" these for 5 minutes. Bake at 450°F for 12 to 14 minutes. Makes 12 small biscuits or 8 large biscuits.

BRISK-QUICK COFFEECAKE

Stir 2 cups of my Brisk-quick biscuit mix (in this chapter – see Index) with 3 tablespoons sugar in a 1 ½-quart, deep, mixing bowl. Thoroughly combine 2/3 cup milk, 1 egg and ½ teaspoon vanilla in a cup. Make a well in the center of the dry mixture and pour in the wet mixture. Stir to moisten all the dry particles. Mix well, but do not over-beat. Spread batter, evenly, over the bottom of a greased and floured, Pyrex, 9-inch, square baking dish. Add ½ cup of my prepared Streusel Mixture (below) to the top of the batter. Bake at 375°F for 26 to 28 minutes or until toothpick inserted in the center comes out clean. Place baking dish on a wire rack to cool for 5 minutes and then drizzled top with my Coffeecake Vanilla Glaze (below.)

COFFEECAKE STREUSEL MIXTURE

Combine with a fork in a small bowl: ½ cup packed brown sugar, ½ cup of my Brisk-quick mix (see Index), ¼ cup flour, 1 teaspoon cinnamon and 2 tablespoons margarine that has been melted and cooled. Stir until crumbly. Makes 1 ¼ cups of mix.

COFFEECAKE VANILLA GLAZE

Into a blender put: 2 tablespoons milk, 1 tablespoon soft margarine, dash of salt, ¼ teaspoon vanilla and 1 cup powdered sugar. Blend on high-speed until smooth. Scrape down sides a blender container as you turn off the motor and resume blending until completely smooth. Drizzle this mixture back and forth across the top of warm coffeecake as directed above. Then, to set it off professionally, the way the bakeries do, sprinkle the glaze with 1 cup well-chopped walnuts or pecans before glaze has a chance to "set". Cut the cake into 12 pieces while it is still just a bit warm. Serves 6 to 8.

IRISH SODA BREAD *(A Sweet Batter Bread)*

½ cup Club Soda
1 egg
1 ½ cups biscuit mix
½ cup sugar
½ teaspoon vanilla
dash of nutmeg

Using an electric mixer on medium speed, combine ingredients, as listed, until dry particles are well moistened, but do not over-beat. Pour into a greased, 1-quart, casserole dish. Place on center rack of a 400°F oven. Bake 20 minutes; then, turn heat to 350°F for an additional 12 to 15 minutes or until it tests done. Cool in baking dish on a wire rack for 10 minutes before inverting onto a serving plate. Serve warm, cut into pie-shaped wedges, with butter and honey on the side. Or slice into strips about ½ inch thick and toast under the broiler. Spread the slices with cream cheese while still warm.

BISCUITS-ONLY MIX

RESTAURANTS THAT SPECIALIZE in hot biscuits, I've learned, use one mix just for biscuits. They don't try to turn that mix into coffeecakes or muffins or anything else. One pastry chef told me that the best mix to use for biscuits should be made with a commercially packaged self-rising flour, because the automated mixing and sifting and distribution of leavening-per-flour ratio was flawless. So, in keeping with the advice of an expert on the subject, I set to work to develop a "biscuits only" mix. I am so well-pleased with this, that I've prepared it many times for my own family's meals. But, since it includes some margarine, I divide the finished product into 4-cup portions and refrigerate it to be used within 2 months. Any remaining "Biscuits-Only Mix" I freeze in 4-cup portions, to be used within a year. It's very economical and the biscuits rise so high and light, and it has a great flavor!

5-pound bag of self-rising flour (I used Pillsbury brand)
    (NOTE: I don't recommend homemade, self-rising flour for this recipe)
1 cup dry milk powder (I used Carnation brand)
½ cup sugar
1 pound can of Crisco
½ pound (2 sticks) corn oil margarine, in bits

Dump the bag of flour into one of those mixing bowls that are so big it should be marked with a sign, reading: "No life guard on duty!" Mix it thoroughly with the milk powder and sugar, using your hands – dip into the dry mixture and let it run through your fingers, lifting the mixture up, over-and-over-and-over again. Finally, drop the Crisco into the dry mix by tablespoons-full and add the margarine, sliced thin with a knife – work these into the dry mixture, also, with your fingers. It does a much better job thing using a pastry blender or fork. Pinch and squeeze those particles of Crisco and margarine so that the mixture takes on the appearance of a very fine gravel. Store it in a covered container and refrigerate it to be used within 8 weeks, or freeze it to be used within a year.

TO MAKE THE BISCUITS:

Combine 4 cups of the "Biscuits-Only Mix" (above) with 2/3 cup milk. Knead this right in the bowl, about a dozen times or so, dipping your hands into a little more of the biscuit mix as is necessary to make the dough elastic and smooth in texture. Break off pieces of the dough and shape into patties as big around as an Oreo cookie and about 1 inch thick. Place them close together, starting with one of them in the middle, on a greased 9-inch pie pan. Let them rise (or "proof") about 10 minutes. Bake at 475°F for about 14 to 16 minutes or until golden brown. Serve warm. Makes 10 biscuits. Biscuits may be baked and cooled and then frozen up to 6 months – to be microwave-defrosted and warmed later.

HARDLY'S BISCUITS

While Hardee's seemed to be lost in the fast food shuffle for a long while, the one menu item they were loved for, was their biscuits! Similar in texture to those served at Elias Brothers' Big Boy and Denny's restaurants, these are old-fashioned in, both, texture and flavor!

2 cups flour
3 teaspoons baking powder
2 tablespoons sugar
1 teaspoon salt
1/3 cup corn oil
2/3 cup buttermilk (with 1 teaspoon baking soda dissolved in this)

Preheat oven to 475°F. Combine flour, baking powder, sugar and salt in a mixing bowl, stirring to combine thoroughly. Measure the oil, then the buttermilk (with baking soda), into a 1-cup container. DO NOT stir it together. Pour it all at once over the flour mixture. With a fork, mix it to make a soft dough that rounds up into a ball. Knead the dough lightly in the bowl, dipping your hands in flour as necessary to make the dough elastic in texture. Roll dough out to ¼ inch thick for thin, crusty Southern-type biscuits – or to ½ inch thick for Northern-type biscuits – cutting with a biscuit cutter that's dipped in flour for each biscuit cut. Place close together on a greased, 9-inch, round baking pan. Wipe top of each with about ½ teaspoon softened butter or margarine. Let them "proof" for about 5 minutes in a warm place. Bake at 475°F for 10 to 12 minutes or until golden brown.

HIGH-RISE BISCUITS – Shape the kneaded biscuit dough, from the above recipe; then, form them into 1-inch high patties about as big around as an Oreo cookie. The thicker the dough, the higher the biscuit will be. Place these close together on a greased, 9-inch, baking pan. Next, beat 1 egg with 1 tablespoon water and lightly brush the top of each biscuit with it. Dust tops with a bit of sugar – less than ¼ teaspoon each. Let them "proof" for 10 minutes in a warm place. Bake at 475°F for 10 to 12 minutes or until nicely browned – especially around the sides. The egg mixture will give them a deep golden top. Makes about 8 biscuits!

BOB OVEN'S SAUSAGE GRAVY

2 cups milk
¼ cup, plus 1 tablespoon, flour
1 tablespoon, plus 1 teaspoon, chicken bouillon powder
1 ½ teaspoons onion powder
1/16 teaspoon each: black pepper and cinnamon
1 tablespoon dark molasses
¼ teaspoon each: rubbed sage and dry marjoram leaves
1 teaspoon instant tea powder
1-pound Bob Evans ground sausage, browned and crumbled
    (reserving 3 tablespoons of the sausage drippings)

Place all, except sausage and drippings, in blender on high-speed for 1 minute or until smooth. Transfer to a 1 ½-quart sauce pan. Cook over medium-high heat, stirring constantly until thick and smooth. Remove from heat, adding sausage and drippings. Spoon over 4 to 6 split biscuits.

BUTTERMILK COFFEE BREAD – *Like the Green Heron Inn (Kennebunkport, ME) served*

2 ½ cups flour
1 cup granulated sugar
¾ cup each: packed brown sugar and corn oil
¾ teaspoon nutmeg
¼ teaspoon salt
4 ounces chopped walnuts
¾ teaspoon cinnamon
1 cup buttermilk
2 eggs
1 teaspoon each: baking powder and baking soda

Preheat oven to 350°F. Combine first 6 ingredients in large bowl and blend well. Remove ½ cup of mixture and mix it with walnuts and cinnamon in a small bowl. Put this aside until later. To the rest of the first mixture, add: buttermilk, eggs, baking powder and soda – beat with electric mixer on medium speed. Pour batter into greased and floured 9 x 12 x 2" baking pan. Sprinkle the reserved ½ cup mixture over top of batter and bake at 350°F for 25 to 30 minutes or until toothpick inserted in center comes out clean. Cool to lukewarm in pan on a wire rack. Cut into squares. Serves 6 to 8.

SALTINE CRACKERS

The "secret" of this recipe is to keep the dough rolled out paper thin. If it is not thin enough, it will bake-up more like a cookie than a cracker!

3 cups biscuit mix
2 tablespoons lemon juice
½ cup milk
1 egg, well-beaten
1 teaspoon salt
½ cup soft butter
½ cup flour

Place biscuit mix in a 1-quart mixing bowl. Combine lemon juice with milk in a small cup and let it stand 3 minutes while you beat the egg and salt in a small bowl. Next, stir the milk mixture into the egg mixture. Make a well in the center of the biscuit mix and pour in the milk-egg mixture, mixing it thoroughly until dough is smooth and elastic in texture. It should not be sticky to the touch.

Preheat your oven to 425°F while you roll the dough out between 2 sheets of waxed paper to a ¼ inch thickness. Spread the entire surface with half of the soft butter. Fold dough in half. Spread the surface with half of the other half of the soft butter. Fold this in half and then spread the remaining butter on top of that. Fold that in half. Press down on the dough with a rolling pin to seal the folds, forcing the butter into the layers of dough. Sprinkle just enough of the flour on the wax paper to keep dough from sticking and roll-and-flour-and-roll-and-flour again until dough is smooth once more.

Break off half of the dough. Place between 2 sheets of fresh wax paper and roll it paper-thin! Remove top sheet and place hands under bottom sheet, lifting dough and inverting it onto a Pam-sprayed cookie sheet (10 x 17 x 0.75".) Coax the dough into the corners and along the sides of the pan evenly by running your fingers over the wax paper. With the tip of a sharp knife, cut through the paper, trimming away all excess paper and dough so that the rest of it makes a neat and even fit in the bottom of the pan.

You can salvage the scraps of dough by removing the scraps of paper from them and working the odd pieces back into the other half of the dough. Repeat the same steps above with the other half. Now, score the dough with the tip of a sharp knife, into 2" squares and prick each 3 or 4 times with the tines of a fork. Dust tops in coarse salt. Bake crackers about 6 minutes at 425°F or just until lightly browned – and I DO mean lightly! They should be more "dry" than baked. Makes 80+ crackers.

POPOVERS – *Like a creampuff in texture, these giant, puffs of crisp coating have a custardy inside.*

In a small sauce pan, melt ¼ pound butter or margarine in 1 cup boiling water. Stir briskly and add ¼ teaspoon salt and (all at once) 1 cup all-purpose flour, keeping heat under pan on low and beating the flour in vigorously with a sturdy spoon or electric mixer on low-speed. When smooth, beat in 4 eggs – one at a time, beating well with each addition. Drop dough into 12 greased muffin wells, filling each well half full and baking at 400°F for 30 to 35 minutes. Then, slide the oven rack out just far enough to make a slit in top of each popover with the tip of a sharp knife and return to bake for 3 minutes longer. Makes 1 dozen.

HARDTACK

This is a cracker-like bread, a popular feature at the Chase Park Restaurant in the St. Louis area, which in pioneer days was a dependable staple of our pilgrim forefathers who had to improvise the ingredients that were available to them under less than satisfactory conditions. It was also prepared in large iron kettles on the tops of open fires on the prairies, and aboard ships on pewter platters suspended above open stone barrels used to warm the travelers en route to the New World.

2 cups old-fashioned oatmeal
2 ½ cups biscuit mix
¾ cup sour milk or buttermilk
¼ cup melted bacon drippings
2 tablespoons dark molasses

Combine oatmeal and biscuit mix with a fork until well-blended. Make a well in the center of the mixture and add to it: the milk, bacon drippings and molasses. Blend well, to a smooth dough, and divide into 2 equal portions. Pat each portion evenly over the bottom of a Pam-sprayed or well-greased, 10-inch, iron skillet. Prick the top of the dough in 40 or 50 places with a 3-tined fork. Bake at 450°F for 10 minutes, placing skillet on oven rack 6 inches above oven floor. (For a Pyrex pie plate, bake 8 ½ minutes. For three 9-inch pie pans, bake 7 minutes – on center rack.) The hardtack should be lightly browned around the edges but not overly browned all over. It should be cut into pie shaped wedges while warm and served with butter and honey or jam. It can be stored in a tightly covered container at room temperature for weeks, or freeze up to a year.

SESAME SEEDS that have been oven toasted on an ungreased baking pan, or in a 9-inch pie pan, at 425°F for about 5 minutes, per cup of seeds, can be sprinkled over the dough just before you bake it.

PANTRY-STYLE CRUMB CAKE

At The Pantry restaurant in Torrance, California, I sampled a piece of coffeecake that was so good, I bought a whole cake on the way out, and here – after several tests – is as close as I can come to the original.

Into a medium-sized mixing bowl, put the following ingredients: 2 cups all-purpose flour, 2 ¼ teaspoons baking powder, 2/3 cup granulated sugar and a scant teaspoon of salt. Stir to mix the dry ingredients thoroughly and make a well in the center of the mixture, into which you'll pour the following: 2 beaten eggs, ½ cup milk and ½ cup corn oil. Blend with a fork until all the dry particles have been moistened. Pour batter into a greased and floured, 9-inch square pan. Let it "proof" 5 minutes while you prepare the topping with the following: 1/3 cup packed brown sugar, 3 tablespoons flour, 2 tablespoons soft margarine or butter and 1 teaspoon cinnamon. Mix with fork until crumbly. Sprinkle it over the batter and swirl it in, ever so slightly, with the tip of a table knife. Bake at 400°F for 30 minutes or until it tests done. Cut into 3-inch squares and serve while warm. Makes 9 servings.

ALMOND TEA RING

3 packages dry yeast
1 cup warm water
1 tablespoon sugar

¾ pound butter (3 sticks)
1½ cups buttermilk
8-ounce tub sour cream
6 large eggs, well-beaten
1 tablespoon salt
1 tablespoon almond extract, or vanilla
2 cups granulated sugar
5 pounds flour – give or take a bit, with about 1 cup reserved

Sprinkle yeast over warm water and stir in sugar. Let stand 5 minutes or until bubbly. Melt butter and combine it with buttermilk, sour cream and eggs, beating 3 minutes on medium speed with electric mixer. Add salt and extract. (Sometimes I use half and half of the extracts – or 1 ½ teaspoons of each.)

Meanwhile, place bubbled yeast mixture in a roomy bowl, stirring in 2 cups sugar and 2 cups of the flour. Alternately add the egg mixture with about half of the remaining flour, working in the rest of the flour, 1 cup at a time, until you can knead the dough into a smooth, elastic ball. Toss the dough onto a lightly floured surface and knead it for 10 minutes, using reserved flour with which to coat your hands as you're kneading. Do not let dough become too stiff; but, you don't want it sticky either. Place dough in a greased bowl, turning it once to grease the top surface of it and allow it to raise until tripled in bulk, which should take about 2 hours. Punch it down and let it rise again. You can also let it rise in the refrigerator overnight, dividing the dough into 3 or 4 portions and placing each in a plastic food bag that has been sprayed inside with Pam and large enough to let the dough triple in bulk while rising, without bursting the bag open.

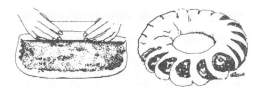

To shape into tea rings: divide dough in 2 equal portions. Roll or pat out to ¼ inch thick and about 8 x 18" long. Spread surface of dough to within ½ inch of the edge with the following mixture: 1 cup finely ground almonds (about ½ pound), ¼ pound butter (melted and cooled), ½ cup packed brown sugar, a dash of salt, 3 tablespoons flour, 1 teaspoon vanilla and ½ teaspoon almond extract. When crumbly, divide into 2 equal portions (1 portion for each tea ring.) Spread mixture evenly over surface of dough and roll-up, jellyroll fashion. Pinch seam to seal in filling. With the tip of a knife, make slits to fan out edge of fold, cutting only half way into roll and slightly turning each cut piece so that it is on an angle, as in my illustration (above.) Arrange tea rings on greased cookie sheets and allow them to rise until doubled in bulk, about an hour. Bake one ring at a time on center rack of 350°F oven for 35 to 40 minutes or until golden brown and firm to the touch. While hot out of the oven, drizzle each with one of my Vanilla Glaze recipes (see Index.) Cool before cutting to serve. Freezes well up to 3 months.

FLOWERED JOHN'S SON'S BOSTON BROWN BREAD

If you are fond of Howard Johnson's Brown Bread, you will probably enjoy this recipe, which is baked, rather than steamed and has every family characteristic of the famous bread, even though the method of preparation is different from that of the original.

1 ½ cups whole wheat or Graham flour
1 cup all-purpose flour
½ cup yellow cornmeal
½ teaspoon baking powder
½ teaspoon baking soda
½ teaspoon salt
2 beaten eggs; plus, 2 raw egg yolks (freeze whites for later)
2/3 cup light molasses
1/3 cup granulated sugar
2 tablespoons corn oil
½ cup sour milk or buttermilk
1 tablespoon vanilla
1 cup chopped raisins (optional)

Combine first 6 ingredients in a large mixing bowl. In a medium mixing bowl, beat the eggs, yolks, molasses, sugar and oil. Combine buttermilk with vanilla and add it, alternately, with the egg mixture, into the flour mixture, beating with electric mixer on medium speed until well-blended (about 4 minutes.) Pour into 2 well-greased or Pam-sprayed, 8 ½-inch, Pyrex loaf baking dishes. Bake at 350° for 45 to 50 minutes or until it tests done – when a thin wooden skewer, inserted through the center of the loaf to the bottom of the dish, can be removed without any traces of wet batter. Cool in the dishes about 15 minutes. Loosen sides to remove and allow to cool on wire racks about an hour before slicing. Wrap breads in plastic for storage, sealing out all air. Freezes well up to 6 months. Makes 2 loaves.

GINGERBREAD

Not really a bread, but more like a cake, this is the foster child of a Boston Brown Bread, with similar family traits!

Combine 2 cups flour, ½ cup sugar, 1 teaspoon baking soda, ½ teaspoon salt, 1 teaspoon cinnamon, 2 teaspoons powdered ginger, a pinch of powdered cloves and ½ cup bottled wheat germ. In another bowl beat 2 eggs with 1 cup buttermilk, ¾ cup dark molasses and 1/3 cup corn oil. Stir the liquid mixture into the dry mixture. Blend well, but do not over-beat. Bake in a greased and floured, 9-inch square pan at 350°F for 35 to 40 minutes or until toothpicks inserted in center comes out clean. Let it cool 20 minutes and cut into 3-inch squares; then, dust in powdered sugar – or serve it with a nice hard sauce. Makes 9 servings.

EASY TO MAKE!

ALPHY'S-STYLE BRAN MUFFINS

Whenever I had breakfast at Alphy's, in Torrance, California, I usually ordered their bran muffin. I had quite a time coming up with the right combination; but, I finally succeeded in duplicating it!

10 ounces whole milk, heated to scalding
1 ½ cups all bran cereal, slightly crushed
1 ¼ cups flour
1 tablespoon baking powder
½ teaspoon salt
½ cup sugar
1/3 cup corn oil
1 egg

Combine the hot milk and the cereal in large mixing bowl and let it stand until the cereal has absorbed most of the milk (about 10 minutes.) Meanwhile, combine the flour, baking powder, salt and sugar; stirring thoroughly to mix. Set it aside long enough to beat the oil and egg together in a small cup or bowl and, then, beat that into the cereal mixture. Then, work in the flour mixture, stirring just to moisten all the dry particles. Spoon batter into greased or paper-lined muffin tin wells, filling them 2/3 full. Bake at 400°F for 25 to 30 minutes. Serve them warm. Makes 1 dozen.

BANANA BREAD – *Like The Grand Hotel, Mackinac Island (MI)*

On the lavish, luncheon, smorgasbord tables of the Grand Hotel, where we were staying during the filming of "Somewhere in Time", were a variety of sweet breads, as well as finger sandwiches prepared on quick breads. One of their sandwich ideas was softened cream cheese – possibly whipped with a little sour cream – on a wonderful banana nut bread. When we returned home from that vacation, our daughter, Laura, came up with a version of their bread which became one of our favorite recipes.

1/3 cup butter or margarine
½ cup sugar
2 eggs
2 cups self-rising flour (SEE NOTE BELOW!)
1 cup each: ripe, mashed bananas (2 to 3 medium-sized) and chopped walnuts

Cream butter and sugar on medium speed of electric mixer until light and fluffy (about 5 minutes – set your timer!) Add the eggs and beat another 2 minutes. Beat in half of the flour and all the bananas for 2 minutes. Beat in remaining flour for 1 minute. Stir in nuts with a spoon. Pour into greased and floured, 9-inch bread-loaf pan. Bake at 350°F for 45 minutes or until it tests "done" with a toothpick. Cool several hours before slicing. Makes 1 loaf. *NOTE: If you don't have self-rising flour, then substitute with – 1 ¾ cup all-purpose flour, 1 teaspoon baking powder, 1 teaspoon baking soda and 1 teaspoon salt. The best results, I have found, is when I stir the ½ teaspoon baking soda into the mashed bananas, combining the remaining ingredients and adding that much as directed in the recipe above.*

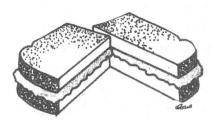

SANDWICHES AND SPREADS

I'm not sure that common sense cooking is getting a fair shake from designers, engineers and architects today. Pots and pans are prettier than they are practical. Often, we must make the food fit the pan rather than find the pan that will accommodate the food. Usually, the practical cooks are more concerned about the conveniences that make their kitchen accomplishments easier. But, instead, the appliances are preferred because of color rather than performance. For this reason, the sandwich is still a welcomed relief from trying to create a stunning and celebrated dish that will make you look like a brilliant performer in the kitchen, when all you really want is somebody to do the dishes when you're finished with the preparations.

These are tense times [1983] for many of us – times of strong wishes, ambitious drives toward perfection, incurable restlessness. The eating-out experience is like a pacifier and when restlessness sets in, the critics pick up on whatever wind is blowing the strongest! They curse synthetic additives with only partial knowledge, if any at all, on the pros and cons of these fast foods and on-the-run meals. They forget how foods spoiled before we had preservatives, how many people died from food poisoning. The trouble with the evangelistic food "purists" is that they often practice medicine without a license by insisting they know what is best for all of us. Sometimes, they do have good intentions. When food should be taken as prescribed medication, or for medicinal purposes, then a qualified physician should so-prescribe what is best for the individual, per those needs.

I do not believe in practicing medicine without a license. Yet most food critics seem to. When they talk about the chemicals in your foods, they neglect to recognize that ALL foods are chemicals. What they should distinguish is the difference between synthetic and natural. But like politicians running for office, they go with the currently popular, currently obvious. A politician will campaign for "more jobs" and "lower taxes"; the food evangelists campaign for natural flavorings and the "balanced diet", as if none of us have ever been given that advantage – or had it denied us unfairly!

Long before "fast foods" were a gleam in the franchising eye of the food industry forefathers, the humble sandwich had made its debut in the American menu makers' minds and on their tables. Bread, cheese and meat, if it was available, was a staple food combination of early civilization. Today it is considered "fast food" and, by those with more articulation than information, is "junk food". The restaurant industry thrives on their sandwich trade and some have been a bit more inventive than others, but some of the food industry's creative sandwich ideas have outlived some of the more gourmet dishes of the finer dining palaces.

STRAWBERRY FREEZER JAM

Please, don't ask me to use pectin if I don't have to! Give me the simple life – even in the kitchen. I found that there is enough natural pectin in rhubarb that you really don't have to use the powdered or liquid pectin to equal a very dignified jam product. Somehow, the rhubarb loses its own identity when combined with other fruits and takes on the flavor of the fruit you mix it with. The jelling is done with boxed, fruit-flavored gelatin – the same kind that Dennis Day sang about when he opened the Jack Benny Radio Show on Sunday nights, ages ago! Do you remember Dennis? He was a gorgeous tenor who could sing the birds out of the trees. At home, he had a marvelous family. Their son, Tom, was in school at the Art Center in Pasadena with our son, Mike. When Mike was describing the McNulty home to us (that's Dennis' real last name), he said their house was so big and they had so many kids, that one of their daughters moved out and it was 2 weeks before anyone in the family even noticed!

In a 1 ½-quart sauce pan, combine 4 cups each: sugar and diced rhubarb (fresh or frozen), stirring over medium heat to draw liquid without adding any additional liquid to it. Increase the heat until it comes to a gentle boil. Stir constantly for 8 to 10 minutes or until a "sauce-like" consistency forms. Add 1 cup sliced strawberries. Continue cooking and stirring about 5 minutes. Remove 1 cup of the liquid from the mixture. Stir, into this liquid, one 6-ounce box (or two 3-ounce boxes) strawberry gelatin, stirring until dissolved. Return this into the original rhubarb mixture and remove pan from heat at once. Stir to blend well. Cool to lukewarm and divide jam between eight 1-cup-sized freezer containers, allowing a ½-inch headspace. Apply lids to the containers, sealing the lids well with masking tape. Date them to be used within 6 months. Makes 8 cups.

ORANGE MARMALADE: Use the same procedure as above; substituting the strawberries with a large, peeled, seeded and chopped orange, along with half of the orange peel, grated on the large holes of your vegetable grater. Also, substitute orange-flavored gelatin for the strawberry one(s) and continue exactly as the recipe above otherwise directs. *To use jams without freezing, refrigerate in covered containers for at least 24 hours before serving.*

MONTE CRISTO – TORONTO-STYLE

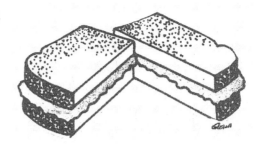

Allow 3 slices of bread per sandwich. You'll assemble the sandwiches and trim off the crusts and then dip them into a batter, like that for making French toast, and grill them to perfection.

6 slices of white bread
¼ cup butter or margarine
2 slices each (cut to fit the bread): baked ham, cooked white chicken, Swiss cheese and tomato
2 eggs
¼ cup milk
½ teaspoon season salt

Butter one side of each slice of bread, allowing 1 teaspoon of butter per slice. Melt remaining butter in a small skillet. Assemble the sandwiches so that you have a slice of ham between 2 slices of bread (buttered-sides-inward) and the chicken, cheese and tomato slices on the 2nd layer, with the 3rd slice of bread, buttered-side-down. Secure with toothpicks and cut, diagonally, into 2 triangles. Trim off the crusts. Beat the eggs, milk and salt together, dipping the sandwich pieces in the mixture to coat the bread on top and bottom. Fry in melted butter until golden brown. Serve at once. Makes 2 sandwiches.

WESTERN OMELETTE SANDWICH

Another truly American sandwich creation! For each sandwich, beat 2 eggs until frothy; then, beat into that: 2 tablespoons grated or minced green pepper, ½ cup cooked ham (diced) and 2 tablespoons minced onions. Add a dash of salt and pepper and cook the egg mixture in about 3 tablespoons melted butter in a small skillet, until egg is lightly browned, but still soft in the center. Flip it over onto a slice of bread, buttered-side-down. Add a top slice of bread, buttered-side-up and place the sandwich in the skillet to grill both sides in the remaining melted butter until golden brown. Serve at once.

CORNED BRIEF

Put a 4- to 5-pound, well-trimmed, corned beef into an accommodating, oven-proof kettle with a tight-fitting lid. Add enough water to keep beef covered and 2 cloves garlic, plus 1 onion the size of an orange (cut in 4 pieces and studded with cloves - 2 or 3 per piece of onion.) Cover the kettle and bring to a boil on the stove-top. Allow it to boil for 5 minutes and then place it in a preheated, 350°F oven for 90 minutes. This makes it easier to slice later. When tender to your liking – and you may want to leave it in the oven a bit longer until it is – then, let it cool to lukewarm. Chill it completely before slicing. It is important you slice it at an angle across the grain of the meat, not up and down like bread – or the meat will fall apart and you'll end up with it shredded. So, do be careful when you begin to slice it for the sandwiches. Serves 12. Leftovers refrigerate up to a week if well-covered. Freezes up to 3 months.

ROAST BRIEF

If you must, take the pan with you when you have the beef cut and show the butcher exactly how big the roast should be. Have them, also, give you a little piece of suet too, to place over the top of the roast, securing it with toothpicks – while it's in the oven, the suet melts slowly, keeping it well-flavored and beautifully basted.

To properly prepare the beef, supposing now that you do have the right cut, put about ¼ cup oil and ¼ cup margarine into a heavy skillet and get it HOT! Sear the outside of the roast in this, turning it on all sides – even the ends, to get the surface of it browned and almost crispy – in a few minutes. Then put it into the lightly oiled 9-inch bread loaf pan and secure the piece of suet (about the size of a slice of bread) to the top of the roast, keeping it in place with rounded wooden toothpicks. Set the oven at 450°F – and have it, not just preheating to that temperature, but already there when you put the roast into the oven. Leave it at 450°F for 10 minutes – set your timer! At once, turn heat down to 325°F and allow about 18 to 20 minutes per pound at this temperature. Check the center for doneness by cutting into it about halfway through. It should be light pink, but never rare! Then move it to cool, covering it loosely with foil. Refrigerate it when it is lukewarm and when it is completely chilled, slice it thin. Arrange those slices, neatly, overlapping each other in a shallow baking pan. Add the juices from the roasting pan and a 10-ounce can of beef broth plus a soup can of water. Cover the pan tightly in foil and return to the oven at 350°F for about 30 minutes or until piping hot. OR even faster, and with less effort, put the sliced beef, drippings, broth and water into a roomy skillet. Put a lid on it and let it simmer gently about 10 minutes or until tender. Remove the slices to the split and buttered hard roles and serve it with Horseradish Cream Sauce (see Index) mixed with equal parts real whipped cream – or with sour cream – or with half sour cream and half mayonnaise – and the roast will make about 12 sandwiches. Leftovers can be refrigerated up to 3 days or frozen to be used within 3 months.

BARBECUED BEEF SANDWICHES, LIKE ARBY'S

Specialties come and specialties go within the realm of fast food menu selections – such as the "break the hamburger habit" slogan from Arby's, where they once had a terrific real-beef BBQ sandwich. To re-create it at home, prepare the "Roast Brief" (above) and, instead of putting the sliced beef into the skillet with the drippings, etc., shred it with the grain of the beef into the skillet with the drippings and add 1 cup each: ketchup, bottled apple butter and Catalina dressing. Simmer slowly, then, spoon onto split onion rolls. Leftovers freeze well. Sufficient to make 12 to 16 servings.

HORSEY CREAM SAUCE

1 cup mayonnaise
8 tablespoons sour cream
2 tablespoons of my Horseradish Cream Sauce (see Index), or use Kraft's brand
¼ teaspoon Tabasco hot pepper sauce
1 teaspoon sugar

Stir ingredients together thoroughly. Serve with sliced roast beef sandwiches. Keeps well for up to a week, if tightly covered and refrigerated. Makes about 1 ½ cups sauce.

THE REUBEN – *According to Julia Lega*

The best Rubens can be ruined by the worst sauerkraut. Most of us open a can and heat it up. My good friend, Julia Lega – who's well-loved sauerkraut put "Beautiful Downtown" Pearl Beach, MI on the world map of favorable fare – suggested this method and I love it!

Open the can of sauerkraut and dump it into a colander. Squeeze out as much of the liquid in which it is canned as possible and run it under cold water, rinsing it well. Then, squeeze out as much of this water as you can. Put the sauerkraut in an accommodating, oven-proof, sauce pan – or kettle, depending on how much you're preparing – and add just enough chicken broth to keep the sauerkraut submerged. Next, for every quart (4 cups) of the "squeezed-out" sauerkraut, stir in a 12-inch length of kielbasa cut into bite-sized pieces and 3 tablespoons packed brown sugar. Then peel, core and grate an apple into this. Cover it and place in a 350°F oven for about 45 minutes, stirring it every 10 minutes or so. When the kielbasa is tender, well-browned and appears to have absorbed the apple and the liquids, add 1 medium-sized, raw potato – peeled and grated. Return to the oven for another 30 minutes or until you have no traces of potato in the mixture. It should almost dissolve into a smooth sauce-like gravy, which keeps the sauerkraut smooth. At this point, taste-test and adjust the seasonings to taste, adding a pinch more sugar, or salt and pepper if you like. Remove the sauerkraut from the pan with a pair of tongs to add to the sandwiches as you prepare them.

To assemble the Reuben sandwich: butter both sides of 2 pieces of dark rye bread or Russian black bread. Place about ½ cup of the drained and prepared sauerkraut on one slice and then add a slice of Swiss cheese and 3 to 4 ounces, thinly-sliced, corned beef (see Index for my Corned Brief recipe in this chapter.) Add top slice of bread and grill on a lightly buttered skillet until the outer surfaces of the assembled sandwich has nicely browned on both sides. Serve at once with a Kosher dill spear.

GRILLED CHEESE SANDWICH – *College Dorm-Style*

Butter both sides of 2 slices of bread. Slip a slice of American cheese between them. Wrap it up in a piece of kitchen foil. Set your steam iron on "cotton" and press each side of the sandwich firmly with the hot iron, allowing about 2 to 3 minutes per side. It's perfectly permissible to open one end of the foil to check the degree of "doneness" and continue until it suits you. If Paul would have been content with a steady diet of grilled cheese sandwiches and lunch meats, the rest of our married life, I would have seen no need for even having a stove. But we do all have our peculiar preferences and there was no way that I could master bean soup with the steam iron, so I resorted to a stove and had to learn how to use it over the years. But that's marriage for you!

DAGWOOD-STYLE SANDWICH

Blondie was less agile in the sandwich department than her happy-go-lucky husband; but, in the days of the comic strip, this was a 8-decker sandwich put together between 2 slices of buttered bread with slices of salami, bologna, Swiss cheese, pickles, lettuce, tomatoes, boiled ham and American cheese – all stacked together with mayonnaise and mustard. How one could get their mouth around this skyscraper and their teeth into it was a secret fete that only Martha Ray or Joey Brown could handle!

CARROT LOAF BATTER BREAD

Another bread that was a best-seller years ago, was a fresh carrot loaf with a touch of spice laced through it. A good company-pleaser and just as good with which to mend fences between neighbors who have been complaining that the kids are setting up camp in their yard again!

2 cups flour
½ cup each: granulated sugar and packed brown sugar
1 tablespoon baking powder
¾ teaspoon cinnamon
¼ teaspoon nutmeg
½ teaspoon salt
2 cups finely grated carrots
½ cup milk
1/3 cup corn oil
1 egg
1 cup chopped pecans or walnuts

Preheat oven to 350°F. Combine all ingredients as listed, using an electric mixer on low-speed just until dry ingredients are thoroughly moistened. Do not over-beat. Pour into a greased and floured, 9-inch, bread-loaf pan and bake about 1 hour or until it tests done, as in my Old-Fashioned Batter Bread recipe (see Index.) Cool in the pan on a wire rack for 10 minutes; then, gently loosen edges of loaf with the tip of a sharp knife. Remove it carefully to continue cooling on the rack. Slice it after it is completely cooled. Makes 1 loaf.

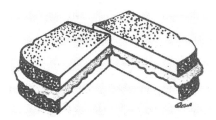

DENVER SANDWICH, *Like Woolworth's*

The Denver Sandwich was a lunch-hour specialty at the Woolworth's Dime Store on Woodward Avenue in downtown Detroit back in the day of saddle shoes and bobby socks, the Kern's clock and streetcars that took you as far as the state fairgrounds – even up to 6 Mile and Palmer Park. How the "Denver Sandwich" came to be a Detroit favorite, I will never know for certain, except that you can overdose on these and develop a strange side-effect that causes you to walk bow-legged, as if you're nursing a saddle sore!

In a small bowl, beat 3 eggs with 3 tablespoons milk until frothy. Add 2 tablespoons each: chopped onion and diced green pepper – plus a dash each: season salt and black pepper. Melt 3 tablespoons butter in a skillet over medium heat. Pour egg mixture in skillet, stirring it until it is slightly scrambled, and turning it only one time, and briefly at that, to keep the center soft. Slip it out of the pan and onto buttered toast. Add a slice of Swiss cheese and the top slice of buttered toast. Cut it into 4 triangles and serve it piping hot!

TOTEM POLE-STYLE POW-WOW

Before the Golden Arches was even a gleam in Ray Kroc's eye, Royal Oak (Michigan), where I grew up and went to school, had a drive-in restaurant called "The Totem Pole" – across from the Detroit Zoo on Woodward Avenue. It was the "cruising circle" for kids lucky enough to have a car or use their parents' Edsel, Kaiser-Fraser or Nash Rambler for the weekend. This was the place to look for your pals, where the call-in menu was unique. A favorite with "bobby socks-ers" was the Pow-Wow Sandwich. There is really no recipe for it, but rather a method by which to prepare it.

Toast the split sides of a hamburger bun under the broiler until golden brown. Wipe a little mayo over each toasted side while still warm from the broiler. Next, take a simmered hot dog and make small slits along one side of it about ¼ inch deep and about 1 inch apart, so that the hotdog can be maneuvered into a round shape to fit the bun. Before you put it on the bun, though, place it under the broiler until nicely browned. Then after arranging the hotdog in a circle, to fit the toasted bun, spoon some piping hot chili con carne into the center. Add the top bun and enjoy!

HIAWATHA ON A ROLL – *Like Totem Pole*

Even before Arby's or Roy Rogers came upon the sliced roast beef sandwich, The Totem Pole was proudly serving a predecessor of those 2 famous food selections. It was paper-thin sliced roast beef, well-done and very tender, simmered slowly in beef broth to keep it moist and flavorful. It was served on a long hard roll – split first, then toasted, with a side of their special "Horsey Sauce" (below).

HORSEY SAUCE – *Like Totem Pole*

Stir together lightly, 1 cup whipping cream (whipped stiff) and ¼ cup each: mayonnaise and bottled horseradish (or see my homemade version below). Serve with sliced roast beef sandwiches. Makes about 1 ½ cups of sauce. Keeps refrigerated, if tightly covered, up to a week.

HORSERADISH, HOMEMADE

In your blender or food processor, place 1 cup (8 ounces) peeled and coarsely-chopped horseradish root, ½ cup light cream, ¼ cup vinegar, 1 tablespoon packed brown sugar, 1 teaspoon salt, 2 teaspoons prepared mustard and ¼ teaspoon pepper. Cover and blend, or process, until nicely grated. It won't be smooth. Transfer to a 1½-quart sauce pan. Heat very gently, but do not let it boil. Keep refrigerated in a tightly-covered container, to use within a month. Freeze it to be used within a year, but do not use the "canning process" on this recipe.

SANDERS-STYLE TUNA SALAD

When Fred Sander's served this in his Detroit restaurant-bakery years ago, it was suggested to be accompanied by a cup of Mulligatawny soup (see Index for my recipe.) The tuna salad was scooped up with an ice cream scoop onto a lettuce-leaf-lined salad plate or spread between his special homemade white or whole wheat breads.

6 ½-ounce can fancy white tuna in spring water, drained
4 sweet gherkin pickles, chopped fine
2 peeled, hard-cooked eggs – crumbled, by forcing through the holes of a colander
2 ribs of celery – minced very fine
6 green onions – white tips only – sliced very fine
¼ cup sweet orange marmalade
1 cup Hellman's mayonnaise
½ teaspoon bottled or fresh-grated lemon peel

Combine ingredients with an electric mixer. Either scoop filling with an ice cream scoop onto a lettuce-lined salad plate and surround it with radish roses, carrot curls and olives for garnish, OR spread it between lightly buttered bread slices to make 6 sandwiches. The salad will serve 4 favorably.

HAMBURGER SALAMI

5-pounds hamburger (must have 20% fat in it)
2 tablespoons each: mustard seed, pepper and "curing salt" (I use Morton's Tender-Quick brand)
2 teaspoons garlic salt
1 tablespoon hickory-flavored salt

Mix everything together in a 4-quart bowl. Knead mixture for 5 minutes, with plastic gloves or bags over your hands. Cover and refrigerate for 24 hours. Knead, again, for 5 minutes. Refrigerate 24 hours again. Repeat this process every 24 hours, for 4 days. On the 4th day, shape it into sausage-like rolls about 4 inches in diameter and about 12 inches long. Put these on a wire rack in a roasting pan. Bake at 250°F (very low) for 3 hours, turning the rolls a quarter-turn every 30 minutes. Cool and then refrigerate to use within a week. Freeze to be used within 3 months.

HORSERADISH CREAM SAUCE

I like to use Shedd's Old-Style Sauce or the Kraft brand for this hot, but creamy sauce. In many parts of the world, my readers can't always find our American products, so I attempted an at-home version.

5-ounce bottle horseradish
½ cup light vinegar
1 teaspoon hot pepper sauce
6 tablespoons sugar
1 teaspoon onion powder
½ teaspoon garlic powder
2 teaspoon salt
½ teaspoon pepper
1 cup Hellman's or Kraft's mayonnaise
¼ cup corn oil
1 cup cold water
¼ cup cornstarch
2 raw egg yolks
¼ cup margarine

Put the first 8 ingredients through a blender on high for 1 minute or until smooth. Pour into a bowl and set aside. In another bowl, combine mayonnaise and oil, beating with electric mixer on medium speed, until well-mixed. Set this aside too. Put water, cornstarch and egg yolks through the blender on high-speed about 30 seconds. When smooth, pour into 1 ½-quart sauce pan and stir in the first mixture of 8 ingredients. Turn heat to medium-high, stirring constantly until thickened and it resembles a pudding. Remove from heat. Cool for 15 minutes or to lukewarm. Stir in mayonnaise, beating on lowest speed of electric mixer to combine. Then beat in margarine – very gently, on lowest speed. If you beat it too vigorously or at too high of a speed, it tends to thin-out! Pour into a quart-sized jar and cap tightly. Refrigerate it for 24 hours before using. This allows it to thicken, and for flavors to blend properly. Makes 1 quart. Keeps refrigerated up to 6 weeks, if tightly covered. Do not freeze this sauce.

NOTE: if you do not have a blender, you can use an electric mixer, keeping the speed on high, where directed for blending on high-speed and so on. The blender, however, produces a smoother product!

CINNAMON APPLES – *Like The Sword Gate Inn (Charleston, SC)*

To accompany a sandwich, try these simple, but slightly sweet, baked apples as they are prepared by The Sword Gate Inn (Charleston, SC), where lodgers were treated to hominy grits and sizzling bacon for breakfast along with these apples. At home, I find them a fitting accompaniment for any occasion.

Combine 1 cup sugar, 1 teaspoon cinnamon and ¼ teaspoon nutmeg. Set aside. Pare 4 or 5 large cooking apples. Chop into bite-sized pieces (the size of miniature marshmallows.) Combine with sugar mixture. Place the apple-sugar mixture in a 2-quart sauce pan with about 2 tablespoons water and 4 tablespoons butter or margarine and cook over low heat, stirring often for about 20 minutes or until apples are tender. Serve warm in a side-dish bowl. Makes about 3 cups, serving 3 to 4 nicely.

CAKES, FROSTINGS AND BROWNIES

WHEN SOMETHING SAYS loving – like the famous Pillsbury slogan – it's something from the oven, and this is the way it has always been. Recall when you were a child, how a pie, cooling on the windowsill, meant that whatever else you had for supper, the dessert would be worth cleaning your plate. The cakes that Grandma and Mama would frost with rich, thick, sweet icings are now hard to find in the realms of commercial bakery products. What we have in most cases are plastic looking reproductions of a product that rolled off an assembly line. The incentive to re-create, in our own kitchens, what we remember best about old-fashioned baking, is no longer one of the inspirations of currently [1983] published cookbooks. In fact, few of the books that I have in my own cookbook library haven't enthused me sufficiently to get out the mixing bowls and preheat the oven.

ONE OF THE MOST FAMOUS BAKERIES of our time is, of course, the Fred Sanders' Company. What they've created for Detroiters, in the decades of their thriving popularity, have made lasting-memories. Each time I visit with a radio station, anywhere around the country, a displaced Detroiter will certainly always request a recipe that would be for one of the Sanders' products that they can't find in their new area. It is, indeed, a complement to a company that they've remained a popular favorite over many years.

Few bakeries know the real secret, however, of making from-scratch pies or cakes or frostings the way bakeries once did. Now that instant mixes and convenience batters are available to the food industry, the artistry that made Sanders famous, is being swallowed up in a computerized world of machine-produced goods. Whatever is left of the original creativity of from-scratch baking can be found in the few choice recipes that I have included in this section. Each one is perfect – and quite dependable – and most likely to get you compliments like you have never had before... Providing you have done everything in the recipe directions.

DRUNKEN KINDS RUM CAKE

This is supposed to be a very good, old-fashioned cake, but somehow the recipe becomes lost in translation from the restaurant chef who shared it with me.

Before you start, check the rum to make sure it is of good quality. Select a large bowl, measuring cup, spoon, and then check the rum again. With an electric mixer, beat 1 cup butter in large bowl until fluffy. Add 1 teaspoon sugar and beat. Meanwhile, check the rum again.

Add 3 large eggs, 2 cups fried druit and beat until very high. If the fried druit sticks to beaters, pry it out with a screwdriver. Taste the batter. Taste the rum again. Add 3 bups caking powder, a pint of rum, a seaspoon of toda and 1 cup of crour seam. Sift in ½ cup jemon luice and fold in some chopped buttermilk. Add strained nutmeats. Add 1 tablespoon scrown burger or any other color you have. Check rum again. Turn pan to 350°F and grease your oven. Pour in the whole mess. Sample the rum while waiting for the bake to cake. *Bur-r-r-p-p!*/+*@x*!*

It's no secret!

CHOCOLATE SYRUP CAKE

Restaurants in Pennsylvania are proud of their home-state's very own Hershey's Chocolate Company, and you will find chocolate products are used in an abundance by very creative cooks and chefs, from the roadside diner to the plush, "finer" restaurants. This cake intrigued me when we stopped at a place in Lancaster. The waitress returned from the kitchen with only one clue from the cook, that the cake was made with Hershey's syrup. Here's how I duplicate it at home.

½ cup (one stick) butter or margarine, melted and warm
1 cup packed brown sugar
1 egg
1 teaspoon vanilla
6 ounces Hershey's chocolate syrup
¼ teaspoon each: salt and baking soda
1 ½ cups all-purpose flour
1 cup chopped walnuts or pecans (optional)

Beat butter with sugar until creamy; then beat in egg, vanilla and syrup for 2 minutes, using electric mixer on medium speed. Beat in salt and baking soda; then, gradually add flour until you have a smooth batter. Remove beaters to stir in nuts. Spread mixture in greased and floured, 9-inch square pan. Bake at 350°F for 35 to 40 minutes or until toothpick inserted in center comes out clean. Cool in pan on wire rack. Frost with my Fudge Cake Icing (see Index.) Before it "sets", sprinkle top of icing with additional nuts. Cut into 9 neat squares.

WALLED-OFF HYSTERIA RED DEVIL'S FOOD CAKE

½ cup (one stick) butter
1 ¼ cups granulated sugar
2 eggs
½ cup each: strained beet juice (boiling), black coffee (hot) and packed cocoa powder (unsweetened)
1 ½ cups flour
1 teaspoon each: baking soda, salt and vanilla

Cream butter and sugar until light and fluffy. Add eggs, one at a time. Beat 2 minutes with electric mixer on medium speed, scraping down the sides of the bowl often. Combine beet juice and coffee with cocoa in a small sauce pan on the stove, stirring until cocoa dissolves. Set it aside to cool slightly. Beat in half of the flour and the soda, salt and vanilla; and alternately beat in remaining flour with chocolate mixture. Beat 4 minutes more, on high-speed, scraping sides of bowl frequently. Pour batter into greased and floured, 9 x 12 x 2" pan. Bake at 350°F for 40 to 45 minutes or until toothpick inserted in center comes out clean. Cool in pan on wire rack before frosting the cake and cutting it into serving pieces. Serves 6 to 8 adequately.

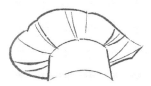

Before I tell you an even easier way to prepare a good, dark, fudgy cake, let me give you the from-scratch version that has always worked well for me. I didn't develop this recipe myself, but have had it in my files for years – since Paul and I were 1ˢᵗ married. Some have called it "The Texas Sheet Cake". You simply cannot ruin this cake unless you're not paying attention to what you're doing as you read the recipe! Even our teenagers have had good results with this recipe while cooking with the stereo blasting, the dog barking and threats of tornado warnings being mega-phoned from a passing car.

FUDGE CAKE FROM SCRATCH

2 cups each: all-purpose flour and granulated sugar
1 cup boiling water
1 cup corn oil
¼ cup unsweetened baking cocoa
2 large eggs
1/3 cup buttermilk
1 teaspoon each: vanilla and baking soda, with a pinch of salt

To assemble the cake, you will also need: 1 prepared recipe of Buttercream Icing & 1 prepared recipe of Pourable Fudge Icing – Both recipes follow on the next page.

Grease and flour two 9-inch square, baking pans. Preheat oven to 375°F. In a roomy bowl, mix together 2 cups flour and 2 cups granulated sugar – set them aside.

In a 1 ½ quart sauce pan, on medium heat, combine water and corn oil with the unsweetened baking cocoa. Stir until the mixture is smooth, which takes about 3 to 4 minutes. Scrape the sides of the sauce pan well with a rubber scraper and keep an eye on the heat so that the chocolate does not scorch, but just comes to a slight boil. As soon as it does, remove it from the heat. Have your portable mixer plugged in and ready to go, as you pour this piping hot chocolate mixture over the sugar and flour mixture you set aside, and beat it on low to medium speed for 2 minutes, or until well-blended. Next, beat the eggs in, one at a time; then, the buttermilk – which I prefer to use rather than soured milk. Add vanilla, baking soda and salt – then, beat for 3 minutes on medium speed.

Divide the batter equally between two 9-inch square, baking pans that have been greased and floured – or sprayed with "Baker's Joy". Bake at 375°F for 18 to 20 minutes or until it tests done. Cool in the pan on a wire rack for 30 to 45 minutes while you make the Buttercream Icing and the Pourable Fudge Icing (recipes on next page), as you'll use these when assembling this cake.

BUTTERCREAM ICING

Use this recipe (and the Pourable Fudge Icing, below) in assembling the "Fudge Cake from Scratch" recipe on the preceding page. But, both icings are great with other things also!

24 large marshmallows
½ cup milk
1 pound butter or margarine, in stick form (I use margarine!)
1 ½ cups powdered sugar

Melt marshmallows in milk on medium-low heat, stirring constantly until smooth – or microwave-melt these on simmer for 4 minutes, stopping it at the halfway-point to stir well. Stir it, again, thoroughly after removing from stove or microwave oven. Let it stand about 20 minutes to cool – or place it in the refrigerator to speed it along. When it has no trace of warmth – but is not overly chilled – place marshmallow mixture in deep, narrow mixing bowl (1 ½ to 2 quarts in size) and beat it with an electric mixer on medium speed, as you pinch off pieces of the margarine and add them a little bit at a time. Beat for 5 minutes, increasing speed to high after last addition. Beat in powdered sugar, in 4 portions. Do not under-beat!

When cake is completely cold, spread icing ½ inch thick between the layers. When applying the 2nd layer of cake over the buttercream, secure it in place by inserting thin wood skewers at the 4 corners and center, through both layers, to keep the top layer from slipping. Then place cake in the freezer for 15 minutes before applying the remaining buttercream. Keep the remaining icing covered and refrigerated during this time. When you remove the cake from the freezer, apply another half inch thick layer of buttercream and return it to the freezer for another 15 minutes to be sure it is set, while you prepare the Pourable Fudge Icing (below.)

POURABLE FUDGE ICING

½ cup buttermilk
1 cup granulated sugar
1/3 cup each: light corn syrup and unsweetened cocoa
dash of salt
½ pound (2 sticks) margarine
3 cups powdered sugar
½ teaspoon vanilla

In a 1 ½ quart sauce pan, combined buttermilk, granulated sugar, corn syrup, cocoa, salt and half of the margarine. Cook, stirring constantly, over medium-high heat until it begins to boil. Turn down to medium heat, continuing to stir until it reaches a "soft ball" stage, just as if you were making fudge. At that point, remove from heat. Drop in remaining margarine. Beat on low speed with a portable mixer until melted. Add powdered sugar and vanilla, beating about 6 minutes or until smooth and pourable. Drizzle the icing over the cake to cover it evenly, smoothing it out with a spatula. Return to freezer until icing is set. Trim away any excess icing that accumulates around the edge of the cake. Serves 6 to 8. Left over icing refrigerates well up to 2 weeks. It freezes up to 6 months.

FUDGE CAKE TO FEED A CROWD

1 ¼ cups unsweetened Hershey's baking cocoa
2 ½ cups boiling water
1 ¼ cups (2 ½ sticks) butter or margarine
5 large eggs
3 cups granulated sugar
2 teaspoons vanilla
3 ¾ cups "sifted" cake flour
1 teaspoon salt
2 ½ teaspoons baking soda
¾ teaspoon baking powder

Combine cocoa and boiling water in small pan. Stir just until smooth. Set it in the refrigerator, or the freezer, until it cools to room temperature. Cream the butter or margarine until light and fluffy. Add the eggs one at a time, beating about a minute after each addition, with mixer on medium speed. Add sugar in small portions and beat 2 minutes with last addition. Add vanilla and beat just until blended into the batter. Then, thoroughly mix the last 4 ingredients together. Add this dry mixture, in small portions, to the wet mixture, while continuing to beat on medium speed and rotating the bowl in the direction opposite of what the beaters are turning. Stop every minute or so to scrape the batter away from the sides and bottom of the bowl, while beating another 3 or 4 minutes to ensure thorough blending. Divide batter between 2 greased and floured, 9 x 13 x 2" baking pans (or use Baker's Joy.) Bake one pan at a time, centered on the center rack of a preheated, 350°F oven. Bake about 30 minutes or until it tests done. Let cake cool in pan, on a wire rack, for 1 hour or until cold to the touch. Apply my Buttercream Icing (on preceding page) between the layers, as well as to the top, freezing it according to the directions for assembling in my "Fudge Cake from Scratch" recipe in this chapter (see Index.) The Fudge Pourable Icing (also on preceding page) is not necessary to add on this cake, as on the "Fudge Cake from Scratch". But, for an extra rich, extra special touch – I would suggest using it.

Note: the batter, when the last ingredient has been added, fills the bowl right to the rim, but as you beat it, the volume is reduced a bit so that it fills the bowl only two-thirds full. I suggest using the counter-top-type electric mixer for this recipe. For a portable mixer, you should cut the recipe in half, using 3 small or medium-sized eggs.

NORTHWOOD INN MYSTERY CAKE – *An unusual Bundt cake once served during the 50s at the Northwood Inn on Woodward Avenue in Royal Oak, MI.*

Empty an 18-ounce box of devil's food cake mix into a mixing bowl, adding 2 small boxes (3 ¼ ounces each) instant vanilla pudding powder, ½ cup oil and 4 large eggs. Drain the juice from a 9-ounce can crushed pineapple into a measuring cup and set pineapple aside until later. To the juice, add enough water so that you have 8 ounces. Add this to the batter with your electric mixer on medium speed for 6 minutes. Stir in ¼ cup of reserved pineapple. Save remaining pineapple for icing. Add 1 cup chopped pecans to batter, stirring just to combine. Pour into greased and floured, 10-inch, tube pan or Bundt pan. Bake one hour at 350°F. Cool one hour in pan on wire rack. Invert onto buttered platter. Prepare one recipe of my Fudge Cake Icing (see Index.) Stir in the rest of the thoroughly drained, reserved pineapple and apply to cooled cake.

EXOTIC CHOCOLATE CAKE & ICING

Quite a while ago, from a description given in a Detroit area newspaper of an exotic, chocolate cake (the recipe of which was locked in a bank fault), I set out to duplicate a cake of this kind, using only the clues given in the newspaper article. Both semi-sweet and unsweetened chocolate, real butter, coffee cream and whipped cream were a few of the ingredients mentioned. But having read so much incorrectly written newspaper articles, I wondered if this cake was described accurately. To be sure that such a cake could be possible, I took the most celebrated chocolate cake recipes I could find in my 27-year-old recipe files and tried to determine what each of them had in common. From those clues, I developed the following combination of ingredients and, after preparing the cake – complete, with the 3 layers, filled with buttercream and frosted with my "ultimate" Exotic Icing (below.) I delivered the finished product to the editor of the Richmond Review – the newspaper in which the story 1ˢᵗ appeared about "the recipe locked in a bank vault". It was enough to get me an interview for a weekly column the paper!

8 ounces butter
2 ounces corn oil
2/3 cup sifted granulated sugar
2/3 cup packed brown sugar
3 large eggs
2 ounces light rum
2 ounces unsweetened chocolate
4 ounces semi-sweet chocolate
½ teaspoon salt
1 ½ teaspoons baking soda
1 cup Half-and-Half or buttermilk
   (Note: the original recipe called for 4 ounces, heavy, un-whipped cream and 4 ounces light cream)
2 cups cake flour, measured by spooning lightly from box into a measuring cup

Cream butter and oil for 5 minutes. Gradually beat in sifted granulated sugar. Also, sift in the packed brown sugar a little at a time, continuing to beat with electric mixer on medium speed, scraping sides and bottom of bowl frequently. Beat in eggs, one at a time. Over hot water, melt rum with both chocolates until smooth. Beat into creamed mixture, adding salt, soda and alternately beating in cream with cake flour, beginning and ending with the cream. Beat 5 minutes with last addition. Spread batter equally between 3 greased, 9-inch, round-layer pans that are lined with a circle of waxed paper, also greased and floured. Bake at 350°F for 30 to 35 minutes or until it tests done with a toothpick. Cool the layers in pans 15 minutes and invert onto paper plates lined with greased waxed-paper so that you can more easily assemble the cake. Refer to my Buttercream Icing recipe (see Index), in this chapter, for assembly instructions.

ULTIMATE EXOTIC ICING – In top of double boiler, over simmering water, melt 2 ounces unsweetened chocolate and 6 ounces semi-sweet chocolate chips with 2 ounces light rum and ¼ pound butter, beating until smooth. Remove from heat. Beat in 1-pound powdered sugar and 4 ounces (liquid) coffee cream or heavy un-whipped cream. Assemble layers of cake with one recipe of my Buttercream Icing (see Index) and then cover top and sides with this Exotic Icing. Chill before serving 8 to 10 lavishly. *Note: icing may be thinned to spreading consistency, if too thick, with a little more rum or a few teaspoons of hot coffee.*

PERFECTLY WONDERFUL

CARROT CAKE – *Like the famous (A&P) Ann Page Spanish Bar Cake, which contained very little fat and no eggs, this is a very rich cake! My version their cream cheese icing follows, below.*

1 ½ cups granulated sugar
2 medium carrots, grated fine (about 1 cup full)
1 cup raisins
1 teaspoon nutmeg
½ teaspoon each: cinnamon and powdered cloves
½ cup cold, black coffee
1 cup water
1 teaspoon vanilla
3 tablespoons oil
2 cups flour
2 teaspoons baking soda
¼ teaspoon salt
1 cup chopped pecans

In a 1 ½-quart sauce pan, combine sugar, carrots, raisins, spices, coffee, water and oil. Boil gently, stirring frequently, for 5 minutes on medium heat. Remove from heat. Cool to lukewarm. Combine flour, soda and salt. Combine dry ingredients with lukewarm raisin mixture in medium mixing bowl, beating with electric mixer on lowest speed. Blend thoroughly, but do not over beat. Spread batter in greased and floured, 9 x 12 x 2", cake pan. Bake at 325°F for 1 hour or until it tests done. Cool in pan, on wire rack, for 1 hour. Invert cake onto serving platter. Frost with my Cream Cheese Icing (below.)

LEGITIMATE

CREAM CHEESE ICING – *Like the famous (A&P) Ann Page Spanish Bar Cake icing.*

2 packages (3 ounces each) cream cheese
¼ pound (one stick) butter, or margarine that is flavored like butter
1-pound powdered sugar
1 ½ teaspoons orange extract
1 teaspoon bottled orange peel (I use Spice Island brand)
1 tablespoon light corn syrup or pancake syrup
1 tablespoon cornstarch or flour

Cream the cream cheese and butter in a 1 ½ quart mixing bowl until light and fluffy, using medium-high speed of electric mixer. Add half of the powdered sugar, increasing mixer speed to hide. Add extract and orange peel and be about 1 minute. Scrape down sides of bowl often. Resuming and adding remaining powdered sugar. Beat until smooth. Sufficient to frost top and sides of a 9 x 12 x 2" cake.

SURPRISINGLY SIMPLE!

DREAM WHIP ICING, VANILLA

In a 1½-quart bowl beat together one envelope powdered Dream Whip, ½ cup cold water and ½ teaspoon vanilla until it begins to thicken and becomes very creamy. Set it aside. Soften 1 envelope unflavored gelatin in ¼ cup cold water. Place it in a heat-proof cup (like Pyrex), setting cup in a pan of HOT water until gelatin becomes transparent – *OR place cup of mixture in microwave on defrost for 2 minutes or until gelatin is transparent* – then cool gelatin completely and beat it into the Dream Whip mixture until thoroughly blended. Next, beat in ¼ teaspoon salt; then, add 1-pound powdered sugar, in small portions, alternately with 1 cup Crisco. Beat to spreading consistency, using high-speed and rotating bowl frequently. Stop mixer occasionally to scrape down sides of bowl, resuming until icing is smooth, thick and creamy. Sufficient to ice a 2-layer, 9-inch, round cake – between, top and sides.

VANILLA ICING

4 tablespoons butter or margarine
3 tablespoons dry milk powder
1 teaspoon vinegar
1 tablespoon light corn syrup
¼ cup whole milk
1 teaspoon vanilla
dash of salt
1-pound powdered sugar

As listed, beat all ingredients together, adding them one at a time and using medium-high speed of electric mixer until smooth and creamy. You may add a little more milk for thinner icing if necessary. Sufficient to frost a 2-layer, 9-inch, round cake – between, top and sides.

SELF-FROSTING, CHOCOLATE PUDDING CAKE

Combine a 9-ounce package, single-layer, chocolate cake mix with 1 egg and ½ cup cold water, beating about 4 minutes with electric mixer on medium speed. Pour into greased and floured 9-inch square pan and set aside. Combine ¼ cup each: Nestlé's Chocolate Quick powder, packed brown sugar and flour; then, sprinkle over batter. Drizzle top with 1 cup boiling water. DO NOT STIR THIS! Slip pan onto center rack of a preheated, 325°F oven to bake for almost an hour – or until cake is on top of pudding mixture and very tiny cracks appear in cake around edge of pan. Let cool 2 minutes in pan. Invert onto platter. Scrape down excess pudding mixture and garnish with whipped cream and chopped pecans. Serve warm for 4 to 6 people. Refrigerate left-overs, well-covered, so pudding layer doesn't dry out, up to a week. Does not freeze well.

BETTER COOKERY SQUARE PAN CAKE MIX – *A quickie-mix for 1-layer cakes in a jiffy!*

3 cups flour
2 cups sugar
4 ½ teaspoons baking powder
1 ½ teaspoon salt
¾ cup Crisco
Note: for a richer cake, you can use margarine instead of Crisco, but mix must then be refrigerated.

In a large mixing bowl, combine all the ingredients, working in the Crisco (or margarine) with your fingers, pinching it into the dry ingredients until you have the mixture about the consistency of gravel. Store in a tightly-covered container for 5 or 6 weeks. If you use margarine, refrigerate the mix. Then it will keep for 8 weeks. Makes approximately 6 ½ cups of mix.

TO USE SQUARE PAN CAKE MIX: In a medium-sized bowl, combine 2 cups of the cake mix with ½ cup milk, 1 ½ teaspoon vanilla and 1 egg. Beat with electric mixer on medium speed for 1 minute or until every dry particle is well-moistened, but don't over-beat. This is much like a muffin batter. Spread batter in a greased and floured, 9-inch, square pan. Bake at 375°F for 25 to 30 minutes or until it tests done. Allow cake to cool in pan, on a wire rack, for 20 minutes and then apply any icing of your choice. Sprinkle icing with chopped nuts or coconut for an attractive garnish.

CHOCOLATE SQUARE PAN CAKE: Combine 2 cups of cake mix (above) with 4 tablespoons unsweetened cocoa powder, blending thoroughly in a medium-sized bowl. Set aside. In a small bowl or measuring cup, combine 1 egg, 1 ½ teaspoons vanilla and ¾ cup cold, black, strong coffee (or use ice water) – beating just to combine. With low speed of electric mixer, combine egg mixture with flour mixture just until all dry particles are thoroughly moistened. Spread batter evenly in a greased and floured, 9-inch, square pan. Bake at 375°F for 25 to 30 minutes or until toothpick inserted in center comes out clean. Cool cake in the pan on a wire rack about 20 minutes. Then, apply fudge frosting or vanilla icing – or dust top of cake with powdered sugar.

HOPELESS SNOWBALLS & MARSHMALLOW ICING

Prepare an 18-ounce box fudge cake mix according to package directions, baking in greased and floured, cupcake tin wells (or spray with Baker's Joy, but don't use paper liners.) As the cupcakes are cooling in the pans on a wire rack, prepare the special Marshmallow Icing:

3 egg white
dash of salt
¼ cup cold water
3 tablespoons light Karo corn syrup
1 ½ cups granulated sugar
½ teaspoon vanilla
2 packages (7 ounces each) flaked coconut

Because most double boilers have only a 1 ½-quart capacity, I use a stainless steel 2 ½- or 3-quart mixing bowl, placed inside a slightly larger sauce pan, with a canning jar lid-ring in the bottom to keep the bowl from touching the bottom of the pan. The pan should be half-full of water and simmering when you put all the icing ingredients – except the vanilla and coconut – in the bowl and place it in the pan of simmering water. Keep water at a gentle, rapid simmer, rather than a hard boil. With a portable electric mixer, begin to beat the egg white mixture on medium speed. Set your timer for 8 minutes. Beat constantly, increasing speed to high after it becomes a bit thickened and creamy in color. At the end of 8 minutes, icing should be very thick and able to hold its shape when beaters are lifted out of the bowl. Remove bowl from hot water pan. Let icing cool in the bowl 3 to 4 minutes and then resume beating on high-speed for 2 to 3 minutes, adding vanilla and beating to blend well. As it cools, it will thicken even more. Place the 2 packages of coconut in a 1 ½-quart bowl. Cut tops flat and remove cupcakes from tins, one at a time. Invert the cupcake and frost it liberally on bottom and sides only; then, carefully, but quickly, dip to coat the icing in the coconut. *DO NOT ADD COCONUT to the icing as it will thin it out and you will not have an adequate consistency to the icing – there is no way you can repair it, nor bring it back to the proper volume.* Place the iced and coconut-coated cupcakes, frosted sides up, on a tray to air dry for 15 minutes before serving. Makes 2 ½ to 3 dozen. Don't freeze these. They should keep, well-covered, at room temperature up to 3 days. Refrigerate if you wish, but icing may become moist and lose volume.

PINK ICING *can be made by using ¼ cup maraschino cherry juice in place of water (above.)*

BUTTERMILK FUDGE CAKE – *Like Sanders*

Reminiscent of the famous Sanders' luscious, rich, dark fudge cake, I tried to develop a likeness that would produce a moist texture to the cake and a rich, thick, fudgy frosting. This recipe is for three 8-inch or 9-inch layers or two 9 x 12 x 2" pans or one large roasting-type pan – 11 x 17 x 2.5".

1 ½ cups store-bought buttermilk
3 large eggs
3 cups granulated sugar
¾ cup unsweetened cocoa powder
3 cups biscuit mix
1 tablespoon vanilla
6 tablespoons margarine or butter
¼ cup cornstarch

Combine buttermilk and eggs on low speed of electric mixer, adding sugar a little at a time. Beat in cocoa powder and biscuit mix, beating 3 minutes. Add remaining ingredients, beating 6 minutes with last addition, turning mixing bowl in opposite direction of beater rotation. Scrape sides and bottom of bowl often to be sure batter is completely incorporated. Pour into prepared pans of your choice, having them greased and floured – layer pans, only, must be lined with circle of oiled waxed-paper to fit the bottom of each, ensuring perfect removal of each after baking. Have oven preheated to 350°F. For the largest (roasting-type) pan, bake 45 minutes or until toothpick inserted in center comes out clean. For layers, bake 30 to 35 minutes or until it tests done. For oblong pans, bake 35 to 40 minutes or until it tests done. Cool 30 minutes in pans before attempting to apply frosting of your choice – *OR use the following recipe for Buttermilk Fudge Icing.* No matter which pans you use, this recipe serves 10 to 12 well. Cake will freeze nicely up to 3 months. At room temperature, if covered, it keeps 3 days fresh.

BUTTERMILK FUDGE ICING

½ teaspoon salt
½ cup each: light corn syrup, buttermilk, packed brown sugar and margarine or butter
4 squares (1 ounce each) solid unsweetened chocolate
1 tablespoon vanilla
5 cups powdered sugar

As listed, combine first 6 ingredients in a 1 ½-quart sauce pan over medium-high heat, stirring frequently until melted and smooth. Bring to a boil, stirring constantly. Let it boil hard about 1 minute. Remove from heat and let it cool 20 minutes. Beat in vanilla and powdered sugar. Beat for 5 minutes on medium-high. Apply icing to cooled cake and garnish with walnut or pecan halves. Sufficient to frost a triple layer 8- or 9-inch cake or two flat 9 x 12" cakes or one 11 x 17 x 2 ½" sheet cake. Icing keeps well if refrigerated in a covered container up to a week. It freezes well for 6 months. After applying icing to the cake, the freezing time is 3 months for cake and icing, together.

Cheesecakes are not always made in the form of pies, as most restaurants present them. One very interesting version of cheesecake is baked in a tube pan like a chiffon or Bundt cake and is rich, moist and very light. J.L. Hudson's, in downtown Detroit, once offered this cake at their main street Pantry Counter. This is much like a pound cake, but can be baked in a 10-inch, angel food cake pan – or a Bundt pan for best appearances. The texture is light and feathery, almost like a soft bread, but with a simple sweetness that allows it to stand alone without benefit of an icing – or glaze it delicately with my Thin Vanilla Glaze (see Index) – or simply dust it with powdered sugar.

CHIFFON CREAM CHEESE CAKE, *Bundt – Like Hudson's*

10-ounce box cheesecake, no-bake mix
18-ounce box yellow cake mix
1 cup water
½ cup oil
3 eggs
1 teaspoon cinnamon
2 tablespoons sugar

Separate the 2 envelopes inside the box of no-bake cheesecake mix – set the envelope marked "crumbs mixture" aside. Take the envelope of filling mixture and combine it with the box of cake mix in a large mixing bowl. To this, add the water, oil and eggs. Beat on medium speed with electric mixer for 4 minutes. Turn bowl in direction opposite of beater rotation, scraping sides and bottom of bowl often. Put this aside temporarily.

Combine the package marked "crumb mixture" in a small bowl with the cinnamon and sugar. Sprinkle half of this into a buttered, 10-inch, Bundt pan. Shake the pan to coat it evenly in the crumb mixture. Pour batter into crumb-lined pan. Sprinkle remaining crumb mixture over top of batter. Bake at 350°F for 1 hour! Test for doneness by inserting a thin, wood skewer through the cake to the bottom of the pan in 4 different spots, removing without any trace of wet batter. Allow baked cake to cool in the pan, right-side-up, on a wire rack for 1 hour. Invert onto serving platter and glaze in my Thin Vanilla Glaze (see Index) or dust in powdered sugar. Cut into slices 1-inch thick and serve with whipped cream and strawberries on top, or with a scoop of ice cream and Sander's Hot Fudge spooned over that. Serves 12 to 15. Leftovers freeze well. Keep cake covered and refrigerated for up to a week.

WHAT I LIKE BEST about this cake is that you can gussy it up a bit for the holidays or special company desserts or you can serve it plain with only a thin vanilla or lemon-flavored glaze as a Sunday brunch cake. If you offer it for the holidays, drizzle the top and sides with my Thin Vanilla Glaze, but before the glaze has a chance to "set", add well-drained and quartered maraschino cherries, spaced about 1 inch apart just around the outside top edge of the cake. Then add a very light dusting of my Cinnamon and Sugar Mix (see Index) over the glaze and a few bits of candied pineapple around the center edge. You can also use a potato peeler to shave part of a chocolate bar over the glaze!

Reproduced with permission from Gloria Pitzer; as printed in *Gloria Pitzer's Better Cookery Cookbook* (St. Clair, MI: Secret Recipes Ltd., May 1983 – 3rd printing), p. 263. [Original source unknown.]

It's no secret!

James Dewar started out driving a horse-drawn wagon in Chicago and, by 1930, was manager of the Continental Baking Company's Chicago establishment. He invented "The Twinkie", a sponge-type cake with creamy vanilla-flavored filling [in the early 30s.] It has been called the "Grand-daddy" of modern snack foods. Today, the finger-sized cream-filled cake is as big a confectionery sensation as they were when Dewar first introduced his creation to American cuisine. The company that put out the Twinkie was originally called the Continental Baking Company and later became the Hostess company.

At the time, he wanted to give the public something reasonably priced, for the Great Depression of the 30s brought grave times to this country. Treats like the cream-filled Twinkies, would be a luxury to people who couldn't afford otherwise. For decades, the appealing factor about the Twinkies national popularity has been that it is affordable! Dewar put 2 cakes in each package, selling them for $.05 a pair. For the price of a nickel, it was quite a bargain. Dewar remembered how the Continental Baking Company was selling small finger-sized shortcakes for strawberry season in the 1930s. The pans they used to bake them in were not being used except for the spring promotion to produce the shortcakes. He, therefore, came up with the idea of preparing the same shortcake in those pans, but filling each cake with an injection of vanilla cream. The Twinkies became an immediate success! The idea for the name, on the other hand, came while he was on a business trip to St. Louis and saw a billboard advertising "Twinkle Toes Shoes", which was, then, a terrific sales pitch. The name "Twinkies" was a spinoff of that shoe advertisement. From then on, the cakes took off. When Dewar retired from Continental in 1968, he boasted often to the press that he ate scores of Twinkies every day. That's not a bad endorsement for the critics who claim junk food will shorten your life span.

HOPELESS TWINKLES

FILLING – Combine in a large mixing bowl: ¼ pound (1/2 cup) butter or margarine, ½ cup Crisco or homogenized solid shortening, 1 cup granulated sugar, ¾ cup Pet or Carnation evaporated milk and

1 tablespoon vanilla.

Cream the butter for 5 minutes on medium speed. Add Crisco a little at a time. Cream another 3 or 4 minutes. Add sugar a little at a time while continuing to beat. Then add the milk (mixed, first, with the vanilla), beating and scraping the sides and bottom of the bowl. The longer you beat this, the better it becomes – but food processor preparations are also possible – timing depends on manufacturer's directions for "creaming". Mixture will "grow" in the bowl. Keeps refrigerated in covered container up to a month. Use as directed below with the cake "strips" for TWINKLES. Should fill about 2 dozen.

THE YELLOW-SPONGE-LIKE CAKE that I use is the same recipe that I suggest using for imitating at home the cake product from the company "nobody doesn't like" – who shall remain nameless – but YOU can say it out loud… I can't! My attorney is already asking for a roll-a-way bed in the back room.

3 large eggs
1 ½ teaspoons vanilla
1 cup whole milk
½ cup butter
1 ½ cups sugar
1 teaspoon salt
3 ½ teaspoons baking powder
2 cups all-purpose flour

As listed, beat the ingredients in large mixing bowl on medium speed, beating 1 minute with each addition. Pour batter into 2 square, 8-inch, greased cake pans or Pyrex baking dishes (or a 13 x 9 x 2" pan.) Bake in preheated, 350°F oven for 30 to 35 minutes – for the 2 square pans – both pans in the oven at same time. For the oblong pan, bake 40 to 45 minutes or until toothpick inserted in center comes out clean. Cool cake in pan on wire rack. Best to use the cake when it is slightly frozen – about 30 minutes in the freezer. Cut cake into bars – 1.5 x 3.5". Put bottom-side of each bar facing up on waxed paper. Spread bottom halves with the Twinkle Filling and put together with an un-frosted bar – sandwich style. Wrap in small plastic sandwich bags or snack-size bags. Seal and date. Freeze up to one year – or refrigerate up to 2 weeks. Makes about 24 cream-filled cakes.

YELLOW COLONIAL CAKE – *Like Sanders*

For over a year, I tested from-scratch recipes for a perfect, yellow, light-as-a-feather layer cake, like the famous Detroit bakery, Fred Sanders, offered. Finally, this recipe developed and is now a successful representation of what a little effort can offer at home. Many caterers have complemented me on the recipe after they've used it. The recipe should be prepared with a counter-top-type electric mixer. But it may be cut in half you wish to use a portable hand-held mixer. Let me emphasize that you must use only BUTTER and your granulated sugar must be SIFTED before measuring! As well, the flour must be sifted, even though the bag it comes in says it has already been sifted. Sift it again! The beating time is also crucial, or the cake will be hard and dry. Don't begrudge one moment of the beating time required.

¾ cup (1 ½ sticks) real butter
1 ½ cups sifted granulated sugar
1 teaspoon each: vanilla and lemon juice
2 large eggs
2 ½ cups sifted flour
2 ½ teaspoons baking powder
1 teaspoon salt
1 cup whole milk

Cream butter with electric mixer on medium speed until light and fluffy. Add sifted sugar a little at a time, continuing to beat. Beat in vanilla and lemon juice, adding the eggs one at a time. Beat 4 minutes, rotating bowl in the opposite direction that the beaters are turning. Stop beaters periodically to scrape down sides and bottom of bowl, and to clean batter from the beaters. Resume beating. DO NOT UNDER BEAT this batter. Combine flour, baking powder and salt; adding mixture alternately to batter, with milk – beginning and ending with flour mixture – and continuing to beat for 4 minutes with last addition. Pour batter into 2 greased and floured, 9-inch cake pans. Bake in preheated 350°F oven for 30 to 35 minutes – placing pans on center rack with 2 inches between them, so the heat circulates evenly around the pans during baking – until cake begins to pull away from sides of pans. Cool in pans on wire rack for 30 minutes. Then remove 1 layer onto a round platter and frost the top; place it in the freezer for 10 minutes before placing 2nd layer on top and completing the frosting application. Makes 2 layers – 9 inches each.

LUNCHBOX BROWNIES with FUDGE CAKE ICING

This is a brownie cake recipe that makes up like a Texas-type sheet-cake, but comes out like a moist, chewy brownie; because you pour the warm frosting over the warm brownies as soon as you take them out of the oven. The frosting forces the brownies to "fall". When they have cooled, and are cut into squares, they have a custardy texture, rather than a cake texture. Originally, I developed this recipe for a bakery in Algonac, MI where we lived many years ago. We were in what my good friend, Bob Allison, once referred to as "Beautiful Downtown Pearl Beach" – a town so small that our City Hall was over a phone booth and if we'd have had a Howard Johnson's, they would've only had one flavor!

The brownie batter:

2 cups each: sugar and flour
1 cup each: water and margarine
6 tablespoons unsweetened cocoa
1/3 cup real buttermilk, *do not use sour milk for this*
2 eggs
1 teaspoon baking soda
¼ teaspoon salt
1 teaspoon vanilla

Stir the sugar and flour together in large mixing bowl and set aside. In 1 ½-quart sauce pan, put the water, margarine and cocoa together, stirring until smooth and cocoa has dissolved. Bring just to a bubble – without letting it boil, so it won't scorch – and immediately pour the hot mixture over the sugar and flour, beating it on medium speed with an electric mixer until smooth. Add buttermilk, beating for 2 minutes on medium. Beat in eggs, soda, salt and vanilla until blended. Pour batter into greased 10 x 17 x 2.5" pan (or 13 x 10 x 2" pan for thicker bars.) Bake at 375°F for only 20 minutes.

While the brownies are in the oven, you should be preparing the icing this way:

FUDGE CAKE ICING

In the same 1 ½-quart sauce pan in which you melted the first mixture of chocolate, etc. – combine 1/3 cup whole milk (not buttermilk, this time) with 1/3 cup margarine, 2 tablespoons unsweetened cocoa powder, 3 tablespoons packed brown sugar and a dash of salt. Bring to a boil, stirring constantly. Let it boil gently for half a minute. Remove from heat. Beat in 1-pound powdered sugar until smooth. Beat in 1 teaspoon vanilla. Stir in 1 cup broken walnuts or pecans (which, by the way, really "makes" it!) Keep the icing warm until brownies are out of oven, using the top of a double boiler over simmering water, or on lowest heat possible on top of stove.

Remove brownies from oven and, at once, pour the icing over the warm brownies. Cut brownies into bars when slightly cool. Makes about 36 bars.

DEVIL'S FOOD BUNDT CAKE

18-ounce box devil's food cake mix
4-ounce package instant chocolate pudding powder
4 eggs
1 cup water (for deeper, darker batter – use 1 cup cold, strong, black coffee)
½ cup oil

Combine all ingredients, one at a time, as listed, beating each addition thoroughly with mixer on medium speed. Pour into greased and floured 9 ½" or 10" Bundt pan (or angel food pan) and bake at 350°F for 50 minutes – or until it "tests" done. Cool right-side-up in pan for 45 minutes. Invert onto serving platter. Drizzle with my Simple Chocolate Cake Glaze (below) or dust in sifted powdered sugar. Serves 8 to 10.

MISS DISGRACED CALIFORNIA PARTY CAKE – *aka: Miss Grace Fudge Ring Cake* – to the above batter, stir in, as the last ingredients: one 6-ounce package butterscotch morsel chips, one 6-ounce package semi-sweet chocolate chips and one 4-ounce package well-chopped pecans. When thoroughly combined with batter, continue as recipe (above) otherwise directs.

SIMPLE CHOCOLATE CAKE GLAZE

2 tablespoons unsweetened cocoa powder
5 teaspoons, cold black coffee
1 tablespoon each: oil and light corn syrup
1 cup powdered sugar
dash of salt

Combine ingredients in a small saucepan and cook over low heat, stirring constantly for 3 to 4 minutes or until mixture becomes smooth and cocoa turns to liquid when combined with the other ingredients. Remove from heat and beat in powdered sugar and salt until smooth. Drizzle over cooled Devil's Food Bundt Cake (above.) Keep refrigerated when not being served.

WASHINGTON APPLE CAKE

The Captain Whidbey Inn (Coupeville, WA) is about a 90-minute drive by car from Seattle. It is a wilderness lodge on Whidbey Island, which attracts weekenders looking for peace and quiet – as well as those wanting good seafood dishes, which is the Inn's specialty. However, as a lovely ending to a beautiful meal, this is one dessert that I cannot resist sharing with you.

3 eggs
2 cups sugar
1 cup corn oil
2 cups flour
2 teaspoon cinnamon
1 teaspoon baking soda
½ teaspoon salt
2 teaspoons vanilla
1 ½ cups chopped walnuts
1 quart *(about 5 medium-sized)*, peeled and thinly-sliced, tart, cooking apples

With an electric mixer on medium speed, beat eggs until thick and lemon-colored (about 4 minutes.) Add sugar and oil. Set aside while you sift flour, cinnamon, soda and salt together. Stir this into egg mixture until all particles are thoroughly moistened. With mixer on lowest speed, add in vanilla and continue beating about 1 minute, thoroughly blending the ingredients. Stir in the nuts. Spread apples in a greased 9 x 13 x 2" baking pan. Pour batter over apples, spreading it evenly to cover bottom of pan. Bake at 350°F for 1 hour or until toothpick inserted in center comes out clean. Cool in pan on wire rack for 30 minutes. Spread top of cake with Apple Cake Icing (below.)

APPLE CAKE ICING – Beat 2 packages (3 ounces each) cream cheese until light and fluffy. Beat in 4 tablespoons melted butter or margarine, 1 teaspoon lemon juice and about 2 cups powdered sugar – or sufficient to give a good spreading consistency to the icing. Spread over cooled cake, which serves 10 to 12 nicely.

GERMAN CHOCOLATE CAKE ICING

No matter what chocolate cake recipe you use, whether it is a boxed mix or "from-scratch" batter, the best way to prepare this traditional dessert cake is to have 2 baked and cooled, 9-inch layers ready to assemble with the following icing:

2/3 cup sugar
2/3 cup canned evaporated milk
2 raw egg yolks
1/3 cup (6 tablespoons) butter or margarine
1 teaspoon vanilla
1 1/3 cup coconut
4 ounces (1 cup) chopped pecans

In a sauce pan, combine sugar, milk, egg yolks and butter or margarine. Cook and stir constantly over medium-high heat until mixture comes to just the start of a boil. Quickly remove pan from heat. Stir in vanilla. Using an electric mixer on low-speed, beat icing until it begins to thicken (about 5 minutes), increasing mixer speed to medium-high. When it has a spreading consistency, stir in coconut and then pecans. Spread icing only between the 2 layers and then over the top of the cake. Do not attempt to frost the sides of the cake. Chill cake about an hour before cutting to serve. Serves 8.

IACOCCA CAKE – *Beer Fudge Spice Cake*

From my "Ask Your Neighbor" recipe journal, I offered this cake to Bob Allison's listeners (October 1972), in response to a listener's request for a good, rich, feathery-light spice cake made with beer.

9-ounce box devil's food cake mix
1 envelope Dream Whip powder
1 teaspoon apple pie spice powder
½ cup light beer
4 tablespoons oil
2 eggs

Combine dry ingredients in one bowl. Combine liquid ingredients in another bowl; then, beat liquids into dry mixture with electric mixer on high-speed for about 4 minutes. Pour into greased and floured 9-inch layer pan or 10-inch, fluted-rim, Pyrex pie plate. Bake at 350°F for 40 minutes or until toothpick inserted in center comes out clean. Cool in pan 15 minutes. Cover with topping and then drizzle with frosting (recipes below) and decorate with walnut halves.

IACOCCA CAKE TOPPING: mix well – ½ cup chopped walnuts, 1 tablespoon sugar and ½ teaspoon cinnamon. Sprinkle over layer before applying frosting (below.)

IACOCCA CAKE FROSTING: combine, in top of double boiler, over simmering water – 6 ounces semi-sweet chocolate chips, 1 ounce (solid) unsweetened chocolate, 1/3 cup Half-&-Half light cream and 2 tablespoons light corn syrup. Stir until melted and smooth (about 12 to 15 minutes.) Beat in 1 ½ cups powdered sugar. Drizzle over topping-covered layer (above.)

One of the best recipes that I ever had was for a brownie mix that kept very well in a covered container in the refrigerator. The brownies were moist and rich and fudgy, like those of the Hostess company – only better! Or so the kids said!

HOPELESS BROWNIE MIX

5 cups sugar
3 cups flour
2 cups unsweetened baking cocoa
1 tablespoon baking powder
1 tablespoon salt
3 ½ cups Crisco

In a large bowl, thoroughly stir together everything but the Crisco. Cut in the Crisco until the mixture resembles gravel. Store in covered container up to 6 weeks in the refrigerator. Freeze it up to 6 months. To measure, lightly spoon mix into measuring cup and level off with flat side of a knife. Makes about 14 cups mix. It will look like a mess of wet sand when you've mixed it all together – but it makes beautiful brownies, sufficient to prepare five 8-inch square pans.

To make the brownies: *beat 2 eggs, 1 teaspoon vanilla and 2/4 cups brownie mix. Stir until nearly smooth. Add ½ cup chopped nuts, if you wish. Spread evenly in a greased 8-inch square pan. Bake at 350°F for 30 minutes or until toothpick inserted in center comes out clean. Cool in pan. Dust in powdered sugar or frost with my Fudge Icing (see Index.) Makes 16 2-inch squares.*

SHARE-A-LEASE BROWNIES

2 ounces (2 squares) unsweetened, solid, baking chocolate
1/3 cup butter or margarine
2/3 cup flour
½ teaspoon baking powder
¼ teaspoon salt
2 eggs
1 cup sugar
1 teaspoon vanilla
½ cup chopped walnuts, optional

Melt chocolate and butter. Mix flour, baking powder and salt. Beat eggs about 2 minutes on medium speed of electric mixer. Gradually add in sugar. Beat in chocolate mixture and vanilla. Mix in flour mixture. (Add nuts, if you wish.) Spread batter evenly over bottom of a greased, 8-inch square baking pan. Bake at 350°F for 25 minutes or until it tests done. Cool in pan. Dust in powdered sugar or frost in my Fudge Icing (see Index.) Cut into 2-inch squares. Makes 16 pieces.

BETTER COOKERY BROWNIE MIX

If you like working with boxed mixes, but wish for a more basic recipe for your brownies – then, try this. It can't be simpler! Trust me! Use only the 2 brand-name products I suggest for perfect results!

1 cup Nestlé's Chocolate Quick Powder
1 cup Bisquick biscuit mix

Mix both ingredients well together. You can multiply the mixture per the amount you wish to use; but, because it is only a cup of each, I prepare it as I need it. *To use this 2-cup brownie mix, add to it:*

2 tablespoons each: oil and water
1 egg
1 teaspoon vanilla

Beat for 2 minutes with electric mixer on medium speed. Spread mixture evenly over bottom of a greased, 9 x 12 x 2" pan (for thin brownies) and bake at 350°F for 25 to 30 minutes or until toothpick inserted in center comes out clean. For thicker brownies, use an 8 x 8 x 2" pan and bake at 350° for 30 to 35 minutes or until it tests done. Cool and dust in powdered sugar, or frost with my Fudge Icing (see Index.) Cut into squares. The 9 x 12-inch pan yields 24 squares, and the 8-inch pan makes 16 squares.

SAUCEPAN PEANUT BUTTER BROWNIES

Decades ago, when the Mills Bakery truck came through the neighborhood, and you wanted him to stop at your house, you'd put a card in the window, reading "Mills". The assortment of freshly baked goodies was overwhelming. One of their specialties (and this goes back to the late 40s) was a chewy peanut butter bar that I was told was NOT baked. This is as close as I could come to the original.

1 cup butter or margarine (2 sticks)
1/3 cup peanut butter
1 ½ cups flour
1 teaspoon vanilla
1 cup dry-roasted peanuts, chopped
2 cups sugar
1 cup water

In large mixing bowl, combine butter, peanut butter, flour, vanilla and nuts, mixing thoroughly. Set aside. In a 1 ½-quart sauce pan combine sugar and water and cook, stirring constantly, until it comes to a boil. Turn heat to low or sufficient to keep mixture just below a boil, continuing to cook and stir to a "hard ball" stage (when a few drops of the syrup form a hard ball when dropped into a glass of very cold water or 250°F on a candy thermometer.) Pour syrup slowly into flour mixture, beating it on medium speed with electric mixer until well combined. Stir until it thickens. Pour into a greased 11 x 7" baking pan (sometimes called a brownie pan.) Chill until set; then, cut into 24 small bars.

BAKERY BROWNIES *(Toronto, Ontario)*

In one of the malls in Toronto, Ontario, there was a bakery that offered beverages along with your choice of the day's selections. These brownies are close to what I sampled there.

1 cup each: granulated sugar and packed brown sugar
2 tablespoons unsweetened cocoa powder
2/3 cup butter or margarine
4 eggs
1 2/3 cups flour
½ cup chopped walnuts, optional

Combine sugars and cocoa, stirring thoroughly. Add softened butter, beating well. Add eggs, one at a time, beating well with each addition. Blend in flour – and nuts, if you choose to use them. When you have a smooth batter, spread it evenly over bottom of a greased 9 x 12 x 2" baking pan. Bake at 350°F for 20 to 25 minutes or until toothpick inserted in center comes out clean. Cool in pan. Frost with my Fudge Icing (see Index) while still warm, if you wish – or dust in powdered sugar. Cut into 36 squares.

SINFULLY RICH!

OATMEAL MUFFIN COOKIES *(Toronto, Ontario)*

These were a featured item in a Toronto bakery – they are made like muffins, but taste like a cookie.

2 cups old-fashioned rolled oats
1 cup packed brown sugar
tablespoons margarine or butter, melted
pinch of salt
1 tablespoon vanilla
½ teaspoon cinnamon
1 cup chopped walnuts or pecans, optional*

*Chocolate (or butterscotch) chips may be substituted for the walnuts or pecans – or may be added in addition to the nuts, allowing a 12-ounce package for this recipe.

Mix oatmeal and brown sugar thoroughly. Work in butter until it becomes intimately acquainted with the other ingredients. Add everything else. Spoon into 12 greased and floured muffin wells. Pack the mixture down firmly with the back of spoon. Bake at 350°F for exactly 16 minutes. Remove pan to wire rack. Allow cookies to cool in the pan about 1 hour. Loosen with the tip of a sharp knife to remove from pan. Makes 1 dozen.

DISGUSTINGLY DELICIOUS!

COOKIES AND CANDIES

COOKIES AND CANDIES really bring out the little child within us all. There is something almost rewarding about simple confections that the food industry has also been able to capitalize on the products of this division with great marketing success. The 1ˢᵗ bakery marketing efforts in the American frontier days included delicacies of French origin, Danish breads and cakes, Austrian strudel and pies of truly colonial persuasion. The candies, which were originally for special religious of observances, have been taken into the fold of a prospering industry and have continued, despite repercussions of the critics, skepticism of sugar and artificial sweeteners, to please the public.

THE NAMES OF THE BRANDS that we remember from our pasts and will recall of our present experiences with confections include Hostess Twinkies, Reese's Peanut Butter Cups, Mallow Cups, Cracker Jack, Niagara Falls and Mackinac Island fudges, Sanders Candy Company, O Henry bars, Baby Ruth, Mr. Goodbar, Life Savers, Tootsie Rolls, Goobers Chocolate Covered Peanuts, Archway, Pepperidge Farm, Oreo and Girl Scout cookies, Stuckey's Pecan Brownies, Keebler Double Chip cookies, Chipperoos, Fig Newtons, and so many more.

When I compiled my favorite cookie and candy recipes for this section, I was really torn between what to keep and what to leave out. I wanted to share with you every single wonderful memory of a pleasing product, you could hopefully imitate in your own kitchen, as a compliment to the original. The array of recipes with which I've been working [since the early 60s], was so good that I had a difficult time deciding which would be the best ones to offer you here.

In cookie-baking, the spirit of "reward" is still there, as it was when we were youngsters, and remains a tradition – we will always find a place and a reason for having a cookie jar in the kitchen. The candy making recipes are, likewise, pleasing imitations of those products I have most enjoyed and those my readers have requested over the years. You will probably want to enjoy trying every one of these recipes – especially at holiday times and when ordinary days should feel like a holiday, too!

Out of the Ordinary!

Years ago, when our 5 children were still in the sandbox set, holding tricycle symposiums in my flowerbeds and declaring our yard a national park for every child in the township, I had this ridiculous maternal notion that a cookie could cure countless conditions. So, I was wrong! Cookies did not remedy a Barbie doll with a missing string in her back or a G.I. Joe without a backpack in the "complete accessory kit", as promised in the catalog. But special cookies from a warm and sunny, semi-cluttered kitchen, did take the "bite" out of a scraped knee and the "owie" out of a bump on the head – and even though it wouldn't bring the pet turtle back to life, a cookie and a kiss from Mom made the world seem a little bit brighter. I doubt that things have changed very much with mothers and their children since my own grew up. Even now, when the boy's come home from college and our daughter and son-in-law stop by, or when our youngest daughter breezes in and out between football games and slumber parties – they all check the cookie jar with the same delight as they expressed when they were youngsters.

FAMOUS NAMELESS CHOCOLATE CHIP COOKIES

My original version had a dozen ingredients. Look at how I shortened it! Still, the results are identical! An interesting note on the popularity of these cookies… A few years ago, [around 1980], I received a letter from Dr. Joyce Brothers, in which this was the only recipe she requested. I sent her the longer, from-scratch version. I hope she has a chance to try this version. One thing I noted about the original cookie is that it has a "sugary" consistency to it. It's almost like a confection. When Amos, himself, was interviewed in Family Circle magazine a few years ago, he offered them the recipe for making his kind of cookie at home. I tried that recipe 3 times and it was NOT one bit like his famous cookies. To be like his product, the cookie must be firm, a little crisp, but not dry, and have a definite brown-sugar-flavor and crunchy-texture to it. You can add chopped raisins to the finished batter and you can double the chocolate chips — but do be sure, if you are imitating the original product, that you include some pecan halves, as well as chopped pecans, for these really "make" the cookie!

18-ounce box yellow cake mix
2 boxes (3 ¾ ounces each) butterscotch pudding powder (NOT instant)
1 ¼ cups mayonnaise
12-ounce package semi-sweet chocolate chips
4-ounce package each: walnut chips and pecan halves

Mix the dry pudding powder with the dry cake mix in a roomy bowl. Combine thoroughly, using a slotted spoon or large meat fork. Then, mix in the mayonnaise; but, don't use an electric mixer! When well-blended, add the chips and nuts. Drop by rounded spoonful, 2 inches apart on an ungreased cookie sheet. Bake 12 to 14 minutes at 350°F. It's important to permit the cookies to cool at least 2 minutes on the baking sheet before moving them, carefully, to paper towels to continue cooling. These are very fragile while warm, but tend to firm-up while cooling. Makes 4 ½ dozen. Keep at room temperature in a tightly covered container for up to a month! They freeze poorly. *Note: If weather is very humid, you'll note that these become quite limp if they stand out, uncovered, for any length of time. If you store the cooled, firm cookies in an airtight container they should remain crisp despite humid weather.*

OATMEAL COOKIES

Cream 1 cup butter with 1 cup granulated sugar and ½ cup packed brown sugar until light and fluffy. Beat in 1 egg, 1 2/3 cups flour, ¾ teaspoon baking soda, a pinch of baking powder, a dash of salt, 1 teaspoon cinnamon and a dash of nutmeg. Stir in 1 ½ cups rolled oats and 1 teaspoon lemon extract. When you have a smooth dough, refrigerate it for 1 hour. Make 1-inch balls and place them 2 inches apart on a lightly greased cookie sheet. Press balls down with the bottom of a glass, greased once and dipped in sugar each time you flatten a cookie. Place a raisin in the center of each cookie. Bake at 350° for 10 to 12 minutes or until slightly browned. Cool on baking sheet for 2 minutes before removing to completely cool on paper towels. Makes 4 dozen cookies.

PEPPER-ITCH ARM MINT MILLIONOS

When we were living in California, it was our pleasure to have, as next-door neighbors, the nicest couple you would ever hope to meet, Dick and Betty Davis. They had come to California from Vermont and had been with the Pepperidge Farm company a long time. Dick had been involved with some of the product developments for Pepperidge Farms and Betty was an executive with the company. I only wish they could've given me a clue on the marvelous cookies that Mrs. Rudkin had developed – but, I was left to second-guessing. Starting with the cookie dough:

½ pound butter
1 ¼ cups sugar
½ teaspoon salt
2 teaspoons vanilla
2 eggs, beaten (about ½ cupful)
1-pound box cornstarch

Beat the butter until light and fluffy on medium speed of electric mixer. Gradually add sugar, a little at a time, beating until smooth and creamy. Add salt, vanilla and eggs. Beat 2 minutes. Remove beaters and work in all the cornstarch with your hands until you have a smooth dough. Drop by small spoonful, 2 inches apart, on paper-lined baking sheets – slightly shaping the spoonful of dough to a flat, oblong, oval form with your fingers. These will spread A LOT!!! Bake at 400°F for 8 minutes or until they are slightly browned just around the edges. Immediately, remove carefully from baking sheet to completely cool on paper towels. Makes 4 dozen single cookies.

They are very fragile while hot! While the cookies are cooling, prepare the mint filling (below.)

12-ounce package semi-sweet chocolate chips
2 ounces solid bitter baking chocolate
4 ounces German Sweet Chocolate bar
3 tablespoons melted paraffin
1 tablespoon peppermint extract

Place all but the extract in the top of a double boiler over gently simmering water. Stir until smooth and melted. Add extract. Remove from heat. Apply the warm chocolate mixture, by spoonful, to the flat side of a cookie and at once make a sandwich out of it by covering it with the flat side of another cookie. Let cookies cool at room temperature until chocolate is set. Then refrigerate in covered container. Makes 2 dozen sandwich cookies.

NEAT MAN MARKET'S FRANGO MINT COOKIES

When Neiman Marcus sells its famous mint-chip filled cookies, you can depend on paying a very good price for them. When I bought some in Chicago [1982], I paid $4 for a 1-pound bag! In my next life, I'm going to eat nothing but Frango Mint Cookies, Sanders' hot fudge sundaes, pizza and strawberry pie from Big Boy!

Begin with the same chocolate mixture that you'd prepare for my "Piper Itch Arm Mint Millionos" Cookies (see Index.) When the chocolate mixture is nicely melted and smooth, in the top of the double boiler (as that recipe directs), pour the mixture into a well-greased, 9-inch square pan. Refrigerate it until it has hardened. Break it up with a hammer into small bits, irregular in shape and size – just as the original is made. To make about 100 cookies, prepare the cookie dough as follows:

1-pound butter
1 cup granulated sugar
2 eggs
2 teaspoons vanilla
4 cups flour
¼ teaspoon salt

Cream butter with sugar. Beat in eggs, vanilla and half of flour. Add salt and work into a smooth dough, using medium speed of electric mixer. Remove beaters and work in remaining flour by hand. Next, work in ALL the broken chocolate bits. Drop by a measuring teaspoonful onto an ungreased cookie sheet, 1 ½ inches apart. Bake at 375°F for 10 minutes. Remove at once to cool on waxed paper.

Out-of-the-Ordinary!

CHOCOLATE CHIP ICE-BOX HOME-STYLE COOKIES

18-ounce package yellow cake mix
1 cup mayonnaise
1 envelope Dream Whip powder
12-ounce package semi-sweet chocolate chips
1 cup broken pecans (these really make the cookies!)
½ cup raisins (optional)

With electric mixer on medium speed, combine first 3 ingredients, beating 4 to 5 minutes or until dough is smooth and comes away from the sides of the bowl. Dump in chips and nuts. Work into dough with a sturdy spoon. Shape dough into 1-inch balls. Arrange balls 2 inches apart on ungreased baking sheet. Bake at 400°F for 12 to 14 minutes or until delicately browned. Let cool on baking sheet 1 to 2 minutes before attempting to remove. These are quite fragile while still warm. Remove carefully with a pancake Turner to continue cooling on paper towels. Makes about 5 dozen cookies.

SPICE CAKE MIX COOKIES

18-ounce box spice cake mix
2 envelopes Dream Whip powder
1 ¼ cups mayonnaise
¼ cup bottled apple butter
½ cup cornstarch

Using medium speed of electric mixer, beat all ingredients about 3 to 4 minutes. Shape into 1-inch balls. Roll balls in granulated sugar, placing 3 inches apart on ungreased baking sheet – they'll puff-up during baking, like a soft cookie; but, then, they settle down to a thin, crispy wafer. Bake 12 to 14 minutes at 400°F, or until nicely browned. Cool on sheets for 1 minute before removing gently with pancake-turner to continue cooling on paper towels or waxed paper until very crispy. Makes 4 dozen.

COOL WHIP COOKIES

18-ounce box yellow cake mix
2 cups Cool Whip
1 egg
2 cups powdered sugar, in a shallow dish

Combine the cake mix and Cool Whip with the egg, beating until smooth. Drop dough by teaspoonful into the dish of powdered sugar, coating the dough evenly on all sides. Place the sugar-covered dough on a lightly greased baking sheet, 2 inches apart. Bake at 350° for 10 minutes or until the tops of the cookies begin to crack. Let cool on cookie sheet about 1 minute. Remove carefully to continue cooling on paper towels or waxed paper. Makes about 3 dozen cookies. *NOTE: you can vary the flavor by using any flavor cake mix, so that it's equal to the 18-ounce-sized box. Strawberry and lemon flavors make delightful variations, with the remaining ingredients the same, as well as baking temperature and time.*

PARADISE CAKES – *Home-Style Cookies – Like Archway*

1-pound butter, softened
6 tablespoons each – powdered and granulated sugars
1 teaspoon vanilla or almond extract
4 cups flour
1-pound shelled pecans, chopped.

Cream butter for 5 minutes on medium speed of electric mixer. Add remaining ingredients, one at a time, continuing to beat. Shape into small marble-sized balls (6 dozen), placing 2 inches apart on ungreased baking sheets. Bake for 20 to 22 minutes at 325°F, or until set, but not browned. While hot, roll each cookie in powdered sugar, about 3 times.

GLOREO SANDWICH COOKIES

When the Washington (DC) Post once interviewed the Nabisco people to ask how they felt about a Michigan housewife, claiming she could imitate their famous chocolate sandwich cookie at home, they were very insistent that it was impossible! Well, I felt if Hydrox could come close, so could I – and I gave the big food company a taste of their own product! To my readers overseas, while I was publishing my monthly Secret Recipe Report, it was a blessing, or so they said!

The cookie dough:

18-ounce package devil's food cake mix
2 eggs, plus 2 tablespoons water
2 tablespoons cooking oil
½ cup bitter cocoa powder

Blend all ingredients together until you can shape the dough into a smooth ball. Let it stand 20 minutes, loosely covered. Form dough into marble-sized balls and place 2 inches apart on greased cookie sheets. Flatten each with smooth bottom of drinking glass, greased once and dipped into Nestlé's Quick powder. (Or use any sweetened, chocolate drink powder.) Bake at 400°F for 8 minutes. Remove cookies at once from baking sheet to paper towels – quickly, flatten each cookie with the back of pancake turner. Makes 96 cookies. Cool for 20 minutes. Prepare the following mixture as directed:

The cookie filling:

1 envelope unflavored gelatin
¼ cup cold water
1 cup Crisco
1 teaspoon vanilla
1 pound, plus 1 cup powdered sugar

Soften gelatin in cold water. Place in a heat-proof cup, in pan of hot water, until gelatin is transparent. Meanwhile, beat Crisco until fluffy, adding vanilla and sugar a little at a time. Beat in gelatin mixture when it is completely cooled, but not "set" or firm. This is used to give the filling stability – as well as protein! When cooled, shape filling into 1-inch balls. Place each between 2 bottom-sides of cooled cookies, pressing gently until filling has spread to the edge of the cookies and rounded-out like the originals. Makes 4 dozen sandwich cookies.

SPANISH PECAN COOKIES

Neiman Marcus, Sanger Harris and Skaggs-Albertson (Dallas, TX), once had a very exclusive recipe for a unique cookie – expensive, but worth it, if you could afford that kind of luxury. When one of my family of readers described the cookie to me and, also, sent a sample – I had the challenge of trying to duplicate them, but the mystery of why these had a hollow center was quite a stumbling block. After dozens and dozens of tests it finally occurred to me that baking soda would create a quick rise in the dough and perhaps this would work. And so it did!

¼ pound butter
½ cup Crisco
2 ¼ cups powdered sugar (do not sift it)
1 tablespoon vanilla
1 teaspoon salt
2 cups (SIFTED BEFORE MEASURED) all-purpose flour
2 teaspoons cornstarch
¼ teaspoon baking soda
4 ounces well-chopped pecans

Cream butter and Crisco for 5 minutes on medium speed of electric mixer. It must be as light as a cloud. Don't begrudge one second of those 5 minutes! Then, gradually beat in the powdered sugar a little at a time. Add the vanilla, salt and half of the flour; then, remove the beaters. Work in remaining flour, sifted twice with the cornstarch and the soda. Work in the pecans. Shape dough into 1-inch balls and place on ungreased cookie sheets, 2 inches apart. Bake at 325°F, for exactly 18 minutes. Dip top of each warm cookie into additional powdered sugar, in a shallow dish. Let cookies cool completely before storing them in a covered container at room temperature. Makes about 3 ½ dozen!

BAKERY SUGAR COOKIES

1-pound butter
1 ½ cups granulated sugar
2 eggs
6 cups sifted all-purpose flour
2 teaspoons baking soda
2 teaspoons cream of Tartar

Cream butter with electric mixer on medium speed until light and fluffy. Gradually beat in sugar in small portions, beating 2 minutes after last addition. Beat in eggs, one at a time. Beat in 2 cups of the flour, soda and cream of Tartar, beating 2 minutes. Remove beaters. Work in remaining flour with a sturdy spoon. Shape into 1-inch balls, placed 2 inches apart on an ungreased cookie sheet. Grease bottom of a drinking glass (just once) and dip glass bottom into sugar, pressing down each ball of dough to a nice even patty. Dip glass into sugar with each cookie pressed, but do not re-grease the glass again. Bake cookies at 350°F for 13 to 15 minutes or until delicately browned. Allow to cool on pan for only a minute. Remove carefully to paper towels to let cookies cool completely. Store in a covered container at room temperature. Makes about 2 ½ dozen cookies. *NOTE: placing half of a walnut or pecan on top of each cookie before baking them really gives them a professional bakery look!*

CORNSTARCH COOKIES

These are delicate and crisp and very rich. There is no flour in this dough – which is, basically, from how I make my Pepper-Itch Arms Mint Millionos.

1-pound butter
2 ½ cups granulated sugar
1 teaspoon salt
1 tablespoon almond extract or vanilla
4 eggs, beaten well – about 1 cup full
2 boxes (1 pound each) cornstarch

Beat the butter until fluffy, adding sugar gradually. Beat in salt, vanilla, eggs and 1 box of cornstarch. Beat until smooth. Remove beaters and work in remaining cornstarch with a sturdy mixing spoon. Chill the dough about 1 hour. Drop dough by teaspoonful, 2 inches apart on an ungreased baking sheet. Flatten each a little with your fingers, pressing a raisin or walnut-half or pecan-half into the center of each. Bake at 400°F for 8 minutes or until the edges of the cookies begin to brown a bit. They are very fragile while hot. Remove carefully to cool on paper towels. Makes 7 dozen.

PAINTBRUSH COOKIES

The JL Hudson's store (downtown Detroit) used to sell these at Christmas time on their main floor near the Farmer Street entrance. Well worth re-creating at home – even if it isn't Christmas!

The cookie dough:

Sift together, twice, 2 ¼ cups flour and 1 teaspoon baking powder – set aside. Cream ¾ cup (1 ½ sticks) butter until light and fluffy, adding ½ teaspoon salt, ½ cup granulated sugar and ½ cup packed brown sugar – then, beat in 1 egg and 1 teaspoon vanilla. Add flour mixture a little at a time until well blended. Roll out and cut with lightly floured cookie cutters. Arrange cookies on lightly oiled baking sheets about 2 inches apart. Use any shape cutters you wish. Meanwhile prepare…

The cookie paint:

Mix together, in a small bowl, 3 beaten egg yolks and 4 tablespoons water. Divide into 3 or 4 smaller containers and add a few drops of food coloring to each cup giving it a lighter color then you want the finished cookie to have, since baking will intensify the color. Use a small, watercolor paint brush to apply designs, print names, sayings, etc., to the top of each cookie. Bake at 400°F or 8 to 10 minutes or until cookies are delicately browned. Remove from pan to cool on paper towels. Makes 5 dozen.

CHOCOLATE CHIP COOKIE BRITTLE

Combine ¼ pound butter and ½ cup Crisco, creaming for 5 minutes until fluffy. Add 2 ¼ cups powdered sugar, 2 teaspoons cornstarch, ¼ teaspoon baking soda and 4 ounces chopped pecans. Work in 1 cup biscuit mix, 1 cup granulated sugar and ½ cup water. Next, work in a 12-ounce package of chocolate chips. Pat into bottom of two, well-greased, 9 x 12" baking pans. Bake one pan at a time in the center of the middle rack of a 350°F oven for 25 to 30 minutes or until "set". While warm, dust top with powdered sugar and cut into squares. Let cool in pan. Remove and place squares and plastic food bags. Seal, label and date. These keep up to a year so you can put some aside for Christmas or even next Easter. Remove from freezer 30 minutes before serving. Makes 6 dozen 1" squares.

BRAVE KID'S CHOCOLATE CHIP COOKIES

"DAVID'S COOKIES", a very popular cookie company in New York, has been producing a double chocolate chip confection that is so rich, memorably delicious and very expensive – as cookies go on the competitive scale – but worth it, believe me! Chances are this product will be giving Famous Amos a run for his money! This is my make-at-home version.

18-ounce package devil's food cake mix (Pillsbury brand preferred)
2 ¾-ounce package finely ground pecans
3-ounce package instant chocolate pudding powder
¼ cup sour cream
1 cup mayonnaise
12-ounce package semi-sweet chocolate chips
3 ¼-ounce package pecans, coarsely broken into pieces

As listed above, combine the first 5 ingredients thoroughly, using an electric mixer. Work in chocolate chips and pecans, squeezing the dough in your hands. The heat from your hands will smooth out the dough; which, at first, will appear to be too dry and crumbly – but the more you work it, like a meatloaf, the better it gets. Drop by rounded tablespoonful onto ungreased baking sheets, 2 inches apart. Bake at 400°F for 12 minutes. Do not overbake! These are such a dark color to start with, that you can't be sure if they are over-baking just by looking at them. Some may burn on the bottom if you do not have the cookie sheet on the center rack, or if you leave them in a minute too long!

IMPORTANT: because the cookies are so fragile while hot, you must let them cool on the baking sheet for 2 minutes before moving them, carefully, onto paper towels to finish cooling. If you let them cool too long on the baking sheet, they may stick to it – return the cookie sheet to the oven for a few seconds to loosen the cookies. Makes 5 dozen.

FROST-'EM-BEFORE-YOU-BAKE-'EM COOKIES

Cut 2 ½ sticks margarine (1 ¼ cups) into bits in a big bowl and cream it with 1 ½ cups firmly packed brown sugar. Beat in 2 eggs. Add 3 ½ cups biscuit mix and 1 ½ cups all-purpose flour. Spread a 7-ounce package of coconut on a cookie sheet and place under broiler until lightly browned. Stir it into batter while still warm. Mix dough thoroughly and chill for 1 hour. Form 1-inch balls and place 2 inches apart on an ungreased cookie sheet. Flatten with greased glass bottom dipped in sugar. Before baking, spread each with a spoonful of frosting – prepared by melting 12-ounce package semi-sweet chocolate chips with 14-ounce can Eagle Brand milk over medium heat, stirring constantly until smooth. While icing is warm, apply to cookies. Bake at 300°F for 18 to 20 minutes or until icing is "set" and edge of cookie is browned. Remove at once from baking sheet. Makes about 4 dozen.

GREENFIELD VILLAGE-STYLE COOKIES

When you visit Greenfield Village (Dearborn, MI), where the Henry Ford Museum is also located, you may be greeted at the town hall with a reception of apple cider and spiced cookies before your tour of the various buildings and enjoy the historical retreat into America's past. Here's my version.

½ cup butter
1 cup sugar
1 egg
1 ¼ cup milk
½ teaspoon vanilla
2 ¼ cups flour
2 teaspoons baking powder
¼ teaspoon salt
½ teaspoon powdered mace
1 egg white, slightly beaten
1-ounce bottle colored cookie sprinkles

Cream butter and sugar. Add egg, milk and vanilla. Beat well. Stir flour with baking powder, salt and mace. Add to creamed mixture. Work into a smooth dough and chill for 1 hour. Shape into 1-inch balls on an ungreased cookie sheet. Then, flatten and brush each with a little slightly-beaten egg white and dust with the sprinkles. Bake at 375°F for 8 minutes or until slightly browned. Makes about 4 ½ dozen.

PATTER PAUL OUNCE BARS

Combine ½ pound butter or margarine with a 14-ounce can Eagle Brand milk and 2 teaspoons vanilla, mixing well. Cover and refrigerate for 4 hours. Next, beat in 2 pounds powdered sugar, a little at a time, until quite stiff in texture. Then, work in two 7-ounce packages of flaked coconut. Pat firmly into bottom of a greased jellyroll pan or 2 greased 9 x 13 x 2" pans. Chill until firm. Cut into 2 x 1" bars. Over simmering water, in the top of a double, melt a 12-ounce bag semi-sweet chocolate chips and 4 ounces Nestlé's Milk Chocolate with 3 tablespoons melted paraffin until smooth. Spear each bar with the tip of a knife. Dip to coat in warm chocolate, letting excess drip back into the pan. Air dry. Store at room temperature in a covered container for weeks. Keep away from humidity or steam.

NEAT MAN MARKET'S LEMON SQUARES

At a famous Texas department store you could, at one time, buy these very rich, very lemony squares for a good price. This is how I recreate these yummy treats at home – starting with the 1st layer:

½ cup (one stick) butter
¼ cup powdered sugar
1 cup flour

Preheat oven to 350°F. Prepare 1st layer – in a small mixing bowl, beat butter until creamy and add sugar gradually. Stir in flour. Beat 2 minutes. Pat mixture into bottom of a greased, 9-inch square pan. Bake for 15 minutes. Meanwhile, prepare 2nd layer:

2 eggs
1 cup sugar
2 teaspoons bottled lemon peel
2 tablespoons each: lemon juice and flour
½ teaspoon baking powder
powdered sugar for dusting

Using electric mixer, mix together eggs and sugar (added gradually), beating thoroughly on medium speed for 2 minutes. Beat in peel, juice, flour and baking powder. Pour over 1st layer, hot out of the oven. Return to bake another 25 minutes, or until a golden crust forms on top. Remove pan from oven and place on wire rack to cool. Cut into 25 squares. Dust in powdered sugar. Serve completely cooled.

GIRL'S SCOOT PEANUT BUTTER SANDWICH COOKIES

Beat well – 2 cups biscuit mix, 2 eggs, 2/3 cup packed brown sugar, 5 tablespoons peanut butter and 1 tablespoon vanilla. Make 6 dozen marble-sized balls. Place on ungreased cookie sheets and flatten each with the bottom of a glass, greased once and dipped in sugar. Do not re-grease the bottom of the glass, but do dip it into the sugar with each cookie flattened. Bake at 350°F for 6 to 8 minutes or until set, but not over-baked. Cool completely before filling with peanut butter icing (below.)

THE ICING: in a small sauce pan, bring to a boil, 1/3 cup milk, 1/3 cup dark corn syrup and ½ cup packed brown sugar. Stir constantly for 5 minutes on gentle simmer. Remove from heat and, at once, stir in 2/3 cup peanut butter and 1 cup powdered sugar. Beat with electric mixer on medium speed until smooth. Next, spread ½ teaspoon frosting on flat side of half the cookies. Press frosting flat with flat side of a second cookie, sandwich style. Makes 3 dozen sandwich cookies.

PEANUT BUTTER COOKIES – *Like you've never had before!*

¼ cup black coffee
1 teaspoon vinegar
2 teaspoons vanilla
2/3 cup oil
1 cup peanut butter
2 cups packed brown sugar
1 cup granulated sugar
3 eggs, beaten
4 cups flour
2 teaspoons baking powder
1 teaspoon baking soda
½ teaspoon salt

Combine everything in order listed, one at a time, in a roomy bowl – beating well after each addition. Work in the flour, baking powder, soda and salt in small portions until you have a smooth dough. Make 1-inch balls, placing them 2 inches apart on an ungreased baking sheet. Press balls down with the tines of a fork, creating a crisscross design on top of each. If fork sticks to dough, dip the fork in a bit of sugar before pressing each cookie. Bake at 400°F for 10 minutes or until nicely golden, but not over-baked. While cookies are still warm, frost them with my warm Fudge Icing (see Index.) Apply warmed icing to warm cookies and, when the icing sets and the cookies have cooled, you have a no-smear icing that will melt in your mouth. Icing is optional, but it makes them stand out! Yields 5 dozen cookies.

CRACKED-TOP GINGER COOKIES – *Like Archway's*

3-ounce box lemon pudding powder, not instant
18-ounce package spice cake mix
½ cup packed brown sugar
½ cup oil
2 tablespoons light corn syrup
2 eggs

As listed, beat all ingredients together thoroughly, adding each ingredient one at a time and beating well with each addition. Dough will be quite stiff. Roll into 1-inch balls. Coat in sugar. Place 2 inches apart on ungreased cookie sheet. Place a raisin or piece of walnut in the center of each ball. Do not flatten! Bake at 375°F for exactly 14 minutes. They will "crack" on top and look like Archway's Homestyle Cookies. Whether, or not, they taste the same…You be the judge! Makes about 3 dozen.

NATURAL VOLLEY GRANOLA

1 cup flaked coconut
4 cups old-fashioned Quaker Oats
1 cup wheat germ
2 cups well chopped walnuts
1 cup packed brown sugar
¼ cup dry milk powder
¼ cup sesame seed

¼ cup honey
1 tablespoon dark molasses
1/3 cup safflower or corn oil
¼ cup butter or margarine

Combine first 7 ingredients in large bowl, working them together thoroughly. Bring last 4 ingredients to boil in small sauce pan. Stir constantly and boil rapidly for 4 minutes. Working quickly, drizzle the hot syrup over the dry mixture and be certain every single piece of the mixture is coated in the syrup. Spread mixture over bottom of greased, shallow, roasting pan – about 12 x 17 x 2" – or use two 9 x 12 x 2" pans. Stir mixture every 5 minutes while baking it at 325°F for exactly 23 minutes. Remove to let mixture cool in pan on a wire rack for 1 hour. Break it up. Store in covered container at room temperature up to 3 months. Makes about 10 cups.

GRANOLA BARS

Combine thoroughly, in large mixing bowl: ¼ cup sesame seed, 2 cups old-fashioned Quaker Oats, ¼ cup dry milk powder, ½ cup wheat germ, ½ cup packed brown sugar, ½ cup shredded coconut and 1 cup well-chopped walnuts. In a small sauce pan, bring to a boil: 2 tablespoons margarine, 2 tablespoons oil, 1 ½ teaspoons dark molasses, ½ cup honey and a dash of salt. Let this boil hard for half a minute while you stir it constantly. Then reduce to a gentle boil for exactly 5 minutes – set your timer! Stir frequently. Pour over dry mixture, coating every single dry particle completely in syrup. Pack mix into a lightly greased jellyroll pan – 11 x 17 x 1". Bake at 250°F with pan on center rack of oven, for 35 minutes (almost drying it, rather than baking it.) Then turn on broiler heat, leaving the pan right where it is letting the top brown just slightly until you can see tiny bubbles here and there. About 1 minute will do it! Remove pan and let cool about 1 hour before cutting into bars. Oiling a pair of kitchen scissors is best way to cut it, as it has a sticky texture. Wrap in waxed paper, wiped in a bit of oil or sprayed with Pam. Makes 48 bars.

KEEP HERS DOUBLE CHIP COOKIES

Sold in supermarkets in paper sacks, the originals have remained the most popular of all commercially prepared cookies. At home – it's still a family favorite for all ages!

1-pound margarine, stick-type (4 sticks)
1-pound brown sugar
2 cups granulated sugar
4 eggs well beaten
2 teaspoons baking soda
1 teaspoon baking powder
½ teaspoon salt
8 ounces shredded coconut – oven toasted at 375°F until browned
1 teaspoon vanilla
6 to 7 cups of flour
12-ounce package each: semi-sweet chocolate chips and butterscotch chips
1 cup chopped walnuts or pecans
2 cups quick cooking oats
¼ cup corn oil

As listed, combine all ingredients in a large bowl. Add only enough of the flour that dough pulls away from sides of bowl and won't stick to your hands. Chill dough for 1 hour. Form into 1-inch balls on ungreased baking sheets, 2 inches apart. Flatten slightly. Bake at 400°F for 10 to 12 minutes. Remove from pan at once to cool completely on paper towels. Makes about 7 dozen. Freezes well up to 1 year.

Family favorites!

KEEP HERS GINGERSNAPS

Cream together ¾ cup butter or margarine and 1 cup packed brown sugar until light and fluffy. Add 1 egg and 1/3 cup dark molasses, beating 2 minutes on medium speed of electric mixer. Work in, as listed: 1 cup (nonfat) dry milk powder, ¼ teaspoon salt, 2 ½ cups rye flour, 2 ¼ teaspoons baking soda, ¼ teaspoon baking powder, 1 teaspoon cinnamon, 1 teaspoon nutmeg, 2 teaspoons powdered ginger and ¼ teaspoon powdered cloves – until dough is smooth. Chill dough 1 hour. Shape into 1-inch balls and roll in sugar, arranging 2 inches apart on ungreased cookie sheets. Do not flatten. Sprinkle tops of balls with a few drops of ice water. Bake at 375°F for 10 minute and pull out oven rack just enough that you can flatten each cookie with a pancake turner that has holes or slots in it. Return cookies to bake another 2 minutes or until firm and tops are cracked. Makes 5 dozen cookies.

CHOCOLATE-COVERED GRAHAM CRACKERS

The crackers:

1 cup self-rising flour
2 cups Graham or wheat flour
1 cup each: margarine and packed, brown sugar
½ cup honey
1 teaspoon vanilla
½ teaspoon vinegar
About ¼ cup milk, or as needed

Combine flours and set aside. Cream margarine, adding sugar a little at a time and beating until light and fluffy. Beat in honey, vanilla and vinegar – work in flour, alternately with enough of the milk that you have a smooth dough that can be shaped into a ball like piecrust. Chill 1 hour. Roll out on lightly floured surface to 1/8-inch thick. Cut into 2.5 x 2.5" squares and place close together on lightly greased baking sheets. Prick tops of each with tines of a fork in several places. Bake at 350°F for 10 to 12 minutes or until lightly browned around the edges. Remove at once to cool on waxed-paper-covered-surface. Flatten each cracker just slightly with back-side of a pancake turner while still warm. Makes about 1 dozen crackers. Prepare the chocolate coating (below.)

CHOCOLATE COATING FOR GRAHAM CRACKERS

In the top of a double boiler, over HOT – not boiling water, stir until smooth:

6 tablespoons melted paraffin
12-ounce package semi-sweet chocolate chips
1 ounce solid, unsweetened, baking chocolate
1 teaspoon vanilla
dash of salt

Keep mixture hot, stirring occasionally to make it smooth, while you pierce the graham crackers with the tip of a sharp knife and dip each to coat them in the hot chocolate mixture. Let excess chocolate drip back into pan. Place on waxed paper to "set" the chocolate. Paper can be peeled away without taking any of the coating with it, once graham crackers have cooled. If you lift the crackers from the paper, instead of the paper from the crackers, some of the coating may stick to the paper. Makes enough coating for 1 dozen squares of graham crackers. Store at room temperature in covered container.

POTATO CHIP COOKIES

There is an unlimited variety of cookies at a neighborhood corner bakery and coffee shop – not yet spoiled by the computerized, assembly-line techniques of the bigger and more complex food corporations – where my family and I stopped, in Ontario, on our way to Niagara Falls. Here is one idea that caught my attention:

1 cup (2 sticks) butter or margarine
½ cup sugar
1 teaspoon vanilla
2 cups flour
½ cup each: well-crushed potato chips and chopped pecans

Cream butter until light and fluffy, adding sugar a little at a time. Beat 2 minutes on medium speed of electric mixer. Beat in vanilla and 1 cup of the flour. Remove beaters and work in remaining flour, chips and pecans by hand. Drop by teaspoonful onto lightly-oiled baking sheets, 2 inches apart. Flatten slightly with bottom of a glass, greased once and dipped into sugar with each cookie flattened. Bake at 350°F for 10 to 12 minutes or until golden brown. Makes about 5 dozen small cookies.

CRACKED-TOP, CRISP SUGAR COOKIES

½ pound (2 sticks) butter
8-ounce carton sour cream
1 tablespoon lemon juice
1 teaspoon baking soda
2 pounds powdered sugar
4 eggs
½ teaspoon nutmeg
2 tablespoons vanilla
6 cups biscuit mix
4 cups flour

Cream butter with sour cream. Beat in lemon juice, baking soda and sugar. Beat until smooth. Add remaining ingredients; but, after adding about half of the biscuit mix, remove beaters of mixer and switch to sturdy spoon. The dough will be a bit sticky. Drop by rounded teaspoonful into small dish of granulated sugar, coating each piece of dough evenly. Arrange these 2 inches apart on ungreased cookie sheets. Press into center – without flattening cookie – a raisin, walnut or pecan piece or a drained, maraschino cherry. Bake at 375°F for exactly 11 minutes. Do not over-bake these! Let cool on pan for 1 minute before removing to cool on paper towels.

NOTE: if you remove them from the pans too quickly, they'll fall apart. They are quite fragile until they have cooled. Makes about 100 small cookies or 50 larger cookies.

HAMTRAMCK-STYLE PINEAPPLE BARS

When I visited a Polish bakery in Hamtramck, MI (Detroit area) many years ago, one of their most popular cookies was their pineapple bars, which have remained a favorite of ours!

5 cups flour
1 ½ teaspoons baking powder
1 cup (2 sticks) butter or margarine
3 large eggs, beaten well
1 cup granulated sugar
1 teaspoon vanilla
½ cup sour cream
½ teaspoon baking soda

Grease a 15.5 x 10 x 1" jellyroll pan – or use two 9 x 12" pans. Combine as listed, blending to the consistency of a pie crust. Divide into 2 equal portions. Pat 1 portion evenly over bottom of a prepared pan. Set aside while you prepare the pineapple filling (below):

2 cans (9 ounces each) crushed pineapple, drained – reserving the juice/syrup
1 cup granulated sugar
5 tablespoons cornstarch
Dash of salt
4 tablespoons butter or margarine

Place pineapple in a 1 ½-quart sauce pan with sugar. Put 1/3 cup of reserved juice/syrup and the cornstarch through a blender until smooth. Pour into pineapple and sugar mixture. Cook over medium-high heat, stirring constantly until smooth and thickened. Add salt and butter. Remove at once from heat. Let cool about 5 minutes. Spread evenly over the prepared half of dough in the pan. Roll out remaining dough between 2 sheets of Pam-sprayed waxed-paper, to the size of the pan, so that when inverted (with the top sheet removed), it fits neatly over the pineapple filling. Peel off other sheet of wax paper, (having used that bottom sheet with which to lift the dough and invert it over the filling.) Dust top of dough with my Cinnamon and Sugar Mix (see Index.) Also, sprinkle it with 1 ½ cups chopped pecans. Bake at 350°F for 30 to 35 minutes or until golden brown. Cut into squares after completely cooled in the pan. Serve as you would a brownie. Makes about 3 dozen small squares.

NIAGARA FALLS FUDGE – *Like Maple Leaf Village offers*

AT MAPLE LEAF VILLAGE, in Niagara Falls, Ontario, the making of fudge before your very eyes has been an art in the form of entertainment for thousands, upon thousands, of tourists each year. The Swiss Fudge people will tell you the recipe is secret. I don't mind! I respect the right to that privilege, but at home we can try to come close to their smooth texture this way… Simply by improving upon my frosting recipe, used for imitating the famous Sanders product. Trust me!

4 ounces unsweetened solid baking chocolate (4 squares)
½ cup milk
¼ pound butter or margarine (1 stick)
2/3 cup light corn syrup
2 cups granulated sugar
3 ½ cups powdered sugar
2 teaspoons vanilla

Put the chocolate, milk, butter, corn syrup and granulated sugar into a medium-sized saucepan on medium to high heat, stirring constantly until melted and smooth – while bringing it to a brisk boil for 4 to 6 minutes. While continuing to stir, scrape down the sides of the pan, also. Remove from heat. With portable electric mixer on medium speed, beat in powdered sugar, a little at a time; then, add the vanilla and beat for 6 minutes. Pour into a well-buttered, 9-inch, loaf pan that is also lined with a strip of greased waxed-paper, placed in the pan so that you have a 2-inch overlap at each end. Chill the fudge several hours or until firm. Use the overlapping waxed-paper ends to remove the fudge loaf from the pan. Slice it as you would a loaf of bread. At the time of this [original] writing, one slice would cost you a $1.89 [Canadian funds.] Each slice is about ½ pound.

TRADITIONAL!

LIFE SLIVERS – *The Candy WITHOUT the Holes*

3 ¾ cup sugar
½ cups light corn syrup
1 cup water
1 teaspoon flavoring oil of your choice (NOTE: this is not extract, but in oil from the pharmacy)
6 to 8 drops assorted food coloring of your choice

Mix together sugar, corn syrup and water in A heavy 2 ½-quart sauce pan. Cook on medium heat, stirring constantly. Bring to a boil. Boil, without stirring, until it reaches 310°F – a bit more than "hard crack" stage (when a few drops of the hot candy, put in cold water, causes the candy to make a "cracking" sound. At that point, remove from heat. Add flavoring oil and food coloring. Pour into foil-lined pan so that it is about 1/8-inch thick. When candy hardens at room temperature, within an hour, you can break it into slivers and dust in powdered sugar. Store at room temperature in a covered container. Makes 2 pounds.

SENSATIONAL!

MALLOW CUP

Just like my Peanut Butter Cups (see Index), this candy is a simple, basic combination. The Boyer Candy Company (Altoona, PA) makes the commercial brand "Mallow Cup" candy. They're easy to find in some areas, but my European readers love the idea of being able to make this imitation.

SHALLOW-CUP MARSHMALLOW CANDIES

8-ounce bar Hershey's Milk Chocolate
4 tablespoons butter
7-ounce jar Kraft Marshmallow Cream
1 cup flaked coconut
24 miniature muffin paper liners

In top of double boiler over gently simmering water, melt chocolate with butter and ½ cup of the marshmallow cream. Stir until smooth. Put coconut on an ungreased cookie sheet in a 375°F oven until lightly browned. Stir coconut frequently to brown it evenly. Cool it and crush it fine with a rolling pin; then, stir into chocolate mixture. Place rest of marshmallow cream, in a heat-proof bowl, in a pan of simmering water until it is of pouring consistency. Divide half of the chocolate mixture between 24 miniature muffin paper liners. Divide the marshmallow equally over that and let it set a bit. Then, divide remaining half of chocolate over the marshmallow layer. Chill until firm. Makes 2 dozen.

SHALLOW MARSHMALLOW SQUARES

Rather than fuss with the paper liners (above), make a quick job of it by altering the shape. Take half the chocolate mixture and spread it evenly over the bottom of a buttered, 9-inch square pan, pouring the warm marshmallow cream over that. As soon as the cream has "set" a bit, spread remaining half of chocolate over the top. Let it stand at room temperature about 1 hour to further set. Cut into 24 squares.

CHOCOLATE ALMOND BARK – *Like Sanders!*

When you look at all the marvelous candies that Sanders offers, be sure to look for their almond bark. If you are not in an area where Sanders products are available, you can try my "poor man's" version; which, while I was living in California, and couldn't find Sanders products, was sufficient to remind me of the days when I had a Sanders right around the corner – and loved it!

12-ounce package Nestle's semi-sweet chocolate chips
14-ounce can Eagle Brand sweetened condensed milk
1 cup chopped almonds

In top of double boiler over simmering water, melt the chocolate and stir in the milk. When piping hot, smooth and completely melted, keep water in lower pan turned to lowest possible heat point and allow chocolate mixture to cook that way for about 20 minutes, stirring occasionally, and scraping down sides of pan often. Then remove from the heat and add almonds. Spread over bottom of greased jellyroll pan, 10 x 15.5 x 1", to a very thin layer. Allow to harden at room temperature. Break into pieces and store in covered container away from warm places or humidity. Makes oodles!

BUTTER PECAN BARK *– follow the same directions (above), but, use Nestlé's butterscotch morsels and chopped pecans instead of chocolate chips and almonds.*

ROCKY ROAD BARK *– follow the same directions (above); except, use chopped walnuts instead of almonds and add 2 cups miniature marshmallows – which you will arrange in the bottom of a greased 9 x 12 x 2" pan, pouring the chocolate mixture over that (covering all the marshmallows) and following the remaining directions (above.)*

TEETH ENGLISH TOFFEE BARS

Combine 1 cup butter, 1 cup sugar, ¼ cup water and ½ teaspoon salt in heavy 2 ½-quart sauce pan over medium heat. Stir constantly until mixture reaches 300°F – or a small amount dropped into glass of cold water "cracks" when it hits the water – called "hard crack stage". You must really watch this carefully or it will scorch! It takes only 20 or 30 seconds for it to go from just right to "uugghh". At once, pour it into an UNGREASED 9 x 13 x 2" pan. Let it cool about 2 hours or until hard to the touch. Melt 3 ounces of semi-sweet chocolate (or 2/3 cup chocolate chips) in top of a double-boiler over HOT, not boiling, water and spread over the hardened candy. Let it set, then invert the pan onto working surface where you can cut or break the candy up into bite-sized pieces – OR while toffee is beginning to cool, and is a bit tacky when you touch it, you can oil a spatula and score the toffee into bars. These should break apart quite easily when you lift one corner with the spatula (rather than inverting the pan when candy is cool) and the entire toffee "sheet" should lift right out of the pan. Then, you can snap the scored portions apart. Makes 1 pound.

RECESS PEANUT BUTTER CUPS

The development of this recipe grew from a request made by a local group of parents whose children followed the Feingold diet to arrest hyperactivity. It became one of my most popular recipes across the country – and when I heard from the people at Hershey's, in Pennsylvania, they were quite upset with my having such a recipe. I assured them that the name "Recess" was drawn from the dictionary definition of the word, meaning "a hidden or secret place" – quite in keeping with the theme of my series. And, because Hershey's makes the famous product by a similar name (of which there are many in various industries, such as Goodyear and Goodrich both making tires), naturally, I recommended using Hershey's chocolate in this recipe. I have had recipes sent to me by those who also try to imitate the famous product, but they each contained powdered sugar and were more like a cookie than a candy. I detected no powder sugar in my samplings of the famous product – so I didn't include it in my imitation.

In top of double boiler, over HOT but not boiling, water, melt one 8-ounce Hershey's milk chocolate candy bar with ¾ cup peanut butter and 4 tablespoons butter or margarine (or 6 tablespoons melted paraffin – optional – but I use it, adding it to the chocolate when I melt it with the peanut butter. It's up to you!) Stir well and put ¾ cup additional peanut butter in top of another double boiler over simmering water – or in a heat-proof bowl in a shallow pan of simmering water. Let peanut butter melt just to a pouring consistency. Have 24 miniature paper liners placed inside cupcake or muffin tin wells. You can place them side-by-side on a cookie sheet, but I like the support that the cupcake tin wells give the papers while the candy is "setting". Next, divide HALF of the chocolate mixture, equally between each of the paper liners. Then, divide ALL the melted peanut butter between them, over top of the chocolate. Finally, divide remaining chocolate over the top of the peanut butter. Let stand, at room temperature, 2 hours to "set". Keep them refrigerated in a covered container up to a week. They'll keep frozen for months – if they even last that long!

NOTE: if you don't want to bother with the cups, grease a 9-inch square pan, spreading half of the chocolate mixture evenly over the bottom and then the peanut butter over that and finely the remaining chocolate mixture over the peanut butter layer. Let it set until firm to the touch and cut into neat little squares. Makes about 36 pieces, depending on the size of your squares.

SOMEWHERE IN TIME – MACKINAC ISLAND

Our reservations were made in February, that year, to spend the Fourth of July week at The Grand Hotel on historic Mackinac Island in Northern Michigan. We had heard, when we arrived, that Universal Pictures was filming a movie with Christopher Reeve and Jane Seymour and that our 2-day stay at the hotel might be disrupted from the usual routine we were used to when we stayed there. The place was booked and we were lucky to have those 2 days because other customers had canceled. The scene when we arrived was one of spectators and glamorous Hollywood activity in the lobby and on the grounds. Paul was just teeing off at the green next to the golf pro shop, the next morning, when we heard a sympathetic moan from the beautiful leading man, himself, as he locked up his bike and headed across the street to the filming activity. I know I should have run after Christopher Reeve for his autograph, but I was in shock!

Later, in the hotel lobby, we watched the scene when Christopher Reeve checks into The Grand and, later, when he and Jane Seymour take a buggy ride away from the entrance of the hotel with Christopher Plummer looking on. Take the time to enjoy seeing the movie they were filming – we've seen it 4 times and can't wait to see it again! It's for everyone who has ever been in love – or who has ever visited lovely Mackinac Island, as we do every summer. In one scene of the movie you'll notice, on the main street of the village, a sign over a shop that reads "Murdick's Fudge", a recipe which I have coveted for years. Finally, after dozens of tests, I came up with the secret for purporting this product at home; although, I've only given you the chocolate flavor here – they have a dozen other flavors to enjoy. It whips up in 5 minutes and, a week later, it's still smooth and creamy.

SOMEWHERE IN TIME CHOCOLATE FUDGE

¼ pound butter or margarine
½ cup light corn syrup
dash of salt
1-pound powdered sugar
6-ounce package semi-sweet chocolate chips
1 teaspoon vanilla

In a 1 ½-quart sauce pan, bring the butter and corn syrup to a boil, stirring constantly. Boil hard for 1 minute; then, immediately, turn heat down to lowest point. Beat in the salt and HALF of the powdered sugar. It will lump a bit, but the electric mixer will smooth it out as you continue beating. Add rest of sugar and raise the heat for 1 or 2 minutes until it shows the 1st bubble of a boil again. Quickly remove from the heat and beat in the rest of the powdered sugar, then the chips until melted and smooth. Next, beat in the vanilla. Pour into a buttered 8- or 9-inch, square pan. Chill 1 hour. Cut into squares. Makes about 2 pounds. To achieve the "Mackinac loaf-style", pack the fudge into a buttered 9-inch bread loaf pan. Chill it several hours, or overnight, and remove it from the pan to slice it as you would bread. You can change the flavor of the fudge by changing the flavors of the baking chips and extract.

P·ie·*Eater's* *·Pie·* ❋ *Digest* ❋

Recipes of enduring significance, in condensed permanent booklet form

PASTRY MYSTERIES SOLVED

WHERE DID THE PIE COME FROM? From the earliest English concoctions which contained magpies. Used during 16th century aristocracy as "Surprise Pies", the crust-covered culinary creation was a fashionable form of regal amusement.

ORIGINALLY COMPRISED OF LEFTOVERS the Colonial American pie was not a dessert, but a side dish. The Colonial cook lined a pan with scraps of bread dough or Hard Tack (Recipe in Revised Bk 1) and filled it with scraps of meats, fruits, nuts, sauce and any other edible leftover.

GOOD FOOD

The Gourmet PIE
An option in COOKING.

Half Baked

✦

MYTH OR REALITY?

PIE CRUSTS WITHOUT ROLLING PINS that taste and look like delicate French pastry is the last word in pie baking. Recipes for these are included in this issue.

FILLINGS, MERINGUE, TOPPINGS, GARNISHES make the easiest recipe look as if it took you all day. Embarrassed by a pie crust that is pale in color with the texture of a biscuit? Simple secrets for copying the restaurant recipes are no longer a mystery to even the beginning cook. The experienced cook will probably wonder why they hadn't thought of these tricks sooner. If fast food reminds you only of the "franchise restaurants"—look again, for these 100 pie and pastry recipes will renew your interest and your enthusiasm in being creative in the kitchen by turning out pies that you thought only a bakery could produce.

LIFE IN THESE UNITED TASTES

PIES AND PASTRIES

IN EARLY AMERICAN TAVERNS, our 1ˢᵗ restaurants in this country, pies were not beautiful nor fancy – but they were good. The custom of baking pies in round, shallow pans (rather than in deep square or oblong pans) originated here for reasons of economy, to stretch scarce food supplies. Originally comprised of "left-overs", the colonial American pie was not a dessert, but a side-dish. The colonial cook lined the pan with scraps of bread dough or Hardtack (see Index for my recipe) and filled it with scraps of meats, fruits, nuts, sauce and any other edible "left-overs".

Fillings, meringue, toppings and garnishes make the easiest recipes look as if it took you all day. Embarrassed by a pie crust that is pale in color with the texture of a biscuit? Simple secrets for copying the restaurant recipes are no longer a mystery to even the beginning cook. The experienced cook will probably wonder why they hadn't thought of these tricks sooner. If fast food reminds you only of the franchise restaurants – look again, for these pie and pastry recipes will renew your interest and your enthusiasm in being creative in the kitchen by making pies you thought only a bakery could produce.

Some cooks still insist that "take-off crusts" give apple pies an even better flavor. Sliced apples are arranged in a pastry-lined pie pan, and the top crust is laid on top, but not sealed to the under crust. When the pie is baked, the top crust is gently lifted off, sugar and spices are sprinkled over the filling and the top crust is carefully put back in place. In experimenting with this colonial technique, I discovered that my Crisco Crust recipe, in this chapter (see Index), works very well.

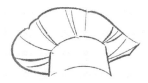

NEAT MAN MARKET'S OPEN-FACE APPLE PIE
– Like that served by the Neiman Marcus – Zodiac Room (Dallas, TX), years ago!

10-inch, partially baked, "Butter Crust" (see Index)
4 to 5 large apples (peeled, cored and thick-sliced) to fill a 10-inch pie plate to the rim
2 cups sugar
1/3 cup flour
1 teaspoon salt
1/3 cup Half-and-Half or light cream
¼ cup milk
½ teaspoon cinnamon

While the "Butter Crust" bakes for 12 minutes at 375°F, place apples in a large bowl. Put everything else through blender, on high-speed, until smooth (about 1 minute.) Pour over apples, coating them well, and then slide rack of oven out just far enough that you can empty the apples and sauce mixture into the hot crust and return it to bake for 90 minutes or until apples are soft. Cover pie loosely with foil for 1ˢᵗ hour of baking! Remove foil for last 30 minutes or so. Serve it warm – a la mode - with vanilla ice cream and caramel sauce, or with shredded cheddar cheese. Serves 6 to 8.

RHUBARB CREAM PIE – *Like the Ox Yoke Inn, located in the Amana Colonies (Iowa), once served a unique rhubarb pie that has been a favorite of mine for many years.*

3 eggs
1 ½ cups sugar
¼ cup light cream or Half-and-Half
dash of salt
pinch of cinnamon
3 ½ to 4 cups well chopped fresh rhubarb (or frozen, unsweetened and thawed)

Beat the eggs with an electric mixer on medium speed until thick and lemon-colored. Add sugar in small portions, continuing to beat; then, slowly add the cream. Next, beat in salt and cinnamon. Remove beaters and stir in rhubarb.

Dust the bottom of an unbaked, 9-inch, single crust (see Index – for my Crisco Crust or Butter Crust recipes), with 1 tablespoon of flour; then, pour in the filling. Place the pie pan on the rack just below the center of the oven and bake the pie at 375°F for almost an hour or until "set". Cool completely before cutting. Serves 6 to 8 well. Garnish tops of servings with slightly sweetened, whipped cream.

COFFEE CREAM PIE – *Randolph, Vermont*

There was a very Victorian "flavored" restaurant in Randolph, Vermont that once served a delicate, coffee-flavored cream pie that was beyond description.

1 cup fine graham cracker crumbs (about 15 cracker squares finely crushed)
2 tablespoons sugar
4 tablespoons butter or margarine, melted and cool
3 cups stiffly with cream
2/3 cup powdered sugar
1/3 cup each: whiskey and Kahlúa
¼ cup instant coffee powder
2 tablespoons hot water

Combine cracker crumbs, sugar and butter; then press into bottom and sides of greased, 9-inch pie pan. Bake 6 minutes at 375°F. While crust cools, prepare filling by gently combining the whipped cream and powdered sugar, using low speed of electric mixer. Stir in whiskey and Kahlúa. Dissolve coffee powder in hot water and fold into cream mixture. Pour mixture into cold crumb crust. Chill 8 to 10 hours or overnight before cutting to serve. Add whipped cream and some shaved chocolate bars to garnish. Serves 6 to 8.

PECAN PIE

Big Boy restaurants have several good pies – this was always one of my favorites. Simple to prepare! Have a good, rich, pie crust handy – I suggest my Butter Crust recipe (see Index.)

2 partially baked 9-inch Butter Crust pie shells (see Index)
¼ pound one stick butter or margarine
1-pound brown sugar
½ cup milk
3 eggs
1 tablespoon vinegar
2 teaspoons vanilla
2 cups broken pecans

Have the Butter Crust pie shells in the oven, partially baking per the crust recipe. In a medium-sized mixing bowl, cream the butter until light and fluffy. Beat in brown sugar, a little at a time, using an electric mixer on medium speed until very creamy. Add milk in small amounts until completely incorporated. Beat in eggs one at a time, then vinegar and vanilla. Beat about 3 minutes on high-speed. Remove the beaters and stir in pecans. Divide mixture equally between the 2 partially baked pie shells. Place the pie pans on a cookie sheet and bake on center rack of 350°F oven for almost an hour or until knife inserted in center comes out clean. Cool the pies before cutting to serve. Garnish top of each serving with a dollop of whipped cream. Each pie will serve 6 to 8 nicely. *If you want to cut the recipe in half, to bake just 1 pie – use 2 medium eggs, in place of the 3 eggs (above.)*

PEANUT BUTTER PIE – *Goody-Goody Restaurant – one of Dayton, Ohio's popular places for great food – had an unusual peanut butter pie that was very similar in texture to my Pecan Pie (above.)*

9-inch, partially-baked, Butter Crust pie shell (see Index)
3 tablespoons butter or margarine
1/3 cup peanut butter
2 cups packed brown sugar
¼ cup milk
2 medium-sized eggs
2 teaspoons vinegar

Prepare the pie shell per recipe directions, baking partially. While pie shell is in the oven, beat butter and peanut butter until creamy, adding sugar a little at a time, until fluffy. Beat in remaining ingredients and pour into warm, partially-baked crust. Place pie pan on a cookie sheet on center rack of 350°F oven and bake for almost an hour or until knife inserted in center comes out clean. Cool before cutting to serve 6 to 8. Garnish each serving with sweetened whipped cream and chopped peanuts.

LEMON CREAM MOUSSE PIE

In a medium-sized mixing bowl, combine a 4-ounce box of lemon-flavored instant pudding powder and 1 2/3 cup milk, beating 3 minutes. Beat in, a little at a time: one 8-ounce package of cream cheese, ¼ teaspoon lemon extract and a pinch of cinnamon. Pour into a store-bought, 9-inch, crumb crust (or see Index for my homemade version.) Chill until firm. Cover it, entirely, with a 7-ounce container of Cool Whip and 1 cup of well-crushed, lemon-flavored, hard candy; adding a touch of cinnamon to taste. Freeze the pie until firm. Cut into neat slices, serving 6 to 8.

MARIE CALIBER'S LEMON CREAM PIE

2 boxes (4 ounces each) instant lemon pudding
3 cups milk
1 envelope unflavored gelatin
¼ cup cold water
¼ cup Triple Sec or orange liqueur (or use 1 ounce brandy flavoring, plus 1 teaspoon orange extract)
8 ounces heavy whipping cream
¼ cup granulated sugar
Dash of salt

1 recipe of my "Butter Crust" (see Index) – prepared and baked completely, then cooled

Combine pudding and milk, beating with electric mixer on medium until smooth. Soften gelatin in cold water. Place in heat-proof cup in pan of hot water (or in microwave on "Defrost" for 1 ½ minutes) until gelatin becomes transparent in color. Let gelatin cool and beat it into pudding. Beat in Triple Sec (or the brandy flavoring/extract substitution.) Spread evenly into cooled, 9-inch pie shell. Beat cream with sugar and salt until quite thick. Spread evenly over lemon filling. Garnish with a few tablespoons of sweet orange marmalade swirled across the top of pie – or with pecan halves and a dash of cinnamon. Chill several hours before cutting, or place pie in freezer for an hour. Serves 6 to 8 nicely.

APPLE CRISP

Mix together until crumbly: ¼ pound butter or margarine, 1 cup quick-cooking rolled oats, 1 cup flour, 1 cup sugar, 1 tablespoon cinnamon and ½ teaspoon salt. Divide mixture in half. Pat one half into bottom of greased 9 x 9 x 2" pan. Over this, arrange 4 cups peeled, cored and thinly-sliced apples – using 4 large, firm and slightly tart apples. Drizzle apple slices with ¼ cup melted butter or margarine and then dust in mixture of ½ teaspoon cinnamon and 2 teaspoons sugar. Pat the other half of the crumbly oatmeal mixture over top of apple mixture. Drizzle with ¼ cup more melted butter or margarine. Dust lightly, again, with more cinnamon and sugar mix. Bake at 325°F for 20 minutes. Increase temperature to 375°F for another 20 minutes or until crust is nicely browned and filling begins to bubble. Serve warm, with ice cream on top, for 6 to 8 sensible people.

APPLE-SOLUTELY PERFECT!

It wasn't until I sampled the pie shops of Southern California that I truly came to appreciate the good-old-down-home-flavor that our moms were known for when we were kids. (My mother made the most mouth-watering apple pie that ever graced a table.) Marie Callender Shops and Restaurants in the Torrance, Long Beach and Lakewood (CA) areas have a delicate, buttery-flavor, apple pie filling. The Polly Pie Shops' apple filling has a bit of spice. The Poppin' Fresh Pie Shops has a hint of nutmeg, I suspect... With some super-sleuthing, I finally arrived at, what I consider, a perfect apple pie!

APPLE PIE

1 prepared, double pie crust recipe – I recommend either my Crisco Crust or Butter Crust (see Index)
2 tablespoons flour
1 cup granulated sugar
1 teaspoon cinnamon
½ teaspoon nutmeg
dash of powdered ginger (less than a pinch)
8 cups thinly sliced, peeled and cored green sweet apples, like Granny Smith
4 tablespoons butter

Partially-bake the bottom crust for 10 minutes at 375°F and remove to a wire rack to cool while you prepare the filling. Combine everything except the butter in a roomy bowl, coating the apples completely. Arrange apple mixture in the partially-baked, bottom crust. Prepare the top crust per the recipe you used. Dot the filling with dabs of the butter and apply the top crust. Seal the edges with a fork dipped in ice water. Make slits in the top for steam to escape. (If using the Crisco Crust recipe, brush with the recommended egg-wash per that recipe.) Preheat oven to 400°F and bake for 45 to 50 minutes on center rack or until crust is golden brown and filling starts to bubble. Cool to lukewarm on a wire rack before cutting into 6 to 8 servings.

STRAWBERRY PIE

Have ready – a 9-inch, single, Crisco or Butter Crust pie shell baked and chilled. Into your blender put 2 cups cold water, a 3-ounce package strawberry Jell-O powder and ¼ cup cornstarch – blend on high-speed until smooth. Pour into a 1 ½-quart sauce pan. Cook over medium-high heat, stirring constantly until smooth and thick, like a pudding. Remove from heat at once. Stir in 1 cup strawberry preserves, 4 tablespoons butter or margarine and ¼ teaspoon vanilla. Pour enough of the warm sauce over bottom of baked pie shell, just to cover it. Arrange a single layer of whole strawberries, hull-side down, using either 1-quart fresh whole berries or a 1-pound bag of frozen whole berries, thawed. Pour about half of the remaining sauce over the berries. Fill the remaining space in the pie shell with additional berries and pour remaining sauce over these. Chill until firm enough to cut into serving pieces – about 2 hours. Top each serving with whipped cream or Cool Whip. Serves 6 to 8.

CRISCO CRUST *(A No-Rolling-Pin Crust)*

6 tablespoons Crisco
1 tablespoon sugar
1 tablespoon milk
½ teaspoon salt
1 cup flour
pinch of cinnamon

1 egg yolk, beaten with 1 tablespoon cold water (for browning crust)

Put the Crisco, sugar, milk and salt in a small, deep mixing bowl. Beat 1 minute on high speed with electric mixer. At once, dump in flour and cinnamon. Beat on high-speed for 30 seconds or until thoroughly combined. Clean mixture off the beaters and spread it all evenly over bottom and sides of a Pam-sprayed, 9-inch, pie pan – or a 10-inch, Pyrex pie plate. Combine yolk and water. Use pastry brush to lap it over the crust's surface. Bake, empty, at 375°F for 18 to 20 minutes or until golden brown.

For top crust: Pat out the single recipe (above) on a Pam-sprayed, waxed-paper-lined dinner plate. Invert crust over the filling in a crust-lined pan, per recipe of your choice. Lift off plate and peel back waxed paper. Make slits for steam to escape. Gently press crust to rim of pie pan with a fork dipped in ice water or flour. Prepare the egg yolk and water as directed above – brush lightly, lapping it, rather than pressing it, over top of crust. Bake per filling recipe directions. Generally, the best temperature is at 375°F for 25 to 28 minutes or until filling begins to bubble and crust is golden brown.

CRUMB CRUST

Put a 10-ounce package of Lorna Doone shortbread cookies (or use sugar cookies or 9 squares of graham crackers) through your blender until finely powdered, using high-speed with an on/off agitation. This should yield about 2 ¼ cups fine crumbs. Dump crumbs into a medium-sized mixing bowl and add 1 envelope (unflavored) gelatin powder, 1/3 cup sugar, ¼ teaspoon cinnamon and ¼ pound (one stick) melted butter or margarine. Mix well and pat evenly over bottom and sides of a well-greased, 9-inch, pie pan or Pyrex pie plate. Bake for 5 minutes at 375°F. Cool and fill as you wish. Makes one 9-inch crust.

RICE KRISPIES PIE CRUST

Melt 4 tablespoons butter or margarine in a small sauce pan over low heat, stirring in 4 cups miniature marshmallows. Add 2 tablespoons milk and stir until marshmallows are melted and mixture is smooth. Remove from heat. Stir in 1 teaspoon vanilla, 4 cups Kellogg's Rice Krispies cereal and 1/2 cup finely-chopped pecans. Pack mixture evenly over bottom and sides of a well-buttered, 9-inch, pie pan or Pyrex pie plate. Do NOT bake this crust! Chill until "set" and fill as desired. Makes one crust.

BUTTER CRUST *(My Most Dependable &Very Favorite Recipe!)*

¼ pound butter – NOT margarine
1 tablespoon sugar
½ teaspoon salt
¼ teaspoon cinnamon
1 cup all-purpose flour

Melt the butter in a small sauce pan on medium heat until it's frothy, but don't let it change color or become the least-bit brown. (I like to put the stick of butter into my heat-proof, 1 ½-quart, glass mixing bowl, placing it in the microwave for 2 to 3 minutes on "Defrost".) As soon as the butter is melted, and while it's still hot, dump in the remaining ingredients. Turn your electric mixer on high and beat mixture in a bowl for about 30 seconds or until it comes away from the center and hits the sides of the bowl. Quickly gather it into a ball and pat it out to cover the bottom and sides of a Pam-sprayed, 10-inch, Pyrex pie plate. (Pyrex plates work best with this very rich recipe.) If you don't have Pam, grease the pan in Crisco only! It might stick otherwise! Bake crust at 375°F for 18 to 20 minutes or until golden brown. Fill as desired. Makes one 10-inch pie crust. *Note: Do not double this recipe. The dough becomes difficult to work with as it cools and, then, it crumbles and breaks apart. Make one single recipe at a time.*

To make top crust: Pat out a single recipe, as given above, on a Pam-sprayed and waxed-paper-lined dinner plate. Invert crust over filling spread in crust-lined pan, per recipe of your choice. Lift off plate and peel back waxed paper. Make slits for steam to escape. Gently press crust to rim of pie pan with a floured fork (or a fork dipped in ice water.) Use an egg-wash if you wish (one egg yolk, beaten with 1 tablespoon cold water and brushed lightly – lapping it, rather than pressing it, over top of crust), but the butter in this crust should allow it to brown beautifully without the wash. Bake per filling recipe directions. Generally, the best temperature is at 375°F for 25 to 28 minutes or until filling begins to bubble up through the slits in the top crust in the crust is golden brown.

1-2-3 PUMPKIN PIE FILLING

1 unbaked 9-inch pie shell
1-pound can pumpkin
14-ounce can Eagle Brand Sweetened Condensed Milk
2 eggs, well-beaten
2 tablespoons each: butter (or margarine) and cornstarch
1 tablespoon pumpkin pie spice, or to taste

Preheat oven to 375°F and partially bake the empty crust for 10 minutes at 375°F. Combine all filling ingredients, beating thoroughly. Pour mixture into pie shell and return to oven to bake for 45 to 50 minutes or until a knife inserted in the center comes out clean. Makes one 9-inch pie. Serves 6 to 8.

BIG PLOY'S CHOCOLATE CREAM PIE

For the best chocolate cream pie, Big Boy Restaurants probably would have been the place to go [in the late 70s.] The recipe is not the same, today – or so it seems – but, this is how I remember it.

1 baked and cooled 9-inch pie shell (see Index for my Butter Crust recipe)
2 boxes, 3 ¾-ounce each, chocolate pudding (NOT instant)
3 cups milk
2 egg yolks, slightly beaten (save and freeze your egg whites for other uses)
4 tablespoons butter or margarine
1-ounce, unsweetened, solid baking chocolate – grated
¼ cup, packed, brown sugar
Cool Whip & Chocolate sprinkles for garnish

Chill crust thoroughly after it is baked and cooled. Empty pudding powder into a 2 ½-quart sauce pan. Beat the milk and egg yolks together well with a fork and stir this into the powder in the sauce pan. Cook and stir constantly over medium-high heat until you see the 1st bubble of a boil. At once, remove pan from heat. With portable electric mixer on low-speed, beat in butter, baking chocolate and brown sugar until smooth. Pour into the chilled pie shell. Return to refrigerator to chill for about 2 more hours or until "firm". Cut into 6 to 8 neat wedges and top each serving with Cool Whip and sprinkles.

SHARE-A-LEASE POWDERED SUGAR POUND CAKE

Make a Sundae Pie with this, rather than brownie squares, the way Hedge's Wigwam once did in Royal Oak, Michigan during the early 50s.

Cream together 1-pound powdered sugar and 1-pound butter until light and fluffy. Add 2 eggs and 1 cup flour, beating 4 to 6 minutes on medium speed with electric mixer. Beat in 1 teaspoon almond or lemon extract and 1 teaspoon vanilla. Then beat in 2 more eggs and another cup of flour. Beat for 3 minutes, then beat in 2 more eggs (total of 6 eggs) with one last cup of flour (total of 3 cups.) Beat 5 minutes, scraping down sides and bottom of bowl frequently. Pour batter into a greased and floured 10-inch tube pan (or two 7-inch bread loaf pans, greased and floured as well.) Bake at 325°F for about 65 minutes for tube pan, or until it tests done by inserting a long thin wooden skewer through the cake to the bottom of the pan – if it comes out clean, remove cake from oven to cool on wire rack. Bake bread loaf pans for 45 to 50 minutes or until toothpick inserted in center of each comes out clean. Cool in pan on wire rack for 45 minutes before removing cake from pans to serving plates. Dust top of cake in powdered sugar while still warm. Serves 8 to 10. Refrigerate, well-covered, up to a week. Freezes well.

FROM-SCRATCH PUMPKIN PIE FILLING

4 eggs, beaten thoroughly
29-ounce can pumpkin
1½ cups granulated sugar
1 teaspoon each: salt and powdered ginger
2 teaspoons powdered cinnamon
¼ teaspoon each: nutmeg, powdered cloves and ground pepper
2 cans, 13 ounces each, evaporated milk (or 3 ½ cups Half-and-Half coffee cream)

2 unbaked 9-inch pie shells (see Index for my Crisco Crust or Butter Crust recipes)

Preheat oven to 425°F. Combine all filling ingredients. Set aside while you partially bake the prepared crusts for only 10 minutes. You can even do this while the oven is preheating, since you want to only "partially" bake them, which prevents the crusts from being soggy after you've baked the pies with the filling in them. You don't even have to let the crusts cool before dividing the filling mixture equally between them. Return the pies to bake at 425°F for only 8 minutes – set your timer! Reduce the temperature, at that time, to 350°F and continue baking for 35 to 40 minutes or until a knife inserted in the center of each comes out clean. Remove pies to cool on wire racks. Keep pies refrigerated when not being served. Makes two 9-inch pies. Serves 12 to 16 nicely.

OHIO LEMON PIE

Make 1 double-crust recipe of my Crisco Crust (see Index) – bottom crust partially baked per recipe.

2 large lemons
2 cups sugar
4 eggs, well-beaten

Slice lemons paper thin, rind and all, and combine with sugar, mixing well with a rubber scraper, just to combine these. Let this stand for 2 hours, covered, at room temperature. Overnight is even better, to completely draw out the lemons' flavor.

Pour beaten eggs into the lemon mixture, combining thoroughly, but lightly. Pour into the partially baked crust and add the top crust as the crust recipe directs, making slits in top for steam to escape. Press rim of crust firmly with a floured fork (or one dipped in ice water) to seal the crusts together. Bake at 375°F for 40 minutes or until you can insert a table knife through the crust and into the filling – about 1 inch from rim of pie – and it comes out clean. Cool before cutting. Serves 6 to 8.

LEMON MERINGUE PIE

Start with 1 box (3 ¾ ounces) lemon pudding and pie filling (NOT instant) prepared per package directions. As soon as the pudding thickens and you see the 1ˢᵗ bubble of a boil, remove from heat and beat in the following ingredients with a spoon:

½ teaspoon lemon extract
2 tablespoons light corn syrup
a dash each: salt and cinnamon powder
4 tablespoons butter or margarine

Pour filling into a baked and slightly cooled, 9-inch Butter Crust (see Index for recipe.) Let the filling cool in the crust for 1 hour before applying the meringue (below.) If the meringue droops and filling doesn't hold its shape when you cut it, you may have applied the meringue too early!

THE MERINGUE – Beat 3 eggs whites until foamy, adding 1 tablespoon light corn syrup and beating until soft peaks form. A little at a time, on high-speed, beat in a 7 ½-ounce jar of Kraft Marshmallow Cream until mixture is very thick – the shape is retained when you draw your finger through it. Apply meringue to the COOLED filling by dropping tablespoonsful around the pie-rim first, then, filling in center with additional tablespoons of meringue. Draw it all together, lightly and gently, with the tip of a spatula. Bake at 375°F for 10 minutes or until golden brown. Let pie cool on a wire rack for 1 hour. Refrigerate for 1 more hour before cutting. To cut through the meringue, without disturbing it or having it stick to the knife, spray the knife blade with Pam or wipe lightly with corn oil. Serves 6 to 8.

BANANA CREAM PIE

2 boxes, 3 ¾ ounces each, vanilla pudding and pie filling – NOT instant
3 cups milk
4 tablespoons butter or margarine
½ cup well-mashed banana (1 small), PLUS 2 large whole bananas, with green tips
¼ cup sugar
9-inch baked and cooled Butter Crust (see Index)

Beat pudding powder and milk thoroughly or put through a blender until smooth. Transfer to a 2 ½-quart sauce pan. Cook and stir over medium heat until you see the first bubble of a boil. Remove at once. Stir in butter and mashed banana. Arrange 1 banana, peeled and sliced ¼-inch thick, over bottom crust. Sprinkle with half of the sugar. Pour in filling and let cool about 30 minutes. Arrange remaining banana, peeled and sliced ¼-inch thick, on top of cooled filling. Sprinkle with remaining sugar. Top with Cool Whip and chill several hours before cutting to serve 6 to 8. Keeps refrigerated, up to 2 days.

SHARE-A-LEASE CHEESECAKE

The crust:

Preheat oven to 350°F. Put ¼ pound butter or margarine in a 9-inch, square pan and into the preheating oven until butter melts. Meanwhile, put a 10-ounce package Lorna Doone Sugar Cookies (or plain sugar cookies) through a blender until fine crumbs. Combine crumbs with 1 envelope unflavored, gelatin powder and ¼ cup sugar. Add ½ teaspoon cinnamon if you wish. Mix it well. Remove pan containing butter from oven as soon as it is completely melted. Mix in crumb mixture, reserving ¼ cup of this and setting it aside to use over filling later, and stir to blend thoroughly. Pat remaining crumb mixture evenly and firmly over bottom of pan. Return to oven to bake exactly 8 minutes – which gives you just enough time to prepare the filling (below.)

The filling:

Mix the following until light and fluffy: 2 large packages (8 ounces each) cream cheese, one 8-ounce carton dairy sour cream, 2 tablespoons butter or margarine, 2 tablespoons cornstarch, 2 large eggs, 1 cup sugar and 1 teaspoon vanilla. Beat with electric mixer on medium speed. As soon as crust is baked, just slip rack out far enough, without even removing pan from oven, that you can pour filling into hot crust. Sprinkle top of filling lightly with the reserved ¼ cup crumb mixture. Return to oven to bake for 30 to 35 minutes or until you can insert the blade of a table knife into the filling, 1 inch from the edge of pan, and it comes out clean. Cool about 30 minutes before cutting to serve – OR chill it thoroughly and serve it quite cold with whipped cream or Cool Whip to garnish each of 8 servings.

BLESSED CHEESECAKE

This was one of the most celebrated cheesecakes to ever grace a New York state table, as it was prepared by a group of Catholic nuns who sold these to raise money to aid their community. Made with Kahlúa or Tia Maria (liquor) – it is VERY good. If you do not use Kahlúa, which is a chocolate-flavored liquor, you may substitute a 1-ounce bottle of rum flavoring and increase the chocolate by 1-ounce (1/4 cup) semi-sweet chocolate chips, melted and smooth.

The crust: Roll 24 Oreo cream-filled cookies into coarse crumbs, using your rolling pin, or put through your blender on high-speed, until texture is equal to gravel. Mix these well with 1 envelope unflavored gelatin powder and 1/3 cup melted butter. Press into bottom of greased 9-inch square baking pan. Set aside while you make the filling.

The filling: Over hot water, melt a 6-ounce package semi-sweet chocolate chips until smooth. In a bowl, beat 2 large packages (8 ounces each) cream cheese until fluffy; adding melted chocolate, an 8-ounce tub sour cream and ¼ cup each – cornstarch, melted butter and Kahlúa or Tia Maria (or use the substitute given above.) Beat in 3 eggs for 6 minutes on high-speed. Pour into prepared crust. Bake at 350°F for 35 to 40 minutes or until knife blade inserted 1 inch from the edge of the pan comes out clean. Cool before cutting into 8 serving pieces. Garnish with Cool Whip or whipped cream.

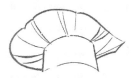

BREAKFAST PIE & VANILLA GLAZE

Years ago – while living in Algonac, MI – we often visited a bakery and restaurant, where breakfast and homemade cakes and pastries were a specialty. On Sunday mornings, we'd take our boat and the 5 kids up the North Channel of the St. Clair River to the city park, tie up at the public dock and walk over to the Cowboy Restaurant and Bakery for a slice of their warm "Breakfast Pie". To make at home…

Spray a 10-inch Pyrex pie plate with Baker's Joy (or grease and flour well.) Combine the following, in a medium mixing bowl, beating with electric mixer (high-speed) for 1 minute to thoroughly mix:

2 cups each – Bisquick and buttermilk
1 egg, well-beaten
1/3 cup sugar
½ teaspoon vanilla

Spread evenly in the prepared pie plate. Over top of batter, spread lightly, but evenly, one 7 ½-ounce jar, baby food – "Junior", "Apples and Apricots". Set aside – and, in a small mixing bowl, with electric mixer on high-speed for 1 minute or until moist but crumbly, combine the following ingredients:

¼ pound margarine, melted and still warm
½ cup each: packed brown sugar and Bisquick
1 cup all-purpose flour
1 ½ teaspoons cinnamon

Sprinkle this crumbly mixture evenly over the "baby food layer". Bake in a 400°F, preheated oven for 45 minutes or until it tests "done". Allow this to cool in the pie plate on a wire rack for 10 minutes (set your timer) while you prepare the vanilla glaze (below.)

VANILLA GLAZE *for BREAKFAST PIE*

Put in your blender: 1/3 cup milk, 1 ½ cups powdered sugar, 1 tablespoon soft margarine, ¼ teaspoon vanilla and a dash of salt; blending on high-speed for 1 minute or until smooth. After the pie has cooled for the 10 minutes, drizzle this glaze over the top of it and let it cool another 10 or 15 minutes before cutting into 6 to 8 servings. If you apply the glaze when the pie is too hot, the pie may fall and, if you apply it when it has cooled too much, the glaze won't "set" as it should. Pie keeps at room temperature, if covered, for up to a week. It freezes well, to be used within 3 months.

CREAM CHEESE PIE

2 packages, 8 ounces each, cream cheese
2 cups powdered sugar
8-ounce carton Cool Whip, thawed
1 teaspoon almond or vanilla extract

Beat the cream cheese with electric mixer on high speed until thoroughly smooth and creamy. Beat in powdered sugar, a little at a time, until light and fluffy. Turn mixer to lowest speed and add Cool Whip and extract. Pile filling into a well-chilled, 9-inch Crumb Crust or baked and chilled Butter Crust (see Index for both recipes.) Place pie in freezer for about 2 or 3 hours, or until firm enough to cut. Serve it as you would an ice cream pie. Garnish top of each serving with a little canned pie filling, any flavor of your choice – or drizzle it with pineapple sundae topping or chocolate syrup. Serves 6 to 8.

CHIFFON CHEESE PIE

1-pound can Thank You brand vanilla pudding
2 packages (8 ounces each) cream cheese, at room temperature
1 cup powdered sugar
8-ounce carton Cool Whip, thawed
9-inch chilled Crumb Crust (see Index)

Combine canned pudding and cream cheese with electric mixer on low to medium speed until creamy and light. Beat in powdered sugar, a little at a time, and fold in Cool Whip. Pile into chilled crust and freeze until firm enough to cut into 6 to 8 servings. Garnish with canned pie filling or sundae toppings.

DIMESTORE CHEESECAKE

Prepare my Crumb Crust in a greased 9-inch square pan, per that recipe (see Index.) Bake, as directed, for 8 minutes and cool on wire rack for 15 minutes. Then, place crust in freezer while you prepare the filling (below), which does NOT have to be baked.

In a small bowl, beat two 8-ounce packages cream cheese until light and fluffy. Set aside. In a medium bowl, beat two, 3 ½-ounce packages, instant vanilla pudding powder and 3 cups milk until thickened and smooth. Beat cream cheese into pudding, on lowest speed of mixer, until blended. Set it aside. Soften 1 envelope unflavored gelatin in ¼ cup water and, then, place it in a heat-proof cup in a pan of very hot water until gelatin mixture becomes transparent. Cool and beat into pudding and cheese mixture. Beat in 1½ teaspoons vanilla or almond extract. Pour into prepared, chilled crumb crust, using the reserved ¼ cup crumb mixture, per the crust recipe directions, to garnish top of cheesecake filling. Place cheesecake in refrigerator for about 2 hours or until firm enough to cut into 6 to 8 neat squares. Add canned pie filling or sundae fruit topping to garnish tops of servings (or sprinkle with chopped pecans or shaved milk chocolate candy bars.) Keep refrigerated, up to a week. Do not freeze this.

BLUEBERRY OPEN-FACE PIE – *Like Polly Pie Shop's*

While living in California, I was introduced to the Polly Pie Shop in Long Beach. One of my favorite choices was their blueberry pie. It was unlike any other I had ever tried. I thought it was probably a baked, single crust with a top-of-the-stove prepared filling. Rather than a top crust, as traditional pies have, this was topped with a crumb mixture that was, in all respects, like baked and crushed pie crust. Finally, after 6 trial-and-errors in 2 days, I arrived at, what I think is, an on-target imitation!

First prepare two 10-inch Butter Crust pie shells (see Index), baked and cooled per recipe directions. Then, combine ½ cup boiling water with a 3-ounce package black raspberry Jell-O gelatin in a small bowl. Stir until gelatin is completely dissolved, then set aside. Drain 2 cans (15 ounces each) blueberries, setting aside berries and putting the liquid (which equals about 2 cups) into blender. (If berry liquid does NOT equal 2 cups – add enough water or juice to it that it does! If it equals more than 2 cups, remove extra amount.) To the berry liquid, in the blender, add:

¼ cup cold water
1 teaspoon cinnamon
¼ teaspoon salt
½ cup cornstarch
1 cup sugar
3 tablespoons lemonade powder mix (Country Time preferred)

Blend on high-speed about 1 minute or until completely smooth. Pour into 2 ½-quart sauce pan. Cook on medium-high, watching and stirring CONSTANTLY as it will boil-over quickly if unattended! As it thickens like a pudding, remove from heat and stir in one stick (¼ pound) butter or margarine until melted and smooth. Stir in the Jell-O mixture and, then, the berries. Pour into one of the cooled pie shells. It should fill it right to the rim. If you use a 9-inch shell, you will have about 1 ½ cups filling left over. Crush the other baked pie shell and sprinkle it over the top of the filling. Allow 6 to 8 hours for pie to chill properly before cutting to serve 6 to 8 people. Pie should be quite firm when you cut it.

CHERRY OPEN-FACE PIE – *Follow blueberry recipe (above), substituting cherry Jell-O for the blackberry flavor, and using 2 cans (15 ounces each) red, pitted, tart cherries for the blueberries – adjust the amount of sugar and add, to taste, additional sugar if you think it needs it. Proceed as blueberry pie recipe otherwise directs.*

RED RASPBERRY OPEN-FACE PIE – *Follow blueberry recipe (above), substituting 2 cups whole frozen (slightly thawed) red raspberries, plus 2 cups cranberry juice. In place of black raspberry Jell-O, use red raspberry flavor. Proceed as recipe otherwise directs, adjusting sugar to taste.*

PINEAPPLE OPEN-FACE PIE – *Follow blueberry recipe (above), substituting orange or lemon-flavored Jell-O and 2 cans (1 pound each) pineapple chunks, using 2 cups of the canned liquid in the same manner. Proceed as directed.*

GRASSHOPPER PIE

When you visited a Chuck Muer restaurant, this was their desert specialty. It's much like the pie served at Win Schuler's restaurant. So, depending on where you would like to be at the time you prepare this, have it a-la-Muer's or a-la-Schuler's!

When I was invited into the kitchen of Chuck Muer's River Crab restaurant (St. Clair, MI) to observe them preparing some of their dishes, I made a mental note to try this pie at home. With a great deal of work on the exact proportions for making only one pie, while they made up to 15 or 20 at a time, it was indeed a challenge! But this is my version of it – and it is almost as good!

Melt half of a 1-pound bag of large marshmallows with ¼ cup milk in a sauce pan over low to medium heat until smooth, stirring constantly. When completely melted, remove from heat. Stir in 1/3 cup Creme De Menthe liqueur and ¼ cup Creme De Cacao liqueur and refrigerate the mixture until completely cooled. Meanwhile, crush 20 Oreo (cream-filled sandwich) cookies to fine crumbs. Mix well with 1 envelope, unflavored, gelatin powder and 6 tablespoons melted butter. Pat evenly over bottom and sides of a buttered 10-inch Pyrex pie plate and chill. Remove the marshmallow mixture from the refrigerator to a medium-sized mixing bowl. In a smaller bowl, beat 8 ounces heavy whipping cream until it holds its shape. Fold it into the marshmallow mixture, using low speed of electric mixer, just to blend thoroughly. Pile it neatly into the chilled Oreo crust. Garnish top with ½ cup more crushed Oreo cookies and return it to the refrigerator to chill for several hours or until firm enough to cut into 6 to 8 serving pieces. Keep pie refrigerated until served, up to a week. Freezes well up to 3 months.

ICE CREAM SPECIALTIES

MANY OF THE GOOD MEMORIES we have of our own youth have been centered around situations in which we enjoyed a soda or a Good Humor on a stick – the way a Good Humor really should be made – and hasn't been since. I can remember when the Boston Cooler came into popularity and when the "slush" was offered at every 4th of July carnival or amusement park.

HOMEMADE ICE CREAM – WITHOUT AN ICE CREAM MAKER

There is something about store-bought ice cream that tastes more like the cardboard in which it has been packaged than what it was intended to be! So, devising a simple method of making ice cream at home – without an ice cream maker – I have been very fond of these recipes. I've tried to make them without whipping cream, but it was nothing to write home about!

Making ice cream at home can be simple and accomplished without the advertised gadgets for electric ice cream makers – or the kind that Grandma used with the rock salt and the hand-operated crank. In fact, just a freezer container and an electric mixer can give you a very good dessert product that will be reminiscent of any you enjoyed from a commercial food company. Even if you don't make your own ice cream from scratch, you can try the recipes that I have so enjoyed for creating various dishes from store-bought ice creams and sherbet's.

When memories visit you, years from now, you will probably recall among the famous ice cream places were Dairy Queen, Baskin-Robbins, Howard Johnson's, Sanders and Friendly's restaurants – as well as the famous specialties like Sander's hot fudge topping, Eskimo pies, Spumoni (with chunks of cherries, almonds and pistachios included) – as well as, creamy, thick malts and milk shakes. These will remain favorites of an adoring public of loyal fans, despite the critics and experts who would have us replace all these with bean sprouts, alfalfa and carob products.

BASKET & RIBBONS – STRAWBERRY ICE CREAM

3 egg yolks
14-ounce can, sweetened, condensed milk – or use my homemade version (see Index)
1 teaspoon vanilla
10-ounce package frozen sliced strawberries, thawed
16 ounces heavy cream, whipped stiff

In large mixing bowl, beat yolks until smooth – about 3 minutes on high-speed. On lowest speed, add the milk and vanilla, just to thoroughly combine. Drain and dice the berries and, with a sturdy spoon, stir them into the milk. Fold in the whipped cream, very carefully, with a rubber scraper until it is well distributed throughout the milk mixture. Pour into a 2-quart freezer container. Seal tightly. Freeze until firm enough to scoop. Makes about 1 ½ quarts.

FLOWERED JOHN'S SONS' – CHOCOLATE ICE CREAM

13-ounce can Pet evaporated milk
6 ounces (¾ cup) Hershey's chocolate syrup
1 tablespoon granulated sugar
1 ½ teaspoons vanilla
4 ounces heavy cream, whipped stiff

Put the beaters of your portable electric mixer in the freezer. Empty the can of evaporated milk into a 2 ½-quart, aluminum, mixing bowl; placing it, uncovered, in the freezer until small ice crystals begin to form on the surface of the milk at the sides of the bowl. Remove the milk and put the beaters into the mixer, beating the milk on low speed and increasing it to high as it thickens and soft peaks form. This process will take about 8 to 10 minutes. Don't begrudge a minute of the beating time! The more air you can incorporate into the milk, the lighter the ice cream will be. Turn the mixer to lowest speed when the peaks are respectably firm and fold in the syrup, sugar, vanilla and the stiffly-beaten, whipping cream. Return it to the freezer – covering it this time with plastic wrap or heavy foil. Freeze until firm. Break it up with a fork and beat it again until creamy. Next, pack it into a freezer container with a tight-fitting lid and re-freeze it until firm enough to "scoop". Makes a little over 1 quart for about 4 to 6 servings.

PINEAPPLE ICE CREAM *– Follow the above recipe, substituting 6 ounces (¾ cup) bottled, pineapple, sundae topping for the Hershey's chocolate syrup and do as otherwise directed.*

FLOWERED JOHN'S SONS – SPUMONI

1 pint each: vanilla, chocolate, pistachio and strawberry ice creams - softened
1 cup each: toasted almonds, sliced, and shelled pistachios, chopped
10-ounce jar maraschino cherries, drained and halved
2 tablespoons rum flavoring

Lightly oil a ½-gallon (2-quart) freezer container. Spread half the softened vanilla ice cream over the bottom; then, spread half of the softened chocolate over that. Divide the softened pistachio and strawberry ice creams, each, in half. Into half of the pistachio ice cream, mix the almonds and pistachios. Combine the cherries with the rum flavoring, mixing into one half of the strawberry ice cream. Spread the half of the pistachio ice cream containing the nuts over the chocolate layer in the freezer container. Then spread the strawberry-rum ice cream mixture over that. Repeat the layers with the remaining ice creams until all have been used. Pack the mixture down gently, but firmly. Seal tight and freeze until firm enough to scoop. Makes ½ gallon.

THE TASTE OF THE TOWN!

WARREN PIERCE OF WJR – Radio, Detroit, was one of my first radio friends with whom I would visit on the air regularly, giving out recipe secrets from the food industry. When Warren had an evening show, we found that the listeners' responses to the famous "make-at-home" recipes prompted some very interesting challenges. One of our annual visits was at Thanksgiving time, when we would reminisce about one of Detroit's best-loved restaurants known as Greenfield's. One of my favorite duplications was for their pumpkin pie, which I've included in this book (see Index.) Each time I offered Warren's listeners one of the Detroit recipes, along would come requests for even more that I had not yet investigated. So, I would check out the new eating place, taste the house specialty and return to Warren's show with the previously requested recipe. This is how most of the recipes in my collection were originally discovered.

SANDERS' HOT FUDGE was one of the nicest experiences I had in working with imitations of the famous recipes, for John (Jack) Sanders, the grandson and president of the company founded by his grandfather, Fred, was one of the sponsors of Warren Pierce's radio show. Imagine my reluctance to share with his listeners my version of Sander's hot fudge. I had previously had so many threatening letters from food company lawyers that I didn't know what to expect if I heard from the Sanders people! To my amazement, the letter we anticipated did arrive only 2 days after I gave my version of the hot fudge recipe to Warren's listeners. The letter, however, said – if it wouldn't ruin my fun in trying to duplicate these famous dishes, would Paul and I and all the kids kindly accept an invitation from Jack Sanders to tour their Oakman Boulevard Bakery and Confection plant and meet their Head Chef, Edy Mader. It was the beginning of a beautiful relationship, between my Secret Recipes and Fred Sander's products and, I learned, encouraged many out-of-state orders for their products whenever I talked about them during my frequent radio visits around the country. As the slogan for Sanders' Restaurants, Bakery and Candy company said, "When it's from Sanders, even a little is a big, big treat…"

MY VISITS ON THE RADIO WITH WARREN PIERCE are still my favorite experiences in my recipe investigations. I would rather do a radio show with Warren, in fact, than television with anyone else. The audience is responsive and the feeling of having really shared something the listeners enjoy having is very rewarding. When Warren went to London for the wedding of Prince Charles and Lady Diana, he returned with a lovely recipe for me to try that was prepared by a chef who served the Prince and his party on their way to the theater. It was like a gourmet scrambled egg or strata dish that I've included in this book, as best I can come close to what the chef described on Warren's show when he had me on one phone and the chef from London on another. See Index for my Prince Charles' Skillet Strata.

SPEEDY SPUMONI

Soften 1-pint chocolate ice cream and stir in ¼ cup light rum, 1 cup chopped pecans and 10-ounce jar maraschino cherries, drained and chopped. Alternated in layers with 1 pint softened pistachio ice cream and 1 pint softened strawberry ice cream, swirling mixture to marbleized. Seal tightly and freeze until firm enough to scoop. Makes 1 ½ quarts. *NOTE: you can also prepare this spumoni in an oiled bread loaf pan. Wrap in foil, sealing tightly. Freeze until firm, then slice 1 inch thick to serve.*

HOT FUDGE SAUCE – *Like Sanders'*

The interesting thing about recipes and formulas is that you can arrive at the same result with 2 entirely different sets of ingredients – as this hot fudge topping will prove.

Recipe Number 1 – *my own favorite!*

14-ounce can Eagle Brand milk
14 ounces light corn syrup (use EB milk can to measure)
½ pound (2 sticks) butter
12 ounces Nestlé's milk chocolate candy bars – Do not substitute on brand of candy!
a few drops vanilla extract

In top of double boiler, over simmering water, combine all ingredients as listed, stirring about 15 minutes until smooth and melted. Cover and continue cooking for at least 30 more minutes, stirring about every 10 minutes. Cool and put through your blender in small portions, using on/off agitation on high speed until mixture is satiny-smooth. Makes 1 quart. Keeps refrigerated up to a month – reheat in top of double boiler over simmering water. Freezes well up to 6 months.

Recipe Number 2 – Follow the same method as in Recipe Number 1, but with these ingredients:

13-ounce can pet evaporated milk
1-pound Kraft light and dark caramels
½ pound (2 sticks) butter or margarine
12 ounces Nestlé's milk chocolate candy bars – Do not substitute on brand of candy!

BUTTERSCOTCH ICE CREAM SAUCE

½ pound butter or margarine
14-ounce can Eagle Brand milk
14 ounces light corn syrup
3 packages, 6 ounces each, butterscotch morsels

Combine everything in top of double boiler over simmering water, stirring constantly until smooth. Use portable electric mixer to beat for 3 or 4 minutes, or until you have a satiny consistency. Better yet, put mixture through your blender on high-speed, using on/off agitation. Store in a 1-quart, covered container in the refrigerator for up to 6 weeks. Reheat in top of double boiler over simmering water just to warm it before serving over ice cream [or whatever else you wish.] If you want a thinner consistency, dilute sauce with a little hot, black coffee to desired consistency. Makes almost 1 quart.

I HAVE HAD IN MY LIFE as a Secret Recipe Detective, the honor of friendship with many wonderful people in the restaurant industry, but with the exception of the letter I received from President Gerald Ford when he was in the White House and also from Michigan's First Lady, wife of the Governor, Hel en Milliken, here is one I place in equal appreciation—reprinted out of context—because I want you to know this man and his company as we do, as a company built on the principles of caring about their customers and the quality of a product that cannot be equalled. At one time I remember a sign being posted in all of the Sanders Restaurants, which I had visited, that stated, to the effect, "Please do not tip our waitresses. We feel they are adequately paid for the services they render." And I never in those many years, met one of their people who disagreed with that policy. The service was always exceptionally good!

". . .July 31, 1978

Dear Mrs. Pitzer:
How very thoughtful you were to send along copies of "Secret Recipes" and "Second Helping". I had lunch with Warren Pierce a few days ago, and we talked some about the conversations you have had with him on his evening radio program over WJR-Detroit. And, presto, along came the books! You are very kind.
I have listened to the Pitzer-Pierce conversations about Fudge Topping and Devils Food Buttercream Cakes with undisguised joy! You two are just great. It's sad, I think, that KFC and others have been so stiff necked (or is it tight-lipped) about all of this. We should all have more fun at what we do.
Speaking of KFC, my memories of The Colonel go back many years. As a high school senior, I drove to Florida with friends during a spring vacation. A long first day put us in Corbin, Kentucky, where we spotted The Sanders Motel. Of course, we had to stay there, and I can still recall discussing with The Colonel, our common last name.
. . .You, too, are such a good friend of Sanders, and if it would not spoil your own fun with recipes, we would very much like to have you visit us here at the plant. Of course, that invitation includes your children, Mike, Bill, the girls and the whole troop. I'd be happy to line up Edy Maeder, our research Chef. He is a master confectioner from Switzerland who can handle almost as many languages as recipes. . .If you would like to do this, please just give me a call. Meanwhile, I'll be looking forward to another round of "Pitzer-Pierce".

My best to you always—
Sincerely—

JOHN M. SANDERS
Chairman of the Board
Fred Sanders Company
100 Oakman Blvd.
Detroit, Michigan 48203
(1-313-868-5700)

Reproduced with permission from Gloria Pitzer; as printed in *Gloria Pitzer's Better Cookery Cookbook* (St. Clair, MI: Secret Recipes Ltd., May 1983 – 3rd printing), p. 318.

DREARY QUEEN FROZEN CUSTARD

Here is an at-home imitation of the very popular soft-serve custard ice cream product that has made many restaurant names famous [since the 50s]!

Prepare a 3 1/8-ounce package vanilla pudding (NOT instant) with only 1 2/3 cup milk and one egg yolk beaten into it. Stir mixture in medium saucepan over medium-high heat until smooth and mixture "just" comes to a boil. Remove from heat at once and stir in 2 tablespoons butter until melted and smooth. Chill pudding in freezer for about 45 minutes. Beat together ½ pint whipping cream, a dash of salt, 1 teaspoon vanilla and 1/3 cup powdered sugar until very thick and stiff. Beat chilled pudding with an electric mixer for 1 minute. Don't mind the darkened coating on top of the pudding – that blends right back in when you beat it well. Then, thoroughly stir (do NOT beat) the whipped cream mix into the smooth pudding. Transfer to a 6-cup freezer container. Freeze until firm. Break it up in a chilled, stainless steel or aluminum mixing bowl, using chilled beaters on electric mixer. Beat 2 egg whites, in a small bowl, until stiff but not dry; adding 3 tablespoons corn syrup. Set aside. Beat the whipping cream mixture until smooth and creamy. Fold egg white mixture into that, using lowest speed of mixer. Freeze until firm enough to scoop. Makes 1 ½ quarts. Freezes up to 6 months.

DREARY QUEEN – **CHOCOLATE SYRUP** *(Like DQ)*

This is, by far, the easiest way to make a smooth, chocolate syrup that's as great on ice cream as it is stirred into beverages, like hot milk for a hearty cocoa drink – or into cold sodas, malts or milkshakes.

1 cup unsweetened cocoa
¾ cup each: granulated sugar and light corn syrup
1 cup cold water
¼ teaspoon salt

In a heavy, 2 ½-quart sauce pan combine all ingredients as listed, cooking and stirring on medium heat until melted and smooth. Use portable mixer on medium speed to blend mixture, keeping heat low so chocolate won't scorch. Cook for 5 minutes, beating slowly until smooth. Beat in 2 teaspoons vanilla; then, pour into a 1-pint container. Cover tightly and refrigerate several hours before using. Keeps refrigerated up to about 8 weeks. Freezes up to a year.

Nostalgic!

PUDDING ICE CREAM SAUCE

2 packages instant pudding and pie filling (3 ¾-ounce each) – 1 butterscotch and 1 chocolate
4 cups milk
4 tablespoons butter
¼ cup each: maple-flavored pancake syrup and hot, black coffee

In a heavy 2-quart sauce pan, prepare both puddings with the milk, cooking and stirring constantly over medium-high heat until smooth. As soon as you see the first bubble of a boil, remove from heat. Stir in remaining ingredients. Serve, while still warm, over ice cream. Makes 1 quart.

CHOCOLATE ICE CREAM BAR COATING

6 tablespoons melted paraffin
1 ounce unsweetened, solid, baking chocolate
12-ounce package semi-sweet, chocolate chips
5-ounce bar Nestlé's milk chocolate
4 tablespoons butter

Combine everything in top of a double boiler over simmering water until mixture is perfectly smooth, using electric mixer on medium speed while mixture continues warming. Makes enough coating for 6 to 8 bars of ice cream – 3 x 4 x 2". Store leftover chocolate mixture in a covered container in the refrigerator for up to a month. When ready to use again, reheat in top of a double boiler over hot water.

CHOCOLATE SYRUP

In a 1 ½-quart sauce pan over medium-high heat, combine 1 cup each: unsweetened cocoa powder, hot water and maple-flavored pancake syrup. Add ½ cup packed brown sugar and a dash of salt, stirring until smooth and mixture comes to a boil. At once, reduce heat to boil very gently for exactly 3 minutes! Remove from heat. Add 1 tablespoon vanilla. Beat vigorously with a sturdy spoon about 1 minute. Let cool for one hour. Refrigerate it in a covered container to be used within 2 months. Makes about 2 ½ cups of syrup.

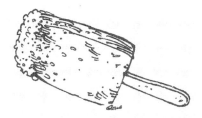

CHOCOLATE-COATED STRAWBERRY GOOD RUMOR BARS

Nothing will ever take the place of the old-fashioned, Good Humor bars, with full-flavored ice cream, coated in thick, rich, deep chocolate that set it apart from any other ice cream bar on a stick. Today, the product, when you can find them, is less than the original I remember from my youth – but thank goodness for memories and for recipes that enable us to imitate our memories at home…

Strawberry ice cream mixture:

3 egg yolks
14-ounce can Eagle Brand milk
1 teaspoon vanilla
1-pint heavy whipping cream, whipped thick but not stiff
10-ounce carton frozen, sliced strawberries

In a large bowl, combine with electric mixer on medium speed, the egg yolks and Eagle Brand milk. Beat in the vanilla until smooth. Fold in the whipped cream. Put the strawberries through your blender, using an on/off agitation on high-speed until berries are puréed. Fold into Eagle Brand mixture and spread into a 9 x 12 x 2" pan that is lined with a sheet of greased foil. Freeze until firm. Cut ice cream mixture firmly into 9 bars, about 3 x 4" each. Make up one recipe of my Chocolate Ice Cream Bar Coating (see Index) in top of double boiler and, while chocolate is still warm, insert flat wooden stick in center of one of the 3-inch-wide ends of an ice cream slice and dip quickly into chocolate, coating evenly. Work with these one at a time! As soon as you have coated one in chocolate, place it on a paper plate and put in the freezer right away – before you do another one. After chocolate is set, wrap each in plastic sandwich bags. Keep frozen up to 3 months.

MARSHMALLOW SUNDAE TOPPING

4 egg whites, at room temperature, beaten with ¼ teaspoon salt until soft peaks hold
1 cup light corn syrup, plus ½ cup MORE
½ cup granulated sugar
½ teaspoon vanilla

Bring 1st cup of corn syrup and sugar to a hard boil in a small sauce pan, stirring constantly and timing it to boil briskly for 2 minutes. Don't over-boil, or topping will be thin. Remove syrup from heat. Let bubbles subside. Resume beating egg whites while pouring in hot syrup in a thin, steady and constant stream. Rotate bowl in direction opposite of beater rotation until incorporated. Bring the other ½ cup corn syrup to a boil for 2 minutes. Resume beating egg mixture, adding this hot syrup in a slow steady stream. Add vanilla and continue beating on high-speed for 6 to 8 minutes or until thick and smooth. Refrigerate to use within 6 weeks. Makes 1 quart.

FUDGESICLES

1 cup Nestlé's Chocolate Quick drink powder (or Hershey's brand)
2 cups dry milk powder
2 ½ cups water

Dissolve the drink powder and milk powder in the water – either beating it with an electric mixer or using your blender to combine until very smooth. Divide mixture up between a dozen, 4-ounce, paper cups and set them side-by-side in a roasting pan, so they don't topple over during freezing. Place a flat wooden stick in the center of each, or use small plastic spoons. Freeze until solid. Remove paper cups by rubbing them between the palms of your hands for a minute – they'll slip right off. Makes about 12.

BEST PUDDING FUDGESICLES – *another good idea for a rich, smooth texture is to prepare 1 recipe of my Fudgesicles (above) and 2 boxes of chocolate pudding, NOT instant, just as the boxes tell you to prepare it. Combine the fudgesicle mixture with the cooled cooked pudding. Divide this mixture between 24 paper cups, at about 4 ounces each. Place flat, wooden stick in center of each or use plastic spoons. Freeze until solid.*

PUDDING POPSICLE

Prepare a 3 1/8-ounce package any flavor pudding (NOT instant) with 1 2/3 cup milk and one egg yolk beaten into it. Stir mixture in medium saucepan over medium-high heat until smooth and it "just" comes to a boil. Remove from heat at once and stir in 4 tablespoons each: butter (or margarine) and light corn syrup. Pour into popsicle molds (or fill 4-ounce paper cups.) Place a plastic spoon or flat wooden stick in center of each and freeze until solid. Makes about eight 4-ounce popsicles.

HOMEMADE PUDDING WORKS WELL in making your own frozen pudding popsicles – not to mention, what a lovely pie filling these mixtures also make. With the addition of one ingredient, the pudding popsicles can be perfect every time. Prepare pudding, and add the other ingredients as the Pudding Popsicle recipe (above) suggests, then add 1 envelope unflavored gelatin that has, first, been softened in ¼ cup cold water and placed over hot water until transparent. It gives it body!

PUDDING-SICLES PDQ

A quick way to make these, is to prepare any flavor (3¾-ounce package) instant pudding with ¼ cup LESS milk than the package directs. Into the prepared and thicken pudding, beat 2 tablespoons light corn syrup and then fold in an 8-ounce carton of Cool Whip. Divide between 8 small (4-ounce) paper cups. Place a plastic spoon or flat wooden stick in the center of each and freeze until solid. To remove the paper cups, rub the frozen cups between the palms of your hands for a minute or so and they'll slip right off.

LOYAL CHOCOLATE PUDDING

3 cups milk
6 tablespoons flour
3 ounces unsweetened, solid, baking chocolate
¾ cup granulated sugar
¼ teaspoon salt
4 tablespoons butter or margarine
1 teaspoon vanilla

Put milk and flour through blender until smooth, using high-speed for about 1 minute. Pour mixture into top of double boiler over simmering water. Add chocolate, sugar and salt. Stir until chocolate is completely melted and mixture begins to thicken. Using a portable electric mixer on medium speed, beat the mixture, while keeping the water in the lower part of the double boiler at a gentle simmer. When thick and smooth, beat in the butter and vanilla just to blend. Remove from heat. Pour into 6 small dessert dishes. Refrigerate to serve well-chilled – or serve it while it is still warm. Your choice.

VANILLA PUDDING

2 ½ cups milk
3 tablespoons cornstarch
¼ cup sugar
½ teaspoon salt
1 teaspoon vanilla
2 egg whites, beaten stiff but not dry

Put milk, cornstarch, sugar and salt through blender on high-speed for 1 minute or until smooth. Pour into top of double boiler over simmering water. Stir constantly until smooth and thickened. Stir in vanilla and fold in the beaten egg whites. Refrigerate several hours before serving to 4.

BUTTERSCOTCH PUDDING

12-ounce package butterscotch baking chips
14-ounce can Eagle Brand milk
¼ pound butter or margarine
½ cup dark corn syrup
¼ cup hot, black coffee

In top of double boiler, over simmering water, combine all ingredients as listed, stirring constantly. When chips have melted, use electric mixer on low-speed to blend completely. Spoon mixture into shallow dessert dishes. Serve completely chilled or warm – both ways are great. Serves 4 to 6.

LEMON ICE CREAM

14-ounce can Eagle Brand milk
6-ounce can lemonade concentrate, frozen
1 tablespoon lemon extract
2 drops yellow food coloring (optional)
1 pint whipping cream, whipped stiff
1 cup coarsely chopped, Lemon Drops, hard candy

In a large mixing bowl, combine Eagle Brand and lemonade, beating until smooth. Add extract (and color, if you wish.) Remove beaters and use rubber scraper to fold in whipped cream, followed by the candy. Pour into a 2-quart plastic freezer container with tight hitting lid. Freeze until firm enough to scoop. Makes almost 2 quarts.

ORANGE ICE CREAM – Prepare the Lemon Ice Cream recipe, above, using a 6-ounce can orange juice concentrate (frozen) rather than the lemonade, and orange extract rather than the lemon. If you choose to add food coloring – add one drop of red to the 2 drops of yellow. Also, substitute crushed, orange, Life Savers candy for the Lemon Drops – following rest of recipe as it otherwise directs.

HOT FUDGE – LIKE BROWN'S

I remember 2 Brown's ice cream parlors [from my childhood in Southeast Michigan] – one in Royal Oak and one in Ferndale. When Brown's went out of business, my dad took over their Ferndale building for his real estate office. That's when I learned how they prepared their hot fudge topping. It's entirely different than Sanders' – with a unique, satiny texture and an unusual flavor!

2 cans (13 ounces each) evaporated milk
2 cups granulated sugar
Dash of salt
1 pound butter – margarine
1/3 cup dark corn syrup
12-ounce package semi-sweet, chocolate chips
1 pound, Kraft's or Brach's brand, light caramels
1 teaspoon vanilla

Put everything, except vanilla, in top of large double boiler, over simmering water, using electric mixer to beat it as it cooks until melted and smooth – about 30 minutes – or put it in blender, in small portions, using medium-high speed. Add the vanilla last and give it another minute or two to blend (or beat). Makes 2 quarts. Keeps refrigerated for 6 weeks, well-covered. Freezes well for about 6 months.

BASKET & RIBBONS CHOCOLATE SYRUP

Of all the recipes, I have tried to develop for various products, this is the most interesting and, because I love the original place, whose products I attempt to imitate, I share this version as often as possible with my radio friends.

1 cup each: unsweetened cocoa powder, hot water and honey
½ cup packed brown sugar
Dash of salt
1 tablespoon vanilla

Place ingredients, as listed, in a heavy, 3-quart sauce pan, over direct heat. Keep it on medium-low and stir constantly until melted, smooth and thoroughly heated. Use electric mixer to beat it while cooking, until it has a satiny texture – or put it through your blender on low-speed for a minute. Refrigerate in a covered container. Keeps for weeks. Freezes for months. Makes 2 ½ cups of syrup.

CAROL SYRUP – CORN SYRUP SUBSTITUTE

Some people, I've been told over the years, are allergic to corn syrup. To help with that problem, I tried to devise a substitute for this product, coming up with the following formulas:

For dark syrup:

2 tablespoons butter or margarine
dash of salt
2 ½ cups water
1 cup packed brown sugar
3 cups granulated sugar
¼ cup dark molasses
½ teaspoon each: vanilla and maple flavoring

Place all but the vanilla and maple flavoring in a 2 ½-quart, heavy saucepan. Cook over medium-high heat, stirring constantly, until mixture comes to a boil. Let it boil hard for 5 minutes – set your timer! Stir often, then, reduce to lowest heat and cook at a gentle simmer, for 10 more minutes. Cool completely. Store in covered container at room temperature to be used within 2 months. Makes 2 cups.

For light syrup: Combine in a 2 ½-quart sauce pan, over medium heat until mixture comes to a boil: 2 cups granulated sugar, ¾ cup water, ¼ teaspoon cream of Tartar and a dash of salt. Reduce heat to simmer. Cover pan and cook 3 minutes, just to reduce crystal build-up on sides of pan. Uncover and cook, stirring often, to "soft ball stage" – when you drop a little from a spoon into a glass of ice cold water and it falls to the bottom in a soft ball. Cool the syrup completely and store in a covered container at room temperature to be used within 2 months. Makes 2 cups.

OTHER DESSERTS, DRINKS & SNACKS

DRINKS AND SNACKS have given an unlikely edge to a suffering food industry that was never anticipated as being possibly successful. Potato chips, pretzels, dips and appetizers have been more than well-received by a public that the industry was once certain had tried everything they could have been offered, and will probably not buy another new idea! How wrong! Whenever a new snack item or beverage has been introduced to the public, it has been received with enthusiasm, until proven unworthy of patronage, because we have become an on-the-run generation of picky eaters. Some just don't want to get involved any longer with a big meal experience. Some don't want to take the time to make the foods and, then, serve them and, finally, clean up afterward. We look for snacks and beverages to serve our guests and to enjoy individually in our most private and leisurely moments.

FROM THE OFFERINGS OF THE FOOD INDUSTRY have come some relatively good ideas, such as the baked potato chip product. Pretzels have gone from the 200-year-old tradition of hard and dry-baked to a soft, bread-like product, liberally sprinkled in salt and topped with prepared mustard and, as a fast food enterprise, has been one of the leading money-makers in the industry.

When it comes to novel beverages, Orange Julius is without competition in the marketplace – using pure orange juice, a healthy product, and their own secret ingredients to produce a frothy, appealing flavor that bears all the characteristics of an orange milkshake. The alcoholic beverages offered, as well, by the better restaurants have been bidding for the customer's attention, as Irish coffee takes on a new look and flavor in an assortment of creations served mostly as an after-dinner beverage. Wines have been flourishing in the United States in the restaurant market, as California, New York and even Michigan join the competition with French wines to bid for customer loyalty.

ORANGE BRUTUS

Remember Brutus? Per old history lessons, he's one of the men who "did in" Julius! (Caesar that is!)

In your blender, put 3 cups orange juice, 1 envelope dream whip powder, ½ teaspoon vanilla and 3 ¾-ounce box instant vanilla pudding powder. Blend until smooth. Pour into a ½-gallon pitcher and stir in 3 more cups orange juice. Makes 6 lovely drinks when served over cracked ice!

SHAMROCK SHAKE

1 ½ cups green, mint-flavored, apple jelly (the kind served with lamb dishes)
2 cups softened vanilla ice cream
1 tablespoon peppermint extract
1 ½ cups milk

Put everything into blender on high-speed using an on/off agitation until smooth. Makes 2 drinks.

MILKSHAKES

WEDNESDAY'S FROSTED DRINK

1 cup milk
½ cup Nestlé's quick chocolate drink powder
3 cups slightly soft vanilla ice cream

Put ingredients in blender, using on/off agitation and blending until smooth. Stop motor occasionally to scrape mixture away from blades and repeat blending until creamy. Makes one serving.

CHOCOLATE MILKSHAKE

6 scoops (1 ½ cups) softened vanilla ice cream
2 ½ cups milk
1/3 cup Hershey's chocolate syrup

Put everything in blender on high-speed, using an on/off agitation, until smooth. Makes 1 very large drink – or 2 reasonable servings.

STRAWBERRY MILKSHAKE

Put in blender – 2 cups softened strawberry ice cream, 2 cups milk, 3 tablespoons Nestlé's Quick strawberry-flavored powder and 3 tablespoons strawberry jam. Blend until smooth. Makes 2 drinks.

VANILLA MILKSHAKE

Put 2 cups milk into blender, adding a 3 ½-ounce package instant, vanilla, pudding powder and 1 ½ cups softened, vanilla ice cream. Blend with an on/off agitation until smooth. Makes 2 drinks.

ORANGE MILKSHAKE

In blender, put 1 cup orange juice, 1 cup softened orange sherbet, ½ cup dry milk powder, ½ cup milk and 1 teaspoon orange extract. Blend until smooth. Makes 2 drinks.

HOMEMADE TEA & COCOA MIXES

TRANQUIL TEA MIX

This is a relaxing combination of natural spices, plus loose tea that you'd drink before bedtime or after an especially hectic day. Blend together thoroughly: ¼ cup dry rosemary, ¼ cup sage leaves and 1/2 cup loose tea. Store at room temperature in a tightly covered container out of direct sunlight for up to 6 months. *To use the mix*: place 1 tablespoon of tea mix in a metal tea ball and brew in 16 ounces of boiling water for 4 to 5 minutes. Makes 2 steaming and tranquilizing cups.

SPICED TEA MIX

Stir to mix well: the finely-grated rinds of 1 orange and 1 lemon, 1 tablespoon cinnamon, ¼ teaspoon nutmeg and a dash of powdered cloves (or 3 whole cloves.) Store in a tightly-covered container out of direct sunlight up to 6 months. *To use the mix*: place 1 tablespoon of mix in a metal T-ball – or make teabags out of coffee filters. Brew in 16 ounces boiling water for 4 to 5 minutes. Makes 2 lovely cups.

FRIENDSHIP TEA MIX

Combine ½ cup orange-flavored, Tang drink mix with ½ cup instant, lemon-flavored, artificially sweetened, tea powder and 2 tablespoons lemonade mix. Combine thoroughly by sifting with a flour sifter into a container. Cover tightly. Keep in dry place out of direct sunlight. *To use the mix*: combine 1 to 2 tablespoons of mix (to taste) with 8 ounces of cold water, stirring until dissolved. Makes 1 serving.

HOT COCOA MIX

Combine 2 cups non-fat, dry, milk powder and 1/3 cup unsweetened, cocoa powder with ¾ cup sugar and a dash of salt. Add 2 tablespoons non-dairy creamer powder. Sift the mixture 4 or 5 times. Store in a tightly-covered container at room temperature. Keeps up to 2 months. Makes about 3 cups of mix. *To use the mix*: place 3 tablespoons of mix in 8-ounce cup. Stir in 6 ounces boiling water, a little at a time, until well-blended and smooth. Add a large marshmallow to float on top. Makes 1 serving.

CLOSE-A-COLA

Don't ask me why I accepted the challenge – and it wasn't even the Pepsi challenge, mind you – but, it seems, most every radio show I have done [1976 to 1983] always brings the same question: "What recipe CAN'T you crack?" [The response] was always, "Cool Whip and Coca-Cola!" Finally, one day, I decided to see just how difficult it would be. 45 days and over 100 tests later, this is as close as I could come… Thus, calling it "Close-A-Cola".

For 1 drink, mix the following ingredients well: ¼ cup cold black coffee, 2 teaspoons Lipton instant lemon-tea powder, 1/8 teaspoon vanilla extract, 1 level teaspoon sugar and a few grains of pepper. Add in equal parts with club soda, pour over ice and enjoy!

VENEERS GINGERALE (SODA) SYRUP – *for homemade golden ginger soda! If you can't find Vernors brand soda in your area, make up a close substitute this way:*

¼ cup packed brown sugar
½ cup light corn syrup
1 teaspoon powdered ginger
2 tablespoons light vinegar
½ cup water

Combine all ingredients in a small sauce pan, bringing it to a brisk boil. Boil hard for 2 minutes. Remove from heat and let it cool. Funnel it into a bottle, to keep refrigerated for months until needed. Makes 1 cup of syrup, which makes 24 ounces of soda.

To use the syrup: by the glass – allow one-part syrup to 2-parts Club Soda, mixing lightly to blend.

BOSTON COOLER

Into your blender, put 1 ½ cups (12-ounces) Vernors Golden Gingerale (Soda) and one BIG scoop of vanilla ice cream. Turn blender on high for about 30 seconds. Pour into a tall frosted glass and enjoy!

FRANKLY CAFÉ "INTERSMASHIONAL" COFFEE MIX

This unique product, by its original identity, is found on the grocer's shelves in red, white and blue cans. At home, I can closely imitate this for half as much as it costs me at the store. Our friends in Europe have enjoyed this "copy-cat" since they can't always find American brand-name products.

FRANKLY CAFÉ MIX [VANILLA]

1 packet artificial sweetener or 1 tablespoon sugar
3 ¾-ounce package instant vanilla pudding powder (Jell-O brand preferred)
1 ½ cups non-dairy creamer powder
¾ cup instant coffee granules (I like to use Maxwell House)

You must use a blender to do this imitation properly. Put all the ingredients in the blender and use an on/off agitation on high-speed until thoroughly blended. Turn off once or twice to stir the mixture away from the blades and scrape down the sides of the container. Resume blending until you can see the color is even and delicately brown. This recipe makes 2 cups of coffee mix, which makes about 48 servings. Store in a tightly-covered container at room temperature for up to 90 days.

To use the mix: place 2 rounded teaspoons of mix in a cup and stir in 7 ounces of boiling water.

To make a smaller quantity, blend thoroughly on high-speed: ½ cup non-dairy creamer powder, ¼ cup packaged instant vanilla pudding powder, ¼ cup Maxwell House instant coffee granules and 1 teaspoon sugar (or artificial sweetener equivalent.) Makes 2/3 cup mix.

BAVARIAN MINT COFFEE MIX – prepare the Frankly Café Mix (above), adding 1 roll of peppermint Lifesavers that has been crushed to a fine powder, continuing as recipe otherwise directs.

IRISH CREME COFFEE MIX – prepare the Frankly Café Mix (above), adding 2 packets (1-serving size each) Carnation brand, hot cocoa mix and continue as recipe otherwise directs. When using the mix (as directed above), also add ½ teaspoon brandy or rum flavoring.

SWITCH MOCHA COFFEE MIX – prepare the Frankly Café Mix (above), using milk chocolate pudding powder instead of the vanilla-flavored and continuing as recipe otherwise directs.

MIX WELL HOUSE COFFEE – *EXTENDER*

Long before the big coffee companies came out with coffee "blends", I was working to develop a homemade extender.

2 cups Minute Rice
1 cup each: yellow cornmeal and Quaker old-fashioned oats
4 cups Nabisco 100% Bran cereal
1 cup dark molasses
1-pound regular coffee grounds

In a dry skillet, over medium heat, brown rice until the color of chocolate. Remove from heat and, while still hot, combine with cornmeal, oatmeal, bran and molasses. Spread evenly between three 9-inch, ungreased, single-layer cake pans. Bake at 325°F for 1 hour. I suggest the 3 round pans as opposed to one large shallow pan, because the mixture will bake quicker, and with a more even browning process, around the sides and in the centers of the 3 smaller pans than in one large pan. While the mixture is still hot, combine it with 1 pound of regular coffee grounds.

TO USE MIXTURE: measure ½ cup Mix for 48 ounces of water and brew by drip or perk method. This is NOT instant coffee. Makes 6 cups.

CALYPSO COFFEE – *This is an after-dinner coffee that I had at The Victoria Dining Room in Niagara Falls, Ontario, and it has been my favorite ever since!*

Pre-rinse an 8-ounce brandy snifter in HOT water. Dry well and wipe the rim with a slice of lemon, dipping the moistened rim into super-fine granulated sugar. It should harden within a few minutes. Meanwhile, add to the preheated glass: 1 shot each – light rum and plain brandy; along with ½ shot Triple Sec, ½ cup hot black coffee and ¼ teaspoon sugar. Garnish with whipped cream and a cherry.

KAHLUA

1-quart water
3 cups sugar
10 tablespoons instant coffee granules or powder
3 tablespoons vanilla extract
A Fifth of 80-proof vodka (750 ml)

Put first 3 ingredients in a heavy, 2 ½-quart sauce pan and bring to a gentle boil – 30 minutes or until consistency is reduced to a syrup consistency. Remove from heat. Cool completely – refrigerating to hasten this. Stir in vanilla and add vodka. Funnel into a dark-tinted 1-quart bottle. Cap it tightly. Let it stand at room temperature for one week before using.

APPLE-DRYING AT HOME

YOU CAN PURCHASE DRIED APPLE SLICES at the supermarket and in health food stores, but it's a shame that more cooks don't try to dry their own – which can be so easily done with the aid of your oven! I was skeptical, until I experimented and found, just like grandma used to do, you merely peel, core and cut the apples into 1/8-inch-thick slices. Place slices, in single layer, on a wire racks and place in your oven. Turn the oven to 150°F and leave them there for 8 to 10 hours, testing them at that time for dryness, by biting into one of them. You must bite into a slice or cut into one to be sure that it is not juicy and, yet, not like a potato chip – entirely without moisture. When all the slices are dried, place in a container with a tight-fitting lid. Don't use metal! Store at room temperature for months!

To reconstitute the dried slices, soak them in just enough warm tap water to keep them submerged – or better yet, in apple cider or apple juice – for about 30 minutes. Then drain and use them as you would canned-apples. Great for pie fillings and other baked goods or desserts.

I liked the appearance of the 2nd test I made better than the 1st test, for I peeled and sliced the apples the 2nd time, dropping the slices into a pan containing 1-quart water and ½ cup lemon juice. I used a French-frying basket to lift out the slices, re-using the juice mixture over and over until all my apples had been soaked and ready for drying. Simply pat the slices with a bit of paper towel before arranging them on the racks. The soaking time ranged approximately from 5 minutes to 10 minutes, depending on how many interruptions I had… *And that includes the nice lady who keeps calling from Toledo, asking me if I can name the person who is buried in Grant's Tomb so I can win 6 free dance lessons at Arthur Murray's nearest studio – which I believe is in Chicago. I told the lady to call my mother-in-law. She probably knew Grant personally. Anyway, she could use the trip to Chicago – it might give her time to forget that she's mad at me for having put that needlepoint picture in our guest room when she stayed here last. The needlepoint read – "There's no place like home!" – but she didn't heed the message, I guess. She stayed a week one night! Interruptions like that can distract you when you're trying to cook creatively...* At least, I must make note to you, if you do prepare the dried apple slices, soak them in the lemon juice and water mixture before drying them and they will have a whiter appearance, as the citrus preserves the natural color of the apples. You can reconstitute the dried apples and put them through your blender, using them in place of fresh apples when making apple butter as well. Six apples, sliced and dried, will fill a 1-quart jar without packing it.

EASIER THAN YOU THINK!

APPLE BUTTER

One of the best additions to pancakes was the offering of apple butter at a restaurant in upper New York State. The apple butter was homemade, from the apples of their adjoining cider mill and orchards. Had I only known, [in the 50s] that I would be re-creating famous recipes [25 years later], I would have paid more attention to what the cook told me she did with the apple butter. All I could remember was that she began with apple juice and lemonade and a little molasses. After several batches that were not even close, I finally came up with the correct combination that, in my memory, duplicated the smooth, slightly-spiced condiment.

6-ounce can lemonade concentrate, frozen
6 ounces "natural"-style apple juice (I used Mott's brand)
2 cups firmly-packed brown sugar
¼ cup dark molasses
4 teaspoons cinnamon powder
1 teaspoon mace powder
½ teaspoon salt
24 firm, semi-large, red apples

Combine everything except the apples in a 2 ½-quart sauce pan, stirring constantly over high heat until it comes to a boil. At once, reduce heat to lowest point and continue stirring until all the sugar has dissolved. Let it simmer ever-so gently while you prepare the apples.

Have a helper – or even two – to peel and grate 24 firm, large, red apples (by weight, before peeling, I had exactly 10 pounds.) Using the large hole of a vegetable grater, grate the peeled apples to almost the cores – you don't want to scrape the casing around the seeds the least bit and have these get into the apples. Keep turning the apple a quarter of a turn as you grate it down close to the core. Discard the cores and combine both syrup and apples in a very large kettle, to be certain all the apples are coated in the syrup. Place this on high heat, again, stirring constantly until it begins to bubble. Remove from heat at once, or it may scorch, and begin putting 2 or 3 cups full of the mixture through your blender to a purée, transferring the purée to a preheated slow cooker or crock pot. When all the mixture has been puréed, cover the cooker with a tight-fitting lid. Be sure there are no particles of food lodged around the rim of the cooker to prevent a tight fit, where heat might otherwise escape and foul up the temperature control. Set heat at high for 1 hour. Then, stir it thoroughly and turn heat to LOW.

Keep it covered and forget about it for 5 hours or longer – depending upon the thickness you wish. The longer it cooks, the thicker it will be. Makes about 3 quarts of apple butter, which can be packed into family-sized freezer containers and sealed securely to be used within a year. Allow to thaw at room temperature when ready to use.

NACHO CHEESE – SPICY

No matter what ballpark or Bar & Grill you go into, today [1983], the hit of the menu seems to be this spicy, cheese sauce mixture accompanied by a plate of corn chips. Not entirely difficult to make, if you can find bottled, hot pickled pepper, using only the juice of that with Cheez Whiz made by Kraft, in proportions to taste – or use this formula, which I serve with a fire extinguisher at our house!

16-ounce jar Kraft Cheez Whiz
¼ teaspoon Tabasco sauce
Dash of cayenne pepper
½ teaspoon black pepper
¼ pound margarine
½ teaspoon garlic salt
1 teaspoon onion powder
1 tablespoon canned jalapeno peppers, chopped –
    or 1/3 of a whole green pepper, seeded and chopped fine

Combine ingredients, as listed, in top of a double boiler over simmering water, stirring until smooth. When thoroughly heated, serve with corn chips. Also, good when served chilled. Keep leftovers refrigerated in a covered container up to a month. Freezes well for several months. Makes 3 cups.

CANAPÉ FRANKS

At a restaurant buffet table, I came across this tasty and truly simple appetizer that has become a family-favorite of ours.

1-pound Ball Park franks
12-16 ounces sliced bacon
1 small box of round, wood toothpicks
1 cup each: ketchup and sugar

Cut each of the franks into 4 pieces of equal length. Cut each strip of bacon into 4 pieces of equal length. Wrap one piece of bacon around one piece of frank, securing with a toothpick and repeating until all the frank pieces have been wrapped in the bacon pieces. Arrange in a single layer in a shallow baking pan. Bake at 400°F for 10 minutes. Remove partially-cooked pieces from pan and place in a slow cooker or casserole dish that will accommodate the pieces so that they fill it half-full.

Combine equal parts ketchup and sugar until you have enough mixture to keep hotdog pieces submerged – I use 1 cup of each. Cover with a snug-fitting lid and oven-bake casserole dish at 325°F for 45 minutes to an hour or until bubbly and thoroughly cooked. If using a slow cooker, turn it on high for 1 hour and then on low for 2 hours, or until time to serve, keeping tightly covered with snug-fitting lid. Serve these while still hot, noting that the toothpicks become nice little handles for picking them up and the heating process does not affect the wood, nor does the wood affect the sauce. Makes 8 to 10 appetizer-sized (4 to 5 pieces) servings. Leftovers can be refrigerated up to a week.

CHEESE WISH

Part of the fun of writing my recipes is coming up with the names for the imitations that will (1) avoid trespassing on the copyrighted or patented trade names of the products I attempt to emulate and (2) waiting for the amused reaction of my readers. This is one of those product emulations that tickles me, because it was our youngest daughter, Cheryl, who came up with the name. In my adventures with Common Sense Cooking, I have discovered several recipes that give both flavor and personality to otherwise plain dishes. I have so many American readers overseas who cannot find brand-named products, that recipes like this one, turn their culinary creations into reminiscent reflections of home.

½ pound each: American cheese slices, cut into bits, and sharp cheddar, grated
¼ cup vegetable oil
2 tablespoons vodka
½ cup dry milk powder
½ cup chicken broth (canned or homemade)

Place everything in top of double boiler over simmering water. Using a portable electric mixer on low, beat it as it melts until completely smooth. Then, put it through your blender on medium speed, using an on/off agitation, for about 20 seconds. Transfer to a container with a tight-fitting lid and refrigerate to use within 6 weeks. Freezes well up to a year. Makes about 4 cups.

LECITHIN is from the Greek, meaning "egg yolk" and is found in all living organisms, plants and animal life. It is a significant constituent of nerve tissue and of brain substance. Composed of units of choline, phosphoric acid, fatty acids and glycerin, it is commercially isolated from eggs, soy beans, corn and egg yolk and used as an antioxidant in prepared cereals, candies, breads and margarine. It works as an emulsifier (a thick liquid.) Lecithin is the one ingredient that will make my "Cheese Wish" exactly like the original product that I attempted to emulate.

If you are familiar with liquid lecithin, purchased from specialty food shops, you can also create the Cheese Wish imitation by combining each of the ½-pounds of American and cheddar with 1 teaspoon of the lecithin and ½ cup of hot broth, beating in 2 or 3 tablespoons dry milk powder to the consistency of hot fudge – or equal to the "original".

IT IS ALSO POSSIBLE TO imitate it by preparing a light white sauce like my "Blender White Sauce" (see Index) – to 1 cup of it, while it is still warm in the top of a double boiler over simmering water, beat in 2 raw egg yolks, stirring until incorporated and smooth. Beat in 4 tablespoons vegetable oil and 1 tablespoon glycerin (from drugstore.) Combine this mixture with 3 tablespoons chicken bouillon powder, ½ teaspoon turmeric, ¼ pound melted American cheese and ¼ pound melted cheddar cheese – and then just enough hot water to give it the consistency equal to the supermarket product.

WELSH RABBIT

In top of double boiler, over simmering water, combine – 1-pound Velveeta cheese, cut into small pieces, and ¼ pound margarine, in bits, with a 10-ounce can cream of celery soup, 1 envelope onion soup mix and ¼ teaspoon Tabasco hot pepper sauce until melted and mixture is smooth. Ladle over buttered toast triangles and serve piping hot. Serves 4 to 6.

SOFT PRETZELS

THE SIMPLE RECIPES that I've told you I personally prefer, are not always the fastest – but how can you argue with the virtues of a 4-ingredient combination that is far superior to what you find in the frozen food selections of your supermarket – or to a product sold exclusively in shopping malls, where it is the only item on their menu. I speak of the SOFT PRETZEL! And I will not get into one of those tacky and senseless debates on the virtues or penalties of a simple food like the "soft pretzel", when it's great-grandfather, French bread, is hardly on the APB of food critics anywhere! Argue, if you wish, about this as a "junk food", but as for myself, I have better options with which to spend my energies. Let me share with you this simple combination of ingredients I developed for this super-snack idea.

1 envelope dry yeast mix
1 cup warm water
1 tablespoon sugar
3 ¼ to 3 ½ cups all-purpose flour

Place yeast, water and sugar in a 1 ½-quart mixing bowl. Give it a stir just to combine it all and set your timer to let it stand in a warm place for 10 minutes. This will allow it to triple in bulk! If it doesn't – the yeast is bad or the water was too hot. Throw it out and start all over again.

With an electric mixer on low speed, work in about half of the flour to a smooth dough. Remove beaters. Work in enough of the remaining flour so that you have a smooth, elastic-type dough that is no longer sticky to the touch. Keep a little extra flour handy in which to dip your knuckles (as in my White Bread recipe directions – see Index) and knead dough for 5 minutes. Do this right in the bowl. Take another bowl the same size and spray it with Pam or wipe it lightly with oil. Place dough in this bowl, turning it over once so that the top is now greased. Spray the inside of a plastic bag with Pam or wipe lightly with oil. Place the bag over the bowl, allowing half of the bag to remain above the top of the bowl, giving the dough room to rise to 3 times its original size in bulk. This takes about 45 minutes – set your timer! It might take a bit longer, depending on the humidity and warmth in the room. If the dough touches the bag at all in rising, it shouldn't stick to it because you have greased it properly.

When dough is about 2 inches above the rim of the bowl, flour your fingers and punch the dough down, kneading it a minute or two. Break apart into 15 pieces and roll them into 12-inch long "ropes". Shape into the popular soft pretzel form by twisting the 2 ends together twice and bringing them down to the center of the "rope". Pinch it together in a, kind of, heart-shape. Arrange on greased cookie sheet and place in freezer, uncovered, for 1 hour. You don't want them to rise any more than they have. Meanwhile, put 4 cups of water in an accommodating skillet with 4 tablespoons baking soda. Bring this to a brisk boil and keep it boiling gently as you lift the pretzels, one at a time, with a pancake turner, slipping it into the water for half a minute. Remove with pancake turner and drain on paper towel. Place 2 inches apart on the greased cookie sheet. Dust in coarse ground salt, or sea salt. Bake in a preheated, 450°F oven for 14 minutes. Remove from cookie sheet at once. Enjoy them while they're hot! Makes 15 pretzels. Serve them with my homemade Mustard (see Index)!

WIND SHOOTER'S BAR CHEESE

A national snack favorite… There are many derivations of this most popular Michigan specialty. The 1ˢᵗ recipe I developed to imitate Win Schuler's product, required several more ingredients than I really wanted to work with. But, the result was perfect! Eventually, I experimented in my Secret Recipes kitchen to streamline the ingredients down to only a few. Each version has its rightful place among the "Haute Cuisine" of fast foods and appreciable snacks. It depends on your personal taste preferences, which recipe to use.

THE ORIGINAL BAR CHEESE SECRET RECIPE

1-pound Velveeta cheese (do not substitute on brand)
½ pound unsalted butter – at room temperature
2 tablespoons onion juice
– bottled or freshly-grated onion, put through blender to purée and diluted with equal parts water
1/8 teaspoon Tabasco, hot pepper sauce
8-ounce package cream cheese, mashed with a fork
5-ounce bottle horseradish
a few drops each – red and yellow food coloring, sufficient to give a bright orange tint (optional)
¼ cup melted and strained bacon drippings

Place all ingredients, just as listed, in top of a double boiler over simmering water. Stir occasionally until melted and smooth. The mixture will appear to be coarse in texture. For best results, put it through the blender on high-speed, using an on/off agitation, for 2 or 3 minutes until satiny smooth – or if you do not have a blender, use an electric mixer on high-speed, beating until smooth. Pour into a container with a tight-fitting lid and refrigerate up to 4 or 5 weeks. Freezes well up to 6 months. Makes about 1 quart – give or take a little!

BAR CHEESE WITH CATALINA

2 pounds Velveeta (do not substitute brand!)
½ pound margarine (2 sticks)
5-ounce bottle horseradish
8-ounce bottle Kraft's Catalina salad dressing
8-ounce tub French onion chip dip

Combine all ingredients in top of double boiler over simmering water, stirring frequently until melted and almost smooth. Cook and stir occasionally for 10 minutes over simmering water, scraping down sides and bottom of pan periodically. Put mixture through blender on high-speed, using on/off agitation, for 2 or 3 minutes. Pour into a 1-quart refrigerator container. Cover tightly. Keep refrigerated up to a month – OR freeze it up to 6 months.

BORED ENDS' COTTAGE CHEESE – *Homemade*

2 cups buttermilk
13-ounce can pet evaporated milk
juice of half a lemon
½ teaspoon salt (optional)

Place it all in the top of a double boiler over hot water and set your timer for 1 hour. Put a lid on the top of the pot and check it when the hour is up to be sure the water in the bottom half is sufficient to touch the bottom of the pan on top. Keep the water hot, but not boiling, and give it a stir or 2, without breaking up the coagulation too much. Let the cheese stand another 40 minutes, uncovered, over the hot water. Line a colander with a large coffee filter and place it inside a larger non-metal container to catch the "whey". Let the cheese drip this way until all of the whey has drained into the container below. Carefully break up the cheese and store it in a covered container in refrigerator for a week. DO NOT FREEZE THIS! The whey can be frozen up to a year to be used in other recipes. Makes 1 cup.

CHEESE-DRAINING (WHEY)

This is a Rube Goldberg method – but it works! And – when you don't have any special equipment for such cookery challenges, as making your own cheese – who's to argue with something that works!

Use an empty 9-ounce plastic Cool Whip container, with lid, well-washed in hot water. With the tip of a sharp knife, make a cut in the form of an "X" about ½ inch in length right through the middle of the bottom of the container. Next, make ½ inch cuts around the bottom edge, about 1 inch apart from each other. Find a Pyrex bowl (NOT a metal container – EVER) the same diameter as the Cool Whip bowl. The Cool Whip bowl will contain the curd and whey when the cooking time is up on the cheese recipes you are using. When you are instructed to drain it in a colander you can use this method instead.

Place the Cool Whip bowl inside the glass bowl, keeping it tightly covered while draining. Let the whey drip into the outer container for 4 to 6 hours per cup of cheese desired. Place 3 paper towels or coffee filters over the top surface of the cheese mixture and press down firmly but evenly with the back of a large spoon to hasten some of the draining of the whey. Repeat 3 or 4 times during the draining process. When no more whey is visibly dripping from the container holding the cheese, transfer the cheese to a storage container. Cover it tightly and refrigerate until time to serve.

SWEETEN HOUSE BREAD PUDDING

Butter 6 slices of white toast – crusts trimmed away. Sprinkle buttered sides of toast with my Cinnamon and Sugar Mix (see Index) to taste. Makes 3 sandwiches out of the 6 slices, placing cinnamon-sugared sides together. Cut each sandwich into 4 strips. Arrange them in a single layer in a buttered 9-inch square baking dish. Sprinkle about ½ cup packed brown sugar over this. Then sprinkle with ½ cup raisins. Combine 4 eggs with 2 tablespoons sugar and 2 cups milk in a small bowl, beating well. Pour over bread pieces. Place baking dish in larger pan with enough water in it to reach halfway up the sides of the dish with the bread mixture. Bake at 375°F for 45 minutes or until "set". Serve warm, topped with sweetened whipped cream or "a la mode", with vanilla ice cream. Serves 6.

POTPOURRI

Entertaining Food & Drinks

FOODS PREPARED for entertaining have always put me in a positive mood… Positive that, if the food is too good, everybody will keep wanting to come to our house and I'll never be asked to theirs! On the other hand, if the food is not as good as it should be, and I fall short of the best cook in our bunch, somebody will be in my kitchen checking my stove for the training wheels they think it should have, considering the results of my cooking skills. So, food for entertaining must be fast, festive and flavorful. But, certainly not to the ridiculous possibility of opening a can of caviar at $18.50 an ounce [at the time of the original writing!] That is, both, elegant and easy, but hardly practical! When folks drop in and wish us happy holidays, it is sometimes without notice and I like to be prepared. While there is absolutely nothing I can do to rid the lamp shades of the cobwebs that suddenly show up in the light, I can at least be glad something in the living room matches. With any luck, if it is mentioned, I'll exclaim promptly: "Oh, don't touch that! That's our daughter's science project. We're observing the mating habits of the harmless house spider!"

At this point, I can whisk everyone into the kitchen where, somehow, Coke splatters on the ceiling seem to go undetected if we turned off the overhead lights and put out some pretty candles. In 2 or 3 minutes, I can be spooning shredded cheddar cheese onto Triscuits, adding a slice of pepperoni and having it all under the broiler while Paul (on cue) delights them with another of his golfing jokes. His old stand-by is the story of his 2 friends on the golf course, noting 2 women on the green ahead of them, playing very slowly. One of the men asked the other if they shouldn't go up to the gals and ask if they minded if the men played through… Or chances were they'd never get off the course. So, one of the men went running up to the ladies and got almost to the green when he darted quickly back. His friend asked what happened and why he hadn't asked about playing through. "I can't do that," the man said. "One is my wife and the other is my girlfriend!" So, the other man offered to go up and ask. He got within a few yards of the ladies and he, also, darted back breathlessly, confessing to his friend… "Small world, isn't it?" By the time they stopped chuckling, the cheese snacks were ready and the egg nog was out of the "icebox" and into the punch cups, diluted with Golden Ginger-Ale (soda) and, depending upon the folks we were entertaining, perhaps a shot of grandpa's favorite rum in each cupful! 2 or 3 of these Yuletide drinks and either Paul's jokes got funnier – or we forgot how many times he told them before.

EGG-NOT

Into your blender, put 2 cups softened vanilla ice cream, ¼ cup light rum, 1 teaspoon nutmeg and 10-ounces Golden Ginger Soda (Vernors preferred.) Blend on high for 1 minute. Makes 4 small drinks.

THE CABOOSE

Made just like a ***GRASSHOPPER***, only using Amaretto rather than Creme de Menthe. Combine in a blender: 1 shot Creme de Cocoa, 1 shot Amaretto, ¼ cup crushed ice and ¼ cup Half & Half light cream. Blend on high for about a minute and serve in a champagne glass with a fleck of nutmeg on top.

HOT BUTTERED RUM

Serve a cup of this brew with my Strawberry Nut Bread (see Index), the idea borrowed from The Country Inn of Berkeley Springs, West Virginia – where owner, Bill North, puts special emphasis on down-home cooking.

Combine 6 cups cider, 3 cinnamon sticks, 4 whole cloves and 1 slice of lemon (about ¼ inch thick), in a sauce pan. Bring it to a boil; then, simmer uncovered for 5 minutes. Pour hot cider through a fine mesh strainer. Discard pieces of lemon. Divide between 8 mugs, pre-rinsed in hot water; and to each serving, add 1 ½ ounces light rum. Float ½ teaspoon butter atop each and add a twist of lemon to the rim of the cups. Serves 8 adequately.

FRUIT SALAD DRESSING

1-pound tub sour cream
7-ounce jar marshmallow creme
Pinch of nutmeg
½ teaspoon almond extract
¼ teaspoon lemon extract

With electric mixer on low-speed, combine ingredients as listed in a small mixing bowl. Keep refrigerated in a covered container for up to 2 weeks to use, as needed, on mixed fruit salad. Makes about 3 ½ cups of dressing – give or take a little.

SWEETEN HOUSE RICE CONFETTI

3-ounce box strawberry or raspberry Jell-O gelatin
¾ cups sugar
2 cups cooked, cold rice (not instant)
1 cup chopped pecans
8-ounce can crushed pineapple, well-drained
10-ounce jar maraschino cherries, drained and each cut in half
2 cups miniature marshmallows
1 cup whipping cream, whipped with 3 tablespoons powdered sugar –
    Or use a 9-ounce carton Cool Whip, thawed

Prepare Jell-O is box directs, stirring sugar into hot Jell-O before it has a chance to thicken. Chill until wiggly but not firm. Stir in cold rice and remaining ingredients in the order given above. Turn into lightly oiled 1 ½-quart container. Cover and refrigerate several hours, or overnight, until firm. As a dessert, serve it in 6 goblet-style glasses. As a salad, serve it on 6 lettuce-lined luncheon plates.

TEXAS FRUITCAKE

Legend has it that Puddin' Hill has the best-darn fruitcake west of the Mississippi – and the recipe for it is a secret that has been closely guarded by a lady named Mary, and her family – who've made it, not just a tradition, but, a reason for celebrating!

1 pound each: walnuts and dates
10-ounce package currants
20-ounce can pineapple chunks
2 jars (10-ounces each) red maraschino cherry
2 cups sugar, divided
1 cup all-purpose flour

6 large eggs
1 teaspoon vanilla
1 ½ cups sugar
¼ pound (one stick) butter or margarine
1 teaspoon each: baking powder, salt, grated orange rind and lemon rind
½ teaspoon each: nutmeg and cinnamon
2 ounces brandy flavoring, or real brandy
1 cup all-purpose flour

Break up walnuts with hammer. Slice dates into 4 pieces each. Mix these with currants and set aside. Put pineapple and its juice with 1 cup of the sugar in a small sauce pan. In another small sauce pan, combine cherries with their juice and the other cup of sugar. Let both pans simmer briskly, uncovered, about 30 minutes. Reserving the syrups, drain each. Set fruits aside to cool, spreading them out over lightly-oiled cookie sheets. Place cookie sheets of fruit in a 350°F oven for 15 minutes. Remove to cool for 15 minutes. Combine with the 1st cup of flour and walnut mixture in roasting pan. Coat every single dry particle of it with the flour. Then beat remaining ingredients as listed on medium-speed of electric mixer for 5 minutes. Pour over floured mixture. Be sure batter coats every piece and absorbs all flour. Pack mixture evenly into bottom of 2 Pam-sprayed, 8-inch, square Pyrex baking dishes that have 2 layers of wax paper on bottom only, placing dishes on cookie sheets to bake at 275°F for almost 2 hours or until toothpick inserted in center of each comes out clean. Cool. Cut each into 2 equal loaf-like pieces. Wrap each in a brandy-soaked cloth and then in plastic bags. Store at room temperature for 30 days to "ripen" before serving. If you use the cakes right away, you can take the reserved syrup from the pineapple and cherries, which you set aside earlier, and combine them in a small sauce pan. Get them piping hot. Remove from heat and measure the syrup. Add half as much whiskey, rum or brandy and brush the warm syrup over the cake-loaves before slicing to serve. Freezes well up to a year. Makes 4 loaves (4 x 8" each). If prepared 30 days before serving, soak and re-soak cloth in liquor during that time, keeping them just dampened. Sealing cakes in air-tight containers – after wrapping in the cloths and in the plastic to keep them moist.

FOOD FOR THOUGHT: Logic is a systematic method of coming to the wrong conclusion with confidence.

ANGEL WINGS

5 egg yolks, well-beaten
5 tablespoons each: sour cream and sugar
1 tablespoon almond extract
¼ teaspoon salt
2 ½ cups flour

Combine all, as listed; and enough more flour that dough is not sticky, but still very soft. Roll small portions of dough at a time to paper-thin on a lightly floured surface. Cut into strips, 2 x 5", and arrange in a single layer on oiled cookie sheets. Fill a deep, heavy sauce pan at least 3 inches deep with oil, heating it to 400°F. Make a 1-inch slit down center of each and draw the opposite ends of the strips through the slit. Drop into the hot oil to fry. They will fall to the bottom of the pan, but will surface in a few seconds as they delicately brown – about 2 minutes. Lift out with tongs and drop into large grocery sack containing about a pound of powdered sugar. Shake the bag to coat the Angel Wings evenly. Makes oodles! *Flavor variations include: substituting for the almond extract – dark or light rum or rum flavoring… Or ginger brandy… Or, in addition to any of these, a pinch of nutmeg!*

REINDEER TEARS – cut the Angel Wing dough into diamond shapes and fry them as directed above.
ELEPHANT EARS – cut the Angel Wing dough to the diameter of a saucer and fry one at a time.

ANGEL AMBROSIA

For this dreamy dessert, bake your own angel food cake or pick one up at the market – tear it apart into bite-sized pieces in a large mixing bowl, adding 7 ounces flaked coconut, 2 jars (10-ounces each) well-drained maraschino cherries, 1-pound shelled pecans or walnuts (broken into odd sized pieces), a 20-ounce can pineapple chunks (drained) and a 10-ounce can Mandarin orange slices (drained.) Lightly mix together with two 12-ounce tubs Cool Whip. Serve in stemmed goblets with macaroons. Makes 10-12 servings.

DRY ROASTED PEANUTS

Spread 3 cups of raw, shelled peanuts over bottom of a shallow, ungreased, baking pan (10 x 13 x 2") and place on center rack of a 350°F oven for 35 to 40 minutes, stirring often. You may have to remove some of the skins of the nuts during baking, as those close to the sides of the pan will brown more quickly than those in the center. Remove when evenly but delicately browned. Allow to cool for 15 minutes. Remove all the skins. Melt ¼ cup butter or margarine in a large skillet, but do not let butter change color, and stir in 1 tablespoon peanut oil. Turn off heat and add peanuts, coating them evenly. Spread in a single layer on paper towels and dust with salt. Store in covered container at room temperature.

CHEESE CRACKERS

1 cup flour
1/3 cup butter (not margarine)
2 ounces (a scant cupful) shredded cheddar cheese
a dash or 2 of cayenne pepper
1/8 teaspoon paprika
1 ½ tablespoons of cold water

Mix flour with butter until crumbly, using pastry blender or 2 forks. Work in cheese, cayenne pepper and paprika. Sprinkle mixture with cold water, mixing as you would a pie crust dough and trying not to handle it too much. Shape into ball and roll out ¼-inch thick on floured surface. Cut with small round cookie cutter dipped in flour. Transfer circles to a Pam-sprayed or lightly-oiled cookie sheet, placing 1 inch apart. Preheat oven to 350°F and bake 8 to 10 minutes. Remove carefully with pancake turner to let crackers cool on paper towels. When completely cooled store them in a metal tin with a tight-fitting lid at room temperature for 7-10 days. Makes about 3 dozen crackers.

SNACKING CAKE – *Here's a mix-in-the-pan quickie company cake!*

1 ½ cups Bisquick biscuit mix
¾ cup granulated sugar
½ cup mayonnaise
1/3 cup Hershey's chocolate syrup
2/3 cup black coffee
1 tablespoon each: vanilla and light vinegar

Grease and flour an 8-inch square pan. Into the pan, dump all the ingredients (without stirring in-between) just as listed. Then, mix well with a fork. Bake at 350°F for 50 minutes. Dust with powdered sugar and sprinkle with chopped nuts and/or maraschino cherries. Serves 6.

BACON CHIP DIP

16 ounces sour cream
8 ounces cream cheese
1 teaspoon hickory salt
½ pound bacon, fried crispy and crumbled
3 green onions, scissor-snipped

Using an electric mixer on medium speed, combine sour cream and cream cheese. Beat in salt. Remove beaters and stir in bacon and onions. Keep refrigerated in a covered container for 24 hours before serving. Makes about 3 ½ cups.

CREAM CHEESE DIP

2 packages (8 ounces) cream cheese, soft
1 cup real mayonnaise
1 tablespoon beef bouillon powder
1 teaspoon each: onion powder and garlic powder
3 tablespoons dry minced onion flakes

Beat cream cheese and mayonnaise until smooth. Beat in remaining ingredients. Makes 3 cups. Keep refrigerated for 24 hours before serving.

COMPANY CHEESE BALL

2 packages (8 ounces each) shredded cheddar
8 ounces cream cheese
2 jars (4 ounces each) craft bacon flavored spread
1 teaspoon hickory salt
2 tablespoons horseradish cream sauce

Put everything in a medium-size bowl and mash it with a potato masher – or use your fingers, which were invented before forks. Squeeze the ingredients together until they all cling lovingly to each other. Shape into 2 balls of equal size – about the size of a croquet ball. Roll each in finely crushed pecans or walnuts and arrange on saucers, wreathed in fresh parsley sprigs. Chill cheese balls, wrapped well in plastic wrap, until time to serve. Keeps refrigerated well, if covered, for up to a week. Each ball, accompanied by assorted crackers, will serve about 8... Or 4, with bad manners.

"DIETING" DISHES

If not for nutritional reasons, most folks diet for vanity's sake because they want to look as good as the "people images" that are constantly being thrust upon us through product advertising, television personalities and fashion promotions. The need to identify with the image is a form of hunger. It's a hunger to be approved, to belong and to be comfortable about belonging, as well as to be appreciated. We want to fit in rather than stand out and being overweight poses a problem with many people's sense of self-worth as confined to how they look, rather than how they behave.

As we are forced into this "mold", keep in mind that dieting is not necessarily right for everyone. There are those, who are perfectly healthy and have good feelings about themselves and the world around them even though they are 10 or 15 or 20 pounds overweight. You know your own body and how it functions and what satisfies it physically and emotionally better than anyone! If your choices, now, include things you eat without really enjoying them, you can begin to exercise, instead of your "will" power, your "won't" power – and refuse to keep on eating what is not good for you and what you don't really need, replacing it with something you do enjoy and that will benefit you in nourishment, either emotionally or physically. The WON'T power exercise for me meant no bread, no potatoes, no pastries, no gravy, no greens or other starches. It worked beautifully. For you, it might not be satisfactory. So, you can choose another course of action. I merely wish to share my experience with you because it worked for me.

What works for one person, may not work for another; but sharing the secrets of a weight loss diet that works, is too good to ignore. Even if you, personally, are not interested in losing 10 pounds, you probably know someone who is! The diet industry pulls in millions and millions of dollars every year, developing new gimmicks, pills, plans, menus, clubs and published materials about losing weight. I have tried them all in my adult life – and never with success! So, I finally developed my own diet. And it worked – for me!

It's not really a diet, but a new pattern of eating that can, if I wish, serve me all my life. The best way to learn any new pattern of behavior – whether it is eating or dancing or jogging or working – is to break it down into small manageable parts and work through them step-by-step! This is not a diet to be used, discarded and taken up again. It is a way of life at the table. It is a new attitude towards food – what they can or cannot do for your health, your appearance and your emotional well-being. You cannot tailor your eating habits to other people's demands. Like a male obstetrician, telling you he knows just how you feel in the 10th month of your pregnancy – nobody really knows, but YOU!

This diet happened to work for me, the same way another diet worked for Jean Nidetch before she put Weight Watchers into operation. She talked about the success of her own diet experiences with others in her home, who shared the disappointments of not losing weight. She was not a nurse, nor a doctor, nor even a qualified nutritionist when she started Weight Watchers. When she sold the organization to the Heinz Corporation, she had made many people happy with her plan for weight loss! Weight Watchers grew to become one of the most successful divisions of the food industry. But the point is, she had an idea, had proven that it worked for her, and could share that experience, giving advice to others, so that it could work just as well for them.

This chapter is a reprint of recipes I used (from my Dieters Digest booklet, published in 1979 and 1980) and the thoughts and philosophies that helped me!

Dieter's Digest

Diet Recipes of enduring significance, in condensed permanent booklet form

Diet Basics

FICTION FEATURE

Selling Points

WHAT WORKS FOR ONE PERSON may not work for another, but sharing the secrets of a weight loss diet that works, is too good to ignore. Even if you personally are not interested in losing 10 pounds (or more as the case may be)—you probably know someone who is! The Diet Industry pulls in millions and millions of dollars every year, developing new gimmicks, pills, plans, menus, clubs and published materials on the subject of losing weight. I have tried them all in my adult life—and never with success! So I finally developed my own diet. And it worked!

The Impossible Diet

Special Request Feature

LIFE IN THESE UNITED TASTES

IT IS NOT REALLY A DIET, but a new pattern of eating that can, if I wish, serve me all of my life. The best way to learn any new pattern of behavior—whether it is eating or dancing, or jogging, or working, is to break it down into small, manageable parts & work through them step by step! This is not a diet to be used, discard, taken up again. It is a way of life at the table. It is a new attitude toward foods—what they can or cannot do for your health, your appearance, your emotional well-being.

YOU CANNOT TAILOR YOUR EATING habits to other people's demands. Like a male obstetrician telling you he knows just how you feel in the 10th month of your pregnancy—nobody really knows but YOU!

❁ WAIST ❁ WATCHERS

Reproduced with permission from Gloria Pitzer; as printed in *Gloria Pitzer's Better Cookery Cookbook* (St. Clair, MI: Secret Recipes Ltd., May 1983 – 3rd printing), p. 356.

WAIST WATCHERS INTERNATIONAL

There is no safe way in the world to lose weight in a rush. All you're doing by taking it off FAST is risking throwing your body into shock! This happens when a pattern of eating is suddenly altered.

Foods are like chemicals – and when certain chemicals are combined, certain results are achieved. All a diet is doing for you is changing the combination of chemicals (foods) so that you are producing results that alter the physical condition and still not jeopardize your health and emotional well-being. Many diets are severely damaging to the mental and emotional stress of the individual. So, you must regard any diet as, simply, a new pattern of eating habits. For want of a better title, I refer to this as "Weight Snatchers International" - because we are dieting to snatch away pounds without forfeiting our health and certainly without giving up the best tasting and the most satisfying choices of foods.

Water is very important in any diet – whether it is counting calories or carbohydrates – because it washes the food away before it has a chance to be absorbed by the system. If you practice drinking water with everything you eat – half a glass before a meal, sips during the meal and half a glass after the meal – you will not only not feel hungry for several hours, but you will not be converting the food you eat in to pounds and inches you don't need nor want! I found that filling a juice container that had a tight-fitting lid with 2 quarts of water 1ˢᵗ thing in the morning was a big help to me and reminded me to drink the water [throughout the day]. There were days when I would be super-busy in the office and hours would pass without my taking a drink of water. So, I put the water container where I could notice it often and stopped every chance I had to drink just a bit. Whenever I did this, I noticed a drop in my weight within a day or two. Water in tea, coffee or bullion does NOT count. You must still drink plain water to "wash away" those foods that would ordinarily turn into unwanted inches or pounds.

THE EASY WAY!

The easy way to diet is to realize that the best diets are planned on sound principles of nutrition, but they must also be designed to give, both, variety and eating pleasure. Dr. George Christakis, who was director of the New York City Department of Health, Bureau of Nutrition and Associate Dean of Community Medicine at the Mount Sinai School of Medicine, proved that if we remove the personal and social pleasures, which the experience of eating provides, we also provoke psychological isolation, boredom and depression, which leads to stress. Stress then leads to over-eating again!

BARBARA WYDEN said it best when explaining the philosophy of dieting: "Diet," she said, "is a magic word to most Americans. Talk of any weight-reducing regimen – all-liquid, high-protein, egg and fruit, steak and celery – and the 79 million Americans who are overweight become as spellbound as children hearing 'Hansel and Gretel' for the first time." Her article appeared in the New York Times Magazine (9/13/70) and I take it out every so often to remind myself that most diet lore is wistful delusion, that excessive weight is not so much a result of WHAT we eat, but as of HOW we eat and what our individual attitudes toward foods really are.

DESSERTS from D-Zerta became a life-saver whenever I wanted a snack and couldn't think of anything sinfully delicious (plus, low-cal and low-carb!) Prepare the gelatin per box directions, but substitute sugar-free soda for the required water in the directions. Sugar-free cola and the cherry gelatin is very good! Sugar-free 7-UP or Vernors goes well with the strawberry-flavored gelatin, also!

WAIST WATCHERS **ICE CREAM** – made with 1 cup frozen heavy cream, whipped stiff, and 1 cup slightly-set D-Zerta gelatin (any flavor.) Freeze until firm. Beat, again, until fluffy; then, freeze once more – this is about as close as you will come to a "Weight-Watcher" frozen dessert.

WAIST WATCHERS **LEMON CHEESECAKE** – made with one envelope D-Zerta lemon-flavored gelatin, prepared per envelope directions and placed in refrigerator until it is syrup-like, but not firm. Meanwhile, beat together: 8 ounces cream cheese, ¼ cup heavy (un-whipped) whipping cream, 1 cup sour cream and 1 teaspoon vanilla or lemon extract. When smooth and creamy, fold in the syrup-like gelatin mixture. Grease a 9-inch layer cake pan and dust it evenly over the bottom and sides with ½ cup finely crushed pecans or walnuts. Shake out the excess nuts, but reserve them for the top of the desert. Pour in the cheese mixture. Sprinkle top with the remaining nuts. Chill until firm. Garnish each "reasonable" serving with whipped cream. Serves 8.

WAIST WATCHERS **CHERRY CHEESECAKE** – Following the directions above for the lemon-flavored cheesecake – substituting cherry-flavored gelatin (prepared with sugar-free cherry soda rather than water, as called for on the package) and, instead of vanilla or lemon extract, use almond extract. Follow as directed above, adding a small dollop of whipped cream and dark chocolate shavings to garnish. Remember the "reasonable" serving rule!

WAIST WATCHERS **WALNUTS** – Sauté 1 cup broken pecans and 3 cups broken walnuts in ¼ pound butter or margarine, melted in a large skillet, for about 5 minutes. Stir constantly to coat well in butter. Transfer nuts to baking sheet, in single layer. Bake nuts in a 350°F oven for 15 minutes. While hot, sprinkle in ½ cup Brown Sugar Twin. Allow to cool. Store at room temperature in covered container. [Variations below.]

WAIST WATCHERS **SPICED WALNUTS** – substitute 3 tablespoons season salt and ¼ cup grated Parmesan cheese for the Brown Sugar Twin (above.) Follow recipe as otherwise directed.

WAIST WATCHERS **CHOCOLATE-COVERED WALNUTS** – follow the sauté and baking directions above – but coat in the following mixture (made in top of double boiler, over simmering water, stirring until melted and smooth): 1-ounce unsweetened solid baking chocolate, ¼ cup oil, ¼ pound butter or margarine, 4 tablespoons melted paraffin (optional), ¼ cup Brown Sugar Twin and 4 bars (3/4 ounces each) "diabetic" semi-sweet or milk chocolate candy. Freeze or refrigerate, breaking mixture into bite-sized pieces.

WAIST WATCHERS SALAD DRESSING

Mix well: 1/3 cup water, 1 teaspoon beef bouillon powder, ½ cup dark vinegar, 1 tablespoon liquid artificial sweetener, 1 teaspoon hickory salt and 1 cup corn oil. Keep refrigerated. Makes 2 ½ cups.

WAIST WATCHERS CREAMY DRESSING

Mix together well: 1/3 cup mayonnaise, 2 tablespoons heavy cream, ¼ teaspoon dry marjoram leaves, ¼ teaspoon dry dill weed, 1 tablespoon dry minced parsley, 1/8 teaspoon garlic salt and ¼ teaspoon pepper. Refrigerate up to a month. Makes ½ cup.

WAIST WATCHERS ALL-PURPOSE DRESSING

Mix 1 recipe of my creamy dressing and 1 cup of the Waist Watcher Salad Dressing (both, above) with 1 cup of my Maurice Dressing (see Index.) Pour over tossed greens, combined with chopped green onions and olives, 2 slices of bacon (crispy-fried and crumbled), sliced zucchini and fresh mushrooms.

CUCUMBER MOLDED SALAD

Empty 2 envelopes from a box of D-Zerta lime-flavored gelatin into a 1 ½-quart bowl or mold. Bring 2 cups of Fresca (sugar-free soda) to a boil and stir into gelatin until dissolved. (Putting it in your microwave on defrost for a few minutes, will also dissolve it well – or place gelatin mold in pan of hot water and stir until clear.) Then stir in 1 ¾ cup COLD Fresca. Add ½ cup chopped pecans, 1 teaspoon lemon extract and 1 medium-sized cucumber (peeled and sliced or cubed.) Chill until firm. Un-mold onto a serving platter. Then, whip 3 ounces of cream cheese with 3 tablespoons each: heavy whipping cream (un-whipped) and mayonnaise, until fluffy. It should be like a thick, creamy frosting. "Frost" entire surface of the molded gelatin with this mixture, just as you would a cake! Sprinkle the surface with chopped olives and a few tablespoons of chopped pecans or walnuts. Serves 6.

KETCHUP – *WITHOUT COUNTING (Low-Carb Diet)*

Combine thoroughly, in this order: 6-ounce can tomato paste, ¼ cup corn oil, ¼ cup margarine, 2 packets Sweet & Low artificial sweetener, 2 tablespoons light vinegar and 5 tablespoons chicken bouillon powder. Keep refrigerated up to a month. Makes 1 ¼ cups or 25 tablespoons. One tablespoon of commercial ketchup has about 4 g of carbohydrates and 1 tablespoon of this has only 0.8 g.

STEWED TOMATOES

Plunge whole tomatoes into boiling water for 1 minute and, at once, into ice water for 1 minute to peel easily. Heat these in one recipe of my PDQ Barbecue Sauce (see Index) and ¼ cup of my low-carb Ketchup (above.) Chill thoroughly, keeping tomatoes in just enough mixture to be submerged, then add 1 diced and seeded green pepper, plus 2 diced ribs of celery. Serves 6.

BIG PLOY'S CANADIAN CHEESE SOUP

Like the Big Boy Restaurants serve, this has a good, rich, smooth base. When I'm on a diet and I make it at home, I use canned chicken broth – or as directed below, with milk, when I'm not dieting.

1-pound Velveeta cheese, cut into small cubes
1 teaspoon paprika
1 cup milk (or canned chicken broth)
2 jars (3 ½ ounces each) baby food chicken
1/8 teaspoon pepper
1 teaspoon onion salt
2 tablespoons butter
pinch of parsley

Melt cheese with paprika and milk (or broth) in top of double boiler, over simmering water. Stir until smooth. Add remaining ingredients. Serve piping hot. Freezes well up to 6 months. Makes 4 servings.

CHEESE SAUCE

In a 1 ½-quart sauce pan, combine: 1 cup mayonnaise, a 10-ounce can cream of celery condensed soup, a 10-ounce can cheddar cheese soup, 1 teaspoon onion salt, ½ teaspoon sugar (or a pinch of Sweet & Low), 1/8 teaspoon curry powder and 1 tablespoon dry minced onion. Cook on low to medium heat, stirring constantly until smooth and well-heated. Makes 3 cups sauce. Do not freeze this.

HERRING SALAD

Rinse well, the hearing fillets of an 8-ounce jar, preferably packed in "wine sauce". Remove as many of the onions as possible. Now, mix the fillets with ½ cup mayonnaise, ½ cup sour cream, 1 teaspoon dry dill weed and 1 freshly diced tomato – seeded as much as possible. It can be kept in a covered container in the refrigerator for 4 or 5 days. Eat as a salad or a fidgety-time snack.

MIXED SALAD

Combine 1 peeled and diced zucchini, 2 diced ribs of celery, an 8-ounce can mushrooms (undrained), 10 or 12 stuffed green olives (sliced) and 2 green onions (scissor-snipped) with enough Italian dressing to submerged it all in a covered container. Refrigerate 24 hours to marinate the flavors. Enjoy it as a salad or a snack.

SALADS CAN BE VERY deceiving – especially when you're eating out and on a low-carb diet! Chick peas, croutons, beans and creamy dressings can set you back a whole week if you're watching your carb-intake. I always carry those 1-serving size packets of Herb Ox bouillon in my purse. Those little packets are a good way to add flavor to an otherwise flavorless "diet" dish when you're eating out!

EGG SALAD WITH ZIP

After you have peeled 4 hard-boiled and chilled eggs, take a wire French frying basket with about ¼-inch holes and force the eggs through the mesh into a mixing bowl. Combine it well with ½ cup mayonnaise, ½ cup sour cream, a 3 ½-ounce jar baby food strained ham, ¼ cup dill pickle (diced) and 1 packet of Sweet & Low artificial sweetener. Scoop onto 3 lettuce-lined plates with a sprig of parsley.

ITALIAN SALAD

Peel and slice one large cucumber paper thin. Also, slice paper thin, a zucchini of equal size, but do not peel it. Combine these with enough Italian dressing to coat well and garnish with sliced, green, stuffed olives. Serve chilled.

FRUIT MAURICE

Peel and cube a whole cantaloupe. Hull and slice 1 pint of strawberries. Combine these and add 1 cup, scissor-snipped, fresh spinach in bite-sized pieces and a quarter head of iceberg lettuce, also cut into bite-sized pieces. Add 8 or 10 cherry tomatoes, cut in halves, and 2 cups diced and cooked chicken. Drench it all in my Maurice Dressing (see Index.) Serves 3 to 4 well.

MELON WALDORF SALAD

Combine 1 peeled and diced cantaloupe, 1-pint halved strawberries, 1 cup broken pecans, 2 ribs diced celery and 2 cups of my Maurice dressing (see Index.) Serves 4.

SHRIMP MAURICE SALAD

Rinse and mash a 6 ½-ounce can of tiny shrimp. Mix with 1 cup of my Maurice Dressing (like J.L. Hudson's – see Index), 1 minced rib of celery, 8 or 10 chopped black olives, ¼ cup chopped walnuts, and 2 ounces Swiss or Muenster cheese, cut in ¼-inch cubes. Spoon into lettuce-lined bowls to serve 4.

MOCK POTATO SALAD

Peel and cube 3 zucchinis. Simmer in just enough water to cover, with a dash of salt, until tender. Drain and chill. Mix with 1 cup diced mushrooms, 1 cup diced black olives, ½ cup diced dill pickles, 1 large diced tomato, 3 snipped green onions and 3 hard-boiled eggs (chopped or crumbled.) Coat well in one recipe of dressing from my Macaroni (or Potato) Salad, Like the Colonel's (see Index.) Serves 6.

MUSHROOM MEATLOAF

In being mildly aware of the carbohydrate content of mushrooms, I noted ½ cup of fresh sliced mushrooms (1.2 ounces) has about 1.5 g of carbs, while a 4-ounce can has about 2.9 g, varying slightly between brands. To help lose excess water build-up that causes about 10 to 15 pounds of our weight, Adele Davis suggests eating mushrooms. Be cautious, however, if you're watching your sodium in-take. The nicest part of this recipe is that it never tastes like a diet recipe! I even prepare it for company in the form of one-inch meatballs, submerged in my Barbecue Meatball Sauce (see Index.) Complement the meatloaf or meatballs with either bottled ketchup or my homemade version (see Index.)

3 pounds ground beef
3 eggs, beaten
1 large cucumber, peeled and well-diced
7 green onions, scissor-snipped fine
1 teaspoon onion powder
5 tablespoons beef bouillon powder
8 ounces heavy cream, un-whipped
3 tablespoons each: Worcestershire sauce and soy sauce
1 teaspoon liquid artificial sweetener
½ cup each: shredded cheddar cheese and Parmesan cheese
8-ounce can mushrooms, drained and well-diced or finely-chop

Mix all ingredients as listed. Pack into 2 oiled, 8-inch, loaf pans. Spread 1 tablespoon ketchup over top of each. Loosely cover in foil. Bake at 375°F for 45 to 50 minutes. MICRO-BAKE – using oiled Pyrex loaf dishes and covering loosely in doubled sheets of plastic wrap – on "Full" power for 8 minutes and then "Roast" for 10 minutes. Place on countertop without uncovering for 8 minutes. Good hot or cold. One loaf serves 4 to 6. Freeze up to 6 months.

CHOP SUEY

2 cups left over pot roast or pork roast, diced
3 cups of my High Ends Gravy (see Index)
1-pound can beans sprouts, drained
6-ounce can bamboo shoots, drained
2 green onions, scissor-snipped
3 ribs of celery, diced
½ cup broken walnuts
1 tablespoon soy sauce

Combine, as listed, and heat carefully on low. Serve as you would stew. Feeds 6 famously.

CRUSTLESS PIZZA – *Have all you want of this dish, if you're following a low-carb diet!*

4 tablespoons oil
1 ½ pounds ground beef
1 small zucchini (or medium cucumber)
½ teaspoon garlic salt
1 tablespoon dry oregano leaves
½ teaspoon onion powder
2 green onions, minced
2 tablespoons beef bouillon powder
2 eggs, beaten
8-ounce can mushrooms, drained
2 large tomatoes, sliced
½ cup grated Parmesan cheese
8 ounces shredded mozzarella cheese

Brown the ground beef in the oil on medium heat. Grate the zucchini or cucumber directly into the beef. Stir until browned and season well with the garlic, oregano and onion. Blend again and remove from heat. Let cool 10 minutes. Beat eggs into the beef mixture – but do it quickly so the heat of the beef won't "set" the eggs. Add mushrooms and spoon it into an ungreased, 9 x 12" pan or Pyrex dish. Arrange tomatoes on top. Sprinkle evenly with Parmesan. Next, cover with mozzarella. Loosely place a sheet of foil over the dish. Bake at 350°F for 25 minutes. Then, place 3 inches from broiler heat for 5 or 6 minutes, until mozzarella bubbles and begins to brown. Makes 12 lasagna-like servings.

MICROWAVE DIRECTIONS: Place in a 9 x 12" Pyrex baking dish and cover with doubled plastic wrap. Set on "Roast" for 12 minutes; then on full power for 2 ½ minutes. Let stand for 5 minutes before removing plastic and serving. (You may also add a 10-ounce package of frozen asparagus or a 1-pound can of green beans (drained) to the top with the sliced tomatoes, for added nutrition and flavor.

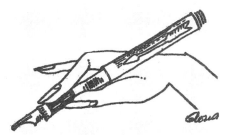

BEHIND THE SCENES

PRIVATE INVESTIGATOR OF SECRET RECIPES or "The Recipe Detective" are the names that my friends in radio and newspapers have given to me, and I enjoy living up to that assignment! I enjoy working with these recipe secrets, but most of all, I enjoy writing about them. I've been writing all my life… Going way-back to when I was in grade school. I was always writing a book, or a poem or a short story. It was a way of life from my earliest memories – a way over which I seem to have no personal control! I had to write… Preferably about what I knew best at the time. Little did I know that what I would come to know best would be cooking! The one year that I spent at Michigan State (when it was still a college, mind you – you figure that out! Sophia Loren and I are the same age – and while we may have the same measurements, 36-28-36, mine are neck, wrists and ankles, I'm afraid) … Was one year in which I learned 2 important things – I could not pass my Creative Writing course and I was "kicked out" of Home Economics! My Creative Writing instructor told me that I typed a neat looking paper and probably should be a secretary, for I would never make it as a writer. My Home Economics instructor advised me to spend the rest of my life having my meals delivered, for I was always finding fault with the way so many cookbooks were written.

I took a position with the J Walter Thompson Advertising company in Detroit, working as a secretary to the copywriters. I met my husband, Paul, there when he returned from a 4-year tour of service with the Air Force. We started dating and one year later we were married. That was 1956. Bill was born over a year later, and then Mike came 20 months after that, and Debbie came along 20 months after that. I lost 3 babies in the next 3 years, but Laura was born in 1964 and Cheryl came 20 months after that. During those years, Paul was working for a sign company in Mt. Clemens, Michigan – where, in the 20 years he spent with them, he did everything from drafting to purchasing agent to account rep! I kept up with my writing, always working for one of the suburban papers and constantly free-lancing to magazines. When Redbook sent me $500 for my "Young Mother's Story" submission in February 1963, called "We'll Never Live with In-Laws Again", I put part of the money into a typewriter, as I had always had to borrow one before that. I wanted a typewriter more than Reagan wanted to be president! I put a lot of miles on that $39.95 machine – I designed a column for weekly newspapers and mailed out samples to over 300 newspapers. Within a year, I had acquired 60 regular papers for my "No Laughing Matter" column and another column I called "Minding the Hearth". Columbia Features in New York offered me a contract and, for a year, I allowed them to syndicate the column in competition with a new humorist, Erma Bombeck! (Right church, wrong pew for me!) When a big city paper carried Erma's column, Columbia placed mine in their competing paper. I split with Columbia on a 60/40 basis (I took 40) and finally, by mutual-agreement, we broke the contract. I was on my own.

HOW SECRET RECIPES BEGAN

When Columbia Features and I parted company, they had acquired only 2 additional papers from me and lost several more. Within 6 months, I had regained all my original papers and was syndicating the column from our dining room table, where we then lived in what my friend, Bob Allison, called "beautiful downtown Pearl Beach" – a town so small that I told people City Hall was over a Dairy Queen, our McDonald's had only one arch and, if we had a Howard Johnson's, it would've had only 3 flavors! We had a 9-year old station wagon at that time. It burned oil and barely got Paul to work and back without something breaking down! I rode a bike to and from the Pearl Beach post office every day where I mailed out my columns and, then, looked for responses to ads I had placed in the Tower Press and Grit magazines for recipes on 4x6" cards that enabled you to imitate famous dishes at home.

BOB ALLISON's "ASK YOUR NEIGHBOR"

I was a regular participant on Bob Allison's "Ask Your Neighbor" radio show that aired 5 days a week for 2 hours in the morning. I used Bob's program for asking for food information that I needed for my weekly columns. Bob's audience was very helpful in supplying me with answers. To reciprocate, I would reply to some of the requests made by his audience when they called into Bob's show. It was a unique format in that one could not simply call in a recipe or information simply because they wanted to share it with others. The information or the recipe had to, first, be requested by a previous caller. Many of my first "Secret Recipes" were developed because of requests made specifically by Bob's callers for such dishes as The Colonel's secret spices, Arthur Treacher's fish batter, Sander's hot fudge, Win Schuler's bar cheese and so on.

At the suggestion of one of Bob's callers that I should put all my column recipes into a book, I wrote my 1st edition called "The Better Cooker's Cookbook". In less than a month, I had sold 1000 copies. I wasn't satisfied with the book, so I didn't reprint it – but, decided that it might work out better if I could do those recipes monthly. So, in December 1972, I put together my 1st issue of what came to be my "Secret Recipe Report", a newsletter that, for 106 consecutive monthly issues, brought me in contact with the many so-called secrets of the commercial food and restaurant industry. I probably wouldn't have done the monthly, except for a falling-out I had with the editor of a small-town paper for which I was writing a food column. I had published some of my 1st attempts at duplicating famous dishes in that column and the response was beautiful, until I offended one of the papers biggest advertisers with a rendition of their cheesecake… "The kind that nobody doesn't like." The editor told me I would have to go back to standard recipes like macaroni and cheese, meatloaf or chocolate cake – or I could pick up my check. I told him to MAIL it to me. That's when I decided it was time to launch my own paper. That afternoon, put out my charter issue, sending samples of it to those whose names and addresses I had on file from having written to me at the paper. That was the beginning of "Secret Recipes"!

THE DIRECTION WAS ALREADY DETERMINED FOR ME!

WHEN I LOOK BACK now, I realize that I was so busy trying to prove that others were wrong about me, I couldn't see how events were taking place that would sooner or later put me where I had always wanted to be – writing for a worthwhile living, while making living worthwhile! In high school, I pestered the school newspaper sponsor, Mr. Rosen, to let me be on the staff. He had no hope for me at all as a reporter! I was secretary of the Senior Class, January 1954, and Judy Guest was secretary of the June 1954 Senior Class. Judy was on the staff of the paper; but, even then, it was well-known that she hoped to write "the Great American novel"– and that she did, 20 years later, with Academy Award-winning "Ordinary People"! Judy's great-uncle was Edgar A. Guest and Bud Guest, a famous radio commentator, was her uncle. It was only natural that writing would run in her family. We were friends because we liked each other and were both involved with the same school activities. I was always glad that we continued to keep in touch, if only at Christmas, for nobody appreciated Judy's eventual success with "Ordinary People" as I probably did, knowing how long she had wanted to accomplish that work. Somehow, despite my personal objections to the direction in which I appeared to be going, it was just as likely that I would accomplish a properly-written cookbook. Even in high school I was put on 2-weeks' probation with the cooking class instructor, for having disregarded the recipe for a pie crust we were assigned to prepare in class. Mine was a recipe that I still use – and have published in this book – for the "No Rolling Pin" crust. Apparently, it's true, that "Life" is what happens to us while we're busy making other plans.

DIVIDENDS

Every successful accomplishment with my writing, after high school and the one year in college, was involved with recipes and cookbooks and restaurants. But I couldn't see that it was a kind of calling. I saw it only as an interest that temporarily kept me writing and making a worthwhile living at it.

WDEE-Radio, in Detroit, gave me a portable radio or a recipe that took 1ˢᵗ place in a contest they conducted – and in 1962, it was WBRB, in Mt. Clemens, that gave me a check for 1ˢᵗ place in their recipe contest. Soon after that, Better Homes & Gardens sent me a check for a recipe in a contest they had conducted. WJ BK-Radio gave me a maple stereo and radio set for their most unusual experience while listening to the radio, in 1964, when I wrote them about our "Picnicking in the Snow". Again, the story was food related, including recipes for having a cook-out on the beach at Metropolitan Park in the middle of winter, with the radio going to keep us in the proper mood. It was all leading to my eventual work in the food industry – but, I couldn't see that at the time I could only see that I had to write and with any luck at all, luck would be when preparation and experience met opportunity. The opportunity was close at hand.

A MEAL BY ANY OTHER NAME

FAST FOOD RECIPES were not published in the best-sellers – and these were the restaurants where families were apt frequent if they wanted a meal that was affordable! Paul and I could take all 5 of the children to Capri's, an Italian restaurant down the road from us in Pearl Beach, and we could feed the whole family for less than $10, providing we ordered the large pizza with only pepperoni and cheese on it and one soft drink for each of us. It was not for substance that we ate out. It was for entertainment. We could take the kids to McDonald's and it did the same thing for us that going to the movies did for our parents. It was an affordable pleasure. It was a diversion from meatloaf and pot roast and peas and carrots. It was a treat. We looked forward to it. We felt good about the experience and even better after it was over. It carried us through a long week of paying the utilities, insurance, house payments and car payments and grocery expenses. When we had to have our 10-year-old station wagon repaired, we had to skip eating out that week. If one of us had to see the dentist, it might be 2 or 3 weeks before we could afford to eat out again. We may do with what we had. We could make the most of what we had. In the 50s and 60s and early 70s, this is the way parents raised their families, budgeted their earnings and allowed for their pleasures. Things changed, as well they should. Women went out to work. If they weren't working to supplement the family income, they went to work for their own satisfaction. Whatever the reasons, families changed. Eating at home became less and less appealing – and less and less convenient. Homes were built with smaller kitchens and bigger bathrooms. Microwave ovens were more affordable – and defrost and heat became more popular.

WE WANTED OUR CAKE AND WE WANTED TO EAT IT, TOO!

We wanted to eat out at a price we could afford; and, when we couldn't afford to eat out, we wanted to dine-in as if we were eating out! At the time, there were few recipes for this kind of cooking. We wanted to spend less time preparing the foods and less money on the ingredients and still serve a dish to those who shared our table with us that would be equal to – if not better than – anything we could buy in a restaurant or from a supermarket. For all of these reasons, I have pursued the investigations of the food industry with the greatest joy and the utmost care, translating into recipes, those secrets that I have been able to decipher.

THE FIRST TELEVISION APPEARANCE

IT WAS THE WORST POSSIBLE TIME to launch a new business. The unemployment rate was terribly high. There was a newsprint paper shortage. There was a gasoline shortage. But I couldn't pass up the opportunity to at least try to have my own publication. It was something I had always wanted to do. I couldn't tell Paul. I knew that! He would have been far too practical to have approved of my starting my own paper, so I enlisted the help of our children. I was taking in ironing at the time, at $5 a basket, and sometimes earned as much as $50 a week. The money was supposed to supplement Paul's paycheck, which – as soon as we found could make ends meet – we discovered somebody had moved the ends. So, I took what money I could from the ironing earnings and bought a mimeograph. I kept it in a big box in the utility room under my sewing table. Paul would hardly pay attention to what I wanted him to think was only sewing paraphernalia. For 9 months, I mimeograph, assembled and mailed out about 100 copies a month of my newsletter. Bill and Mike helped assemble it and Debbie help me test the recipes and address the copies. I don't know how we ever kept it from Paul for that long, but I couldn't tell him what I was doing until I could assure him that I could make a profit. All I was doing was breaking even. Then Dennis Wholley, at Channel 7 in Detroit, called and said somebody had sent him a copy of my newsletter. He was tickled with the crazy names I gave the recipes and the home-spun format. He wanted the entire family to be his guests on his "A.M. Detroit" show on November 14 – which was also our Laura's birthday. I couldn't keep it from Paul any longer, because I couldn't pass up an opportunity to promote the paper on a popular local television show. He took it quite well, considering the state of shock he must have been in at my announcement. But we took all 5 of the kids with us across town, in a blizzard yet, with Laura having a bout of car-sickness during the hour's drive there. And, during that experience, we met Coleman Young, the recently elected mayor of Detroit, who was also a guest on the show. All of Pearl Beach must have been tuned into a.m. Detroit that morning, with half of the population gathered at the Pearl Beach post office, watching the portable set there.

It brought us many new orders for our newsletter and it wasn't long before CKLW's Bob Heinz asked us to appear on his show on New Year's Day. We, again, took the family over to Windsor, Ontario – across the Detroit River – for another exciting experience and hundreds of letters that followed, wanting to subscribe to the newsletter. By that time, Paul was giving me every evening of his time when he came home from his own job at the sign company, plus all the weekends just to fill the orders. My list of "Secret Recipes" had grown to 200 and we offered them, on 4 x 6" cards [that I printed on my mimeograph], at $.25 each or 5 for a dollar. It was quite a packaging process to fill the combinations of orders, so I put all those recipes into a book. It was going to be our "only" book on the subject, since most of the recipes were "fast foods" – but, as it turned out, it was only the 1st of a series of 5 books. After "Book One" took off and became a very good seller, I did a Bicentennial American Cookery book as a limited edition and was pleased when the Henry Ford Library at Greenfield Village in Dearborn, Michigan ordered copies for their Bicentennial collection. That was July 1976. Paul was going to quit his job.

<u>RECIPES TESTED TO TURN OUT RIGHT</u>

PAUL GAVE HIS BOSS TWO WEEKS' NOTICE and left his job of 20 years to devote full time to helping me with the recipes and the newsletter. The subscriptions had increased from less than 100 to over 3000 in a few months. Bob Allison's "Ask Your Neighbor" show was still one of our favorite contacts and before we knew it, we became a sponsor of Bob's show. It was just prior to buying advertising time on Bob's show that one of his audience had called in a request for a fish batter like Arthur Treacher's. The caller specifically asked on the air if Gloria, the Recipe Detective, might give the recipe try. I did, and went back to the phone with each of several developing steps, waiting for the response of Bob's audience to each. The 1st several recipes were not quite "on target". I wanted the recipe to be exactly like the famous batter of the fish and chips chain. Each step came closer and closer to the perfect duplication, and each was reported over Bob's show. Finally, with the club soda and pancake mix combination, the radio show's audience was so enthusiastic that they sent a copy of the recipe to Carol Haddix, who was then the Food Editor of the Detroit Free Press. She tested the recipe and published it with an endorsement, that she felt it was "right on target". Within a few weeks, another request was made from Bob's audience for a hot fudge topping like Sanders had, which was the largest confectionery and bakery in Michigan – if not, at least the most popular. Again, I sent the final recipe, after several tests and just as many failures, to Carol Haddix. She published it with her "on target" endorsement. It proved to be a protection for our recipes that both Bob Allison's radio show and the Detroit Free Press had records of each recipe in the various stages of development for when others came along a few years later attempting to copy my recipes – period-paragraph-and-semi-colon, I could validate the originality of each of the recipes that were taken and published without giving credit to me as the originator.

Once the Free Press carried our recipes on a regular basis, the wire services picked up interest in my recipes and the National Enquirer sent a photographer and free-Lance writer to interview us. While there were 100 or more newspapers carrying stories about our recipe duplications, I must admit, that the article in the National Enquirer was probably the most accurate. They were very thorough in putting the story together. There wasn't even one mistake in the recipes, which many papers made in typographical errors of sorts. The free-lance writer of that story in the National Inquirer was Carole Eberly, [1983] publisher of the Michigan Journal and author of a collection of recipes from Michigan.

THE PHIL DONAHUE SHOW

It was 1977, and we were considering a move from Pearl Beach to St. Clair, since our 80-year old house was already packed, wall-to-wall and floor-to-ceiling, with recipe books and newsletter inventory. Just about the time we planned our move, the Phil Donahue show called and invited us to Dayton, Ohio to appear on their program there. I had to decline. We already had more work than we could handle and I had found that television appearances were merely food demonstrations that I did not enjoy experiencing. I enjoyed my radio work more, and the number of stations on which I had become a regular participant had grown to include over 100 across the country and in Canada.

We were settling down in our new house in St. Clair, with our office in the basement. We outgrew that arrangement in a short time and rented a larger office uptown. But the books became more successful than we anticipated and the newsletter circulation was growing to over 10,000. Soon, I found that we had to put the business back into our home. I couldn't depend on being in a writing mood between our regular "office" business hours of 8 AM to 5 PM. Some of the radio shows that I took part in were on-the-air at midnight, especially my favorite visits with KMOX in St. Louis and WGY in Schenectady. With my files and reference materials at the office and me, at home on the telephone with the radio shows, the arrangement was not satisfactory. So, Paul and our 2 sons remodeled our two-car garage, attached to the kitchen, and we moved the operation back there; where, for the next 4 years, the business ran quite smoothly.

We were receiving about 1000 letters a day from the radio shows that I took part in and the newspaper stories that I was more-or-less an acting consultant on subjects related to "fast food". In the spring of 1981, our old friend, Carol Haddix, ran a story about our new book of "Homemade Groceries" in the Chicago Tribune, where she had just been assigned the food department. The Donahue Show people called once more and requested our appearance. We had just done a PM Magazine show with Detroit and had declined an invitation to appear in New York on Good Morning America, as well as declining an opportunity to have People Magazine interview us – and I still wonder why in the world I said I would do the Donahue show! I think it was because I had just tangled with Grit, the weekly newspaper in Pennsylvania, over giving credit to the Food editor's teenage daughter for having developed a fish batter like Arthur Treacher's, using club soda and pancake mix – and received an apology on the back page of one of their issues, placing the item between an ad for corn and callous remover and waste cinchers. I was also tangling with Jove Publications, who were pressing hard to sell their "Junk Food Cookbook", using my recipes, word-for-word, with credit going to somebody else. I wanted to establish the fact that I was very much in business and willing to protect my copyrighted property with the same enthusiasm and sincerity as the major food companies had exhibited in protecting theirs from my imitations. (And believe me, we've heard from all the big ones!)

So, on July 6, Paul and I flew to Chicago, staying at the Hyatt O'Hare, and did the Donahue show live – for an entire hour – on July 7, flying back that same afternoon. The next day, 15,000 letters waited for us at the St. Clair post office. And every day for 4 months, we picked up thousands of letters – having received by Christmas, well over 1 million letters, requesting information on how to acquire our books, which were still available only by mail from our address. We were bogged down with an unexpected response. It was an experience of mixed blessings!

THE SURPRISE – A DREAM COME TRUE!

If you've ever seen 1 million letters, you know how we felt when we tried to handle the overwhelming response! It was exhausting! Our home, which was both our office and our sanctuary, became like a factory, with people helping us to process the mail, eventually having to return thousands of the orders to the customers with our deepest regrets that we could not, in all fairness to them, delay their order. The onslaught of mail had forced us to do this. We were all working from 7 AM until 1 or 2 AM the next morning just to open and read the mail. Our phone bill had been buried in some of that mail and in a month's time, being something like 23 to 24 days behind in opening the mail, our phone was shut off for non-payment of our bill. As soon as we realized what the mail was doing to us, we tried to get Donahue's people to stop the continued scheduled showings of our appearance. But that show remained on their repeat schedule for almost a year, playing in the Panama Canal zone, Greenland, Iceland, Australia and on hundreds of small town stations. Most of the letters requested a sheet of "free" recipes that were included with the order blank for a self-addressed stamped envelope to us. The offer would have been good for us, if it had only been shown that one time – the day on which we appeared on the show – but for nearly a year afterward, the requests still came, as did the complaints and the threats to report us to postal authorities for not having sent those "free" recipes, tore us apart emotionally and physically! Some people did not include their self-addressed-stamped envelope. Some envelopes were addressed to themselves, such as Joe Smith, but in care of OUR address instead of THEIR address. It was a confusing mess! Some people wrote threatening letters that they hadn't received their orders and were turning us over to the postmaster general as frauds! I laid my head on my desk many a time, in tears of anguish and fatigue. The family was falling apart. We couldn't print our books fast enough, to fill all the orders! Then the post office, in delivering the thousands of books that we DID mail out, lost some, destroyed some, and delayed and even miss-directed other orders.

MISTAKES

We talked about making a move to California in the fall of 1981. I really wanted to move out there, where my sister, Hazel, and her family were living. Our son, Mike, was living in Pasadena, then, and it seemed like it would be a lovely chance for us to…begin a new life in Los Angeles! We thought that, by moving to California, it would be a new beginning. Leave all our problems behind us in St. Clair. We were mistaken. In the effort to relocate, we notified our subscribers – then, at 15,000 – that we would cease publication with the October 1982 issue of the recipe newsletter and we would take our books off the market for several months to make the move to Los Angeles. I went out there in March, while Paul remained in St. Clair so Cheryl could finish the school term. At Easter, they came out with our daughter, Debbie, and her husband, Jim. By that time, I had bought a lovely mobile home for [Paul, Cheryl and I] in a very nice park. It was going to be "country club living!" Everybody said so! We enrolled Cheryl in a high school there. She hated it! After a week, she was so ill from disliking the new experience, I had to bring her back to St. Clair, where Paul was still trying to close-up our office.

My father had suffered a stroke during that week and, when I saw how hard my mother was taking his death, I took her back to California with me. She was to stay month – or until Paul and Cheryl could come back out while Debbie and Jim moved into our St. Clair home. Within the month that my mother was with me in California, I began to miss all the things about St. Clair that originally attracted me to move there. I missed the friendliness of the town. I missed the security of being able to walk the streets without having to fear harm from my fellow man, which in Los Angeles was not easy to do! Life in California was hectic and fast-moving. Too much importance was placed on being on the go and having a good time. I couldn't work there! My new book, which should've been 75% finished, to replace the original 5 books by October 1, was only 1% finished. There was no peace or contentment.

When it was time to take my mother back to Michigan, I knew I was going to have to tell Paul and Cheryl that we couldn't move out there permanently. Cheryl might've been willing to give it another try, if it would make Paul and I happy, but I couldn't see where she would have much of a life for her last 2 years in high school. I wanted to get back to work and back to familiar and peaceful surroundings, where I could test new recipes and write an inspiring collection of new dishes and new information on the food industry. I couldn't do that in Los Angeles. Seeing the barbed wire and tall concrete block walls around the mobile home parks, the condominiums and the school yards made me suddenly appreciate the freedom of living in a small town. I was ready to go home. I remembered what Dick Syatt, one of our radio friends, had told me about finally getting everything you ever wanted, when he said, "Hell is God, giving you what you thought you wanted." Sometimes we need to have something, lose it and get it back again, before we can really appreciate what we have. I had that chance and I am so glad for it. It was a time to learn and to grow.

MINDING THE HEARTH

I am resigned to my life with an armchair quarterback, for I know that the garlic in our matrimonial gladiola patch is PRO FOOTBALL! From September to March, every year, there is always going to be a gigantic communication gap in our house. The art of conversation isn't really lost. It's merely hidden behind the pre-game warm-up, installing a power offense which will take advantage of decent, but not blinding, speed in the backfield in a right-handed attack with a lot of blocking in a size-out pass pattern. I guess the reason I'll never win an argument with my husband in the fall is that I can't understand one single word he says. I even tried to leave him once during an NFL game, but it wasn't until the Super Bowl was over (5 months later) that he even noticed I was gone.

I admit, I don't know much about football, but I still insist it isn't quite fair that the fellow who worked so hard last season, doing a terrific job as quarterback, wasn't promoted to HALF-back this season! Anyway, the last time I tried to cultivate an interest in the game was the time my husband called me in to watch the last 2 minutes of an exciting game. (Mind you, I use the term "exciting" very loosely!) I guess it was exciting. Paul kept jumping up and down, hollering, "Look at them go!" All I learned from that experience, was that 2 minutes of football is equal to 20 minutes of Daylight Savings Time. An ordinary Sunday afternoon at our house would begin as he slipped into his George Blanda sweatshirt and punted his bottle of Ironized Yeast Tablets across the room, then he would step up to the TV set and announce, "Gloria, is there anything you'd like to say to me before football season begins?"

Perhaps you understand why every fall I join Parents Without Partners. Because my husband would only notice me if I were to run through the living room with… a number on my back. I can forgive him a lot of faults, especially during football season, but not insisting that we disconnect my grandmother's pacemaker because it was interfering with the TV reception during a big game! When he asked if I had anything to say to before he turned on the set, it was no wonder I replied, "Do I have to say it all now?"

"Woman! You know better than to speak to me during an instant replay!" he snapped.

"All right," I screamed. "Why do you love football better than you love me?"

"I don't know," he said, scratching his head. "But, I love you better than basketball! … Love you? Of course, I love you! That's my job. I'm your husband! Besides, I love EVERYBODY!"

"I suppose you'd like to have dinner in the living room, in front of the TV," I said tartly. "Or should I time it for the half-time extravaganza?"

"Half-time will be fine. By the way," he asked, "what are we having for dinner?"

"Film clips of last Sunday's roast!" [I answered.]

"That's not funny," he snapped. "I'm getting hungry!"

"Good!" I said bitterly. "Then the pre-dinner line-up includes whose off-sides that can set the table while I give you a slow-motion replay of how your son kicked the oven door while I was pampering a Boston butt cuss (to see an illegal substitution for pork roast) to see and spelled out Billy Sims with 659 parsley flakes on a field of mashed potatoes."

"Okay," he chuckled. "I can take a joke as well as the next guy. But, what are we really having for dinner?" He asked.

"PICKLED PIGSKIN – that's what!"

WITH ALL THIS INFORMATION IN MIND, you must now understand why it is that I have never written a book for women. I thought I did not have enough information to hold a woman's interest for more than one or 2 chapters. But I do NOW, and I'm going to entitle it *"EVERYTHING YOU NEVER WANTED TO KNOW ABOUT FOOTBALL – and were sorry you asked!"* Football season, the punt of no return, is that once-a-year experience that makes me wonder, as my husband sits, watching one game after the other on TV, why he hasn't worn out HIS end zone! It's my own fault. I tried to cultivate an interest in the game so that we could share something besides the absence of conversation between us on weekends from September through February. But looking back, it seems that all we have been able to share, instead, is the compelling urge to see this season over with. I want to see it over with, so that we can be a family again, and my husband would like to see it over with, so that he can see how closely he came to determining the winning team at the Super Bowl!

My armchair quarterback keeps giving advice on every play. Every time this happens, I expect Tom Landry to stretch his arm right through our picture tube and point at my husband, insisting, "Hey, you – you with all the advice! Go in for Dupree!"

Mind you, this is the same man who has committed to perfect memory such statistics as how many touchdowns and yards run, his favorite player has mastered, but he can't remember his own shirt size, where he left his car keys, our kids' middle names, nor his mother's telephone number!

But, at least, he is not as emotional over the game as some husbands I know. Just last weekend, I visited my friend while she was in traction in the hospital, bandaged from head-to-toes like an Egyptian mummy – while her apologetic husband leaned over her, explaining, "Honey, if I've told you once, I've told you 100 times… NEVER walk in front of the TV during a 95-yard punt return!"

I SUPPOSE, ONE THING I CAN ALWAYS DO, while he watches television football games, is the grocery shopping. After all, somebody must! We can't eat without groceries. While I have tried to train Paul for retirement, by trying to teach HIM how to shop for the food, I don't believe he is ready, yet, for his "solo flight" down the aisles of the A&P!

I'm the food-shopper with outstanding guilt-complex who is driven to ask poor souls with 4 items in their arms to go ahead of me – unless they've brought their lunch with them and are prepared to spend a month in line behind me, explaining the 3 carts of groceries to the person behind me who has never had feed a family of teenagers. One must chance that while you are permitting all those nice people to pass you up with their one or 2 items more than the express line will allow and YOUR ice cream is in the puddle on the floor under your cart that is being mopped up by a disgruntled stock boy! Things like this occasionally afford me the reputation of being recognized by butchers everywhere as, "Here comes that nut who always has to see the other side of the roast!"

FINAL FOODS FOR THOUGHT

RECIPE FOR LIFE

Take yourself;
Peel off all layers of egotism and self-pity,
Cut out all seeds of unkind thoughts and
All unhappy emotions.
Remove all prejudices and worries.
To this add:
One firm belief that life is worth living.
Mix well with one practical idea that you are somebody!
Season with a sense of humor and optimism;
Sweeten with love.
Then add one strong determination
To live at your highest, every hour of the day,
Come what will.
Garnish with smiles and pleasant words.
Serve with gentleness and courage.
Note the effect!

GOD GIVES JOY that we may give;
He gives us joy that we may share;
Sometimes he gives us loads to lift
That we may learn to bear.
For life is gladder when we give,
And love is sweeter when we share,
And heavy loads rest lightly too,
When we have learned to bear.

YOU CAN'T CHANGE THE PAST,
but you can ruin a perfectly good present by worrying over the future.

If true happiness is acquired through persistence and patience, it would be like the fable of the elderly Chinese profit who asked for a needle when none could be found. However, somebody offered him a crowbar and a file. He was pleased and assured his friends that it was only a matter of time before he could produce the needle he wanted.

WHEN IT COMES TO USING MY HEAD in the kitchen, I can't ignore some of the neat tricks I have come across for using food ingredients to solve other problems. So, I must share these tips with you.

 Did you know…

For BEE STINGS, you can ease the pain until you get to the doctor's office by covering the wound with a paste made of water and Adolph's meat tenderizer powder.

If you BURN yourself on a stove or iron, until you can get medical attention, cover the burn (if it's only a small area, of course) with a paste made of water and baking soda, which relieves the pain.

For POLISHING bathroom chrome – try toothpaste and rinse it off with a damp cloth. For silver plate or sterling silver – make a paste of cigarette ashes and water. Rub vigorously and rinse with warm water, repeating until silver is shiny again!

Pen INK, printing ink and other such stains can be removed by applying hairspray to the spot, then rinsing carefully in cold water and blotting it dry with a terry-cloth towel. Repeat until it's removed.

If you SPILL FOOD on your clothes while you're eating out, order a glass of club soda and dampen the stain with a napkin that has been dipped into the soda.

For a STY near the eyelid, I've had relief many times by holding a wet, warm tea bag on it. Something in the tea bag causes the sty to break and drain.

For shining COPPER-bottom pots and pans, apply vinegar and then salt, rinsing it under cold water and repeating the mixture in equal parts until copper is bright again!

For BETTER SCRAMBLED EGGS – add 1 tablespoon small curd cottage cheese to each beaten egg before pouring it into the prepared skillet.

For BETTER GRAVY from a canned product – combine cans of, both, beef and chicken gravies in equal parts and add a fleck or 2 of powdered cinnamon and a dash of Sweet Vermouth – to taste.

The CN TOWER IN TORONTO serves their orange sherbet packed into a hollowed out orange shell, having removed about a 1-inch slice from the top. The sherbet filled orange shells are frozen solid before serving and a long-stemmed maraschino cherry is placed on top of each one with a sprig of fresh peppermint leaf. The orange sections that were removed from the shells, I was told, were frozen to be used in their ambrosia salad. (See Index for my Angel Ambrosia recipe.)

An ASPIRIN TABLET added to a vase of water containing fresh-cut flowers seems to keep the flowers looking fresh longer.

Shine the LEAVES OF YOUR HOUSEPLANTS with a paper towel dipped in milk and allow to dry.

For GUM in hair or on fabric, rub with peanut butter until it loosens and wash with Dawn dish soap.

If you bought one of those "bargain" rolls of PLASTIC KITCHEN WRAP that sticks to itself – so that you can't unroll it – put it in the freezer for a little while.

BATTERIES seem to extend their "life" and POPCORN will pop better, if you keep these in the freezer.

For HEALTHIER HOUSEPLANTS, save your egg shells. Put them through your blender with cold water and use the mixture on your plants. Works well on outdoor tomato plants, too! The water in which you boiled eggs, when cooled, is also good for using on your plants.

What to do with that last bit of JAM or JELLY in the jar? Add a little corn syrup to it. Mix it well and use it over pancakes.

Rinsing PEELED BANANAS in lemon juice and dusting in sugar will keep them white for nice desserts or salads. However, lemon juice on fresh-sliced bananas, to be used in a pie filling, must be blotted-well on paper towels, or the lemon juice will cause the cream filling to break down and become soupy.

Use PAM spray on your car door lock when you have a severe cold weather threat. Then spray your car door key in a little Pam and you won't have trouble getting it open.

BACON that is sliced and packaged, separates perfectly for frying if you roll up the slab beginning at the Nero side. Unroll the slab and roll it in the other direction from the other end. Note: bacon curls, while it fries, if the heat is too high.

Set saucers of VANILLA EXTRACT around a room that is freshly painted to rid the air of offensive paint odors.

Keep a CORKED BOTTLE of wine on its side so that the cork will remain wet from the wine, which causes the cork to swell and prevents any air from getting in the bottle. If a corked bottle of wine is kept in an upright position, the cork dries out and the wine can take in air, causing it to lose everything it's worked for – before its time!

For a HEART-SHAPED CAKE for Valentine's Day – bake 1 layer in an 8-inch round cake pan and another layer in an 8-inch square cake pan. Cut the round layer in half and place each half against adjacent sides of the square layer.

AFTERTHOUGHTS ON BETTER COOKERY

THE GOOD LORD HAD INTENDED FOR ME to be a gourmet cook, I would've been born with Teflon hands! Don't misunderstand – I like to cook! But I do not wish to spend more time in the preparations as is necessary.

NO ONE APPRECIATES good food as much as I do. Don't ask me how I know – I just do. It does not concern me how a dish has been prepared, if it tastes great and looks good on the table! A gourmet cook would never agree with this philosophy. However, anyone can become a gourmet cook, that is, if that is what you wish. All you need are numerous ingredients of good quality, a lot of time and patience and twice as much money – not to mention, and unblushing candor for admitting without modesty you are a "gourmet" cook. This admission will intimidate many people just as easily as being faced with the admission that somebody is a terrific dancer, a great singer or an exceptional parent. And while it is perfectly acceptable and not the least bit conceited to say one is a "gourmet" cook, there is still a tendency to back off from them because you know how many failures you have experienced and how skilled you would like to be in the kitchen, if only you had the time and the energy – and a generous allowance with which to buy all the right ingredients.

BETTER COOKERY is my answer to the "gourmets", who insist that "fast food" tastes like cardboard – and, sometimes, the various menu selections really do! But there are many family-type restaurants within the division of the fast food industry that turn out exceptional meals for very reasonable prices, even giving senior citizens discounts and paying careful attention to how children are serviced. When you're a gourmet cook, you naturally have a throbbing desire to enjoy perfection with every dish, whether you're preparing it, or someone else! To a gourmet cook, compliments go with the territory – failures don't! They expect EVERY dish to be perfect enough to warrant a complement!

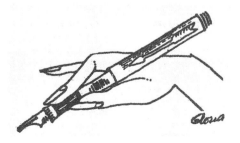

RECIPE INDEX

Original back-cover, as printed in *Gloria Pitzer's Better Cookery Cookbook* (St. Clair, MI: Secret Recipes Ltd., May 1983 – 3rd printing). Reproduced with permission from Gloria Pitzer.

Back-cover photo, as printed in *Gloria Pitzer's Better Cookery Cookbook* (St. Clair, MI: Secret Recipes Ltd., 1995). Reproduced with permission from Gloria Pitzer.